Yale Western Americana Series, 18

EDITORIAL COMMITTEE

William H. Goetzmann
Archibald Hanna, Jr.
Howard Roberts Lamar
Robert M. Utley

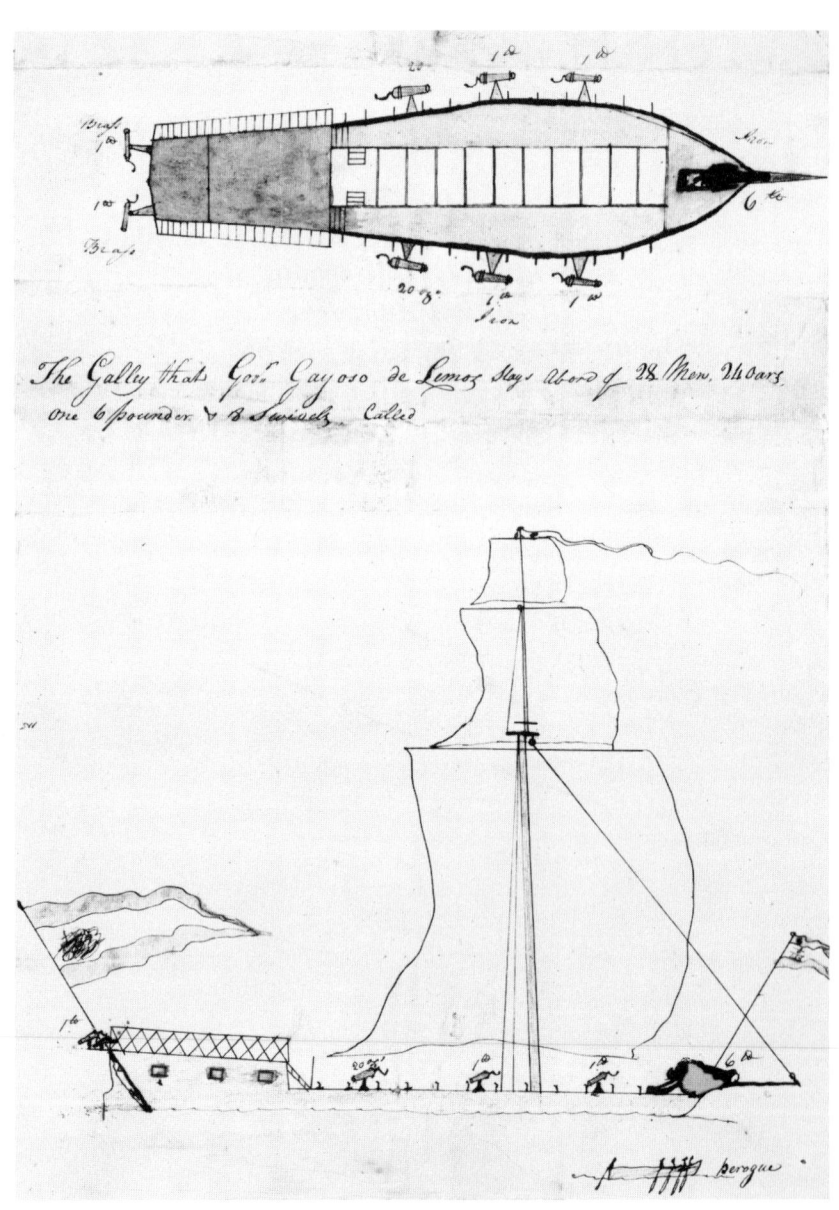

The galliot of Governor Gayoso de Lemos in 1798

SPANISH WAR VESSELS ON THE MISSISSIPPI

1792-1796

Abraham P. Nasatir

Yale University Press | New Haven and London

1968

Copyright © 1968 by Yale University.
Designed by John O. C. McCrillis,
set in Baskerville type,
and printed in the United States of America by
Connecticut Printers, Inc., Hartford, Connecticut.
Distributed in Canada by McGill University Press.
All rights reserved. This book may not be
reproduced, in whole or in part, in any form
(except by reviewers for the public press),
without written permission from the publishers.

Library of Congress catalog card number: 68–13920

Preface

In the early days of my professional career I chose Spain in the Upper Mississippi–Missouri Valley as my field of research. To start my collection of archival documentation, I had two one-year fellowships in the archives of Spain. There I collected—in the form of copies, transcripts, photostats, and notes—as nearly complete collections of the correspondence of the lieutenant governors of Upper Louisiana and of the post commanders as I possibly could. In addition, beginning in 1924, I procured documentary material on the over-all policy of Spain and selections of correspondence of the peripheral post commandants. Out of this collecting came a number of studies, and, especially during the 1930s, a coterie of excellent students worked with me, translating, editing, and writing dissertations. Of my own works, several have appeared, but two large projects long ago completed were not published.

Among the documents that interested me, I discovered a number of diaries relating to the frontier of Spanish Louisiana, and letters of the commandants of the Spanish navy that patrolled the Mississippi. These I carefully translated and edited, and at my request, my colleague Professor Frank Johnson wrote a story to accompany the translations of the diaries. I then permitted the project to lay in storage, but a year ago, on the advice of the executive editor of the Yale University Press, I revised some of it, rewrote the entire introduction, and revised a good many of my editorial notes to both the narrative and the diaries.

In the interval between my first engagement upon this material and my recent work on it, some of it appeared in print. The diary of Rousseau was published in translation, unedited, by Lawrence Kinnaird, in his *Spain in the Mississippi Valley*. I carefully compared my translation with his and noticed a number of slight differences. Kinnaird has given a polished translation and made the document into a literary product—which it most certainly is not.

Therefore I myself have held to a literal translation. Where I differed in a number of small instances with the Kinnaird version I took the original to my colleague Professor Elizabeth M. Brown, who carefully studied the texts, and I have followed her in my renditions. The appearance of Kinnaird's translation has also saved me a number of minor errors, and I have corrected several of his.

Professor Jack D. L. Holmes in the meanwhile went to Spain, discovered several of the diaries, and published them in Spanish in a very limited and expensive edition. In many instances he has corrected the Spanish in the originals and made a number of changes. He also split certain ungrammatical and long and unpunctuated Spanish paragraphs into sentences—sometimes, I believe, misreading the text. In a few instances only, however, have my copies differed from his printed versions, these occasioned in most cases by his omitting a sentence or line. I have fully edited the diaries, and to the major one have added some parts that Professor Holmes did not find. Professor Holmes also translated into English Gayoso de Lemos' report on his trip to Illinois; in this case he omitted a paragraph and, in reprinting the document in Spanish, made a number of changes.

The records of naval life on the Mississippi at a critical moment in the history of the Spanish-American frontier are contained in this volume. In translating literally the basic diaries and not attempting to make nice writing out of down-to-earth prose, my idea was to render the words of the diarists in their own manner and way of expression and in as close to a word-for-word rendition as possible in straightforward English. Since the documentation of the subject is so voluminous and the letters of the commandants so numerous, no attempt has been made to refer to every document available. To hazard a guess, I would judge that I have used 70,000 out of the more than 200,000 pages of transcripts in my private collection, and have referred in notes to roughly about 8 to 12 per cent of my documentation on the materials contained in this volume. In choosing, I made certain selections that will not only support the materials (practically unknown in detail) but also guide future students interested in the field. While this has, of course, necessitated many multireference footnotes, the citations were increased further by the lack of a diary for one of the expeditions, which necessitated the use of complete, detailed letter-writing by the participants.

The writers of the documents herewith included often recorded their facts—and especially proper names—phonetically; and in their thinking in one language and transposing into the language in which they wrote, they often spelled differently the names of persons, Indian tribes, and places. Despite some inconsistency, I have kept the spelling of proper terms in the precise fashion in which they were recorded in the text of the original documents (in most cases), and where necessary have added an editorial note of identity. In many cases I have given the various spellings of the same place upon their first mention in the documents and thereafter kept the original spelling in the text.

Although the documentation covers principally the period 1793-95, I have extended the story narrative at both ends in order to give a rounded account of the setting and the problems of the Spanish naval war vessels on the entire length of the Mississippi River from its mouth to above Prairie du Chien, and to give a very short and cursory outline of the story till the end of the Spanish regime in the Mississippi Valley. This narrative reflects parts of my over-all topical interests as well as my writings and publications in the field.

I cannot refrain from expressing my deep gratitude to many persons who have aided me in my work. They are far too numerous to mention here individually. My former students who have aided me have been mentioned in many editorial notes. But to one I must make special reference. Miss Frances Coughlin spent more than two years working by my side and produced an excellent dissertation, from which I have drawn freely. While I did most of the translating and guiding, she did a masterful job of synthesis and made it much easier for me to compile and write the editorial notes. My former colleague for many years, Professor Leslie P. Brown, now happily enjoying his work as Professor Emeritus of Romance Languages, gave me of his time and vast knowledge for over twenty years. He went over my original translations with close attention and saved me from falling into many errors. Certainly his expertise of romance languages saved me from many a pitfall. Also, in going over my translations in preparation for this edition, I have had the cooperation and aid of his wife, Elizabeth M.

Brown, Professor of French, who happily is still actively a colleague and who has carefully gone over the few diaries and letters written in French. My more recent colleague, Professor Thomas Case of the Spanish department, has given me of his time and knowledge in reviewing the documents in Spanish.

My grateful appreciation is most willingly given to my colleague and associate Noel M. Loomis, with whom I have worked for the past six years and with whom I joined in writing and translating the documentary materials that I discovered in various archives relating to Pedro Vial and the Roads to Santa Fé—materials that recently appeared in print. Noel Loomis has given to me unstintingly of his time that I might not fall into errors in the use of English, and has seen to it that my writing could be understood by readers. Finally, I am indebted to David Horne, then of Yale University Press, for his seeking me out and his aid and generous advice and help, which have led to the appearance of this work in print.

My wife also has made an important contribution to all my work in these historical matters. Not only has she shown great understanding while I have been engaged on the peregrinations necessary to gather material and while I have been closeted in my study to make those materials publishable, but she has kept friends and advice-seekers at arm's length, and has foregone the material pleasures enjoyed by most women, which might have been hers with the money that I spent on research and travel if I had been contented with the more prosaic aspects of college teaching.

A. P. N.

San Diego State College
January 1966

Contents

Preface	v
1. The Threat of the Kentuckians	1
2. The Spanish Fresh-Water Fleet	22
3. Key Site for a Fort at Ecores à Margot	59
4. *La Flecha* Reinforces New Madrid	74
5. Fort San Fernando Established at Barrancas de Margó	85
6. Intrigue with the Kentuckians	119
7. The Fleet Leaves the Upper River	132

DOCUMENTS

1. Diary of Captain of the Army Don Pedro Rousseau January 5–March 25, 1793	149
2. Diary of Juan Barnó y Ferrúsola November 9, 1793–February 16, 1794	189
3. Diary of Gayoso de Lemos' Expedition on *La Vigilante*	232
PART I: April 16, 1795–[September 7, 1795]	238
PARTS II AND III: October 6, 1795–December 8, 1795	288
PART IV: December 9–29, 1795	315
4. Gayoso de Lemos' Trip to Illinois: A Report 1795	327
Index	343

Abbreviations

AGI	Archivo General de Indias (Seville)
AGS	Archivo General de Simancas, Sección Guerra Moderna
AHAP	American Historical Association *Papers*
AHAR	American Historical Association *Annual Report*
AHR	*American Historical Review*
AHN	Archivo Histórico Nacional (Madrid), Sección Papeles de Estado
HAHR	*Hispanic American Historical Review*
IJHP	*Iowa Journal of History and Politics*
leg.	legajo
LHQ	*Louisiana Historical Quarterly*
MVHR	*Mississippi Valley Historical Review*
MHS	Missouri Historical Society
P de C	Archivo General de Indias (Seville), Sección Papeles de Cuba
res.	reservada
Sto. Dom.	Archivo General de Indias (Seville), sección Audiencia de Santo Domingo
WTHSP	West Tennessee Historical Society *Papers*

1   The Threat of the Kentuckians

The shifting borderlands of the area now occupied by the United States have not always been determined in North America.[1] Long before the United States was formed, there was a three-cornered rivalry for America among Spain, England, and France. This was altered by the Treaty of Paris of 1763, which reduced the conflicting powers to two as the result of France's exclusion from continental North America. Within a few years, however, the United States entered the contest, which again became a three-way conflict, with the borderlands shifting more rapidly than before. During the latter part of the eighteenth century, then, Spain was confronted anew by aggressors—not two, as before, but now three, for the French tried to recover what they had previously lost. This four-way conflict (three against one, as far as Spain was concerned) centered in the Mississippi Valley and existed in spite of treaty-written boundaries and the creation—on paper, at least—of the independent United States.

Spain occupied the Mississippi Valley, which she had inherited, or won, from the French, and found herself squeezed between the United States and England, with France very active subversively. Since she was determined, at all odds, to use the Mississippi Valley area as a huge wilderness buffer to protect her far more important colonial empire in the commandancy-general borderlands of the Southwest and her still more important empire deeper in the viceroyalty of New Spain, she had to fight to keep the shifting frontiers from getting out of hand and putting her in a secondary position.

Spain held a paper title to the entire area west of the Mississippi River and to East and West Florida by virtue of treaties following various wars, having been victorious in some and vanquished in

   1. See my presidential address before the Pacific Coast Branch of the American Historical Association given at the University of California at Los Angeles in August 1964: "Shifting Borderlands," *Pacific Historical Review, 34* (1965), 1–20.

others. By the Treaty of Paris she lost East and West Florida to England but recovered them by the Treaty of Paris of 1783, and promptly wanted to consolidate her holdings in the Southeast. Her desire for international prestige caused her to battle diplomatically and to intrigue actively in order to remain in possession of a large area to which the newly created United States held nominal title. England, too, fought for control of the Northwest and of the Upper Mississippi Valley. France since 1763 was left without ownership of territory, for she had given her claims east of the Mississippi River to England and west of the river, together with the Isle of New Orleans east of the river, to Spain. Thereby Spain controlled the mouth of the river.

Both Spain and France, who resented having been forced by military defeat to lose territories that had belonged to them, schemed and sought vengeance in the American Revolutionary War. When both fought England in that revolt of thirteen of England's colonies, Spain won back some of her territory—East and West Florida.

France had never reconciled herself to the loss of Louisiana, and even though, theoretically, her friendship with Spain was an important reason for the transfer of 1763, she had a change of heart and tried to get it back almost immediately. Perhaps French diplomacy was not wholly committed to the recovery, but since the Frenchmen in North America were, the attempts continued at intervals[2] until, in the 1790s, she went to greater and greater lengths to regain it. Finally, Napoleon literally stole it back from Spain under the guise of the polite term "retrocession."[3] In the meantime France's lack of real estate "back of the United States,"

---

2. My former student Ronald D. Smith, now of Arizona State University, has written a doctoral dissertation entitled "French Interests in Louisiana: from Choiseul to Napoleon" (University of Southern California, 1964), based on my collection of transcripts. In it he discusses these matters in detail and also cites printed materials.

3. In 1789 a serious recommendation was made by a responsible French official, Eléonore François-Elie Moustier, Minister of France to the United States, 1787–89. He sent a *mémoire* to the French foreign office suggesting that France recover Louisiana. His plan was either to convince Spain that that province was of no value to her, or else offer it in exchange for Guiana or Jamaica, which France was to capture from the English. After carefully sizing up the situation, Moustier concluded that the best solution of the Louisiana problem for Spain, the colony of Louisiana, and France would be for the latter to take over Louisiana; the time was propitious for such a move.

while England and Spain both had territory there, and the attempts of all three nations to strangle or to "guide" (control and perhaps dismember) the young new—and perhaps unwanted—independent United States made Louisiana's possession loom larger in the minds of Frenchmen. Moreover, the Revolution had made France into a crusading nation, feared by all others, and brought her into war against almost every European power, with her successes even pushing England and Spain into a precarious alliance. But alliance or no alliance, Spain in the Mississippi Valley feared England, France, and the United States, and considered them ominous threats to her empire in North America.

Technically, then—and in effect, as well—the Treaty of Paris of 1763 removed the French from continental North America and at the same time swept the old Spanish frontier at Los Adaes (which had been the Franco-Spanish border for half a century) eastward to the banks of the Mississippi River, while at the same time it jumped the British border from the Appalachian Mountains westward to the banks of the Mississippi. In reality, what had been a small annoyance on the Red River (French traders at Los Adaes and among the Indians) had been traded for a mortal danger on the Mississippi River, putting Spain into an even more precarious situation. Spain knew also—and soon had it affirmed—that, however bad a neighbor or enemy France was, England was far more dangerous. She later discovered, of course, that the United States was still worse.

The chief problem of the Spanish Court for some time, however, was English encroachment into Spanish Louisiana, for English traders dealt almost at will with Indians in Spanish territory. Forts did not stop them, and at least one reason for Spain's entrance into the war against England in 1779 was her desire to remove the British threat to Louisiana. This she did when she recovered East and West Florida, and when she in fact held onto the territory east of the Mississippi as far north as the Ohio River. Yet in the Upper Mississippi Valley it was different, and as a result of the war, in spite of the technical and actual defeat of the British, it was England who gained control of the trade in that entire area.[4]

---

4. See A. P. Nasatir, "Trade and Diplomacy in the Spanish Illinois 1763–1792" (doctoral dissertation, University of California, 1926). The writer has since published some parts of that work and many additional studies relating to the Upper Missouri and Mississippi Valleys.

For Spain there was the constant threat of an armed British invasion from Canada, which had been attempted ever since the treaty of 1763 and, although practically dispelled for two years by an Anglo-Spanish alliance that lasted from 1793 to 1795, while Spain and England were both fighting France, was renewed actively after the Treaty of Basel. The treaty took Spain out of the war in 1795 and led to war between Spain and England in late 1796, with consequent threats of armed invasion of Louisiana, Florida, and even Santa Fé and other parts of the Spanish empire. Those threats, however, are not the subject of this book; rather, it deals with aggression against the Mississippi frontier by the French and the Americans: the defense of Spain's Mississippi frontier.

France, although without territory on the North American continent, still had the Bourbon Family Compact and was an ally of Spain up to the time of the Revolution in 1789. However, the situation in Louisiana was not only different from that in France, but peculiar. Most of the inhabitants were French, and their objection to the cession of Louisiana to Spain in 1763 was particularly vocal, though perhaps not unanimous. While many of them became reconciled to Spanish rule under the popular regimes of Luis de Unzaga and Bernardo de Gálvez, there were always those who never ceased to hope and work for the return of France. Attempts to deliver the province to France were made while Ulloa was attempting to establish Spanish rule in Louisiana, during and after the American Revolution and especially after the outbreak of the French Revolution, when they became persistent, continuous, and insistent. This latter event provoked an outburst of enthusiasm for the former mother country and renewed attempts to return to French rule.

In 1790 and 1793 French Louisianians petitioned the National Assembly of France, requesting reannexation of the colony to France. New Orleans was filled with Jacobins, the "Marseillaise" was sung, and Republican clubs were formed. Since Jacobins were active in other parts of the province, Spanish authorities were greatly alarmed, fearful that if France should attack Louisiana, its inhabitants might rise up in revolt against Spain and Louisiana would be lost. War then broke out between France and Spain, and in 1793 the colony's trade with France was cut off. While New Orleans merchants led revolutionary demonstrations at home, repeated threats of armed attack by French forces against both Upper and Lower Louisiana further aggravated the situation and kept Governor Carondelet in constant fear of French aggression.[5]

In point of fact, Carondelet's fears were not unfounded. The French Republicans, burning with revolutionary ardor and militant spirit, eagerly sought someone to liberate Louisiana, whose inhabitants, still French-speaking, were begging to return to French rule. In 1792 several plans for the conquest of Louisiana and other Spanish provinces were presented to the Girondin government of France, and out of them grew the famous Genêt affair, which will be discussed later.[6] Edmond Charles Genêt's plans failed, however, and Jean Antoine Joseph Fauchet, who succeeded Genêt as French minister to the United States, ended it by issuing a proclamation that forbade all Frenchmen to violate the neutrality of the States.[7]

Genêt was not the only Frenchman to plan an expedition against Louisiana. There were others, as, for example, Captain Muhlberger of the artillery at Lille in 1794.[8] But France was too busy in Europe, and when in 1795 the peace of Basel made Spain her ally instead of her enemy, France turned to diplomacy to obtain the retrocession of Louisiana, finally consummating that bit of statesmanship when Talleyrand won the secret treaty of San Ildefonso of October 1, 1800.

The third source of aggression against Louisiana were the Americans of the western United States. Before the American Revolution, the chief threat had been from the encroachment of British traders, but as the result of a great expansionist movement that began into the Old Southwest (the area west of the Appalachians, south of the Ohio, and east of the Mississippi) during the Revolution, soon there were a number of firmly established American settlements in the Ohio and Mississippi Valleys, and as the republic

---

5. See my former student Ernest R. Liljegren's article "Jacobinism in Spanish Louisiana 1792–1797," *Louisiana Historical Quarterly*, 22, 3–53. This is treated below, pp. 135–36.

6. See below, pp. 74ff.

7. Lee Liljegren, *LHQ*, 22, 3–53.

8. Prospectus of two expeditions on Spanish territory, signed by Muhlberger, Captain of Artillery of the First Company of the Charante, Lille, 18th of Nivose, An II (January 7, 1794), Archives Nationales (Paris), Section Colonies, Ser. C13A, Vol. 51, folios 5–6. There were many other proposals for expeditions.

grew, it pushed with increasing vigor against Spain's frontiers in Louisiana and the Floridas.

The treaty of 1783, which set up the independent United States, posed some serious problems. The first was caused by Spain's closing the Mississippi River in 1784 to all commerce but Spanish. Since the Mississippi was the natural highway for the inhabitants of the Ohio and Mississippi Valleys, not only had they enjoyed free navigation of the river since the treaty of 1763, but during the American Revolution, Spain had granted navigational rights to the Americans to help them defeat the British. The war was hardly over, however, when Spain denied the river to the Americans and immediately precipitated a conflict with the American West. After some twenty years of usage, Americans had come to regard free navigation of the Mississippi as one of their inalienable rights. Furthermore—and more importantly—it was the only economically feasible means of transporting their produce to outside markets. They therefore considered it essential to their prosperity and were not disposed to give it up without a struggle. The problem became a matter of diplomatic negotiation as early as 1782 and remained a vexing question until the Treaty of San Lorenzo el Real was signed in 1795.

A second problem that strained relations between Spain and the United States was the boundary of West Florida. While England, in her peace treaty with the United States, had set the southern boundary at the 31st parallel and granted Americans the free navigation of the Mississippi, Spain, with good reason, considered the Yazoo, at 32° 26', the northern boundary of West Florida. As for the navigation of the Mississippi, England had had neither the right nor the power to grant it to the United States. In the treaty with Spain, also made in 1783, England omitted all references to the navigation of the Mississippi and ceded East and West Florida without stipulating the boundaries of the latter. According to the British Order in Council of 1764, they included Natchez and all the territory north passing through the parallel of the junction of the Yazoo and Mississippi Rivers (32° 26'). Consequently, both Spain and the United States had legal claims to the territory between 31° and 32° 26', from the Mississippi to the Chatahoochee on the east, and including Natchez and the heart of the southern Indian country. The Spaniards, moreover, held on to the disputed territory by right of possession, which had been established when Gálvez took Natchez from the British in 1779. Since the Americans refused to accept Spanish possession, the boundary dispute and the question of navigation of the Mississippi became the topic of long and acrimonious dispute. Spain and the United States negotiated these questions from 1783 to 1795 and even longer.

Behind those problems lay the deeper issue of economic and political control of the rich Mississippi Valley. Both governments realized that a fundamental matter was at stake, and were determined not to yield. Negotiations were conducted first in the United States, then transferred to Madrid, but brought no results. When in 1793, as a consequence of the French Revolution, Spain and England became allies against France, once again the United States profited from Europe's wars. In July 1795 Spain signed the Treaty of Basel with France, thereby breaking her alliance with England. Now threats of English aggression against Spanish possessions in North America were no longer restrained. Almost immediately Spain was alarmed by rumors of a proposed British attack on her Gulf colonies, and the Spaniards knew well that in case of such an attack the aid or at least the neutrality of the United States was imperative for the preservation of the Spanish empire. (In the Nootka Sound controversy, when a British attack threatened, Spain had been fearful that the States might give England permission to cross the Old Northwest to get at Spanish Louisiana—and it could have happened, given the relations between Spain and the United States at the time.) Thus it was to gain American friendship and support against threatened British hostilities that Godoy, in Spain, finally decided to yield to American demands on the navigation and boundary questions. On October 27, 1795, the Treaty of San Lorenzo el Real—Pinckney's Treaty—was signed, by which Spain granted to the Americans free navigation of the Mississippi with the right of deposit at New Orleans for three years, and established the boundary between the United States and West Florida at the 31st parallel.

While American and Spanish diplomats were negotiating over the problems, however, the men of the American West attempted to take matters into their own hands. The frontiersmen were restless, independent people, accustomed to making their own laws and with little respect for the weak and far-off Federal government. International law and lengthy negotiations meant nothing or little to them. Their immediate problem was the necessity for free navigation of the Mississippi, and if it could not be obtained in any other way, the Westerners were ready to use force—their own.

The frontiersmen likewise paid little attention to Spanish claims to the disputed territory east of the Mississippi. What they wanted, they took—and frequently their wants ran to the lands along the east bank of the Mississippi, south of the Ohio. Consequently, one of the main problems of Spanish defense in Louisiana after the American Revolution concerned threats of attack from independent and lawless bands of Westerners. François Luis Hector, Baron de Carondelet, governor and intendant of Louisiana, received a steady flow of reports of and about proposed American invasions of his territory, most of which were to originate in the Ohio country. Although none of the attacks was ever fully realized, many were planned and some were begun. Thus the Spanish officials in Upper Louisiana were forced to maintain a constant state of alert against surprise attack.

Faced with threats of aggression from three different sources— British, French, and American—Spanish officials in Louisiana had few means of adequate defense. The province was normally an economic burden, requiring a subsidy, or *situado,* to be supplied, and since the Spanish Court was loathe to put any more money and resources into the colony than absolutely necessary, the governors and other officials were constantly pleading for more troops, artillery, munitions, and money. The defenses, in truth, were pitifully inadequate: a thin line of scattered military outposts, stationed in wooden and earthen forts incapable of withstanding anything stronger than Indian attacks or small bands of white men without artillery. These were the defenses of Louisiana's 500-league frontier.[9]

---

9. Carondelet to Las Casas, New Orleans, September 30, 1793, Archivo General de Indias (Seville), Sección Audiencia de Santo Domingo, *legajo* 2580. Carondelet to Alcudia, No. 18 *reservada,* New Orleans, September 27, 1793, Archivo Histórico Nacional (Madrid), Sección Papeles de Estado, leg. 3898. Draft (Carondelet) to Las Casas, No. 158, res., New Orleans, April 15, 1796, Archivo General de Indias (Seville), Sección Papeles de Cuba, leg. 153A. Carondelet to Gayoso, New Orleans, August 8, 1796, P de C 23; Carondelet to Las Casas, No. 163 res., New Orleans, November 1, 1796, P de C 1447.

Governor Esteban Miró[10] and Intendant Martín Navarro[11] had developed and initiated a four-point plan for the defense of Louisiana. When Carondelet took over the province in 1791, he continued to use the methods begun by Miró but made many changes in the original plans. The first point of defense concerned the control of the Indian nations inhabiting the territory between the Spanish and American frontiers in the Southeast. Miró's aim was to erect a barrier of Indian nations by making the Southern

10. Esteban Rodríguez Miró (1744–95) was born in Catalonia and entered the Spanish army as a cadet at the age of sixteen. He served in the campaign of 1762 against Portugal. In 1769 he arrived in America, where he served as aide-de-camp to Bernardo de Gálvez in the West Florida campaign. Subsequently he was promoted to colonel and commander of the regular Louisiana regiment. When Gálvez left Louisiana in 1782, Miró became acting governor; and when Gálvez was promoted to viceroy, Miró was appointed governor, on August 19, 1785. He was advanced to the rank of brigadier general in 1789. When Navarro retired as intendant on May 10, 1788, the office of intendant was combined with that of governor until Carondelet assumed office on December 30, 1791. Miró returned to Spain and defended himself against the charges of intriguing with Wilkinson in order to make a yearly profit of $2,000 on the purchase of Kentucky tobacco. Shortly before he died, Miró was promoted to field marshall. He married Celeste C. C. Macarty of a wealthy Creole family.

Miró was popular in Louisiana, and his conduct in office commands respect. Militarily, his policy was strictly defensive. He sought to control the southern Indians through Alexander McGillivray and Panton, Leslie and Company, and he showed himself anxious to avoid a rupture in the troubles with Bourbon county (1785) and in relations with Georgia land companies. The celebrated intrigue with Wilkinson was initiated by the latter and carried on by Miró only under minute instructions from Madrid. Economically, Miró's administration of Louisiana was mild and beneficial. He encouraged commerce and agriculture, opposed the establishment of the Inquisition, and restored New Orleans after the fire of 1788. Authorized by the royal order of 1788, Miró encouraged foreign immigration and the partial opening of the Mississippi. He knew French well and had some knowledge of English.

Though Miró's administration and policies have been much discussed, there is no complete biography of him. The best approximation is Caroline Burson, *Stewardship of Esteban Miró* (New Orleans, 1940). See also C. E. A. Gayarré, *History of Louisiana, Spanish Domination*, 3 (4 vols. New Orleans, 1903); Alcée Fortier, *History of Louisiana*, 2 (4 vols. New York, 1904); A. P. Whitaker, *Spanish-American Frontier* (Boston, 1927). Miró's extensive correspondence is found in the P de C and in the AHN. There is a *residencia* of Miro's administration in Madrid.

11. Martín Navarro, *contador* and later intendant of Louisiana. During Gálvez' campaign against the English, he was left in charge of civil matters in New Orleans. He intrigued with the Western settlers and settlements to induce immigration to Spanish Louisiana, and was hostile to the Americans. Navarro was a gifted and intelligent man who had a long residence in Louisiana, during which he won the esteem and respect of all classes of men. He was transferred to Spain in the spring of 1788. Navarro was appointed intendant of Louisiana on February 24, 1780. Draft of his

tribes allies of the Spaniards, through economic rather than military means. By concluding treaties of defensive alliance with the Choctaw, Chickasaw, and Creek nations, he sought to bring the Indians under Spanish protection and to exclude the introduction of American influence. Spanish control was to be maintained through the monopoly and regulation of Indian trade, the contribution of supplies and presents, and the influence of Indian chiefs. Actually, the services of two British traders were most important in securing such control—those of Alexander McGillivray, a quadroon Creek, and of William Panton of Panton, Leslie and Company (in 1783 the largest tradinghouse in East Florida). Though both men were of great value to Spain, they were British, and dependence on British traders to control the Indians was in the long run an uncertain and dangerous policy.

Carondelet's Indian policy differed from Miró's in that it was of an offensive rather than a defensive nature: where Miró's Indian alliances were strictly defensive and pacific, Carondelet sought offensive military treaties with the Indians; where Miró discouraged hostilities toward the United States, Carondelet incited the Indians to attack and plunder Americans who ventured into Spanish domain. Indeed, Carondelet considered the use of Indian allies one of the best means of defense against American aggression. Since the value of Indian warriors rested upon the Spaniards' ability to unite all the tribes into a single confederation capable of united military action, Carondelet worked at drawing the Creeks

---

título is in Sto. Dom. 2606. He served 22 years in Louisiana. At his own request he was relieved of the intendancy by royal order of February 25, 1788, which retired him on half pay with rank of *intendente*. On his return home, since Spain was satisfied with his conduct, he was not only consulted on important matters other than those concerning Louisiana and Florida commerce, but was sent on a mission to France and England. In 1790 he returned to Spain, shortly thereafter incurred the disfavor of the King, and was banished from the Court for two years. In March 1793 he petitioned the King for *agregado del Consejo de Indias*. He died probably in 1794. Navarro was an official of unusual liberality and breadth of vision. (See A. P. Whitaker, ed., *Documents Relating to the Commercial Policy of Spain in the Floridas and Louisiana* [Deland, Fla., 1931], pp. xlii–iii, 232, 233, and other documents in the volume. Navarro's "Reflections on the Present Conditions of the Province of Louisiana," dated September 24, 1780, is in the Bancroft Library and is printed from other copies with erroneous dating in Manuel Serrano y Sanz, ed., *Documentos históricos de la Florida y la Luisiana* [Madrid, 1912], pp. 361–71; and in J. A. Robertson, ed., *Louisiana under Spain, France and the United States*, *1* [2 vols. Cleveland, 1911] pp. 241–78.)

away from the United States and eventually even gained the friendship of an American faction among the Chickasaws. In addition to wooing the Creeks, Chickasaws, and Choctaws, he added a fourth tribe to Spain's Indian allies in the south—the Cherokees. The climax of Carondelet's Indian policy in the Southwest was reached in the Treaty of Nogales, signed October 28, 1793, after negotiation by Manuel Gayoso de Lemos.[12] That treaty not only

---

12. Next to the governor general, the most important Spanish official during the 1790s was Manuel Gayoso de Lemos, governor of Natchez. Jack D. L. Holmes, *Gayoso The Life of a Spanish Governor in the Mississippi Valley 1789–1799* (Baton Rouge, 1965) appeared too late to be used in this volume. Gayoso was born in Oporto, Portugal, in 1747, of a Portuguese mother and a Gallego father, serving as consul there. He received a large part of his education in England and thus acquired a perfect knowledge of English, which was to prove valuable later. He entered the Spanish army as a cadet in 1771, was promoted to sublieutenant in 1772, and in 1779 became a sublieutenant in the grenadiers. He was promoted to full lieutenant in April 1781 and to captain on June 25, 1782. On September 20, 1786, Gayoso received the rank of lieutenant colonel and in 1789 was promoted to full colonel, assuming command as governor of Natchez. Most of his time in the service was spent in Portugal, at the court at Lisbon, at Cadiz, and on the seas.

In 1787 Gayoso was called to Madrid and given a special commission as governor of the Natchez district, which was chosen to try out a new Spanish policy of immigration—that of assimilating Anglo-American settlers into a Spanish colony. He served as governor of Natchez until late in 1797, when he was chosen to replace Carondelet as governor general. His rule was marked by mildness and exceptional honesty. A polished gentleman, with a likeable personality, he had the esteem of the inhabitants and gave Natchez a gay, hospitable tone and an air of culture.

Also an energetic and able official, Gayoso played a leading role in the affairs of Louisiana during his residence there. He negotiated with the Choctaw and Chickasaw Indians for the cession of land at Nogales and supervised the erection of the highly important fortifications. Not only was he in charge of the founding of the fort of San Fernando de las Barrancas, but he negotiated the cession of that territory from the Indians. Gayoso made a military tour of inspection of the Upper Mississippi settlements and carried on the negotiations with the Westerners, especially as regards their Spanish intrigues. Upon the promotion of Carondelet, Gayoso became governor general at the end of 1797, and remained such until his death on July 18, 1799, at the age of 48. Gayoso died a poor man. He was married three times, first to a Portuguese lady who died shortly after arriving in Natchez in 1790. His second wife was the daughter of an influential planter at Natchez and died three months after their marriage. His third wife was the sister of his second wife, Margarita "Peggy" Watts, who was seventeen years old at the time of her marriage. Gayoso had sons by his first and third wives, the last being only two years old when Gayoso de Lemos died. (S. C. Arthur and G. C. Huchet de Kernion, *Old Families of Louisiana* [New Orleans, 1931], pp. 281–82.) (See A. P. Nasatir and E. R. Liljegren, "Materials Relating to History of Mississippi Valley," *LHQ, 21* [1938], 3–73; Irving A. Leonard, "A Frontier Library, 1799," *Hispanic American Historical Review, 23* [1943], 21–51; autobiography of Gayoso de Lemos, signed at Natchez, February 11, 1794, P de C

created a Spanish-protected confederation of the Creeks, Choctaws, Chickasaws, and Cherokees, but established a mutual territorial guarantee, agreed that the Spaniards deliver an annual gift to each tribe in its own territory, and gained the Indians' consent to the admission of Spanish commissioners among them. These last two provisions were important in that the first gave Spain an excuse to send troops into the Indian country, thus preparing the way for the establishment of future Spanish posts in Indian territory, and the second was necessary to maintain Spanish control and influence over the savages.[13]

Despite Carondelet's great faith in Spain's Indian allies, however, the savages were in reality fickle, undependable, and incapable of united action. Moreover, both Miró and Gayoso recognized a point that had eluded Carondelet: as military allies, the Indians cost more than they were worth. Indeed, the effect of Carondelet's aggressive Indian policy was, on the whole, detrimental to Spanish interests in Louisiana. It not only interfered with the development of the intrigue for the secession of the West —for, as Indian attacks increased on the American frontier, the intrigue suffered—but it also had a bad effect on the diplomatic negotiations being carried on between Spain and the United States.

The various objectives of Spain's high policy obviously were not consistent: it sought simultaneously (1) to keep control of the river by cutting off navigation; (2) to keep the West from exploding by allowing some traffic to highly selected favorites, but not allowing enough to make it possible for hordes of rough boatmen and Westerners, equal to the conquest of Louisiana, free use of the river; (3) to promote the secession of the West, so that the West would place itself under Spanish control in exchange for navigation rights of the Mississippi; and (4) to entice from that same

---

125; *Real despacho* as colonel, dated San Lorenzo, October 21, 1790, P de C 570A; *Nombramiento* as governor of Natchez, P de C 566. Gayarré, *History of Louisiana*, 3; A. P. Whitaker, *Spanish-American Frontier* and *The Mississippi Question* [New York, 1934]; S. F. Bemis, *Pinckney's Treaty* [Baltimore, 1926]).

13. Treaty of Nogales, certified copy encl. in Carondelet to Alcudia, No. 22 res., New Orleans, December 5, 1793, AHN 3898. Five original copies of the treaty are in P de C 2353; additional copies are in P de C 121 and 2363. The treaty is printed in M. Serrano y Sanz, *España y los Indios Cherokis y Chactas* (Seville, 1916), pp. 91–92. The governor related the negotiations and occurrences of the signing of the treaty in Carondelet to Alcudia, No. 26 res., New Orleans, January 24, 1794, AHN 3899.

West the immigrants who would make Louisiana prosperous and populous enough so that Spain would have no fear of the West. These somewhat contradictory aims served to make the Mississippi frontier an exceedingly sensitive one: tension, strain, and endless rumors of war and threats of aggression plagued the lives of Spanish officials. But despite all tactical advances and retreats, the grand issues remained clear. The frontiersmen knew as well as Jefferson that, in the latter's words, "there is on the globe one single spot, the possessor of which is our natural and habitual enemy. It is New Orleans, through which the produce of three-eighths of our territory must pass."[14] And Miró's successor at New Orleans, the Baron de Carondelet, prophesied that "if such men [that is, 'the prestigious and restless population' of the West] come to occupy the banks of the Mississippi and Missouri, or secure their navigation, doubtless nothing will prevent them from crossing and penetrating into our provinces on the other side. ... In my opinion, a general revolution in America threatens Spain unless the remedy be applied promptly."[15]

In 1795, however, the Treaty of San Lorenzo el Real at one stroke destroyed Spain's laboriously constructed Indian policy in Louisiana and Florida. By giving to the United States jurisdiction over nine-tenths of the Southern Indian tribes, the treaty nullified the Spanish-protected confederacy and voided Spain's numerous treaties of alliance and commerce with the Southern tribes. Moreover, in establishing complete reciprocity in the Indian trade, it destroyed Panton's monopoly and threatened the firm of Panton, Leslie and Company with ruin. Since it was not put into effect immediately, however, Spain did not abandon her Indian policy until the spring of 1798.[16]

The second means by which Miró and Navarro tried to check

---

14. Jefferson to Livingston, Washington, April 18, 1802, in P. L. Ford, ed., *Writings of Thomas Jefferson, 8* (10 Vols. New York, 1892–99), 143–47.

15. Carondelet's military report to Las Casas, New Orleans, November 24, 1794, encl. in Carondelet to Alcudia, No. 48 res., P de C 2354. It is printed in Robertson, *Louisiana under Spain, 1,* 293–345, and elsewhere. It is also found in British Museum, Additional Manuscripts, Vol. 17567, folios 22–63 v; extracts printed in L. Houck, *Spanish Régime in Missouri,* 2 (2 vols. Chicago, 1909), 9–17 (from Carondelet to Aranda, the original of which is an AHN 3897).

16. There were, of course, other reasons for the failure of the Spanish Indian policy.

American aggression was countercolonization. Spain sought to curb growing American power in the West by increasing the population of her border provinces. To accomplish this she used two methods: one, employed chiefly in Lower Louisiana, was the continuation of her old policy of bringing in loyal Spaniards from other colonies; the other attempted, through a liberal extension of immigration privileges, to draw American settlers from the United States into Spanish territory, thereby filling Louisiana and West Florida with potential defenders—fighting fire with fire.

To attract American settlers, Navarro recommended the extension of commercial privileges and the granting of free trade to the inhabitants of Louisiana, for only thus could the province become prosperous, and only a prosperous colony would attract settlers. Miró tried to encourage immigration by relaxing trade restrictions and reducing transit duties for the Americans. He also offered free land grants to all who would settle on Spanish soil and take the oath of allegiance to the King. Finally, the royal order of December 1, 1788, greatly liberalized the immigration system in Louisiana and West Florida.[17] Where before, only Spaniards and Catholics were permitted to settle in Spanish colonies, the order of 1788 encouraged the immigration of aliens and Protestants from the American West. Protestants would be tolerated, but public worship in that Church would not be, for the Spaniards' hope was eventually to transform the Protestant American settlers into loyal Catholic subjects of the Spanish King, and the settlers were supposed to take an oath of allegiance to Spain and bring up their children in the Catholic faith.

Although Miró's policy of countercolonization resulted in the establishment of a new post at New Madrid and an increased population in the Natchez district, on the whole it was a failure. Despite the great liberalization of Spain's immigration system, the Americans enjoyed many more political and religious privileges in the United States. Furthermore, freedom from commercial restrictions in the Spanish province was uncertain and depended largely upon the degree of enforcement demanded by Spanish officials.

17. See Valdés to Miró, Madrid, December 1, 1788, AHN 3888 bis; this letter encloses the instructions as agreed in the meeting of Junta de Estado (later called Consejo de Estado) at its meeting of November 20, 1788. See Nasatir and Liljegren, *LQH, 21,* reprint p. 12.

Another factor in or reason for the failure of countercolonization was that the Spanish colonial system forbade certain activities that Western Americans were accustomed to enjoying: local self-government, public Protestant worship, and indulgence in land speculation—one of the frontiersmen's favorite sports. Moreover, the Hispanicization of frontier Americans could not be made effective.

On the other hand, at the end of the Spanish regime by far the greater number of inhabitants in the Missouri-Arkansas area (excluding the capital, St. Louis) and perhaps also in Lower Louisiana (excluding New Orleans) were Americans. Indeed, Carondelet did not like Miró's policy of countercolonization, for he saw that it was filling the colony with them. Fearing their spirit of independence, he proposed to stop completely their indiscriminate immigration into Louisiana and to admit only a selected few who wanted to farm. Gayoso agreed, and he went further, regarding French settlers with the same suspicion. He believed that only a small, picked number of each nationality should be permitted to enter Louisiana and West Florida, preferring to populate the province with Spaniards, Germans, Hollanders, Flemish—and some French royalists.

By means of land grants and other inducements, Carondelet tried to stimulate the immigration of settlers from Europe, giving preference to Roman Catholics. Spanish agents were sent to New York and Philadelphia to entice European immigrants from the United States, and Carondelet made use of promoters such as Felipe Enrique Neri, Baron de Bastrop, and Don Josepha, Marquis de Maison Rouge, to bring Flemish and German settlers into Louisiana. Like Miró, however, Carondelet failed to populate the province.

Although opposed to Miró's countercolonization policy, Carondelet agreed with Navarro that free trade was the key to Louisiana's prosperity. Granted free trade, he believed, the province could soon equal or surpass in fertility, cultivation, commerce, and wealth the states of the Western United States. If Spain would grant the Americans free commerce with Louisiana, Spain's revenues would multiply through increased trade, and New Orleans would become the principal mart of the United States and Europe. The colony's prosperity would result in the rapid population of both banks of the Mississippi and Missouri Rivers with colonists who would be warlike, energetic, and loyal subjects, protecting the inner provinces—Texas and New Mexico—from foreign invasion.[18]

The third point in the Spanish program of defense encouraged intrigues with certain leaders in the American West to bring about the separation of Kentucky and other Western settlements from the Federal Union, as well as the establishment of an independent nation in the West under Spanish protection. With the United States split into rival republics, Spain could follow the old principle of divide and rule, playing each power against the other to her own benefit.

As a matter of fact, discontent had developed in the West shortly after the Revolution, setting the stage for the intrigue that Spain wanted—and which stemmed from Spain's own actions. The Westerners, disgusted with the failure of the Federal government to obtain free navigation of the Mississippi, were determined to have it, either by an armed invasion of Louisiana or by secession from the Union and establishment of a pro-Spanish state to deal separately with Spain. They were also tired of the mishandling of Indian affairs, for the border settlements lacked sufficient means of defense against not infrequent Indian raids. Their discontent was increased when the United States refused to join the French Republic in its war against England and Spain. Resentment of the whiskey tax added fuel, and in Kentucky dissatisfaction grew because of Congress' refusal to admit Kentucky into the Union as a state: the Westerners thought they had been sold out by the Easterners in the proposed Jay-Gardoqui treaty in 1786. In short, they were a long way from Philadelphia, and most of them were individualists or they would not have come West in the first place.

So strong was the frontiersmen's dissatisfaction with the Federal government that by the end of 1786 many Westerners were openly advocating secession from the Union and the establishment of a Mississippi Valley republic. Naturally, it was from Western discontent that the frontier intrigues with Spain developed, initiated by Americans whose eyes were on personal gain. Spain was moved by her official fear of the aggressiveness of the American frontiers-

---

18. Carondelet to Aranda, No. 1 res., New Orleans, June 10, 1792, AHN 3898; draft in P de C 2362; copy annexed to Carondelet to Las Casas, No. 33 res., New Orleans, June 10, 1792, P de C 152B. Carondelet to Alcudia, No. 36 res., New Orleans, June 3, 1794, AHN 3899.

men who might descend on New Orleans and take by force what Spain was unwilling to concede: it was for her own safety to deal with them and take advantage of the discontent.

Perhaps the first overtures were made to Diego de Gardoqui, Spanish minister at Philadelphia, by James White, a delegate to Congress from North Carolina, in August 1786. White spoke of the Westerners' concern with the free navigation of the Mississippi and suggested that in all probability the Western settlements would be willing to secede from the United States and place themselves under Spanish protection in return for free use of the river. A few months after Gardoqui reported this interview with White to the Spanish Court, without committing himself to its support, a second overture was made to the Spanish minister in Paris, the Conde de Aranda, by a French chevalier named Pierre Wouves d'Argès, who had just returned from three years in the wilds of Kentucky. D'Argès' suggestion dealt more with the seduction of American settlers and their removal to Spanish soil than with the separation of the West. He believed that Spain could strengthen Louisiana and weaken the West by attracting American frontiersmen into Spanish territory. Once his plan was approved by the Court, d'Argès returned to the United States to put it into effect but found himself blocked by both Gardoqui and Miró, each interested only in his own plan. Thus failing to secure necessary support, d'Argès finally returned to France in 1789 without having accomplished a thing.[19]

The third and most important overture was made to Miró by James Wilkinson,[20] merchant and self-styled leading citizen of

---

19. These matters are dealt with in print in many places. Mention should be made here of Bemis, *Pinckney's Treaty;* Whitaker, *Spanish-American Frontier;* J. Navarro Latorre and F. Solano Costa, *Conspiración Española 1787–89* (Zaragoza, 1949); T. M. Green, *Spanish Conspiracy* (Cincinnati, 1891). See also references given in note 20.

20. James Wilkinson was born in Calvert County, Maryland, in 1757. He was a military man and took an active part in the American Revolution. Hard-drinking and dominated by a passion for intrigue and a greed for money, he was involved in the Conway Cabal against Washington, and, as a clothier general, his accounts were irregular. Wilkinson carried his propensities for intrigue into the West, where he supplanted George Rogers Clark as leader. He opposed Humphrey Marshall and advocated separation from Virginia. He sought to turn the "prevalent discontent, intensified by Jay's proposed treaty, to his own financial gain." This was the motive behind the conspiracy with Spain. Through personal interviews and specious memo-

Kentucky. An incorrigible schemer, Wilkinson saw in Kentucky's discontent an opportunity to gain personal commercial privileges from Spain, as well as a possible chance to become a leading figure in a new Western republic—and perhaps even more. In the summer of 1787 he descended the Mississippi to New Orleans, where he presented to Miró and Navarro a memorial regarding condi-

rials, Wilkinson succeeded in making a good impression on Miró. He was enabled to dispose of his goods in New Orleans and sought further to secure a monopoly of Kentucky trade with the capital. He was successful enough to avail himself of the local agitation for statehood to convince Spain that he was looking toward disunion, and for a few years not only did he gain the monopoly he sought, but his fellow Kentuckians entrusted him with produce for the New Orleans market.

Nonetheless, Wilkinson's varied enterprises in land speculation, farming, trading, politics, and intrigue were not profitable. He was prompted to re-enter the army, leaving his business affairs to Harry Innes, and led forces against the Indians north of the Ohio in March 1791. In October of the same year he was made a lieutenant colonel in the regular army, and in March 1792 was promoted to brigadier general under Wayne. He soon quarreled with his superior and opposed him openly. His position as an officer in the army did not preclude further relations with Spain: he reported Clark's activities to Carondelet and urged action against the Kentuckians. But in 1795, when Gayoso de Lemos ascended to New Madrid for an interview, Wilkinson refused to meet him.

Wilkinson was later implicated with Burr, and his efforts to further Jefferson's plans for exploring the Louisiana purchase coincided both with his presumptive connection with Burr and with his intention to engage in the fur trade, allied with A. Chouteau. This enterprise led to three preliminary ventures up the Osage, the Mississippi, and the Missouri, the latter undertaken by his son, J. B. Wilkinson. He died in Mexico.

Whatever his character and success, Wilkinson's personal gifts were remarkable. Of him it is well said that "nature had endowed him with a passport which insured his favorable reception wherever he was seen and heard—a language which captivated the hearer—a courtesy of style which disarmed suspicion—a countenance open, mild and beaming with intelligence; a carriage firm, manly and erect; manners bland, accommodating and popular" (Burson, *Stewardship*, p. 151).

There is a large literature on Wilkinson, much of it biased: James Wilkinson, *Memoirs of My Own Times* (3 vols. Philadelphia, 1816); D. Clark, *Proofs of the Corruption of General James Wilkinson* (Philadelphia, 1809); Filson Club *Publications*, No. 31 (Louisville, 1926); R. O. Schreve, *The Finished Scoundrel: General James Wilkinson* (Indianapolis, 1933); J. R. Jacobs, *Tarnished Warrior* (New York, 1938); A. P. Whitaker, "James Wilkinson's First Descent to New Orleans in 1787," *HAHR, 8* (1928), 82–97; W. R. Shepherd, "Wilkinson and the Beginnings of the Spanish Conspiracy," *American Historical Review, 9* (1904), 490–506, and "Papers Bearing on James Wilkinson," ibid., pp. 748–66; Green, *Spanish Conspiracy;* Gayarré, *History of Louisiana, 3;* J. A. James, *George Rogers Clark* (Chicago, 1928); T. Bodley, *Life of George Clark* (Boston, 1926); Whitaker, *Spanish-American Frontier;* Bemis, *Pinckney's Treaty.*

tions in the American West. In the memorial[21] Wilkinson pointed out the growing discontent in the West, both with Spain for closing the Mississippi and with Congress for doing nothing about it. The Western population was rapidly increasing, Wilkinson said, and unless Spain should do something about the situation, the frontiersmen would descend upon Louisiana to open the river by force. He then offered two ways to avert an invasion: one was to build a Spanish party in Kentucky through manipulation of commercial regulations and to foment a revolution that would result in Kentucky's secession from the Union and her establishment of a republic under Spanish protection; the other was to adopt a liberal immigration policy designed to depopulate Kentucky and draw the Americans into Louisiana. Whichever course Spain might choose, Wilkinson offered himself as her sole agent in Western America, asking in exchange certain personal favors, fees, and commercial privileges.

Miró and Navarro gave Wilkinson's proposals their hearty approval and immediately forwarded them to the Court, but no reply was received until a year and a half later, when the decision of the Junta de Estado[22] reached New Orleans. Although the proposal to foment a revolution was rejected, the Spanish government declining to form any connection with the Westerners until their independence should be established, Miró was authorized to continue correspondence with Wilkinson. On the matter of navigation and commerce the Junta declared that all Americans were to be permitted to navigate the Mississippi as far as New Orleans subject to a 15 per cent duty, which Miró was authorized to reduce to

---

21. Wilkinson's first memorial of September 5, 1787, and the decision of the Junta de Estado upon it is found in AHN 3893A; translated in Shepherd, *AHR, 9,* 749-50; printed in Spanish in M. Serrano y Sanz, *El Brigadier Jaime Wilkinson y sus tratos con España para la independencia del Kentucky años 1787 a 1794* (Madrid, 1915) pp. 19-20. The original in English is in the Louisiana Historical Society; the memorial in both English and Spanish was enclosed in Miró to Valdés, No. 13, New Orleans, September 23, 1787. It is printed in Filson Club *Publications,* No. 31, pp. cxix-xxxix. In Spanish, together with other documents, it is also found in Navarro Latorre and Solano Costa, *Conspiración Española*. In this latter volume, pp. 185-202 and taken from AHN 3888 bis, in Wilkinson's first letter to Miró and Navarro, dated August 22, 1787, as well as Wilkinson's memorial. See also Whitaker, *HAHR, 8,* 82-97.

22. See Nasatir and Liljegren, *LHQ, 21,* reprint p. 12; see also pp. 8-9 for Spanish colonial correspondence and policy making.

6 per cent in certain cases. However, instead of making Wilkinson Spain's sole immigration agent in Kentucky, the Junta established the general policy of immigration already discussed. While Miró's correspondence with Wilkinson continued as long as Miró was governor general, the intrigue lapsed when Carondelet took office in 1791 and was not resumed in earnest until early in 1794.[23]

The Treaty of San Lorenzo el Real destroyed the Kentucky intrigue as well as it did Spain's system of Indian alliances. Then, when countercolonization proved a failure under both Miró and Carondelet, Spain's only remaining means of defense lay in the fourth point of Miró's original program: defense through a system of military fortifications, to be supported by a squadron of war galleys—a fresh-water navy—on the Mississippi River. It is this last point in Spain's program of defense on her Mississippi frontier, and particularly the part played by the galleys, that interests us in this volume.

Military defense in Spanish Louisiana was conspicuously shallow and notoriously inadequate. When Carondelet became governor general at the end of 1791, most of the colony's fortifications were simple earthen structures, which in some localities were being washed away by riverfloods and which were often surrounded by rotting palisades that could scarcely withstand musket fire. Carondelet looked over the defense situation and reported in January 1792 that the lack of defenses and forces was so great that Louisiana would not be able to repulse an attack from even five or six thousand Americans. The task of defending her 500-league frontier, stretching along the Mississippi from Balize and the Delta to the Ohio River, seemed insurmountable to Carondelet, with his thinly scattered ill-defended outposts and the depleted forces of the colony. Miró had said much the same things before.

All the persistent rumors of Americans arming to descend the thinly populated and practically unfortified Mississippi frontier, and especially the persistently recurring reports of invasion plans under George Rogers Clark, had forced Miró to think about American threats as a constant and increasing factor in the complex of forces constituting his plans for defense of his colony. He there-

---

23. Carondelet's intrigues with Wilkinson are discussed, below, p. 119–31.

upon had asked the Spanish Court, and formally requested permission, that he be allowed to station a galley and three gunboats at Natchez—a move that initiated a period of tenseness and implicit warfare with all the new forces stirring on the continent, contributing a picturesque and little-known chapter to the history of the Mississippi River.

2   The Spanish Fresh-Water Fleet

In any plan of defense of Louisiana four widely scattered points had to be considered: defense at the mouth of the Mississippi, defense at the mouth of the Ohio, defense of the entire length of the Mississippi, and maintenance of law and order in the capital. For the defense of a province so spread out and so exposed to surprise attacks from Indians as well as from American and British aggressors, Carondelet thought a force of at least four battalions was necessary. The first he proposed to establish at New Orleans to cover the detachments at Placaminas (Plaquemine) and San Juan del Bayú; the second, at Pensacola, would cover Movila (Mobile), San Marcos de Apalache, and Tombigbee; the third, at Natchez, would cover Nogales, Baton Rouge, Gálveztown, Natchitoches, Ouachita, and Punta Cortada; the fourth, at New Madrid, would cover Arkansas Post, Barrancas de Margó (Chickasaw Bluffs), St. Louis, and Ste. Geneviève. In addition to those four battalions, Carondelet believed that the province needed a naval force of six galleys to patrol the Mississippi River.[1]

While Carondelet's recommendation for a squadron of river galleys was carried out, his constant pleas for more troops were never answered. In 1792 the fixed Regiment of Louisiana (the only corps of regular troops in the colony) consisted of three battalions,[2] and at the end of 1796 it still consisted of only three battalions. At full strength the regiment was supposed to number 1856 officers and men,[3] but it never achieved that strength during Carondelet's tenure: in 1793 it was short about 300 men, while in the summer

---

1. Carondelet to Floridablanca, No. 1 res., New Orleans, January 23, 1792, AHN 3898; Carondelet to Alcudia, No. 18 res., New Orleans, September 27, 1793, AHN 3898; draft in P de C 178A. Carondelet to Las Casas, No. 1 res.

2. Carondelet to Floridablanca, No. 1 res.

3. The full regiment included a colonel, a lieutenant colonel, a commander, a sergeant major, 3 adjutants, 6 standard bearers, 27 captains, 27 full lieutenants, 27 sublieutenants, 78 sergeants, 58 drummers, 213 corporals, and 1507 soldiers (statement of Distribution of the Regiment of Infantry of Louisiana, New Orleans, De-

of 1794 he reported that 300 men and 19 officers were lacking.[4] The number continued to diminish, and, despite Carondelet's frequent solicitations, reinforcements failed to arrive. At the beginning of 1796 some 400 men were lacking, and by December the number had risen to 467. While in December 1796 the regiments totaled 1389 troops, 1018 of whom were on detached duty at the outposts of the colony, the only forces left to defend New Orleans were the remaining 317 troops plus a force of 200 men from the second battalion of the Regiment of Mexico. The outposts of the province were similarly ill defended: although Pensacola had 379 men, none of the other posts even approached that figure, the usual complement being closer to 100 or even 50 or less.[5]

One of the reasons that Louisiana was always short of men, munitions, and fortifications throughout the period of Spanish rule is that the military branch of the colony never did receive a regular allotment for its expenses. The annual military expenses varied, of course, from year to year, but on the whole they showed a steady increase, because new settlements required new fortifications. Not only did the acquisition of England's West Florida posts in 1783 double Louisiana's military expenses, but during 1791, 1792, and 1793 new forts at Nogales, Placaminas, and New Madrid added even more. Such extraordinary outlays had to be met with subsidies, which the Court was very loathe to grant. Indeed, the lack of a regular allotment for the military branch in Louisiana caused the ruin and decay of the fortifications of the province, since there was no money for repairs.[6] Moreover in 1796 Carondelet wrote that an annual expenditure of 200,000 pesos for mili-

---

cember 1, 1796, P de C 178B). The Louisiana regiment was made up of some of the worst of the Spanish soldiery. Their excesses created much friction between the inhabitants and the government. At one time Carondelet stated that two-thirds of them should be imprisoned for their delinquencies, but that in view of the crisis he did not dare punish them. (Liljegren, *LHQ*, 22, 19.)

4. Carondelet to Alcudia, New Orleans, July 31, 1793, printed in American Historical Association *Annual Report 1896*, *1*, 996–99; Carondelet to Alcudia, No. 34 res., New Orleans, May 1, 1794, AHN 3899; draft in P de C 178A; copy in Carondelet to Las Casas, No. 113, New Orleans, May 1, 1794, P de C 152B. Carondelet to Alcudia, No. 43 res., New Orleans, August 18, 1794, AHN 3899.

5. See distribution as given in Carondelet to Godoy, New Orleans, January 9, 1796, annex No. 5 to Carondelet to Godoy, No. 67 res., New Orleans, January 9, 1796, AHN 3886; Carondelet to Gayoso, New Orleans, August 8, 1796, P de C 23; Statement of Distribution of the Regiment of Infantry.

6. Carondelet to Las Casas, No. 442, New Orleans, September 30, 1792, Sto. Dom. 2580.

tary expenses alone was necessary to maintain the posts along the Mississippi frontier in a state of defense adequate to repel American and English aggressors. He suggested that for 2,000,000 pesos Louisiana could be put on a war footing that would assure the defense of the colony.[7]

Upon the establishment of peace with France, Carondelet renewed his requests for troops, and urged that not only the Regiment of Louisiana be completed but that another complete regiment of infantry and a second company of artillery be sent from either Spain or Mexico. The lack of a regiment in Spain would hardly be noticed, he said, while it was sorely needed in Louisiana, which was surrounded by Indians, threatened by American aggressors, exposed to the intrigues of French enthusiasts, and inhabited by 20,000 slaves who were eager for liberty.[8] Carondelet did not get the land forces he considered necessary, but he was successful in obtaining a royal squadron of galleys—naval vessels—on the Mississippi at the beginning of 1792.

It appears that the first suggestion made by a Spanish official for the use of war galleys on the Mississippi above New Orleans had been made by Miró in January 1787,[9] caused by reports of George Rogers Clark's activities against Louisiana. It was obvious that the American Revolution had brought changes necessitating modifications in the defense strategy of Louisiana: with the hordes of restless American frontiersmen pushing toward the Mississippi, clamoring for the free navigation of the river and for an extension of the American frontier to the 31st parallel, it was imperative that Spain occupy that territory in order to defend Louisiana against American seizure. Recognizing the changed situation in Louisiana, Miró strengthened the defenses of Natchez and requested permission to station some armed vessels there.[10] He also suggested a lookout on an island some 110 to 160 leagues above the town to watch

---

7. Carondelet to Las Casas, No. 162 res., New Orleans, November 1, 1796, P de C 1447.

8. Carondelet to Godoy, No. 67 res., and esp. annex No. 5; draft [Carondelet] to Las Casas, No. 158 res., New Orleans, April 15, 1796, P de C 153A.

9. Miró to Marqués de Sonora [José de Gálvez], No. 4 res., New Orleans, January 17, 1787, AHN 3885 bis.

10. Threats of American settlements at Chickasaw Bluffs and Walnut Hills (Nogales), along the east bank of the Mississippi, appeared in 1784 and 1785. In the fall of 1785 several commissioners for a proposed settlement at Walnut Hills appeared at Natchez to demand that the Spaniards surrender the town and recognize the 31st parallel boundary, and there were persistent rumors of 2500 armed men under

descending vessels and descending enemy expeditions in order to warn Natchez of their approach. The lookout was to be manned by a detachment of eight men and a pirogue, to be changed every two months. Miró estimated that the cost of the proposed fleet's maintenance would not be excessive, amounting only to salaries for the *patrones* and sailors, plus two rations pay daily to each soldier who should serve with the detachment and help row the pirogues.[11]

Miró's request was approved, but for several reasons he delayed putting it into execution. Not only had Clark's threats of attack vanished, but in the summer of 1787 Wilkinson arrived in New Orleans with the assurance that Louisiana would not be disturbed by American attacks during the time that his propositions were pending in the Court. Therefore, to avoid unnecessary expense, Miró postponed the stationing of war vessels at Natchez.[12] Wilkinson's assurances during his absence from Kentucky proved false, however, for in January 1788 the captain general at Havana informed Miró that a party of Americans was assembling on the Tennessee River to attack the province. Ordered to prepare for its defense, Miró arranged to station vessels at Natchez and send a small detachment to the head of an island a few leagues below the mouth of the Arkansas River.[13]

Two pirogues, manned by their *patrones*, two sergeants, and twelve soldiers, were to be stationed at the Arkansas Post under the orders of Josef de Vallière, the commandant there, to whom Miró sent instructions for the maintenance of the detachment: one of the pirogues, garrisoned by its patrón, a sergeant, and six soldiers, was to be stationed at the head of an island about four or five leagues below the mouth of the Arkansas River; the men were to build a shelter and were to watch the river for groups of descending *chalanes* or *berchas*;[14] sentinels were to be kept day and night,

---

Clark and Montgomery at the mouth of the Ohio ready to descend and capture Natchez. But Miró expected the commissioners, and no invasion occurred.

11. Miró to Sonora, No. 4 res.; Miró to Navarro, New Orleans, January 29, 1788, P de C 27; draft of reply and original in P de C 87. This is translated in Lawrence Kinnaird, "Spain in the Mississippi Valley," *AHAR 1945, 3,* 237-39.

12. Kinnaird, *AHAR 1945, 3,* 237-39; Miró to Sonora, No. 4 res., and draft of reply, Aranjuez, April 21, 1787, AHN 3885 bis.

13. Miró to Navarro, New Orleans, January 29, 1788, P de C 27; draft in P de C 87; printed in Kinnaird, *AHAR, 1945, 3,* 237-39.

14. The *Chalán* was a type of flatboat, the *bercha* a keeled barge. For further details see below, p. 51. For *patrón*, see below, p. 31, n. 26.

and frequent changes of the guard were to be made. If they should sight any invaders, they were to descend immediately to warn Natchez—that is, if there should be a group of four or more large chalanes or more than twelve berchas.[15] The entire fleet of war vessels—a galley, two gunboats, and a galiot—were under Captain (made lieutenant colonel in the Regiment of Louisiana) Alexandro de Boulliers.[16]

Boulliers' instructions were specific. Since at Natchez that little fleet was to be kept ready to leave on two hours' notice, the sailors were restricted from land duty and several hours' rowing practice daily was recommended. They were, of course, to defeat and capture any enemy boats descending the river with hostile designs. The moment he heard that enemy vessels were descending, he was to order his fleet up the river to a place where both banks were flooded, so that enemy flatboats would be unable to land, and he was to await them there, arranging his four vessels so they could fire from all four fronts as much as possible in order to withstand the numerical superiority of the enemy. If the enemy, discomfited by the naval might of Spain, yielded forthwith, Boulliers was to disarm them, throwing the arms in the river if there should be too many of them to load in the galleys; then he was to station the flatboats in the river, place his own vessels outside as guards, and escort the captives to Natchez. However, if Boulliers should fear

---

15. Draft of instructions to commandant of Arkansas post (drawn up by Miró), New Orleans, January 30, 1788, P de C 2361. There is an original of this in the Bancroft Library; printed in Kinnaird, *AHAR 1945, 3*, 239–41.

16. Copy of instructions to Don Alexandro de Boulliers, signed by Miró, New Orleans, February 24, 1788, P de C 5; Miró to Grandpré, No. 333, New Orleans, February 26, 1788, P de C 5; Miró to Grandpré, No. 334, same date, P de C 5. Boulliers was a captain with the rank of lieutenant colonel in the Louisiana regiment.

Miró's suggestion for a permanent fleet at Natchez in 1787 was the first made by the Spaniards for the use of war galleys on the Mississippi River above New Orleans. The plan was approved by the Court and put into operation in 1788. (See Miró to Sonora, No. 4 res., New Orleans, January 17, 1787, AHN 3885 bis; draft of reply, Aranjuez, April 21, 1787, ibid.; draft [Miró] to Navarro, New Orleans, January 29, 1788, P de C 87; copy of instructions to Alexandro de Boulliers, signed by Miró, New Orleans, February 24, 1788, P de C 5.)

Miró's plan to station Boulliers with a small fleet at Natchez early in 1788, mentioned above, gave Gayoso de Lemos the idea. Gayoso, governor of Natchez, included the notion of establishing a small squadron of galleys to cruise on the river above New Orleans as part of his plans for the defense of Natchez and Louisiana. He suggested the plan to Carondelet, who acted upon it immediately. He wrote the Court for permission but went ahead with the plan, establishing the naval flotilla in January 1792 and appointing Rousseau as commander of the river fleet.

that they might escape from Natchez, he was to take them down the river to the capital. On the other hand, if, instead of yielding, the Americans should open fire, he was forthwith to sink their boats. Miró emphasized that Boulliers was to explain carefully the necessary naval operations and to stress the glory of victory, to keep up the morale among Spanish soldiers and sailors, and to assure the men that they had no need to be intimidated by any superiority in the numbers of the enemy. For, indeed, there was an ominous disproportion of physical weight: 150,000 inhabitants of Kentucky (including a more than fair proportion of rough riflemen, none too delicate about treaties, boundaries, and prescriptive rights) and only some 15,000 in all Louisiana and Spanish Illinois.[17] But the expected American expedition did not come, the rumored army of frontiersmen dissolved into the unknown, and in April, Miró received word from Wilkinson, speaking optimistically of the prospects for the separation of Kentucky and the fulfillment of Spain's desires concerning Western America. Miró consequently turned his attention to the Western intrigue as the solution to his problem of defense against the American aggression. In the meantime he had initiated naval activities in the Mississippi—activities with which Carondelet would be in full accord.

Further rumors of aggression came in occasionally, but they never materialized. At the end of 1790 Clark was reported to be marching at the head of 700 men to take possession of the entire east bank of the Mississippi, from lower Coles Creek to the mouth of the Ohio—but he failed to appear,[18] and Miró apparently felt

17. The census of 1785 gives 31,433, a doubling of the population since 1769, when it was 13,538. The number of free colored persons was about 1100, and of slaves and whites there was nearly an equal division—hence the figure 15,000. (Gayarré, *History of Louisiana, 3,* 170–71.) The population in 1788 was 42,346 (ibid., p. 315).

Miró wrote Gálvez on April 15, 1786, that if Louisiana were intended to serve as a barrier to the Americans, it could not do so unless there would be a considerable increase of its population. This could be obtained only through commerce and agriculture—the one requiring protection, the other assistance. Commerce cannot prosper without freedom and unlimited expansion. Agriculture needs laborers. Both are needed to supply a means of paying the expenses of the colony, to secure His Majesty's possessions and rights, and to make his power and arms respectable. (Ibid., pp. 173 ff.)

18. Miró stated in 1792 that during his term in office as governor general of Louisiana he was threatened four times by armed men and/or expeditions from the Ohio:

(1) By Brigadier Clark in 1786. This threat vanished when publicized to the Assembly of Virginia by Wilkinson. (See among other *informes* those of Sainte

felt that the influence of Spain's American friends engaged in Western intrigues was strong enough to prevent any group of Americans from actually invading Louisiana.[19] Even so, toward the end of his term he ordered Commandant Ignacio Delinó at Arkansas Post to establish a permanent guard detachment at the mouth of the White River, with the result that a corporal and four soldiers were assigned to the White River station.[20]

A more substantial step toward militarizing the Mississippi was intiated in 1791, when a post and a fort were carved out of the wilderness and meanderings of the river at Nogales, in response to the bold enterprises of American land speculators. In 1789 the Georgia state legislature had authorized the South Carolina Yazoo Company and had given it a large grant of land on the east bank of the Mississippi, extending from near Natchez to the Yazoo River, including the area known as Walnut Hills. The well-instructed and accomplished intriguer Dr. James O'Fallon became the agent of the South Carolina Company, which proposed an independent American colony at Walnut Hills under Spanish authority. Since this was obviously a Trojan horse, Spanish officials forthwith re-

---

Geme Beauvais, November 15, 1786, printed in Kinnaird, *AHAR 1945, 3,* 190–92. These were enclosed in Cruzat to Miró, St. Louis, December 2, 1786, which is printed in ibid., pp. 192–93.)

(2) By Captain John O'Sullivan from the district of Franklin, of which Gardoqui advised Miró as did also Wilkinson.

(3) By the English colonel John Connolly, who was commissioned by the governor of Canada to Kentucky to induce those inhabitants to attack Louisiana, of which Gardoqui and Wilkinson informed Miró. (See Gardoqui to Floridablanca No. 308, New York, January 12, 1790, and annexes, AHN 3894.)

(4) By Doctor O'Fallon, agent of the South Carolina Yazoo Company, of which Miró was informed by Wilkinson (J. C. Parish, "The Intrigues of Doctor James O'Fallon," *Mississippi Valley Historical Review, 17* [1930] 230–63; C. H. Haskins, "Yazoo Land Companies," in American Historical Association *Papers, 5* [New York, 1891] 61–103).

(See Miró to Campo de Alange, Madrid, August 11, 1792, Sto. Dom. 2588; copy in Missouri Historical Society, Papers from Spain, No. 84, and in British Museum Additional Manuscripts, Vol. 17567, folios 65–96. Cited with short summary and part translated in A. P. Nasatir, *Before Lewis and Clark, 1* [2 vols. St. Louis, 1952], 157–60. Recently printed in Spanish in Jack D. L. Holmes, *Documentos inéditos para la historia de la Luisiana 1792–1810* [Madrid, 1963], pp. 16–63.)

These threats are discussed in many places and are perhaps most easily accessible in Whitaker, *Spanish-American Frontier.*

19. Delinó to Miró, No. 26, Arkansas, December 28, 1790, P de C 16; Draft [Miró] to Delinó [New Orleans], February 11, 1791, P de C 17.

20. Carondelet to Delinó, New Orleans, January 7, 1792, P de C 18.

jected it and prepared to hold the disputed territory with a sizeable military establishment. Under Gayoso de Lemos' direction they selected a site for a fort and began to build.[21]

On December 30, 1791, the Baron de Carondelet succeeded Miró as governor general of Louisiana. Unlike his mild, equable, patient predecessor, the nepotistically appointed Carondelet was a choleric and quick-nerved warrior, a strategist of wide views and agile combinations, but often deficient in precise knowledge of the instruments and conditions of the game he was taking over and somewhat deficient, it may be, in practical realities. But he had in recompense a prophetic vision of the magnitude of the issues at stake: he had imagination and the sense of a great role to be played. His clear, small, rather effeminate yet firm handwriting can still be seen in the many thousands of pages of manuscripts and letters in the archives of Spain and elsewhere. Write he most assuredly could—and did. Fearful of any slight whisper, rumor, or unconfirmed event, he tended to magnify every report of activity among the American backwoodsmen into a threat of attack on Louisiana. He got excited and wrote at length and with great patience; he reported in detail to his brother-in-law, Luis de Las Casas, the captain general at Havana, and the Duque de la Alcudia in Spain. But no one should sell Carondelet short: although basic patterns he knew and over-all strategy he might see, the wherewithal to carry them out was not always at hand. However, he was to defend Spain's possessions and govern Louisiana as long as he was governor general, to the best of his ability.

As we have seen above, Carondelet looked over the state of

---

21. The principal account is in Miró's letter to Valdés of May 22. See also Gayoso to Miró, No. 84, Natchez, May 10, 1791, P de C 2352; and his Political Report dated Natchez, July 5, 1792, P de C 2353, in Robertson, *Louisiana Under Spain, 1*, 271–89. See also the accounts in A. P. Whitaker, "South Carolina Yazoo Company," *MVHR, 16*, 383–94; Parish, *MVHR, 17*, 230–63; Haskins, *AHAP, 5*, 61–103; Gayarré, *History of Louisiana, 3*, 272–300; Whitaker *Spanish-American Frontier*, pp. 126–33; Burson, *Stewardship of Miró*, pp. 174–85.

Nogales was established to prevent an American land company from occupying the territory around the mouth of the Yazoo River, thus threatening Spain's entire plan of defense on the Mississippi River. Fearing that the Americans might establish a settlement despite Spanish opposition, Miró decided to put a fort there and sent Gayoso de Lemos to explore the mouth of the Yazoo. The fort was established in 1791, with Elías Beauregard as its first commandant. (Gayoso to Miró, No. 84, Natchez, May 10, 1791, P de C 2352.)

Louisiana defenses and found it very sorry indeed.[22] Gayoso de Lemos, governor of Natchez, then presented him with a plan of defense for the Natchez district,[23] which Gayoso believed to be the key to the defense of the whole of Louisiana. Among the points in his plan was the completion of the fort at Nogales begun in 1791, completion of the repairs to the fort at Natchez, and, above all, the establishment of a small squadron of galleys to cruise on the river above New Orleans.[24] Perhaps Miró's plan to station Boulliers with a small fleet at Natchez early in 1788 gave Gayoso the idea for putting a squadron of galleys on the Mississippi, or perhaps it seemed to him the most obvious answer to the defense of Spain's long frontier in Louisiana; probably both reasons contributed to his decision. Gayoso certainly felt that no suitable measures had been taken to keep the Anglo-Americans out of Louisiana, and he did not believe that Indian alliances or intrigues with the Western-

22. Carondelet to Floridablanca, No. 1 res., New Orleans, January 13, 1792, AHN 3898.

23. "Estado político de la provincia de la Luisiana," Natchez, July 5, 1792, in Robertson, *Louisiana Under Spain, I,* 271–89.

24. Spaniards had used galleys, galiots, and *lanchas cañoneras* on the Lower Mississippi below New Orleans and of course at the mouth of the river. And except for the suggestion of stationing a small fleet at Natchez in 1791, the activities of the galleys to the end of 1791 were confined to the lakes and river surrounding New Orleans and on the lower river. Throughout 1791 and probably during 1790 also, there was a galiot at Natchez. In 1792 Rousseau mentioned that *La Flecha* arrived in Nogales from New Madrid. Perhaps it had ascended the river to deliver supplies and war materials. (Rousseau to Gayoso, Nogales, March 9, 1791 [1792], P de C 40.) Early in 1791 Gayoso ascended the river to the mouth of the Yazoo in a galiot accompanied by a convoy of vessels bringing men and materials to construct a post at Nogales (Miró to Sonora, No. 4 res., New Orleans, January 17, 1787, AHN 3885 bis; Gayoso to Miró, No. 84, Natchez, May 10, 1791, P de C 2352).

In 1723 it was proposed in Louisiana that the French put a *galère* and a *demigalère* on the Mississippi to navigate between New Orleans and Illinois, but the purpose of the galère was to be purely commercial and the proposition was not adopted. (N. M. M. Surrey, *Commerce of Louisiana during the French Régime 1699–1763* [New York, 1916, p. 73.)

Wilkinson in 1787 in New Orleans saw a number of galleys there. In his opinion they were too heavy and unmaneuverable for service on the river, and he suggested that the type of vessel used by the Americans on the Delaware River against the English fleet would be better. (W[ilkinson] to Carondelet, Fort Jefferson, February 26, 1794; trans. encl. in Carondelet to Las Casas, No. 113 res., New Orleans, May 1, 1794, P de C 2354.) On January 6, 1792, Gayoso wrote Carondelet that the "Floating forces are indispensable on this river, since without them the fortifications which exist and which may be constructed would be of much less usefulness" (P de C 2353; see also Gayoso's "Estado político," July 5, 1792, P de C 2353).

ers were sufficient to accomplish that purpose without the support of military defenses.

Gayoso believed that 2 galleys, each equipped with 24 oars, 3 *lanchas cañoneras*[25] equipped with 12 oars, and one galiot or large felucca with 12 oars would be sufficient for the naval defense of the Natchez district. Armament for the squadron should consist of one 12-caliber cannon and 12 swivel guns for each galley, and one 8-caliber cannon at the prow of each lancha cañonera with 2 swivel guns at the stern; the galiot was to be furnished with 8 brass swivel guns. The war-time crew of each galley was to include a patrón,[26] 24 oarsmen, one artilleryman with 6 assistants, and a garrison of 20 soldiers—all under the command of the captain of the ship. The war dotation of each gunboat was a patrón, 12 oarsmen, one artilleryman with 4 assistants, and a garrison of a sergeant and 8 soldiers. When unarmed, the galleys required only a patrón and two sailors, while a patrón and one sailor were sufficient for the gunboats. The galiot was to remain armed at all times and be under Gayoso's direct command; its regular dotation was to consist of a patrón and 16 oarsmen, with a sergeant or corporal and 8 soldiers comprising the war-time garrison.[27]

Carondelet acted immediately upon Gayoso's suggestion to establish a river squadron. In January he wrote to the Court, requesting permission to base 2 galleys equipped with 24 oars and armed with 12-caliber cannon, and 3 *lanchas cañoneras* equipped with 12 oars and armed with 8-caliber cannon, at Natchez to patrol the Mississippi River above New Orleans.[28] Without waiting for a reply to his request, he then proceeded to form a squadron of galleys for service on the Mississippi, probably utilizing for that purpose several light vessels that were doing duty along the Gulf Coast and on the lakes and river around New Orleans. By the end

---

25. The *lancha* was a small edition of the *lanchón,* or barge. *Lanchas cañoneras* or *barcos cañoneros* were used by the Spaniards as small gunboats to support their squadron of war galleys. For further details see above, p. 50–51.

26. The patrón was the captain, sailing master, or navigating officer of a riverboat —the steersman, although he was not considered a naval officer.

27. Note on the floating forces needed for the defense of Natchez, signed by Gayoso de Lemos, New Orleans, January 7, 1792, certified copy signed by Carondelet and enclosed in Carondelet to Floridablanca, No. 1 res., New Orleans, January 13, 1792, AHN 3898.

28. Carondelet to Floridablanca, No. 1 res.

of January the organization of His Majesty's Light Squadron of Galleys on the Mississippi River was complete, and Carondelet appointed Captain Don Pedro Rousseau[29] as commander of the new river fleet.[30]

29. The first commander of the Spanish squadron of galleys on the Mississippi River was Captain Don Pedro Rousseau, a Frenchman who entered the service of Spain about 1779 to serve the King faithfully for 24 years. Little is known concerning his life before he attached himself to Spain, except that he distinguished himself as commander of a corsair during the early days of the Revolution. When Spain entered the Revolutionary War, Rousseau joined Gálvez' naval forces and was put in command of the brigantine *Galveztown*, operating in the gulf waters off the Florida coast. While serving under Gálvez he captured the English sloop *West Florida* on Lake Pontchartrain, receiving two serious wounds during the boarding. He aided in the conquest of Movila and forced the port of Pensacola with Gálvez on board his vessel. For his meritorious services he received the special thanks of the King and, at the end of the war, was granted the "aggrégation" at New Orleans, where he established his home and married.

During Miró's term of office Rousseau served for two years at the post of Natchitoches. Early in 1792 he assisted in the capture of William Bowles, delivering him to Havana at the order of Carondelet. In January 1792 Carondelet appointed him to command the newly created squadron of galleys on the Mississippi River. One of his first assignments was the delivery of artillery to New Madrid in 1793, when that post was threatened by an attack from the Ohio. The following year he led an expedition of the galleys to New Madrid to aid in the defense of Upper Louisiana against the projected Clark-Genêt expedition. For a while Rousseau was stationed at Fort Placaminas to guard the mouth of the Mississippi against an attack from the sea. In 1795 he aided Gayoso de Lemos in the establishment of San Fernando de las Barrancas. (Carondelet to Las Casas, No. 138, New Orleans, July 30, 1792, P de C 1441; petition of Rousseau to the King, New Orleans, November 15, 1803, printed in Houck, *Spanish Régime in Missouri*, 2, 324–26; Houck, *History of Missouri*, 2, 142, n. 50; Nasatir and Liljegren, *LHQ*, 21, reprint p. 47, n. 105. Draft of Certificate of Carondelet, New Orleans, August 5, 1797, P de C 23. There are many letters in P de C 209, 210, and 211.)

Throughout his career as commander of the galleys Rousseau suffered from ill health, but until the expedition to Barrancas it never interfered with his work. Life on the river boats was rugged, however, and Carondelet's constant fears of attack kept the squadron always on the move, so that Rousseau found little time to rest and recuperate. In the summer of 1794, arriving at Nogales after six months on the upper river, he complained of a bad case of insomnia, and late fall found him at Natchez convalescing from a fever, probably malaria. (Rousseau to Carondelet, Natchez, n.d. [March 17–31?, 1793], P de C 118; Rousseau to Gayoso de Lemos, on *La Venganza* at Nogales, June 29, 1794, P de C 209; Rousseau to Carondelet, on *La Venganza* at Nogales, June 29, 1794, P de C 210; Rousseau to Carondelet, Natchez, November 30, 1794, P de C 210.) He recovered sufficiently to lead the squadron to Barrancas early in 1795, but his health was broken and he was unable to take a very active part in the construction of Fort San Fernando. While at Barrancas he developed a severe hemorrhoid condition, which caused him infinite suffering and crippled him so that he could hardly perform his duties. By the time the galleys redescended to New Orleans, after nearly a year on the upper river, Rousseau's health was so poor he was forced to retire to his home for treatment and rest.

THE SPANISH FRESH-WATER FLEET 33

Naturally, Carondelet had stepped into his position as governor general of Louisiana to face a complex set of factors in a time of great tension. Knowing French and Spanish but no English, and not acquainted at all with Spain's empire in the Mississippi, he had to evaluate the many and complex factors involved, but he

---

(Gayoso to Carondelet, San Fernando, July 18, 1795, P de C 198; Gayoso to Carondelet, No. 18 res., New Madrid, September 22, 1795, P de C 32; Rousseau to Gayoso, on *La Venganza*, October 12, 1795, P de C 211; Rousseau to Carondelet, on *La Venganza*, at San Fernando, December 8, 1795, P de C 211; Rousseau to Carondelet, New Orleans, January 18, 1796, P de C 129; draft in P de C 33.)

Early in June 1795 Carondelet informed the Court of Rousseau's part in the establishment of Fort San Fernando de las Barrancas and requested that in recognition of his services there and as commander of the river squadron he be granted a promotion to the rank of lieutenant colonel. He repeated the recommendation in February, and in April, Rousseau received the formal notice of his promotion. (Carondelet to Alcudia, No. 53 res., New Orleans, June 10, 1795, AHN 3899; copy in P de C 2351. Rousseau to Carondelet, on *La Venganza*, San Fernando des Ecores, August 22, 1795, P de C 211. List of subjects recommended by Carondelet for promotion enclosed in draft [Carondelet] to Prince of Peace, No. 73 res., New Orleans, February 10, 1796, P de C 178A; Rousseau to Carondelet, New Orleans, March 5, 1796, P de C 33; Las Casas to Governor of Louisiana, Havana, April 11, 1796, P de C 153A; Rousseau to Carondelet, New Orleans, April 20, 1796, P de C 33.)

After 1796 Rousseau's naval activities were confined to the gulf waters off the Florida coast. In 1799 he participated in an expedition to regain the fort of San Marcos de Apalache from the Indians, and a year later, while in command of *La Leal*, he captured two ships from the English. In 1801 he intercepted several vessels carrying artillery and ammunition to William Bowles, and burned one of Bowles' schooners. Finally, upon order from Governor General Salcedo, he took two galleys and a bombardier to the relief of Fort Apalache when Bowles and his Indians threatened it with attack. In November 1803 he requested the King to grant him retirement with a pension in the city of New Orleans. Rousseau had ten children at the time, the eldest, Don Pedro Andrés Rousseau, serving as a cadet in the Regiment of Louisiana. (Petition of Rousseau to the King, in Houck, *Spanish Régime*, 2, 324–26; draft to Rousseau, New Orleans, November 25, 1800, P de C 69; Nasatir and Liljegren, *LHQ, 21*, reprint p. 47, n. 105.)

Rousseau was generally acknowledged as a brave and zealous officer by his superiors and seems to have been well liked by the men who served under him. Carondelet reported that he "manifested great zeal in the service of His majesty and activity, and courage and boldness and vigor." The records show only one complaint against him, made by Portell in the fall of 1794. (Draft [Carondelet] to Alcudia, New Orleans, September 27, 1793, P de C 178A; Gayoso to Carondelet, Natchez, April 4, 1793, P de C 2363; also printed in Houck, *1*, 410–12. Draft of Certificate of Carondelet.) According to Portell, Rousseau was petulant, like all his countrymen. Moreover, he did not understand the Spanish service, and Portell was afraid he would counsel the militia at New Madrid to refuse discipline. Apparently he discovered his fears to be groundless, however, for he made no further complaints against the captain. (Portell to Gayoso, New Madrid, October 20, 794, P de C 47.)

Rousseau's correspondence while commanding the river galleys and while he was at Natchitoches is contained in widely scattered legajos in the P de C. His activities

did not fail to understand the value of the Mississippi River, at once the prize of the game of empire and one of its chief instruments. Both as soldier and as statesman, Carondelet did show a keen appreciation of the double nature of the Mississippi itself.

The Mississippi River forms the central artery of a vast network of rivers and streams that drain the huge area lying between the Appalachian Mountains and the Rockies. With its more than forty navigable tributaries, it forms a great inland navigation system, and in Carondelet's time it opened illimitable domain to venturesome settlers, traders, and trappers. From the viewpoint of its Spanish defenders, it took its rise in the far north and flowed down to about the area of Cape Girardeau, just above the mouth of the Ohio. Its bed, which lies below the surrounding prairie country, is fairly level and is bordered by abrupt wooded bluffs.

From Cape Girardeau to the gulf—the military highway of the Spanish regime—the river flows through a broad alluvial plain varying from thirty to sixty miles wide, with the heights of the valley thus rising at a considerable distance from the river. Along the east bank of the Mississippi runs a low plateau that begins near the Illinois and extends into the neighborhood of Baton Rouge. At several points along the river this highland strikes the water, forming a series of low bluffs, as, for example, near the present site of Memphis[31] and at a number of points between Vicksburg and Baton Rouge, including the site of Natchez. Everywhere else the shores of this erratic, ever-shifting river are flat and unstable.

---

during 1792 to 1796 are detailed in the admirable unpublished master's thesis of my former student Frances Coughlin, "Spanish Galleys on the Upper Mississippi" (Claremont College, 1945). Some of his activities during the same period have been discussed below, pp. 63 et seq. Rousseau's *nombramiento* as captain of infantry with salary of lieutenant dated El Pardo, January 15, 1794, is in P de C 566; royal order of February 27, 1798, for salary as captain and rank of lieutenant colonel *graduado* is in P de C 1502; index to royal order granting salary of captain of infantry, March 13, 1798, is in P de C 560.

30. Services of Pedro Rousseau, New Orleans, November 15, 1803, printed in Houck, *Spanish Régime*, 2, 324–26. Las Casas approved Rousseau's appointment in September 1792, at the same time approving Carondelet's measures for defense of Louisiana and his appointment of Guillermo Duparc as Rousseau's second in command of the squadron (Las Casas to Governor of Louisiana, Havana, September 3[2?], 1792, P de C 152A).

31. The diaries below, pp. 172–74, 185–86, 216–17, 279–83, describe the Barrancas à Margot. Gayoso in his letter to Carondelet, No. 17 res., New Madrid, September 16, 1795, describes the Barrancas de Prud'homme, P de C 2364; printed in Spanish in Holmes, *Documentos*, pp. 253–59.

During the period of Spanish occupation of Louisiana there was only one spot on the west shore all the way from Cape Girardeau to the gulf high enough to escape inundation at flood time; this was the "small prairie" located about a league below the mouth of the St. Francis River. On the east bank, 18 miles below the mouth of the Ohio, a precipitous cliff called the Iron Mine rose 200 feet above the river, and extended some thousand yards. Below the Iron Mine the shores of the river were low and swampy until the Chickasaw Bluffs appeared, some 210 miles to the south, and from Chickasaw Bluffs on to the mouth of the Yazoo, both banks of the river were swampy, covered with high reeds and cypress trees. Just below the mouth of the Yazoo River the series of highlands closing the valley on the east reappeared to form the bluffs at Walnut Hills; from there to Baton Rouge they ran close to the river's shore, often dipping into the water itself to furnish several excellent sites for towns. Below Baton Rouge the east bank was an endless succession of low cypress swamps subject to inundation in flood time.

This was the great central artery: into it flowed many others, all of commercial and military importance. Carondelet, musing on their great distances and silent menace, knew that he must put his little army in boats to cope with such fantastic problems of logistics, for, measured from New Orleans, one climbed this wilderness empire by a giant stair, whose steps were successive rivers. It was 100-odd leagues to the first northern bastion of Nogales, on the Yazoo—more than a month away—another 120 leagues on to the Arkansas, another 50 leagues to the St. Francis, 100 leagues more to the Ohio, and 60 on to the Missouri. To far-off St. Louis, all-important anchor of the line, it was some 500 leagues or—more important measure—three months' time under favorable conditions (four months or more, often enough). To New Madrid,[32] sen-

---

32. Between St. Louis and New Madrid were: Ste. Geneviève, 20 leagues below St. Louis and a league away from New Bourbon, and Cape Girardeau, about 20 leagues below Ste. Geneviève and above the mouth of the Ohio River. Below New Madrid about 100 leagues was the Arkansas Post, and between those two points there were no other white settlements until Barrancas de Margó was built on the east bank in 1795. Arkansas Post was not on the Mississippi River but some distance up the Arkansas. There was a small detachment at the mouth of the river (or at the mouth of the White River). There was also a naval station at the mouth of the Ohio. One hundred leagues below Arkansas was Nogales on the east bank of the Mississippi at the mouth of the Yazoo River, and about 40 leagues below the mouth of the Yazoo was Natchez.

tinel station for the increasing volume of traffic down the Ohio, one counted 300 or 400 leagues, depending on the height of the river, and from 75 to 90 days of upstream struggle; to Barrancas de Margó, at the Chickasaw Bluffs, 340 leagues from New Orleans at low water or 60 to 75 days' transit time; to the flourishing community at Natchez, almost a neighbor of the capital, one had to spend nearly a month of hard travel. Upstream, one did not travel on the Mississippi but rather fought one's way.[33]

Although Carondelet was unable to obtain the additional land forces he thought necessary for the defense of Louisiana, he was successful in securing the establishment on the Mississippi River of a royal squadron of galleys that became a key to his entire program of defense of the Spanish empire in the Mississippi Valley. Since the Mississippi served as the main highway for the entire valley, the importance of a naval force on the river was obvious. Two physical features of the Ohio-Mississippi River system made it conceivable that this miniature armada might stand off the rush of invading Westerners. One was the Falls of the Ohio, which prevented the frontiersmen from bringing vessels of comparable size into the Mississippi; the second was the ill-defined, swampy shores of the river, which made it impracticable for superior forces of Westerners to land and bring their fire power to bear on the galleys. On the river itself the heavier armament of the galleys and their vastly superior maneuverability as compared with clumsy flatboats would enable a smaller force to fight under heavy odds with some prospects of success.

While the river galleys served as a link among Louisiana's scat-

---

33. There are a number of descriptions of the Mississippi River and posts during the Spanish regime: V. Collot, *A Journey in North America* (2 vols. and Atlas, Firenze, 1924); A. Stoddard, *Sketches of Louisiana* (Philadelphia, 1912); Philip Pittman, *Present State of the European Settlements on the Mississippi*, ed. F. A. Hodder (Cleveland, 1906); Perrin du Lac, *Travels in the Two Louisianas* (London, 1807); Paul Alliot and Gayoso, printed in Robertson, *Louisiana under Spain*, *1*. Gayoso and Rousseau among others describe parts of the river in their diaries and letters. Journal of John Halley in 1789 and 1791 in the Durrett Collection of the University of Chicago gives an interesting account of a boatman's visit to the Spanish commandant at the mouth of the Arkansas. See also John Pope, *A Tour through the Southwestern Territories* (Richmond, 1792); Francis Baily, *Journal of a Tour in Unsettled Parts of North America in 1796 and 1797* (London, 1856).

Many of these points are discussed and precise locations given as mentioned in the diaries of the voyages on the Mississippi given below, pp. 149–326.

tered outposts and in time of danger afforded much-needed support to harassed post commanders, the main purposes of the fleet were to defend Louisiana against every attack and to preserve the province from illegal infiltration. Whenever the Spanish outposts were threatened with attack, the galleys were used to transport reinforcements of troops from one fort to another, as well as to deliver needed supplies and munitions to threatened river posts. When invasion was expected by water, the squadron stood by to lend naval aid and to carry garrisons and troops from abandoned posts or down the river for safety. During times of threatened invasion the galleys were used to convoy commercial vessels loaded with provisions and munitions up the Mississippi. Without the galleys to patrol the upper river, enemy bands could easily have gone into Upper Louisiana from the Ohio to attack and capture the isolated and ill-defended posts of the upper province. Indeed, their mere presence frequently deterred groups of American aggressors from attacking, because the Americans could not bring boats anywhere near the size of the galleys past the Falls of the Ohio. In fact, descending flatboats, unless in great numerical superiority, were helpless against the Spanish fleet.

The naval vessels also cruised at key points on the river to inspect descending boats for suspicious persons or hidden arms and to watch for signs of an invading party—prepared to stop it, if not too large, or else descend to give warning to the posts below. The four chief cruising stations on the Mississippi were: (1) at the mouth of the Mississippi—Balize and Placaminas; (2) between Nogales and the mouth of the Arkansas River; (3) just above the Nogales fort; and (4) opposite the mouth of the Ohio River. They were also used to cruise on the Upper Mississippi as far as Prairie du Chien.

Besides their military uses, the Spanish river galleys fulfilled many domestic purposes in Louisiana. Their duties consisted in transporting men, materials, and supplies for building new military posts along the river; giving added force for defense against Indian or white attacks and aggression; acting as a police force to maintain law and order so as to protect the commerce of the King's vessels from Indian attack or white pirates; aiding in the capture of criminals; delivering the annual presents to the Indian nations and impressing the savages with Spain's naval power and prestige; playing an important role in the postal system; and assuring the prevention of smuggling by English or American merchants and traders. Even though the galleys were never tested by an actual attack, the Spaniards' use of the river squadron on the Mississippi may certainly be judged successful.[34]

At the time of its formation in January 1792 His Majesty's Light Squadron of Galleys probably comprised five galleys, two galiots and one lancha cañonera. Shortly there was added a heavy galley (*La Leal*) and two more galiots,[35] which did not form a regular part of the river squadron. The section of the river over which each vessel was to operate depended on its size. The largest, *La Leal*, which was completed at New Orleans toward the end of 1793, built at the expense of the officers of the fixed Regiment of Louisiana, was used exclusively on the river below the capital, the lakes, and the gulf. Of much greater tonnage than the others, it was capable of going to Havana,[36] but by the same token, it was incapable of running the sand bars, the whirlpools, and the narrow chutes of the Mississippi above New Orleans.

The next largest galleys were *La Victoria* and *La Luisiana*,[37] originally confined to the middle reaches of the river, from Natchez and Nogales to New Orleans. While Rousseau considered

---

34. The documentation of these points is far too great to cite individually. Many are illustrated in the diaries below, pp. 149–326.

Manuel García, commandant of the squadron, wrote Gayoso de Lemos, New Orleans, July 14, 1798 (P de C 1501B): "The galeras are worth their weight since they conserve free navigation of the seas to all King's vessels, assures the King his immense possessions on the Mississippi and the entrance to it, commanding respect of our residents [*vecinos*] and of the numerous and barbarous Indian nations."

35. *La Fina*, which usually worked with *La Leal* on the lower river, and *La Vigilante*, which belonged to Gayoso de Lemos and was stationed wherever he happened to be. See below, p. 242, n. 4.

36. Carondelet to Alcudia, No. 15 res., New Orleans, August 27, 1793, AHN 3898; draft [Carondelet] to Alcudia, New Orleans, September 27, 1793, P de C 178; draft [Carondelet] to Metzinger, New Orleans, March 24, 1795, P de C 28; Carondelet to Las Casas, No. 125 res., New Orleans, October 20, 1794, P de C 1447; draft in P de C 152B. Draft [Carondelet] to Las Casas, No. 127 res., New Orleans, November 5, 1794, P de C 152B; Las Casas to Carondelet, Havana, December 23, 1793 [1794], P de C 152B; passport of *La Leal*, New Orleans, April 10, 1794, P de C 21.

37. *La Luisiana* was slightly smaller than *La Victoria*. In August 1796 the complete crew of *La Luisiana* consisted of 1 patrón and 35 sailors. *La Victoria's* crew was incomplete—32 sailors and 1 patrón. (*Relación* of patrones and sailors of the crew of *La Victoria*, signed by Barnó y Ferrúsola, and idem for *La Luisiana*, dated today, August 24, 1796, signed by Metzinger; both relaciones were enclosed in García to Carondelet, No. 67, on *La Venganza*, San Fernando, August 24, 1796, P de C 33.)

them too large and too heavy to ascend the river as far as Barrancas de Margó, early in 1796 both galleys ascended to Barrancas successfully, the next year they reached New Madrid, and *La Luisiana* continued on to St. Louis (since the Spaniards feared for *La Victoria* because of the strong currents between New Madrid and St. Louis, it descended instead to the capital).[38] Both galleys carried about 32 or 34 oars; they were heavy enough to carry a more formidable armament than their lighter sisters—a 24- (sic) caliber cannon, 2 4-caliber cannon, and 8 swivel guns each. Their crews consisted of a patrón, 32 to 35 sailors, and one *proel*.[39]

The 3 remaining galleys in the squadron—*La Venganza* (the flagship), *La Castilla*, and *La Felipa*—were about the same size and tonnage, and formed the main body of the Spanish squadron on the upper river. They carried about the same number of oars[40] as the 2 larger ones, but a lighter armament, each galley being equipped with one 18-caliber cannon and 8 swivel guns. These 3 galleys ascended with the squadron on its first trip to New Madrid in 1794, continued to serve on the upper river in the vicinity of Chickasaw Bluffs and New Madrid from 1794-96, and ascended to St. Louis in the summer of 1797.[41]

Two smaller vessels—the galiots *La Flecha* and *La Activa*—were regularly attached to the river squadron. They were simply smaller copies of the larger galleys, carrying 14 to 16 rowers and an armament of 8 bronze swivel guns. Both were stout and serviceable vessels, capable of encountering more diverse river conditions than any of the other members of the fleet. Whereas *La Flecha* made

38. Rousseau to Carondelet on *La Venganza* at San Fernando, October 9, 1795, P de C 32; same to same, Ecores à Margot, November 23, 1795; Rousseau to Gayoso, November 25, 1795, P de C 211; Metzinger to Gayoso, on *La Luisiana*, March 11, 1796, P de C 48; Grandpré to Carondelet, Natchez, February 5, 1796, P de C 212B; Barnó y Ferrúsola to Carondelet, San Fernando, April 10, 1796, P de C 33; Howard to Carondelet, New Madrid, April 7, 1797, P de C 35.

39. The *proel* was a seaman stationed at the prow of the boat.

40. The crew of *La Venganza* in August 1796 consisted of 34 sailors, 1 patrón, and 1 proel. *La Felipa*'s crew at the end of 1795 included 34 sailors when complete. (Draft [Gayoso] to Rousseau, New Madrid, December 3, 1795, P de C 130. *Relación* of crew garrisoning *La Venganza* during August 1796, signed by García and enclosed in García to Carondelet, No. 67.)

41. Draft of secret instructions to Rousseau, drawn up by Carondelet, New Orleans, January 15, 1794, P de C 2354; another draft, P de C 2352. There are many letters that could be cited, especially the letters of Rousseau and García on *La Venganza*, 1792-97.

many voyages to the upper river beginning in 1792 and, in fact, spent most of its time there, *La Activa* was not on the upper river as constantly. Both were left there, stationed at St. Louis, in 1797, and furnished the post with naval and patrol support against English and American aggressions. Making reconnaissance and patrol voyages as far as Prairie du Chien after the turn of the century, *La Flecha*, under the command of Santiago St. Vrain, was stationed in St. Louis permanently, while *La Activa* was under the command of Roberto Macay and stationed at New Madrid.[42]

La Vigilante,[43] the third Spanish galiot to see service on the Mississippi, was not a member of the squadron but was used by Gayoso de Lemos for his official trips on the river. It was made over into a galiot in 1794 from a *lanchón* that the commandant of New Madrid purchased for the royal service from a trader named Bartélemi Tardiveau.[44]

42. Relación of patrones and sailors who garrison *La Flecha*, signed by Bernardo Molina, enclosed in García to Carondelet, No. 67. For *La Flecha* on the river to New Madrid in 1792 and 1793, see Rousseau to Gayoso, on *La Venganza*, Nogales, March 9, 1791 [1792], P de C 46; Log of La Flecha, below, pp. 154.

For *La Flecha's* later activities see A. P. Nasatir, "Anglo-Spanish Rivalry in the Iowa Country 1797–1798," *Iowa Journal of History and Politics*, 28, (1930), 337–89, where diary of *La Flecha* to Prairie du Chien under the command of Molina in 1798 is published. There are several other such diaries for 1801, etc., under the command of Santiago de St. Vrain. See below, pp. 141–43.

43. *La Vigilante* was armed with 8 swivel guns and a 6-pound cannon mounted on the prow. There is much correspondence relating to it. On its purchase and Rousseau's opinion of it, see Rousseau to Gayoso, on *La Venganza*, Nogales, June 29, 1794, P de C 209; Rousseau to Carondelet, same date, P de C 210. Portell to [Carondelet], New Madrid, July 15, 1794, P de C 29; Carondelet to Rendón, New Orleans, October 16, 1794, P de C 618; certificate of purchase of a lanchón from Bartolomé Tardiveau, signed by Portell, New Madrid, July 22, 1794, enclosed in ibid.; draft [Rendón] to Gayoso, New Orleans, November 20, 1794, P de C 581A. There is a drawing of *La Vigilante* in the MHS, and it is published in Leland D. Baldwin, *Keelboat Age on Western Waters* (Pittsburgh, 1941).

44. Bartélemi, or Bartolomé, Tardiveau was a French trader who negotiated with Congress on behalf of the people of Illinois. He was born, probably in Nantes, about 1750 and came to America in 1777. He was twice captured by the British and once imprisoned in Halifax. In Philadelphia in 1778 he taught French, then migrated to Kentucky, engaged in trade, and was a landowner and politician. He was a friend of Wouves d'Argès. Tardiveau went to Kaskaskia and saw Cruzat in St. Louis, and Peyroux in Ste. Geneviève. He settled for a while in Vincennes, acted as an interpreter, and drew up several memorials on the Western country. He proposed to deliver tobacco in New Orleans annually for six years and wrote letters to Crevecoeur giving a contemporaneous account of conditions, especially economic conditions, in Kentucky and Cumberland. Tardiveau was a judge at Kaskaskia, carried

The final member of the Spanish river squadron was the lancha cañonera *El Rayo,* a small gunboat equipped with 8 oars, carrying a crew which, when complete, consisted of a patrón, a proel, and 8 sailors or oarsmen, and armed with a single 12-caliber cannon probably mounted on the prow. With the squadron on the upper river most of the time, it spent most of the year 1795 cruising at the mouth of the Ohio.[45]

The river war-vessel was a long, smartly designed ship constructed on a stout ribbed keel, effectively streamlined for breasting the swift river current, except that the hull was widened near the stern to accommodate a relatively large cabin. The deck of the boat was covered, except for the section where the rowers' benches were placed, and the sides were close to the water, except where, toward the stern, they were built up to form a cabin. The cabin occupied well over one-fourth of the boat, its flat roof being railed in to form a second half-deck. The vessel was equipped with a high mast carrying as many as three sails for use on the infrequent occasions when travelers on the winding Mississippi could expect a favoring wind. It was also equipped with a rudder and helm, and carried anchors, grappling irons for use in boarding enemy vessels, and stream cable, probably used for cordelling.

Always accompanied by a number of pirogues, or round-bottomed dugout canoes, used for express mail service, scouting messenger service, detached duty, and other purposes, the galleys' chief means of propulsion were oars and sails. However, when a strong headwind made rowing too difficult, they sometimes resorted to

---

on negotiations for the Scioto French emigrés, settled some of them in Spanish Louisiana, and went to New Orleans several times. He then moved to New Madrid and became a Spanish subject, being interested in mills in that area and associated in business enterprises with Audrain and others. He died February 22, 1801. See Howard C. Rice, *Barthélemi Tardiveau: A French Trader in the West* (Baltimore, 1938). My former student Mary Jane Richards has written a good honors paper (in my possession) on Tardiveau based on my collection of manuscripts. See also Houck, *History of Missouri* and *Spanish Régime in Missouri,* consult indexes; C. W. Alvord, *Kaskaskia Records 1778–1790* (Springfield, 1909). "B. Tardeveau; a French man, of considerable abilities, with the arts & address peculiar to his nation, he speaks and writes Inglis elegantly—& is a great schemer both in politicks & commerce, but always deceives himself" (James Wilkinson to Andrés L. Armesto, New Orleans, September 14, 1789, P de C 2373).

45. Ferrúsola to Carondelet, on *El Rayo,* New Madrid, March 28, 1795, P de C 32; another letter written on same day, P de C 31, *Dotación* of artillery considered necessary in the plazas and forts of the province (of Louisiana), n.p., n.d., P de C 122A.

cordelling. They seldom if ever used poling or punting, since they were all equipped with a large number of oars and rowing was much faster.[46]

Captain Pedro Rousseau served as the first squadron commander, under the immediate and strict command of the governor general.[47] And never was a Spanish fleet commander obliged to make a months'-long expedition into the Upper Mississippi, confronting endlessly changing and unpredictable conditions, without the comfort of explicit instructions from his chief covering every conceivable—and on occasion, inconceivable—circumstance. All commanders were required to send detailed reports to the governor general. On financial matters Rousseau also reported to the intendant general, and reports on the fleet's activities around the Natchez district were always sent to Governor Gayoso de Lemos.

The squadron had a physician or surgeon who traveled with it (in 1795 the fleet surgeon was Dr. Luis Fauré), and sick sailors were usually sent to the nearest post hospital.[48] From 1794 to 1796

---

46. See diaries below, pp. 149-326. Draft of instructions to the commanders of the galiots, galleys, and boats of the light squadron that ascended to New Madrid under Captain Rousseau (drawn up by Gayoso), opposite the Yazoo, March 11, 1794 [1795?], P de C 2363; Instructions to ———, signed by Rousseau, same place, on *La Venganza*, March 24, 1795, P de C 2364; Rousseau to Carondelet, Natchez, November 30, 1794, P de C 210.

47. From 1792-96 Captain Rousseau served as squadron commander, being replaced by Manuel García in 1796. Commanders received orders from the governor general, although Gayoso de Lemos, governor of Natchez, sometimes gave him instructions, usually at Carondelet's request. Gayoso de Lemos was commander-in-chief of all the Spanish naval forces on the upper river in 1795, and consequently gave orders in addition to Carondelet's. (Gayoso to Carondelet, on *La Vigilante*, New Madrid, October 2, 1795, printed in *AHAR 1896, 1,* 1093-95. This is from P de C 178A; another copy in P de C 178B; certified copy in P de C 2364. See Anthony Wayne's letter addressed to General or Commanding Officer of the Spanish arms and troops on the western bank of the Mississippi, printed in *AHAR 1896, 1,* 1091-92. These are all enclosed in Carondelet to Alcudia, No. 62 res., New Orleans, November 1, 1795, AHN 3899.

When the ships were on detached service they received orders from Carondelet or Gayoso de Lemos.

48. Most common diseases in the squadron were scurvy and fever, probably malaria. Severe cases of scurvy were usually sent to New Orleans, since the outpost hospitals did not have means for treating scurvy adequately.

Luis Fauré, "médico y cirujano mayor" of the squadron, was born in La Rochelle, France, about 1763, and entered the Spanish service as "médico y cirujano" of the Royal Hospital at Natchez on April 15, 1785. Between 1794 and 1798 he also served in the posts of Nogales, Barrancas, and Baton Rouge. He was appointed surgeon for

the squadron also had a *contador,* Don José Zamora, who accompanied it on the expedition to the upper river in 1794 and again in 1795. Entrusted by the intendant with funds to cover the expenses of the galleys while they were on the upper river, his duties included paying the wages of the soldiers and sailors attached to the squadron, settling accounts for supplies and services furnished by post commanders, and arranging for the dismissal and hire of personnel.[49]

Each individual galley did not at first have a naval officer in command; instead, one officer served for two or more boats, communicating his orders to the crew through the patrón. Since this system did not prove satisfactory, however, at the instance of Rousseau each vessel, by 1793, was supplied with a commanding officer who exercised absolute control over all the sailors and land troops on board his ship, always being subject himself to the squadron commander or his second.

Relations between the naval officers and the post commandants were usually prescribed by detailed instructions from the governor general, issued each time the squadron or any of its vessels ascended the river or was stationed at a particular post. His instructions to the commanders in the squadron were always extremely detailed, attempting to cover every contingency that might possibly arise. Carondelet himself left little to the initiative of his naval officers, even going so far as to suggest the procedure to be used by the galleys in battle, prescribing when and how they were to attack and when and under what conditions they were to retreat.

The size of Spain's naval forces on the Mississippi was probably

---

the boundary commission in 1798 but perhaps did not serve. He held land on Cole's Creek. Fauré's service record is in P de C 161A.

49. Rendón to Gayoso de Lemos, New Orleans, March 30, 1795, P de C 48; Trudeau to Portell, No. 35, St. Louis, June 8, 1795, P de C 127; draft [Gayoso] to Zamorra, New Madrid, October 5, 1795, P de C 130. Zamora to Gayoso, San Fernando, October 29, 1795, P de C 48.

José Zamora, second lieutenant of the New Orleans militia, performed the duties of *contador* of the Mississippi squadron under Rousseau in 1794. He was born in La Coruña about 1759, and served in the office of the *Contador de Reales Rentas* beginning in 1785. His accounts kept as contador of the squadron and at San Fernando are in P de C 533B; his service record is in P de C 565. According to Gayoso de Lemos, Zamora fulfilled his duties perfectly and with zeal that merited only the highest commendation (Gayoso to Carondelet, San Fernando, July 18, 1795, P de C 198; same to same, No. 18 res., New Madrid, September 22, 1795, P de C 32).

between 280 and 300 men,[50] though rarely was the fleet complement complete. Ideally, there was not only a patrón, who supervised the mechanics of navigation, took orders from the commander, and occasionally was used to command a galley in the absence of its commander for short trips on the river, but also a proel. Good sailors, however, were scarce in Louisiana, making it very difficult to keep complete crews on the war galleys. Usually crews were recruited in New Orleans or Natchez, but by the time the galleys reached the upper river, many replacements were necessary. While desertions were high, sailors quit often, and replacements were frequent; punishment for deserters when caught was not severe. As a whole, sailors in the river squadron were coarse, hardy men, who resented discipline and were quick to desert if they did not like their treatment.

The sailors were paid at a higher rate than Spanish land troops in Louisiana. Their wages ran from 11 to 15 pesos a month, plus daily food rations, which consisted mainly of biscuits made from wheat flour, supplemented by beans, salted meat, rice, and corn ground into gruel or on the ear. (Although fresh wild meat was fairly abundant, fresh fruits and vegetables were not, and the result was the prevalence of scurvy.) When soldiers were used for rowing the galleys, they received 2 *reales* a day in addition to their regular pay, and sailors who did extra land duties were paid at the same rate. Galley commanders received 30 pesos a month plus the regular table allowance[51] for Spanish naval officers.

Discipline was fairly strict and burdensome, though not severe. Since rum and whiskey were forbidden on board the galleys, offenders were sternly punished and their liquor confiscated. Punishments for insubordination or disorderliness might vary from fatigue duty to whippings to imprisonment, depending on the

---

50. This estimate is based upon the crews of the 5 galleys and 2 galiots in the squadron, plus the galley *La Leal* and the galiots *La Fina* and *La Vigilante*. In the *estado* given Gayoso de Lemos in 1799, the squadron then consisted of 4 galeras, 3 lanchas cañoneras, 3 galeotas, and a bombadera (not including some of our galleys but containing others). It listed all told: 264 oars and 229 crew, lacking 86 men to complete their complement in full, which would make the full complement total 315 (encl. in Gayoso to Saavedra, New Orleans, June 9, 1799, AHN 3901; the *estado* is dated New Orleans, June 10 [sic], 1799).

51. Barnó y Ferrúsola to Carondelet, New Madrid, May 9, 1795, P de C 31.

nature of the offense. Stealing and grave insubordination were punishable by lashings, or *casión,* administered without mercy or contemplation. The sailors lived constantly under the eye of two masters—the patrón of the vessel, responsible for all matters pertaining to navigation, and the officer in charge. They were absent from home in a dull and hostile climate for long months, and even at a center of civilization like Natchez, official orders required them to be kept separate from the garrison troops and to spend a number of hours a day in naval exercises on the river. Grumbling and quarrels were thus constant[52] and desertions quite naturally commonplace.

The river war-galleys—or fresh-water navy—organized in late January 1792 by order of Carondelet, and under the command of Pedro Rousseau, probably stayed at New Orleans until around the end of February of that year, when Carondelet ordered Rousseau to ascend to Natchez to cooperate with Gayoso de Lemos in its defense. The reason for that order was the arrival in the capital of frequent and continuous reports that the United States was trying to attract Spain's Indian allies and was threatening the Spanish settlements along the Mississippi. When Rousseau reached Natchez with the squadron in March, Gayoso immediately sent him to Nogales. Available evidence indicates that the galley *La Venganza* and the gunboat *El Rayo* were stationed at Nogales under Rousseau's command from March until July 1792, while the rest of the squadron remained at Natchez.

Little evidence is available at the present time about the activities of the member ships of the squadron during its first year. Most likely the majority of the vessels remained in the lower part of the river between Natchez and New Orleans, although in March 1792 Rousseau mentions that *La Flecha* arrived in Nogales from New Madrid. He himself was with the squadron during the entire latter half of 1792 at Natchez. In January 1793 the tensions in the Mississippi Valley frontier rose to such heights that Rousseau was ordered to ascend the river, thus beginning the really important ac-

52. The above account is based upon various letters and instructions from Carondelet and Gayoso de Lemos to officers of the river fleet; on letters from the said officers to Carondelet and Gayoso, and from Rendón; on letters of the squadron commander to officers under him; and on the diaries given below, pp. 149-326.

tivity of the galleys, especially in the defense of the upper part of the river and valley.[53]

The galleys sailed in some formation when they set out up the river, usually at a distance of a precise interval—one-half a line or a cordelle. The squadron had, of course, to navigate the Mississippi: it had to cope with wind, weather, and water—impersonal and maddening opponents. Indeed, each season contributed its own hazards to river navigation. While there was a well-defined season for descending the river during or just after the spring floods, there was no good season for ascending it at such time. When the Mississippi was in flood, it was nearly impossible for the heavy galleys to make way against it. In summer, when the river was low, the route was much longer and the channels often so shallow and so full of bars, or *baturas,* that the galleys had great difficulties. In late fall and winter, when the river was somewhat higher, storms, snow, sleet, icy head-winds, and floating chunks of ice made the slow progress up the river an endless test of endurance. At any season the lack of wind or a strong opposing wind was liable to delay the progress of vessels depending on sails.

Under all conditions the current was the first obstacle. At New Orleans it ran steady and strong at nearly six miles an hour, making it very difficult to push heavy galleys. On the upper river it ran three to four miles an hour, depending on the season and the flood conditions. High, dense forests along the river bank often blocked the wind from the water and prevented the use of sails. It was therefore necessary to hug the shore, where the current was less strong and where countercurrents might even help the boat along. At a bend, however, the full weight of the current swept against the outer bank, bringing progress to a stop. Thus at every bend of the tortuous river a boat finding itself on the outside had to cross the river to take the quiet inside bank. But in crossing the full current of the stream, a boat would lose one-half mile of distance, to be made up by heavy rowing before the boat reached the next bend—which was soon enough. In one section of the river, boats were known to stem the current 54 miles, in order to gain 5

---

53. Rousseau to Gayoso, on *La Venganza,* Nogales, March 9, 1791 [1792], P de C 46; Carondelet to Las Casas, No. 138, New Orleans, July 30, 1792, P de C 1441; Beauregard to Gayoso, No. 185, Nogales, November 10, 1792, P de C 46; many other letters of Carondelet and Gayoso de Lemos; and especially Rousseau's letters dated July through December, 1792.

miles as the crow flies. Similar conditions, though not so extreme, occurred at intervals of every 15 or 20 miles.[54] All told, men counted 390 bends between New Orleans and St. Louis.

Yet steadily, if slowly, the boats crept up the river.[55] They usually stopped for lunch-time respite and to rest the men. Half-rowing, half-feeling their way up the quieter edges of the current, the crews had to look out for other perils. Rocky cliffs extending into the water and rock obstructions in the river bed caused dangerous whirlpools; sand bars and islands lay ever in wait, constantly forming, continually shifting, sometimes—especially in cloudy weather or at dusk—too well concealed. And despite all vigilance of the lookout, a galley would occasionally ground humiliatingly. Then there was nothing for it but to have the crew plunge into the water and, while the patrón endeavored to lever the boat one way and another, tug and haul it off by main strength.

Every mile or so there were other obstacles to be avoided. Not only could floating logs entangled with loose masses of debris, known as "floating islands," severely damage even a galley, but hulls could be ripped by "planters" and "sawyers." The former were logs whose root ends had become fixed in the river bottom, the free ends tilting a little downstream by the action of the current. They were concealed spikes ready to impale any vessel. Sawyers were much the same, except that the downstream ends were

---

54. Usually vessels going upstream sought to avoid strong currents in the Mississippi River between the mouths of the White and Arkansas Rivers by using a channel that connected the two rivers about 18 miles inland from the west bank of the Mississippi. On reaching the mouth of the Arkansas, the vessels ascended that river to the channel, crossed over it to the White River, and descended again to the Mississippi, thus avoiding 22 miles of strong current. See diaries below, pp. 149–326; see esp. 167, 250 n. 22.

55. Three to 7 leagues a day was the average rate for the galleys, and Gayoso on *La Vigilante* offered the sailors an extra dollar and a *filete* for each day they made seven leagues or more as an incentive to make them row faster.

The rate of travel on the Mississippi naturally varied according to season and type of vessel. Vessels rowed by 20 men could make 6 to 7 leagues a day upstream, rates of progress being in direct proportion to the size of the crew. Descending vessels naturally traveled faster than upstream. Whereas it took 3 to 4 months to ascend to St. Louis from New Orleans, the return trip could be made in 12 to 25 days; rate of travel downstream ranged from 25 to 40 leagues a day. See diaries below, pp. 149–326; see esp. pp. 220–21. A. P. Nasatir, "Anglo-Spanish Frontier in the Illinois Country during the American Revolution," *Journal* of the Illinois State Historical Society, *21* (1928), 329.

free to sway up and down with the motion of the current. If they could be seen breaking the water, they were not so dangerous, but since the "sleeping" sawyers never broke surface, they could sweep up unexpectedly and damage the bottom of a boat passing over them.

To make the most of countercurrents and quiet stretches, and to avoid all such destructive and baffling obstructions to river traffic, required experience, skill, and always exhaustive labor and aching endurance. Under such conditions three to seven leagues a day was the normal schedule. Come nightfall, the galleys anchored and found camp sites as they could along the river banks, if they were not flooded, or on an island, if one was available—but always at a spot where there was only one channel in the river. If no camp site was available, they might eat and sleep as best they could aboard the vessels. No one was allowed to forget that he was in an army on the river, nor Captain Rousseau, that he was a Spanish official. For in all night encampments strict regulations governed the conduct of ships and crews. A guard was mounted on each galley, sentinel watch kept throughout the night, and one pirogue dispatched across the river to station itself on the opposite shore, to see that no unchallenged vessel of any description should pass during the night. As for Captain Rousseau, each day he was obliged to draw up a detailed account of the squadron's affairs for transmission to New Orleans.

Natchez was a sort of advanced base for the squadron: repairs could be made there and the galleys careened so as to reduce the necessity for long round trips to the capital. Also, Gayoso de Lemos, governor of Natchez, was from time to time empowered to give commands, and in 1795 he himself was to command the squadron on the Upper Mississippi. As post commander, he had the additional duty of taking prisoners and sick sailors from the galleys and furnishing supplies.

Especially from Natchez upriver was the squadron to engage in patrols and the policing of river traffic, and sections of the river were assigned to certain galleys and *galeotas*, for river traffic was high during the Spanish regime. The Spaniards, for their own use, largely adopted the mode of transportation and communication in general use among the French inhabitants—namely, navigation by the river waterways. They used the same types of boat, modified some, and assigned different names for other of the vessels. They introduced many variations: bullboats, canoes, pirogues, *radeaux,* chalanes, flatboats, broadhorns, barques, berchas, lanchas, lanchones, keelboats, feluccas, shalops, frigates, brigantines—all these and more figure in the story of the struggle to master the continent through its rivers.

Most primitive of all was the bullboat, made of large buffalo hides stretched over a willow framework and calked with grease or tallow, and occasionally used in emergencies by travelers in the Missouri region. The canoe, adopted by the French from the aborigines, was made of birch bark, cedar splits, and ribs of spruce covered with yellow pine pitch. While it was light and strong and especially adapted for the upper waters of rivers, where portages would be necessary, it was in use throughout the province by colonists as well as Indians.

Another primitive boat of great versatility, a conspicuous member of the river parade in the Spanish regime and still much in use, was the pirogue, a dugout made from the trunk of a large tree: the cypress was considered best, although the Indians had used cottonwood. It could float, according to the inhabitants of the region, on a heavy dew, yet its freight capacity was considerable. The smaller pirogues could carry a ton, while larger ones, ranging up to forty or fifty feet long and as much as five feet wide, could carry fifty tons. Their passenger capacity ran as high as thirty men, although occasionally one meets references to pirogues that could carry fifty. They were furnished, ideally, with a sail, but oars had to be the principal means of propulsion. An oar at the stern was sufficient to guide them, though larger pirogues were sometimes furnished with a rudder. Since both the trapper and the Indian trader made extensive use of this light-draft, capacious river craft, at the end of the season heavily laden pirogues went with ease from the fur center of St. Louis to New Orleans with precious cargoes of pelts.

For heavier cargoes two types of craft—under many names—provided the staple of river transport. The first was the flatboat, essentially a raft with roof and sides—a large, flat-bottomed, square-built boat of great width, with no keel. Its sides were usually built up some three or four feet and a greater or lesser proportion of the deck space could be roofed over to provide shelter for a family, livestock, or goods in transit. The second basic type was the keelboat, a carefully constructed craft built on keels with ribs and covered with planks. It was a long, slender boat—some forty to eighty feet long and from seven to ten in beam. Fully loaded, it drew only about two feet of water. The central part of the craft was usually covered over with a kind of cabin or cargo box; indeed, a trip in one was described as similar to traveling in a wooden jail. With a freight capacity ranging between fifteen and fifty tons, the keelboat was a jaunty, efficient little vessel, as adapted as anything afloat could be to beating up the long river with a paying cargo.

A larger edition of the same type of boat bore usually a different name—barge in English, lanchón in Spanish. Much wider than keelboats, probably varying between twelve and twenty feet in beam, they averaged thirty to forty tons burden and required a crew of fifteen men or more. The barges were fitted with square sails and steered with a rudder, with those on the Mississippi usually covered their full length. Widely used by Spanish officials in the royal service, lanchones were equipped with both oars and sails.

All boats except chalanes were rowed both up and down stream. Ordinarily, one oarsman was provided for every three thousand weight in the boat. While smaller editions of lanchones, the lanchas were equipped with masts and sails and used sometimes also as small gunboats, berchas were the favorites of merchants and traders on the Upper Mississippi.[56]

    56. Lanchones were used for the royal service—to deliver supplies and munitions to outposts, to carry gifts to Indians, and for a variety of other services. Two lanchones, *El Príncipe de Asturias* and *La Céréz*, were used extensively in the upper river during the last decade of the 18th century. The first was stationed for several years at New Madrid; the second operated between Natchez and New Orleans. During the period of the threatened attack in Upper Louisiana the commandants of New Madrid and St. Louis frequently supplemented the defense of their posts by arming a lanchón to provide them with support.
    Bercha, referred to by the French as *berge* and perhaps by the English as barge, closely resembled a keelboat. Larger than a lancha, the bercha was smaller than a lanchón. Average size was 12 to 14 oars, plus a mast, sails, and rudder. Gayoso de Lemos had a bercha of 12 oars; a *berchita* had 10.
    The *goellette* was a goleta or schooner type.
    In Lower Louisiana the Spaniards frequently used the *falua* or felucca for government service. It was a swift-sailing, open boat similar in construction to a longboat and propelled by oars and sail. Large feluccas used by officials for traveling on the river were sometimes provided with awnings to serve as shelter against sun and rain. The vessels varied in size; Gayoso's felucca at Natchez in 1794 carried 14 oars.

Whenever the wind was favorable, sails were used. Otherwise, because of the winding course of the river and the height of its banks, sails were not dependable. In times of low water, punting, or poling, was sometimes resorted to as a means of propulsion, although, being a very slow and laborious process, it was seldom used by the Spaniards on the Mississippi, oars generally being preferred. Cordelling or towing vessels up river was also used and in the Illinois area was even more common than rowing. A cordelle was a rope or cable fastened to the top of the mast, then passed through a ring on the bow of the boat. The end of the cordelle was pulled from shore by twenty to thirty men, who walked along a towpath on the river bank.

Chalán was the Spanish name for a flatboat, while bercha, lanchón, and lanchas were the names of various imperfectly distinguished types of flatboat, ark, or broadhorn used by immigrants and in commerce. "Broadhorn" or "ark" was the whimsical popular Western name for the ubiquitous flatboat—the first, because of the two long sweeps near the stern, which would keep the boat in the middle of the current; the second, because of the hopeful clutter of household gear of the immigrants, who often brought cows, chickens, cats, and dogs aboard, making it a tragi-comic travesty of the biblical ark. Some of the wealthier immigrants floated south in capacious arks furnished with neat cottages, brick fireplaces, and a stable for animals. Most sought a "hazard of new fortunes" with such just pathetic household stuff as they had been able to accumulate at the points of embarkation. Poultry and cattle shared a rough cabin at one end of the ark; barrels and boxes of clothing, dishes, provisions to use or sell were distributed carefully—if the traveler was at all prudent—so as to keep the craft in balance.[57]

57. For a comprehensive description of French river boats on the Mississippi see Surrey, *Commerce of Louisiana*. See also Beverly W. Bond, Jr., *Civilization of the Old Northwest* (New York, 1934); Baldwin, *Keelboat Age*. With these accounts as bases, I have added a few varying notes taken from the diaries below, pp. 149–326, and various other letters and documents from 1792–96. In my discussion of boats and dress, which is by no means a full one, I have taken the liberty of using a few facts which chronologically are dated beyond the 1792–97 period of this account.

Among others the following give good accounts and descriptions of boats; F. A. Michaux, *Travels in America Performed in 1806* (London, 1809); John Bradbury, *Travels in the Interior of America in the Years 1809, 1810 and 1811* (Liverpool, 1817, reprinted in R. G. Thwaites, ed., *Early Western Travels*, *5* [32 vols. Cleveland, 1904–06]); Christian Schultz, Jr., *Travels on an Inland Voyage—Performed in*

Broadhorns in commerce were fully as picturesque, lumbering heavy-laden down the stream piled high with flour, salt, kegs of whiskey, salted pork, boxes of ham and bacon, awkwardly answering to the straining sweep to find the channel past a sand bar or elude an eddy that would pile them up helplessly on the bank. On the broadhorn or keelboat the red-shirted crew were a splash of color. And always there was music. No boat was complete without a fiddler perched on the cabin or on a barrel of flour, who scraped away hour after hour, while the men joined in singing, handling their oars or poles in time to the music. Mile after mile the rough ballads of the West or the touching grace of French folk songs sounded out muted across the stream and echoed from strange cliffs and new headlands.

Every vessel that managed to float, or drift, down river as far as control points at Nogales or Natchez had run the gantlet of Spanish posts and guard vessels. Though the downstream traffic was less cruelly arduous than the trip upriver, it also furnished hourly hazards of planters and sawyers, concealed rocks that could smash up the bottom of a boat, whirlpools, and other obstacles. And often enough travelers who had come down from the Ohio had experienced murderous Indian attacks, so the Spanish section of the river seemed to them more peaceful.

As far south as the Arkansas, floating at night was too dangerous: every vessel had to tie up prudently at nightfall, for a sudden fall of the river might leave one end stranded on shore and open the seams of the boat. But in flood, below the Arkansas, one could venture to float downriver on clear, moonlit nights, and then, indeed, the semitropical land became a thing of wonder and enchantment. Moreover, because of its being flooded, the river reduced the danger of Indian attack. The channel was an intermittently "luminous track in the moonlight," with dense cypress swamps soft and mysterious in the half-light. And since the awesome quietness kept

---

the Years 1807 and 1808 (2 vols. New York, 1810); Marion Tinling and Godfrey Davies, *The Western Country in 1793* (San Marino, 1948); Zadoc Cramer, *The Navigator* (Pittsburgh, 1808; many editions both before and after 1808); Stoddard, *Sketches of Louisiana;* Seymour Dunbar, *History of Travel in America* (New York, 1915). On the ark and broadhorn see W. W. Carson, "Transportation and Traffic on the Ohio and the Mississippi before the Steamboat," *MVHR,* 7 (1920), 28–29.

voices low and intimidated until the mood changed, quavering voices might begin some ballad sung along the Loire:

> Dans mon chemin j'ai rencontré
> Trois cavalières bien montées,
> L'on, ton, laridon, danée
> L'on, ton, laridon, dai.[58]

To the galleys charged with policing the river, however, the delicacy and complexity of their task precluded much appreciation of the romantic charm of the scene. Traffic was steadily increasing

---

58. Canadian oarsmen measured the strokes of the oars by songs, which were usually sung responsively between the oarsmen at the bow and those at the stern. On occasion the steerman sang, and the men responded in chorus.

John Bradbury supplies three verses of the most famous song of the Missouri oarsmen; its touching puerility can be appreciated in the adjoining translation by Bradbury:

I

> Behind our house there is a pond
>   Fal lal de ra
> There came three ducks to swim thereon:
> All along the river clear,
> Lightly my shepherdess dear,
>   Lightly, fal de ra.

II

> There came three ducks to swim thereon,
>   Fal lal de ra.
> The prince to chase them he did run
> All along the river clear,
> Lightly my shepherdess dear,
>   Lightly, fal de ra.

III

> The prince to chase them he did run,
>   Fal lal de ra.
> And he had his great silver gun
> All along the river clear,
> Lightly my shepherdess dear,
>   Lightly, fal de ra. etc.

Other songs are cited in Baldwin, *Keelboat Age*, pp. 91–94. See also J. Hall, *Letters from the West* (London, 1828); H. and E. Quick, *Mississippi Steamboating* (New York, 1926). The song quoted in the text is in Brackenridge's *Journal*, reprinted in Thwaites, *Early Western Travels*, 6, 63, 89. See also R. H. Gabriel, ed., *The Pageant of America*, 2 (15 vols. New Haven, 1926-29), 196.

throughout the last phase of the Spanish regime, partly because of the steady growth in population along the Ohio and on the upper river, partly because of the relaxation of trade regulations induced by the diplomatic intrigue of Wilkinson and others. Perhaps a new era was inaugurated when Wilkinson, in the spring of 1789, accompanied a consignment to New Orleans, with a flotilla consisting of 25 boats loaded with the tobacco crop of Kentucky,[59] flying the flag of Kentucky, and carrying swivel guns and 3-pounders. From that point on, river traffic steadily augmented, and the keeler and boater took shape as definite Western types.[60] From the end of April to the middle of June 1795 Colonel Gayoso recorded the passage of at least 25 chalanes past Barrancas de Margó. Then, too, the milder immigration regulations encouraged a steady influx of homesteaders. John Pope, who traveled in 1791 from Pittsburg to New Orleans, recorded the fact that, in spite of hostile Indians, numbers of boats were passing down the river. Near the Arkansas River he was hailed by a boy transporting buffalo meat to a settlement of thirty families.[61]

Spanish trade and immigration regulations were complex, however, and not all the traders or settlers were fastidious about their tactics. The irrepressible Wilkinson, for instance, on an occasion when he sent his partner, Hugh McIlvain, downstream with a cargo, instructed him to "make a present" to the commandant at New Madrid and push on. At Natchez he was to "put on his best Bib and Tucker," declare that he had come down to settle, and give the oath of allegiance. This done, he was to "make the commandant" a present and go on to New Orleans, at which point he was to flatter the governor's expectations of furthering Spain's political interests in Kentucky, so as to derive his own trading profit from official concessions.[62]

---

59. Baldwin, *Keelboat Age*, p. 28; F. A. Ogg, *Opening of the Mississippi* (New York, 1904), p. 441; Burson, *Stewardship of Miró*, p. 158, gives statistics.

60. Baldwin, *Keelboat Age*, p. 28.

61. John Pope, *A Tour through the Southern and Western Territories of the United States of North America, the Spanish Dominions on the Mississippi, and the Floridas* (New York, 1888), pp. 22–36; Baldwin, *Keelboat Age*, pp. 32–33.

62. Baldwin, *Keelboat Age*, p. 28. Wilkinson engaged Hugh McIlvain, a merchant of Lexington (secret partner of Wilkinson), in 1791 to take 120 hogshead of tobacco to New Orleans, where he was to be governed by Philip Nolan in disposing of it. Philip Nolan was in business arrangements in New Orleans, acting for James Wilkinson. (Whitaker, *Mississippi Question*, pp. 142, 299.)

Such wily rascals kept up in Spanish officialdom a certain sense of strain and suspicion, and so, too, did the outright smugglers. Certain Americans who descended the Ohio River into Spanish Louisiana carried on a regular contraband trade in the Spanish posts of the upper province. On the pretext of trading with the American settlements of Kaskaskia and Cahokia, a number of American berchas ascended the Mississippi to carry on a contraband trade with St. Louis and other posts in Spanish Illinois. It was difficult to control such illicit trade, for unless the American boats were actually found trading on the west bank of the Mississippi, they could not be seized. The commandant of the galiot cruising at the mouth of the Ohio River was instructed, therefore, to watch closely for any kinds of vessel loaded with American or English goods tied up on the west bank. If one showed some indication of intent to unload or sell its merchandise without official permission, the commandant was forthwith to confiscate the vessel, make an inventory of all its goods—to be signed by the boat's patrón, the commandant, and two witnesses—and send everything to the commandant of New Madrid for action.[63]

Even legitimate settlers availing themselves of the new immigration policy, which tolerated the presence of non-Catholics as long as they did not publicly practice their religion, were a source of difficulty. They were not allowed to bring any prohibited goods into the province with them, and the general rule for all galley commanders was to confiscate such prohibited goods as were found on boats descending the river.[64] Gifts to the Chickasaw Indians were allowed to enter duty free, but firearms had to be recognizable trading guns—no swivel guns or cannon. Such illicit items were to be seized.

Governor General Carondelet, however, never allowed his naval or post commanders to forget the statesman in the policeman. It

---

[63]. Draft [Carondelet] to Langlois, October 17, 1794, P de C 126; Langlois to Carondelet, No. 14, New Madrid, February 6, 1795, P de C 31; García to Gayoso, San Fernando, August 12, 1796, P de C 50; another same date, P de C 33. draft [Carondelet] to García, New Orleans, August 27, 1796, P de C 129.

[64]. In practice, however, the Spanish authorities often showed leniency in individual cases, particularly when the foreigner was an American coming with his property to settle permanently in Louisiana (Rousseau to Gayoso, on *La Flecha*, January 15, 1793, P de C 207B; draft [Gayoso] to Carondelet, No. 22 res., on *La Vigilante*, 4 leagues above New Madrid, October 6, 1795, P de C 128).

was necessary at all times to tread delicately; the West was to be kept pacified, though not allowed to pour, at its torrential pleasure, through the great province. No one was to be offended, but everyone was to be kept in order. Any just complaint of an American, Carondelet declared, would be sufficient cause for a subordinate's removal from office. Carondelet wrote to Thomas Portell,[65] at the passport control station of New Madrid, that he was to "welcome Americans to New Madrid with the softness and sweetness proper to the Spanish Government," to allow them to look at the fort out of natural curiosity, but to keep alert at all times for spies. The commander of the galiot cruising on the Ohio was also specifically enjoined in the same sense to show consideration to legitimate American traders—in particular to the magnates of Kentucky.[66]

Between the Ohio River and Natchez the Mississippi ran through almost virgin wilderness, broken slightly only by the small village of New Madrid and the isolated fort of Nogales. On the interminable reaches of the silent river, galleys and galiots maintained their constant patrol, maintaining the *imperium* of distant Spain in the empty land. It was a satisfaction to all when descending vessels hove in sight, and an occasion for due formality. A war vessel, which was required to fly its flags so that it might be prop-

---

[65]. Thomas Portell was born in Gerona, Cataluña, on February 12, 1739, and became a cadet on August 1, 1754. The son of a captain, he served in the infantry of Guadalajara for 29 years. He was made captain in 1776 and went to America in the expedition to Havana in 1780. In September 1791 Portell arrived in New Madrid to take over the command of the post from Pedro Foucher. Little is known of his earlier life except that just prior to coming to Louisiana he served as commandant of Fort Apalache in West Florida. He remained as commandant of New Madrid until the summer of 1796, when he was replaced by Carlos Dehault Delassus. Portell returned to New Orleans. In command at Fort St. Marks in Florida when Augustus Bowles attacked, Portell surrendered the fort. For this act he was court-martialed for cowardice, and when the case was settled five years later, he was dismissed from the Spanish service. While Portell was in command of New Madrid, he never showed signs of cowardice. He was a zealous servant of the Crown and worked hard to keep up the defenses of that important point of defense of the Spanish empire against constant threat of attack from the Ohio. (See Nasatir and Liljegren, *LHQ, 21,* p. 35; Houck, *History of Missouri;* A. P. Nasatir, "Anglo-Spanish Frontier on the Upper Mississippi 1786–1796," *IJHP, 29* [1931], 155–232. I have collected a great deal of Portell's correspondence during his regime at New Madrid. A short biographical sketch is contained in Portell to Prince of Peace, New Orleans, March 29, 1797, AHN 3900.)

[66]. See Vallé to Lorimier, Ste. Geneviève, October 7, 1794, P de C 210; Carondelet to Portell, New Orleans, July 17, 1795, P de C 22.

erly recognized, was approached by the King's ship, whose commandant boarded the newcomer with great courtesy. The commandant paid a ceremonial visit to the patrón of the boat, questioned him as to the cargo, and requested to see all the books and papers, written or printed, sealed or loose. Works on such harmless subjects as literature, art, and medicine were promptly returned; books on law, constitutions, or government, however, furnished an anxious moment. These, as well as frankly seditious literature,[67] were confiscated forthwith. Sealed letters were also the occasion for some alarm. They were placed in a box, which was thereupon sealed and sent on to the governor at Natchez, usually on the descending vessel itself. If, however, there was some reason for questioning the innocence of such sealed documents, the commander of the vessel was regretfully obliged to take charge of the box in which they were sealed, and accompany the suspicious boat to Nogales. Since arms and munitions of war were *prima facie* objects of suspicion, Spanish warships were strictly instructed to confiscate them, regardless of their destination. The warships also examined Spanish trading vessels or pirogues and looked at their passports and visas. Sometimes, of course, the commander of a warship was happy to meet some descending chalanes, for he would often purchase from them meat, bacon, salted pork, and other food items.

There was one notable exception to the courtesy and consideration naval officers were instructed to extend to travelers on the Mississippi: the Frenchman. All Frenchmen were regarded with deep distrust, and their passports examined with particular care. Should any Frenchman be found carrying inflammatory literature or symbols of the French Revolution, he was to be put in irons, and the galley was posthaste to deliver him to the jail at Nogales.[68]

Indians had a special part in the life of the galleys and vessels on

---

67. The alarm over James Puglio's *El Desengaño del hombre* created a widespread hunt for copies of that dangerous book. Orders were given on the frontiers to keep it out. The Inquisition had proscribed seditious books and papers in 1790. See J. Rydjord, *Foreign Interests in the Independence of New Spain* (Durham, 1935), p. 128 et seq.; and by same author, "The French Revolution and Mexico," *HAHR*, 9, 60–98. See also L. E. Fisher, *Background of the Revolution for Mexican Independence* (Boston, 1934).

68. There is a veritable mine of documentary evidence in the Spanish archives concerning this problem. For some indications of materials see Nasatir and Liljegren, *LHQ, 21*, 3–75; Liljegren, ibid, *22*, 46–97; James, *Clark*; Gayarré, *History of Louisiana, 3*; Whitaker, *Mississippi Question*.

Many French royalists were permitted to colonize in Louisiana.

the river. Frequently a native canoe or pirogue slipped alongside and invited the crew to trade. This, however, was most expressly forbidden; nor were any of the crew allowed to buy the Indian's annual gifts after they had been distributed. On the other hand, it was the galley commanders' duty to win the friendship of any savages they met on the river; to this end they had ready small gifts of food, brandy, gunpowder, or such miscellaneous merchandise as was kept aboard for that special purpose. And a mark of special distinction, highly prized by the Indians, was to take a chief aboard for a private cruise.[69]

Such were the daily duties of the squadron,[70] carried out by their crews, bedeviled by the plagues of black flies, gnats, and mosquitoes that flourished in the humid, swampy regions along the Mississippi. The river was a noble prize, but only to be held by the sternest exertions, even when there were no threats to its possession other than those offered by nature itself. But there *were* others, and the galleys soon became pawns in a tenser game than searching carousing keelers for suspicious literature. Toward the end of their first year of service, 1792, the political thermometer rose acutely, and the most important Spanish contribution to the history of Mississippi River traffic—light war galleys and galiots for service on the Mississippi above New Orleans—were soon put into activity higher and higher up the river.

[69]. See among illustrative documents: draft of secret instructions to Rousseau given by Carondelet, New Orleans, January 15, 1794, P de C 2354; another draft in P de C 2352. Rousseau to Carondelet, on *La Venganza* at Ecores, April 26, 1795, P de C 198; Rousseau to Rendón, on *La Venganza* at Ecores, April 25, 1795, P de C 602B; draft [Carondelet] to Rendón, New Orleans, April 7, 1796, P de C 89; same to same, New Orleans, April 11, 1796, original and draft, ibid.; Rendón to Vilemont, New Orleans, April 16, 1796, P de C 129; García to Gayoso, on *La Venganza* on Arkansas River, May 31, 1796, P de C 212A; Folch to Carondelet, San Fernando, June 7, 1796, P de C 33; diaries below, pp. 149–326. Rousseau to Carondelet, *La Venganza*, 25 leagues below New Madrid, April 22, 1794, P de C 210; and at Ecores, April 24, 1795, P de C 211, and April 26, 1795, P de C 198.

[70]. Both government and private boats also carried on the mail service, for none was established in Louisiana under Spanish rule. On occasion a mail service and special expresses were established between government posts. Special rapid mail service known as express vessels were also used by the government—especially express mail pirogues, which afforded the fastest means of communication between the posts and the capital available in Louisiana during the Spanish regime. Gayoso de Lemos believed that the most rapid mail service was a combination of express pirogue and overland special service (messenger service). Sometimes mail was carried overland by messengers on horseback.

3 Key Site for a Fort at Ecores à Margot

In the fall of 1792 Carondelet received reports of threatened American attacks against three different points in the province. Thomas Portell at New Madrid wrote that the Indians in Cumberland were restless and that the Americans suspected the Spaniards of inciting them. He feared the Americans might use the savage unrest as a pretext to attack New Madrid. This was further indicated by rumors that preparations for war were being made in Kentucky and at Fort Pitt—where General Wayne had 5,000 men, and where 150 flatboats were being built—and that two bodies of troops of 1500 men each were descending to the mouth of the Tennessee and the Cumberland.[1] While Portell feared that the Americans might establish settlements at Muscle Shoals or on Margot River or on both, Carondelet was afraid that the Americans were threatening Nogales. In December, Zenon Trudeau[2] at St.

---

1. Portell to Carondelet, No. 96, New Madrid, November 15, 1792, copy certified by Carondelet, encl. in Carondelet to Las Casas, No. 61 res., New Orleans, December 21, 1792, as was also Carondelet's letter to Gayoso, New Orleans, December 18, 1792, P de C 1442. See also draft of Las Casas' reply attached, dated Havana, February 4, 1793, ibid.; Carondelet to Aranda, No. 26 res., New Orleans, January 8, 1793, AHN 3898.

2. Zenon Trudeau, lieutenant governor of Spanish Illinois at St. Louis from 1792-99, was born in New Orleans on November 28, 1748. He was well educated, entered the army at a youthful age, and rose to the rank of lieutenant colonel and captain of the grenadiers. He married Eulalie Delassise in 1781 and had several sons, one of whom became surveyor general of Louisiana. On July 22, 1792, Trudeau took command of St. Louis as lieutenant governor of Upper Louisiana. He performed his duties faithfully and in 1797 was given an opportunity to retire on a pension. He refused because he thought he was needed while Spain was at war with England, and remained in office until the summer of 1799, when Carlos Dehault Delassus replaced him. In 1803, rather than serve outside the province, he requested the pension previously offered him and asked to remain in Louisiana. A few years later he died in the parish of St. Charles. Trudeau was an efficient and well-liked administrator, and possessed a friendly disposition, a pleasing personality, and a very mild temper.

Trudeau entered the service as cadet October 1, 1769, was a sublieutenant in

Louis reported that he had definitely heard that the Talapuches and Cherokees were planning to attack Cumberland, and he was concerned that the Westerners would use this as a pretext to invade Illinois, whose position was very weak.

Carondelet informed Trudeau that the news of an attack on Cumberland was false, but should any attack occur he was to use all available forces in Illinois, together with whatever aid he could get from the British and Indians, to repel it; in case of necessity he could call on Lorimier and his Indians for additional support.[3] Portell's reports concerning an American threat from Cumberland seemed serious enough to Carondelet, however, to warrant strong action, and he resolved to reinforce the threatened post at New Madrid. He gave orders to Trudeau[4] and to François Vallé[5] at

---

1772, lieutenant in 1778, *capitán graduado* in 1780, lieutenant of grenadiers in 1784, full captain in 1786, and brevet lieutenant-colonel in 1796. He took part in the campaigns of Baton Rouge in 1779 and of Pensacola in 1781, and when Natchez was threatened in 1787 he arrived with a detachment of troops to reinforce it. He lost 3500 pesos in the New Orleans fire in 1788. There are two service records of Trudeau dated 1793 and 1795 in P de C 161A.

See Nasatir and Liljegren, *MVHR, 21*, reprint p. 65, n. 143; Houck, *History of Missouri*, 2, 57–58; Trudeau to Carondelet, No. 3, St. Louis, July 25, 1792, P de C 25A; Nasatir, *IJHP, 29* (1931), 172; Secret General Orders to be observed by Don Carlos Howard, P de C 2365; printed in MHS *Collections, 3* (1908), 71–91, and also in Houck, *Spanish Régime in Missouri*, 2, 123–32; extracts printed in State Historical Society of Wisconsin *Collections, 18*, 449–52. Collot, *Journey*, 2, chap. 29. I have collected as nearly a complete file as was possible of Trudeau's correspondence and documentation. Trudeau deserves a biographer. Some materials and/or correspondence of his has been published in several of my publications, e.g.: *IJHP, 29*, 155–232; "Anglo-Spanish Rivalry on the Upper Missouri," *MVHR, 16* (1929–30), 359–82, 507–30; "Jacques Deglise on the Upper Missouri" and "Spanish Exploration of the Upper Missouri," *MVHR, 14* (1927), 47–71; "John Evans: Explorer and Surveyor," *Missouri Historical Review*, 25 (1931), 219–39, 432–60, 585–608; *IJHP, 28*, 337–89; *Before Lewis and Clark*. Many more will appear in my as yet unpublished "Imperial Osage: A Documentary History of the Osage Indians during the Spanish Régime."

3. Trudeau to Carondelet, No. 46, St. Louis, December 18, 1792; draft of reply attached thereto, New Orleans, January 29, 1793, P de C 23A. See also Diary 1, entry for January 24, below, p. 160.

4. Carondelet to Trudeau, res., New Orleans, December 22, 1792, Bancroft Library; printed in Kinnaird, *AHAR 1945, 4*, 107–08.

5. Carondelet to Vallé, New Orleans, December 22, 1792, MHS, Vallé Collection, No. 2; draft in P de C 205.

François Vallé, *fils*, was the son of the first Spanish commandant of Ste. Geneviève, who in his time was the wealthiest man in Spanish Illinois. The elder Vallé migrated to Kaskaskia from Canada, moving from there to Ste. Geneviève when Eastern Illinois was ceded to England. In 1777 young François married Louise Char-

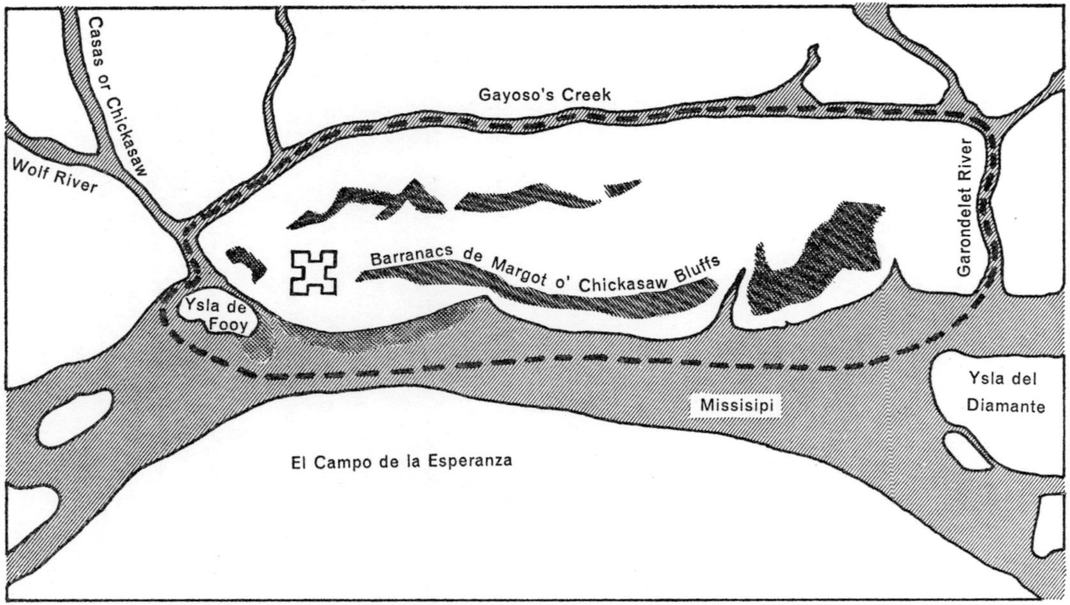
Casas or Chickasaw
Gayoso's Creek
Wolf River
Garondelet River
Barranacs de Margot o' Chickasaw Bluffs
Ysla de Fooy
Ysla del Diamante
Missisipi
El Campo de la Esperanza

St. Louis and Ste. Geneviève to dispatch their militias to the aid of Portell the moment the latter's post should be attacked, and to prevail upon the Indians to march with the militia to the defense of New Madrid. Strongly suspicious of the intentions of the American Army, Carondelet warned Trudeau to prepare for the attack but to avoid showing hostile intentions; the newly created freshwater fleet was now to be used and to meet the test of mobility along the whole Mississippi frontier. The critical nature of the moment persuaded Carondelet to send the commander of the squadron himself—Captain Pedro Rousseau, in whom Carondelt had great faith—with reinforcements for the threatened fort. He ordered Rousseau to ascend to New Madrid, deliver the reinforcement of men and munitions he carried for the post, and return, stopping on his descent at Ecores à Margot (another name for Chickasaw Bluffs or Barrancas de Margó) to examine the bluffs for a suitable site for a fort. If, during his ascent, he should learn of the siege or fall of New Madrid, he was to return to Nogales at top speed, taking care not to approach land on the east bank of the Mississippi. To replace the arms, munitions, and men taken from Natchez to New Madrid, Carondelet dispatched a galley, together with those materials from New Orleans to replace them, as well as additional troops to complete the garrisons at Natchez and Nogales.[6]

In the meantime Rousseau had received the threatening report and had hurried a pirogue to the capital with pleas for four additional sailors per galley, from six to twelve artillerymen to

---

pentier. At his father's death in 1783 he became head of the largest and most influential family in Ste. Geneviève. When Peyroux was sent to New Orleans in 1794, Vallé was named temporary commandant of the village by Trudeau. His appointment was made permanent in 1796, and he continued to hold office until his death in March 1804. (See Houck, *History of Missouri, 1,* 349–50; *Spanish Régime in Missouri, 1,* 54, n. 4. Trudeau Report of 1798 to Gayoso, dated St. Louis, January 15, 1798, P de C 2365; in Houck, *Spanish Régime, 2,* 247–58. Secret Orders to Howard; Gayoso to Carondelet, New Madrid, September 27, 1795, P de C 43. See also Francis J. Yealy, *Sainte Geneviève* [Ste. Geneviève, Mo., 1935]; W. A. Dorrance, *Survival of French in the Old District of Sainte Geneviève* [University of Missouri Studies, Columbia, 1935]. There is a great deal of Vallé correspondence in the P de C, a part of which I possess in my collection. The Vallé family papers are in the MHS.)

6. Carondelet to Gayoso, res., New Orleans, December 22, 1792, P de C 18; draft in P de C 2362.

man the guns, and additional swivel guns. While these were to prepare the galleys for offensive and defensive action, each vessel was to be commanded by a young captain, a naval officer.[7]

It was early in January that Gayoso received Carondelet's order to send a galley to New Madrid, and Rousseau was immediately sent out on his secret mission, Gayoso himself taking over the command of the squadron during Rousseau's absence. Rousseau left Natchez on January 5 in the galiot *La Flecha*,[8] manned by a crew of 18 sailors and 3 soldiers, armed with 8 swivel guns. By traveling each day from six in the morning until five at night, the galiot reached Nogales on the twelfth. There it was storming, and the bad weather caused a three-day delay. Rousseau was anxious to go, even though he learned from a descending American flatboat that there were only 2,000 poorly disciplined troops, or men, at Fort Pitt, and that they were ready to desert. It was a difficult voyage due to the cold weather, ice, and snow. On January 29 *La Flecha* reached the Arkansas River and was forced to stop there on account of the iron bindings' having broken. Since heavy snow prevented their being able to ascent to the post, they camped for shelter half a league from the Arkansas River. Arriving at Arkansas Post on February 2, Rousseau procured a blacksmith from the commandant to repair a broken rudder. With rain and bad weather further delaying the galiot, it was only on the sixth of February that Rousseau was able to depart for the journey upriver, leaving behind at the post two sick sailors and taking one man from Arkansas Post to replace them.

The cold increased, but strong, favoring winds enabled the galiot to use its sails. When the river began to rise, pieces of floating ice and driftwood made the ascent hazardous. A few days later the galiot passed some rapids that were so strong it took all the oars aided by the sails and a good stiff wind to pass, and even then the whole boat trembled. By February 20 the galiot reached Ecores à Margot, but rain and bad weather continued to delay its progress. Not only did a strong current cause the river to rise two feet a day,

---

7. Rousseau to Carondelet, Natchez, December 17, 1792, P de C 219; Carondelet to Gayoso, res., New Orleans, December 22, 1792.

8. See Log of *La Flecha*, below, p. 153. There is a great deal of correspondence extant in the Spanish archives relative to this trip, but Rousseau's log gives an adequate picture of the expedition. Only the barest outline is given here.

but it was necessary to hug the shore as closely as possible for fear of snags and rocks. During the night of March 2 a gale blew up, uprooting many trees and forcing Rousseau to break camp and travel half a league in the night. Everywhere the Mississippi began to overflow its banks.[9]

At ten o'clock on the morning of March 6 *La Flecha* anchored before New Madrid. Rousseau remained in that post until March 19, during which time he unloaded the three soldiers, two eight-caliber cannons, and other arms and munitions he had rushed to New Madrid from Natchez. After reviewing the militia, he formally handed out commissions that he had brought with him, reconnoitered around New Madrid, and prepared for his descent. On March 19 he left: it was now springtime and the river flooded. He took with him Medad (or Medard) Mitchell,[10] who had been discovered drawing maps of the Mississippi. Since the Ohio River was falling rapidly, Rousseau concluded that by mid-April it would hardly be navigable and thus thought it unlikely that an American attack from the Ohio would occur that year.[11]

La Flecha made the descent to Natchez very rapidly, averaging over 29 leagues a day. The river shores were flooded on both sides except for a small prairie a league below the St. Francis River and at Ecores à Margot. Rousseau carefully noted all the points, islands, and distances for a map he was making. On March 21 he put ashore at Ecores à Margot to examine the bluffs, and almost at the entrance of the Margot River found what he considered to be an excellent site for a fort. Early on the morning of March 26, seven days after leaving New Madrid, Rousseau reached Natchez, where he reported immediately to Gayoso de Lemos, to whom he presented

9. Rousseau to Gayoso, on *La Flecha* on the Mississippi, February 27, 1793, P de C 209; see also Diary 1, below, pp. 176.

10. Medad, or Thomas, Mitchell was sent to New Orleans by Jaudenes and Viar in the later part of 1792 with letters for Carondelet. He asked Carondelet for employment, but since the Governor General did not consider him to be a reliable person, he sent him back to Philadelphia with an answer for Jaudenes and Viar. He was used to contact the conspirators in Kentucky and the Secret Committee of Correspondence of the West. A short biographical sketch signed by Mitchell and addressed to Gayoso de Lemos is in P de C 208A. See Nasatir and Liljegren, *LHQ*, *21*, reprint p. 32. Mitchell copied the maps for Rousseau.

11. See Diary 1, below, p. 185. Rousseau to Carondelet, Natchez, n.d. [March 27–31?, 1793], P de C 118.

three maps, and in April he descended to New Orleans to deliver Medad Mitchell and the maps to Carondelet.[12]

Meanwhile, almost before Rousseau's winter odyssey had begun, other disturbing reports of Western movements had poured into Carondelet, who was harassed with American threats against Nogales and Ecores à Margot. Several enterprises were afoot, he judged, to establish American settlements on the disputed east bank of the Mississippi River. That, of course, would be fatal, for with the east bank once held in force by an enemy at a decisive point, all the defense line north of Nogales would collapse, and with it would go St. Louis and the treasure of the Missouri region, as well as the idea that Spanish Louisiana was a bulwark for the defense of New Spain. Perhaps the most mischievous and effective of the schemes afoot, Carondelet judged, was one to seize the dominant bluffs at Ecores à Margot—San Fernando de las Barrancas, or Memphis, Tennessee. General James Robertson, it was reported, was to make a pretext of taking wheat to the Chickasaw Indians (who were actually in need of it and were courted by both the Spanish and the Americans) in order to descend to the strategic bluffs in the spring.[13]

At Ecores the river spoke in its characteristic manner to determine the struggles of history. A whirlpool forced all vessels, ascending or descending, to run a narrow gantlet within a pistol shot of a portion of the bluffs on which a fort could be located. Obviously, whoever commanded those bluffs commanded the river. Established at Ecores, the Americans could not only intercept Spanish commerce from Illinois but completely cut all communication between Upper and Lower Louisiana, and might even be able to separate Natchez and Nogales from the capital. Capturing the trade of the Chickasaws, they could easily replace Spanish influence over those Indians, and would soon start a contraband trade with the Arkansas, Atakapas, Opelousas, Natchitoches, and Texas Indians, which would be impossible to destroy once it was begun.

12. Ibid. For a discusson of the maps see the introduction to Diary 1, below, pp. 151–52. Gayoso had employed Mitchell to make a copy of Rousseau's map of the Mississippi. (Gayoso to Carondelet, Natchez, April 4, 1793, P de C 2363; printed in Houck, *Spanish Régime*, *1*, 410–12. Gayoso to Carondelet, No. 8 res., Natchez, April 18, 1793, P de C 2363; in Houck, *Spanish Régime*, 2, 4–8.)

13. Carondelet to Aranda, No. 26 res., New Orleans, January 8, 1793, AHN 3898.

From their vantage point at Ecores, the Americans would also be able to build boats large enough to dominate the Mississippi—an impossibility so long as they possessed no settlements on the river below the Ohio because of the difficulties of getting large boats past the falls. With large boats they would have no trouble sending secret expeditions into Lower Louisiana, since the current would be in their favor.

Ecores à Margot was a very important key point—and the fleet of galleys was one of Carondelet's most potent executive instruments in preserving it for Spain. He ordered the galleys to ascend the river to that point, believing that if the squadron could reach the bluffs before the arrival of the Americans, the latter would not attempt to establish themselves there unless they possessed very superior forces. In such an event Rousseau was ordered to retire to Nogales without offering any resistance. However, if the Americans did attempt it, Rousseau was ordered to request them peacefully to stop, and if they did not obey, he was to seize their boats, distributing the maize they had brought to the Chickasaws. In the event that Portell reported the approach of an American expedition large enough to attack the entire province, the galleys were to retire to Nogales, trying to rout the enemy on their descent. Failing that, they were to station themselves beneath the fort at Nogales in order to prevent the expedition from entering Lower Louisiana.

The first step on the part of the Spaniards was to persuade the Chickasaw Indians to permit the establishment of a trading post at the bluffs under the conduct of John Turnbull, an Indian trader friendly to Spain. Through Turnbull's trading post, Carondelet hoped eventually to persuade the Indians to permit the establishment of a Spanish fort at Ecores à Margot.[14] The next step was for

14. Ibid.; Carondelet to Alcudia, No. 9 res., New Orleans, May 24, 1793, P de C 2363; in Houck, *Spanish Régime*, *1*, 413–14. Carondelet to Alcudia, No. 36 res., New Orleans, June 3, 1795, AHN 3899; Carondelet to Las Casas, No. 137 res., New Orleans June 13, 1795, P de C 2364; in Houck, *Spanish Régime*, *2*, 111. Carondelet's Military Report: Carondelet to Las Casas, New Orleans, November 24, 1794, encl. in Carondelet to Alcudia, No. 48 res. New Orleans, November 24, 1794, P de C 2354; in Robertson, *Louisiana Under Spain*, *1*, 293–345, and less accurately in *AHR*, 2. Same information found in Carondelet to Aranda, No. 129, New Orleans, November 24, 1794, AHN 3897; also in British Museum, Additional Manuscripts, Vol. 17567,

Carondelet to secure his own capital, for the threat of war with France was now so manifest that he could not dispatch the galleys to the distant bluffs ill-advisedly. He therefore postponed the sending of his fleet to Ecores for the moment and suggested to the captain general at Havana that if the *paquebot La Borja,* expected at any moment, would consent to guard the coast—the mouth of the Mississippi—until July or until the threat of war with France should vanish, the squadron could be dispatched immediately to Ecores armed with artillery. Carondelet told his brother-in-law that despite everything, he would make all efforts possible, "so that at no time can they impute to me having lost such an opportune occasion to assure to Spain the navigation of the Mississippi, the conservation of the Kingdom of Mexico, and preponderance over the Indian nations included in the area between the Appalachian mountains, the Ohio and Mississippi Rivers and the Gulf of Mexico."[15]

In the meantime, since the galleys could not immediately be readied for the expedition to Ecores, Carondelet fell back on whatever expedients of delay he could command. To Delinó at Arkansas Post went instructions to incite the Indians to assault any American boats descending the river, to shoot their sailors, and to order the inhabitants of his post to capture any enemy vessels.[16] To Rousseau at Natchez went orders to take the fleet upriver to establish a post at Ecores—with the Indians' consent, of course— and Carondelet designated Delinó as its commandant. Delinó was instructed to prepare with the greatest secrecy rations for 200 men and to be ready to embark with the galleys the moment they reached the Arkansas River, probably about the first of June.[17] Orders also were sent by express pirogue to Portell at New Madrid, to prepare secretly ten thousand rations for 200 men to despatch to Ecores as soon as the squadron reached there, probably in July.

---

folios 22–63; extracts in Houck, *Spanish Régime,* 2, 9–17. Carondelet to Gayoso, New Orleans, March 5, 1793, P de C 2353. See also Gayoso to Alcudia, Natchez, February 18, 1794, AHN 3902, in *AHAR 1896, 1,* 1042–45.

15. Carondelet to Las Casas, No. 66, New Orleans, January 24, 1793, P de C 1447.
16. Carondelet to Delinó, res., New Orleans, February 1, 1793, P de C 18.
17. Rousseau to Carondelet, Natchez, n.d. [March 27–30?, 1793], P de C 118; Carondelet to Delinó, *muy* res., New Orleans, April 1, 1793, P de C 19; draft in P de C 208B; copy in Bancroft Library.

New Madrid was also to be ready to supply the new fort with militiamen, workers, arms, and all things useful, and to keep Rousseau informed of the intentions and dispositions of the Americans and Indians toward a Spanish fort at Ecores.[18]

But no sooner had the orders been given than Carondelet had to countermand them. Since war had broken out with France and Carondelet had been ordered to prepare for the defense of Louisiana against surprise attack, all available forces were ordered south with the most vehement insistence. It was impossible to defend both Balize and New Madrid with the colony's few forces, New Madrid being a three-month journey upriver. Carondelet therefore abandoned the defense against the American threat in the upper country to concentrate all his forces against the French threat, fearing that a French expedition of only 800 men and 3 war frigates could capture New Orleans—and with the capital gone, the rest of the province would be lost. Not only did Carondelet fear the weakened defenses of Louisiana, but he was also concerned that the French invasion would be aided by the large faction of French partisans in New Orleans. It was known that some of Louisiana's inhabitants had actually gone to France, laid before the Convention a proposal for a surprise attack on New Orleans, and said that Louisiana could easily be won back to France.[19]

Concentrating on Lower Louisiana's defense and therefore lacking more substantial means of checking the aggressive Westerners, Carondelet addressed a letter to General Robertson, pleading for fair play: Spain, he urged, had not interfered to aid the Creeks in their war against the United States, and he hoped that the States would reciprocally not mix in the affairs of the Chickasaws to the disadvantage of Spain. He advised the Spanish *chargés* in Philadelphia of the changed situation in Louisiana, urging the Duque

18. Carondelet to Portell, muy res., New Orleans, April 1, 1793, P de C 2363. Rousseau approved of Carondelet's choice for a supply base, as New Madrid was more accessible to Ecores à Margot by water than Nogales, and the distance by land was only a day and a half (Rousseau to Carondelet, Natchez, n.d. [March 27–31?, 1793], P de C 118).

19. Carondelet to Gayoso, New Orleans, April 2, 1793, P de C 19; draft [Carondelet] to Alcudia, No. 8 res., New Orleans, May 24, 1793; same to same, No. 9 res., same date; both in P de C 2363, and printed in Houck, *Spanish Régime*, 2, 18–20; *1*, 413–14. Originals are in AHN 3898.

de la Alcudia to use diplomacy and negotiations to end the American project against Ecores.[20]

In June 1793 Carondelet ordered Captain Rousseau to take the galleys downriver to their battle stations before the fort of Placaminas.[21] But it was left to Rousseau's discretion whether to meet the enemy further down or under the guns of the fort. In the event that the enemy should reduce Fort Placaminas, it was up to the galleys to fight a delaying action up the delta to the Détour des Anglais, where the remaining galleys would reinforce them. Throughout the late spring and early summer *La Venganza* and *La Victoria* alternated with *La Luisiana* and *La Castilla* in the defense of the lower-river approach to the capital.[22]

While the summer wore away in anxious tension and the French threats gradually faded,[23] during this period further disturbing reports of American threats to Ecores continued to arrive. The Chickasaw Indians were divided in allegiance: Chief Payemingo supported the Americans, Chief Ugulayacabé adhered to the Spanish cause.[24] In July, Portell at New Madrid was obliged to report by express that General Clark's nephew, Lieutenant William

---

20. Carondelet to James Robertson, New Orleans, May 21, 1793, encl. in draft [Carondelet] to Alcudia, No. 8, res.
Portell said his captain of militia would observe the movements of Robertson and at Ecores à Margot. The captain sailed in a pirogue with 2 men under the pretext of trade but actually to carry out secret instructions. He was to collect information about the movements of the Americans. (Draft [Carondelet] to Portell, New Orleans, July 11, 1793, P de C 124.)

21. Fort Placaminas was constructed under Carondelet's direction at a point about 60 miles below New Orleans called the Placaminas Turn, 18 miles above the mouth of the Mississippi. It was located on the left bank of the river at the mouth of a small creek or bayou called Mardigras, in a moving swamp that extended to the sea. The fort had no land approach and could only be reached by the river. Its position was excellent for the defense of the river's mouth. (Robertson, *Louisiana under Spain, 1*, 161.)

22. Orders to Rousseau and Duparc, signed by Carondelet, June 11, 1793, P de C 19; drafts [Carondelet] to Duparc, New Orleans, June 26, and July 27, 1793, P de C 19 and 20.

23. Fort Placaminas had been greatly strengthened and a royal order of 1793 relaxing trade restrictions in the province had pacified the inhabitants to a large degree (Draft [Carondelet] to Alcudia, New Orleans, September 27, 1793, P de C 178A; Royal Order, June 9, 1793, in Whitaker, *Documents Relating to the Commercial Policy of Spain*, pp. 177–79. See Liljegren, *LHQ, 22*, 7–8.)

24. Ugulayacabé was chief of the Spanish faction and Payemingo chief of the American faction among the Chickasaws.

Clark, had taken three flatboats south loaded with corn, muskets, gunpowder—and whiskey. Lieutenant Clark protested that his expedition had no ulterior purpose—a statement Carondelet did not feel compelled to believe. Actually they were delivered to Payemingo at Ecores, but Gayoso believed that Ugulayacabé would keep the Americans from establishing a fort at Ecores.

Carondelet hoped that the galleys might be the means of an effective check to the probing thrusts of Western aggression against the vital bluffs at Ecores: if Spain could establish a strong fort there in time, only serious military exertions could dislodge it, and there was ground for hope that the resources to this end would not be available to the Westerners.[25] Thus, in August, Carondelet picked up the threads of the combination begun earlier in the year. Rousseau was to mobilize the galleys and go north to New Madrid. His orders were to seize any boats descending from the Ohio with arms and troops, explaining with care and circumstance that Spain controlled the navigation of the Mississippi and could not permit the establishment of foreign posts on the King's river, nor allow Americans to give arms to Indian nations in her territories. In the event that Americans were already established at Ecores, Captain Rousseau was authorized to take a strong line: if possible, he was to persuade them to remove; otherwise, he was to evict them by force of arms.[26]

Portell was similarly instructed to inspect carefully all American boats descending with maize for the Chickasaws and was informed that he should explain to all interlopers, emphatically, that the Mississippi belonged to Spain and that all troops and munitions— other than the recognized trading-guns—must be confiscated. Legitimate traders were not to be bothered, but Spain would not stand for Americans supplying munitions to their only enemy—Payemingo—among the Chickasaw. In the event that this determined stand should provoke an attack on the upper province, Lieutenant

---

25. Portell to Carondelet, New Madrid, May 7, 1793, P de C 26; same to same, No. 161, New Madrid, May 20, 1793, P de C 26, and No. 178, New Madrid, July 5, 1793, P de C 27A; Carondelet to Alcudia, No. 18 res., New Orleans, September 27, 1793, AHN 3898; another of same date, draft in P de C 178A. Gayoso to Carondelet, Nogales, July 25, 1795, encl. No. 1 in Carondelet to Alcudia, No. 15 res., New Orleans, August 27, 1793, AHN 3898.

26. Carondelet to Gayoso, New Orleans, August 15, 1793, encl. No. 3 in Carondelet to Alcudia, No. 15 res., AHN 3898.

Governor Zenon Trudeau at St. Louis was ordered to be prepared to support New Madrid; Louis Lorimier[27] at Cape Girardeau and his Indians were to be summoned to Portell's support; and further

27. Louis Lorimier, founder and commandant of a trading post at Cape Girardeau, was born in 1748 at Lachine, near Montreal Island, Canada. Both he and his father were Indian traders, and together they established a trading post in Ohio known as "Laramie's Station." During the American Revolution young Lorimier, who was a Tory, led many Indian expeditions against the Americans from his Ohio post, until it was attacked in 1782 by George Rogers Clark and he was forced to flee for his life. For a while he stayed at Vincennes; then he crossed the Mississippi into Spanish Illinois to settle in the Ste. Geneviève district, where he was engaged in the Indian trade with Peyroux and Menard in 1787.

Probably early in 1792 Lorimier established himself at Cape Girardeau to found a trading post. In 1793 he took the oath of allegiance to the Spanish King and was given exclusive trading privileges with the Shawnee, Delaware, Loups, and other Indian nations in the Cape Girardeau district. Through his influence and control over these Indian nations he was of great service to the Spanish government in the defense of Louisiana against the many French and American attacks that threatened the province from the Ohio. In the fall of 1795 he was given a large grant of land to form a settlement for Indians, whom he was to entice into Spanish territory from the United States. Lorimier remained at Cape Girardeau until his death in 1812, engaging in the Indian trade and performing various missions for the Spaniards, chiefly in connection with the savages.

Lorimier was not an educated man. He could write his name but was unable to read, and the Spaniards were obliged to employ a secretary, L. Largeau, to take care of his correspondence. He had a great deal of natural intelligence, however, and possessed a high degree of executive ability. Rousseau described him as "an excellent man, very devoted to the service loving the nation and very useful for the upper district." Carondelet gave him credit for his services to Spain, recognized the value of his influence over the savages, but otherwise considered him a selfish man who thought only of his own advancement.

In December 1795 Lorimier requested Carondelet to appoint him to the rank of captain with a lieutenant's pay. The Governor General forwarded the request to Las Casas with a recommendation for favorable consideration in the light of the trader's important services to Spain. Carondelet thought that by rewarding Lorimier, other men like him would be encouraged to employ themselves usefully in the defense of the province. Despite Carondelet's support, Lorimier apparently did not receive the requested position. In January 1803 Lieutenant Governor Delassus repeated the recommendation, suggesting that until the military appointment came through, Lorimier should be made a captain in the militia, for he was then serving as commandant of Cape Girardeau without any rank to make him respected.

In a petition to the Marquis de Casa Calvo, dated Cape Girardeau, August 24, 1804 (P de C 142), Lorimier said that he had become a subject of Spain in 1786, and that due to his influence and long residence among the Indians, the majority of the Loup and Shawnee Indians left the banks of the Miami River and settled in Spanish Illinois. They greatly aided the Spaniards during the period of the intrigues of Generals Clark and Montgomery.

Despite his advanced age, Lorimier petitioned to continue under Spanish rule and to leave the area (already transferred to United States dominion) and start a

help to Portell would come from the presence of the galleys at Barrancas.[28]

Although the expedition of the galleys was planned with care and thoroughness, a very destructive hurricane on August 18 damaged four of the largest vessels, and the repairs, although very rapidly made, delayed the expedition for three months.[29] Carondelet, expecting to dispatch the squadron about the middle of October, drew up a preliminary draft of secret instructions for Rousseau. The squadron was to consist of the galleys *La Venganza*, *La Castilla*, and *La Felipa*, the galiot *La Flecha*, the gunboat *El Rayo*, and a lanchón. It was to pick up men and supplies at New Orleans and Nogales and go full speed to Ecores. Rousseau was to keep a small vessel two points in advance of the fleet, to warn of threatening vessels; at night such small, fast vessels were to return to the squadron to report. In the event that the fleet should meet a hostile expedition, Rousseau was to proceed by reasonable stages. He was first to stop the enemy boats and inquire into the reasons

---

new settlement on the frontiers of Mexico, the governor of which would choose a site for that settlement. The Loups and Shawnee Indians would move with him, and some whites would also join him. Lorimier did not, however, move.

(See Houck, *History of Missouri*, *1*, 331, 363, 364; *2*, 135-37, 171-79, 180-363. Trudeau's Report of 1798, Trudeau to Gayoso, St. Louis, January 15, 1798, P de C 2365; in Houck, *Spanish Régime in Missouri*, *2*, 247-58. Nasatir and Liljegren, *LHQ*, *21*, 34, n. 74; Carondelet to Lorimier, New Orleans, May 8, 1793; and "Journal of Lorimier during the Threatened Genêt Invasion of Louisiana," Cape Girardeau, December 27, 1793-95; both in P de C 2365 and in Houck, *Spanish Régime*, *2*, 51-52, 59-99, resp. Rousseau to Carondelet, on *La Venganza*, Nogales, June 29, 1795, P de C 210; Secret Orders to Howard, signed by Carondelet, New Orleans, November 26, 1796, P de C 2364, in MHS *Collection*, *3*, 71-91; also in Houck, *Spanish Régime*, *2*, 123-32; excerpts printed in *Wisconsin Historical Collections*, *18*, 449-52. Memorandum of Louis Lorimier presented to Gayoso, Cape Girardeau, December 6, 1795, P de C 208A; Lorimier to [Carondelet], Cape Girardeau, December 31, 1795, P de C 211; Carondelet to Las Casas, No. 847, New Orleans, March 30, 1796, P de C 1444; Delassus to Salcedo, Ste. Geneviève, January 13, 1803, in Houck, *Spanish Régime*, *2*, 322. My former student Robert I. Burch has written an excellent master's thesis on "Lorimier, Indian Trader and Spanish Agent" [University of California, Berkeley, 1940]. There is wealth of material on Lorimier in the P de C, copies of most of which I have in my collection. There is a journal of Lorimier's longer than the one printed in Houck, and a letterbook of his, among other documents, in the P de C. Lorimier deserves a biographer.)

28. Draft [Carondelet] to Portell, res., New Orleans, August 6, 1793, P de C 132.

29. Carondelet to Portell, New Orleans, August 23, 1793, P de C 20; Carondelet to Alcudia, Nos. 15 res. and 18 res.; Carondelet to Portell, New Orleans, September 27, 1793, P de C 20; draft in P de C 123.

for their appearance in Louisiana with armed troops. If thereupon the enemy mistreated any of the vessels in the squadron, the galleys were to open fire; if the enemy still refused to cooperate, then, and only then, were the galleys to attack and destroy them. While the primary purpose of the expedition was to carry supplies for the establishment of a post at Ecores, to keep the real aim secret, Rousseau was to say that the purpose of his expedition was to strengthen New Madrid, which was threatened by a party of bandits.[30]

Carondelet's secret instructions for establishing a post at Ecores à Margot were not followed out in 1793. Very probably they were not even sent, for they seem incomplete and are unsigned and undated. Renewed fears of French aggression caused abandonment of the plans for the second time in a year.[31] They also caused Carondelet to turn from the defense of the upper province to what he considered more pressing problems in the capital. Reassured and certainly somewhat relieved by Secretary of State Thomas Jefferson's letter to Spain's agents[32] that the President would endeavor to restrain Americans from participating in hostile expeditions against Spain, he focused all his attention on defense against the French. Not until after the Clark-Genêt threat had disappeared did Carondelet return to his plans to place a Spanish fort at Ecores à Margot.

30. Secret instructions to Rousseau to form a post at Barrancas de Margó (an unsigned and incomplete document) in P de C 2362. It was probably drawn up in October, when he was still planning to send an expedition to Barrancas in the middle of that month.

31. Three expeditions to Barrancas are mentioned in Carondelet's corespondence in 1793: the first in Carondelet to Portell, muy res., New Orleans, January 4, 1793, P de C 19, draft in P de C 208B; the second planned for the spring of 1793, and the third for the fall.

32. Jefferson to Spanish Agents, Philadelphia, August 29, 1793, *AHAR 1896, 1,* 1005; Carondelet to Gayoso, res., New Orleans, October 29, 1793, P de C 2363, in *AHAR, 1896, 1,* 1019-21; Portell to Carondelet, No. 199, New Madrid, October 9, 1793, P de C 27A.

4 *La Flecha* Reinforces New Madrid

It was news from the Spanish chargés in Philadelphia that had caused Carondelet to cancel his plan of sending the squadron of war galleys to Ecores à Margot in the fall of 1793. According to José de Jaudenes y Nebot and José Ignacio de Viar, Citizen Edmond Charles Genêt, the French minister to the United States, was secretly planning an expedition against Louisiana, Providence, and perhaps Canada, with 2 ships of 74 guns and 6 or 8 frigates, and advised that precautions be taken.[1] Shortly thereafter Carondelet was possessed of the declaration of a dubious character named Pierre Pisgignoux, to the effect that the French planned to attack Fort Santa Margarita and several other places in Louisiana before sending their fleet with troops to the mouth of the Mississippi. He named three French revolutionary agents[2] charged with preparing a diversionary attack against the posts of the upper province

---

1. Jaudenes and Viar to Carondelet, Philadelphia, August 21, 1793, printed in *AHAR, 1896, 1*, 999–1000; a copy encl. in Carondelet to Gayoso, New Orleans, October 8, 1793, P de C 20.

Detailed accounts of the Clark-Genêt expedition from the French and American points of view may be found in many sources. We are interested here only in the Spanish point of view of the projected attack against Louisiana. For French and American views see among others the following: F. J. Turner, "Origins of the Genet Expedition," reprinted in *Significance of Sections in American History* (New York, 1932); James, *George Rogers Clark;* E. W. Lyon, *Louisiana in French Diplomacy* (Norman, 1934); Arthur B. Darling, *Our Rising Empire* (New Haven, 1940); A. De Conde, *Entangling Alliance, Diplomacy and Politics under George Washington* (Durham, N.C., 1958); Liljegren, *LHQ, 22,* 3–53; Bemis, *Pinckney's Treaty;* Whitaker, *Spanish-American Frontier.* Correspondence relating to Genêt and Mangourit activities published in *AHAR 1896–97, 1; 1903, 2.*

2. Auguste de la Chaise was a native of Louisiana. His grandfather had come to province in 1723, and the family became one of the most powerful in Louisiana. He was a leader in the Genêt scheme to liberate Spanish Louisiana, and because of his energy, ability, and influence, he was greatly feared by the Spanish officials. As late as 1798, rumors of his presence in the Southwest occasioned plans for his capture. La Chaise entered the French army, became a general, and was killed in Santo Domingo in 1803. (Nasatir and Liljegren, *LHQ, 21,* reprint pp. 35 ff. Description of

preparatory to an attack on New Orleans, and said they were to gain the support of the Americans—i.e. Westerners—as well as the inhabitants of Louisiana, by any means possible.[3]

Carondelet sifted these various reports with care and anxiously contemplated the vast extent of wilderness territory committed to his—and Spain's—guardianship. Since the inconsistencies in Pisgignoux's statement and the mention of the nonexistent (in Louisiana) fort of Santa Margarita led him to believe that Pisgignoux was Genêt's agent and that the attack on St. Louis was a ruse, he ordered the squadron to concentrate at the mouth of the Mississippi, at the Bayou Mardigras. It was a tactically effective move, for, protected there from the enemy's artillery, the galleys could fire on troops landed from the river to attack Fort Placaminas.[4]

The hostile French squadron was expected sometime between the eighth and the fifteenth of November. Weather conditions narrowly limited the period of crisis; if the French did not attack in November, when the east winds prevailed, the immediate threat to the capital would be at an end, because the fierce north winds of

---

La Chaise also given in Trudeau to Lorimier, muy res., St. Louis, December 14, 1793, P de C 195.)

Charles De Pauw was born in Ghent in 1756 and was educated in Paris. He came to America with Lafayette, and after the Revolution married a Virginia lady and settled in the Blue Grass region. His grandson endowed DePauw University. For several years prior to 1793 he had been trading in New Orleans. He made the circuit from Kentucky down the river and returned to the United States by sea. De Pauw had trade connections in New Madrid, Ste. Geneviève, and Avoyelles. In 1792 he seems to have had some connection with emigration to Louisiana, and in that year he was giving information relative to military affairs in the Ohio valley to the Spanish officials. In 1794 he was declared a traitor to the Spanish King, and an order was issued to confiscate his property. This order is in Carondelet to Vidal, New Orleans, April 9, 1794, MHS, Vallé Collection.

Mathurin was a master carpenter.

Descriptions found in *Orden del Gobernador político y militar*, Natchez, November 9, 1793, P de C 123; Gayoso to Barnó y Ferrúsola, Natchez, November 7, 1793; certified copy in P de C 42 and other places, including one signed by Trudeau and dated March 12, 1794, in MHS, Vallé Collection, Env. I.

3. Jaudenes and Viar to Las Casas, October 1, 1793, printed in *AHAR 1896, 1*, 1006. Declaration of Pisgignoux to Spanish ambassador, October 1, 1793, in ibid., 1002-03; also copy encl. in Jaudenes and Viar to Alcudia, New York, October 16, 1793, AHN 3895. See Nasatir and Liljegren, *LHQ, 21*, reprint pp. 31-38.

4. Carondelet to Gayoso, res., New Orleans, October 29, 1793, P de C 2363, in *AHAR 1896, 1*, 1019-21; Carondelet to Alcudia, No. 20 res., New Orleans, November 6, 1793, ibid., 1021-22; Carondelet to Collel, No. 81, New Orleans, November 17, 1793, P de C 20.

December would prevent the French fleet's ascending the delta. By the end of November, therefore, Carondelet could hurry the squadron north in full force to block any attempt from the Ohio.

Despite the desperateness of the threat below New Orleans, Governor Carondelet did not neglect entirely the upper river defense. He sent word to Wilkinson to observe carefully what was going on in Kentucky and Cumberland and to advise him of any movements contrary to Spain's interests. He also felt obliged to detail one galiot to the defense of the upper province. *La Flecha*, one of the trimmest and fastest of the fleet members, hence one of the busiest, was entrusted with the duty of cruising between Nogales and the Arkansas to prevent revolutionary agents from contaminating the upper posts with seditious doctrine and activity. In particular, the galley commander, Juan Barnó y Ferrúsola,[5] was to search

---

5. Juan Francisco José Barnó y Ferrúsola was born in Gerona in 1762, and entered the royal service in Louisiana on May 1, 1788. He was appointed *guarda-almacen,* or storehouse keeper, of the new post of Nogales on January 27, 1791, and held that position until September 1, 1793, although he disliked it and several times asked to be relieved. He was a friend of Gayoso de Lemos, governor of Natchez, who offered him the command of *La Flecha* and ordered him to make the cruise up the Mississippi, the diary of which is presented below, pp. 193–231. He was appointed lieutenant of the militia of Natchez. Carondelet recommended Barnó y Ferrúsola to Rousseau for his knowledge, and he served in several capacities in the Mississippi squadron. At various times during the period 1794–97 he commanded the vessels *La Castilla, El Rayo, La Felipa,* and *La Victoria.* Ferrúsola ascended the river on the cañonera *El Rayo* in December 1794 and joined Langlois at his cruising station before the Ohio. He arrived there in February 1795 and helped Langlois establish the naval station opposite the mouth of the Ohio River. He cruised on the upper river and delivered supplies to the new post at Barrancas until the summer of 1796. In June of that year he was recalled from his Ohio River cruising station to Fort San Fernando, where he was transferred from *El Rayo* to the galley *La Victoria.* Ferrúsola remained at Barrancas until the fall of 1796, when he was ordered to report to New Orleans to take over a new job as keeper of the artillery warehouse in the capital. A few months later he received word of his promotion to the rank of sublieutenant of the army. In 1797 he was appointed *comisario* of the boundary commission. When Carondelet was promoted to Ecuador, Barnó y Ferrúsola asked to go there as well. His petition was granted, and Carondelet appointed him the ad-interim administrator of *aguardiente* of Guayaquil. There he married. Ferrúsola's record in the river squadron was a good one. He got along well with his fellow officers and no complaints were ever made about his conduct. Rousseau considered him a good officer and very brave, and Gayoso spoke highly of his discretion. (See Ferrúsola to Carondelet, New Madrid, May 9, 1795, P de C 31; petition of Ferrúsola, Natchez, November 28, 1795, P de C 21; draft [Gayoso] to Rousseau, Natchez, March 13, 1795, P de C 128; Ferrúsola to Carondelet, New Madrid, December 3, 1795, P de C 32; Ferrúsola to Carondelet on *El Rayo,* Barrancas, March 26, 1796, P de C 33;

with special vigilance for Auguste de la Chaise, Charles De Pauw, and Pisgignoux, capture them, and deliver them to the capital. Gayoso put those orders into execution, issuing instructions to Barnó y Ferrúsola on November 7, the latter leaving Nogales on November 9. Gayoso wrote to the commandants of Nogales, Arkansas Post, and New Madrid by express, warned them of the threatened French invasion, and alerted them to watch out for the revolutionary agents, giving descriptions of the three most wanted of them and telling the commandants to arrest them and send them under guard to Natchez, irrespective of their passports.[6]

Jaudenes and Viar continued their diplomacy in Philadelphia but realized quickly that diplomacy alone was inadequate for dealing with men of direct action like the French republicans and American frontiersmen. They went on with their work as informants,[7] however, by filling in the activities, work, and proposals of the three agents so hunted for by the officials of Louisiana. More-

---

García to Carondelet, No. 53, on *La Venganza*, San Fernando, June 20, 1796, P de C 33. List of subjects recommended by Carondelet for promotion enclosed in draft [Carondelet] to Prince of Peace, No. 73 res. There is a signed copy by Carondelet dated New Orleans, February 6, 1796, in Carondelet to Las Casas, No. 155 res., P de C 1447, wherein Carondelet recommends Ferrúsola—then lieutenant of militia, captain of a galiot, and employed on the Mississippi since the year 1793—to the rank and salary of sublieutenant in the army. See draft [Carondelet] to Joseph de Ville [Degoutin], New Orleans, September 16, 1796, P de C 130; draft [Carondelet] to García, n.p. [New Orleans], September 17, 1796, P de C 129; draft [Carondelet] to Degoutin, New Orleans, November 22, 1796, P de C 130; Rousseau to Carondelet, on *La Venganza*, Nogales, June 29, 1794, P de C 210; Gayoso to Carondelet, No. 2 muy res., New Madrid, September 22, 1795, P de C 2364; draft to Ferrúsola, New Orleans, March 9, 1797, P de C 35.)

6. Carondelet also strengthened the forces at New Orleans, ordering Gayoso to send him reinforcements from Natchez. See Carondelet to Gayoso, res., New Orleans, October 29, 1793; Gayoso to Carondelet, res., Natchez, November 5, 1793, P de C 208A; Carondelet to Alucudia, No. 20, res., in *AHAR 1896, 1*, 1021-22; Gayoso to Portell, res., Natchez, November 4, 1793, P de C 208A; Instructions to Ferrúsola, signed by Gayoso, November 7, 1793; certified copy in P de C 42; draft in P de C 123. Carondelet to Gayoso, New Orleans, November 27, 1793, P de C 20.

7. For this story see Liljegren, *LHQ, 22*, 3–53, and more esp. Nasatir and Liljegren, *LHQ, 21*, reprint pp. 35-37, where citations are given, particularly concerning Pisgignoux. See Pisgignoux to Portell, Pittsburg, November 11, 1793, P de C 27B; certified copy in P de C 1447. Audrain to Carondelet, Pittsburg, November 28, 1793, P de C 207B; Jaudenes and Viar to Jefferson, New York, October 2, 1793; certified copy in Las Casas to Alange, No. 24 res., Havana, November 9, 1793, in Archivo General de Simancas, Sección Guerra Moderna, leg. 7235; Jaudenes and Viar to Carondelet, New York, October 2, 1793, encl. in ibid. This Las Casas letter to Alange is an important dispatch.

over, when Medad Mitchell approached them with a proposal or plan for checking the French project against Louisiana, Jaudenes and Viar thought so well of it that they gave him letters of recommendation and expense money and sent him overland to New Madrid as an informing ambassadorial agent to the officials along the Mississippi River.[8]

Because of the inescapable condition of Carondelet's position at the lower end of the river, removed by many hundreds of miles from decisive events at the upper part of the province, he had to reconstruct the situation as best he could from murky informants who were often glibly lying (or at least so he thought) about events that dated back weeks and months in time. A very stormy petrel of this nature was the herald of the Clark-Genêt expedition, that same Medad Mitchell who had once been taken into custody because of his indiscreet map-making on his neighbor's river. To Portell at New Madrid about December 1, to Gayoso de Lemos some three weeks later, and to Carondelet on December 26, Mitchell brought a full and detailed account of the expedition. George Rogers Clark had been appointed major general of the Kentucky forces, with authority to appoint officers for an army of 5,000. However, money was lacking; Clark was quarreling with Dr. James O'Fallon, land agent, incendiary writer, and influential politician with a considerable following among Kentuckians; and Congress was expected to interpose its authority to stop the invasion in order to avoid war with Spain.[9]

The military problem posed for Carondelet by an attack in force against Upper Louisiana was a difficult one. The squadron could conceivably prevent the eruption of armed vessels from the Ohio, but it was not possible to prevent an enemy from proceeding overland to Kaskaskia, crossing the river at that point, capturing St. Louis, and attacking New Madrid by land. Moreover, in all the

---

8. Jaudenes and Viar to Las Casas, New York, October 8, 1793, encl. in Las Casas to Alange, No. 24 res.; Las Casas to Alange, No. 374 res., Havana, February 21, 1794, AGS 7235; Report of Mitchell to Jaudenes and Viar, New York, October 3, 1793, encl. in Las Casas to Alange, No. 24 res.; Carondelet to Las Casas, No. 99 res., New Orleans, December 30, 1793, P de C 1447; copy in P de C 152B. Trans. of [Mitchell] to Carondelet, encl. No. 1, ibid.; Gayoso to Carondelet, No. 16 res., Natchez, December 23, 1793, encl. in Carondelet to Alcudia, No. 23 res., New Orleans, January 1, 1794, AHN 3898. See Nasatir and Liljegren. See also Diary 2, below, pp. 206–07; 209 n. 51.

9. See references above, n. 8.

upper province, 500 leagues above the capital, there were only 90 regular troops and 200 militia. Nor could Carondelet be happy with his poor defenses and paucity of troops for the protection of Lower Louisiana. It looked dark. Not only could the Spanish bulwark in the Mississippi fall, but also Carondelet feared for the safety of Santa Fé and the Kingdom of Mexico. Carondelet was informed—mistakenly, as it proved later—that Santa Fé was but 22 days march from St. Louis[10] and that the invaders planned to extend their conquest to include the *Provincias Internas.*[11]

Despite his pessimism, Carondelet was determined to utilize every possible means at his command for the colony's defense. Seeking to take advantage of Spain's alliance with England, he even requested John Graves Simcoe, lieutenant governor of Upper Canada, to send a corps of 500 men to the aid of St. Louis, even though he did not think that the aid, even if granted, could arrive in time.[12] On top of all that, even with the French threat of attack by sea no longer a threat, the colony upon whose resources alone Carondelet could rely was not entirely dependable: not only was it full of internal foes ready to join the Franco-American forces, but should the French Convention publish its decree of liberty, there was danger of a Negro uprising.

In a game where all the odds seemed hopelessly against Spain, the squadron was the one effective resource. Since the enemy could not bring vessels of equal weight and fire power down the Ohio, the full squadron could stop an enemy expedition at the mouth of the Ohio or below that point. In addition, Trudeau at St. Louis was ordered to concentrate all available resources, including the

---

10. See Nasatir and Liljegren, *LHQ, 21,* 36. See also Carondelet to Branciforte, New Orleans, April 23, 1796, AGI, Estado Mexico, leg. 5; same to same, June 7, 1796, in Nasatir, *IJHP, 29,* 178–81.

Noel Loomis and I have recently concluded from our study of Pedro Vial that the 22 days distance from St. Louis to Santa Fé was after all not "too mistaken." This notion of St. Louis being 22 days distant from Santa Fé remained in the Spaniards' minds for a long time, creating a fear for their northern possessions. (See e.g. Nasatir, *Before Lewis and Clark, 1,* 79, 113; and Nasatir, *IJHP, 29,* 155–232.)

11. Carondelet to Las Casas, No. 99 res.; Carondelet to Alcudia, No. 23 res., New Orleans, January 1, 1794, AHN 3898; draft in P de C 178B.

12. In *IJHP, 29,* 181–83, I discuss this and give citations to letters. See also Trudeau to Carondelet, letters No. 166, St. Louis, March 20, 1794, P de C 125; May 3, 1794, P de C 139. The correspondence between Simcoe and Carondelet went through Trudeau (Trudeau to Carondelet, New Orleans, January 3, 1794, P de C 21).

Indians, who were almost always counted as a military force in Carondelet's plans, at Fort Céleste in New Madrid, until the galleys should arrive. If overwhelming pressure should compel them to retreat further—to Nogales—they were, above all, to save the cannon of St. Louis and New Madrid or to destroy them rather than see them captured.

If all went badly in the upper province, the defense of the entire province was to be staked on holding Nogales. Governor Gayoso de Lemos, who did not always concur in his superior's views, was in agreement as to that. But to defend his district, he begged his superior for more men and, above all, more war vessels and transport. Carondelet, troubled by the ever-present possibility of revolt on the part of subjects "seduced by vain love of a deceitful liberty," did not feel able to send reinforcements; but, because they were needed to defend New Orleans and the province depended on the preservation of the capital, he promised Gayoso he would rush them north if word should come that the enemy had forced the entrance of the Mississippi. Gayoso found such a promise painful. While reinforcements could perhaps be rushed from the capital in six weeks time, by then the fate of the province could well have been sealed through the capture of Nogales. On the other hand, Gayoso did somewhat strengthen Nogales and also Natchez, where a volunteer corps was created under his own personal command and with distinctive uniforms.[13]

Early in January 1794 a still more ominous cast was given to the situation by news brought back from the Falls of the Ohio by Ezekiel Dwet, a Dutch resident of the Natchez district, that the French were building boats at the Falls, at Limestone, and at Fort Pitt, and—disastrous addition—that they were stopping all chalanes

13. Carondelet to Las Casas, No. 103 res., New Orleans, February 8, 1794, P de C 1447; draft in P de C 152B, and encls. therein. Las Casas to Alange No. 374 res.; Carondelet to Gayoso, New Orleans, January 15, 1794, P de C 21; Gayoso to Carondelet, No. 15 res., Natchez, December 22, 1793, P de C 42. Relación of what is necessary of Natchez in order to defend the upper river, Natchez, December 21, 1793, encl. in draft [Gayoso] to Carondelet, Natchez, December 22, 1793, P de C 27B; Gayoso to Carondelet, No. 18 res., Natchez, January 21, 1794; copy attached to Carondelet to Las Casas, No. 103 res., P de C 1447. Gayoso to Alcudia, res., Natchez, February 18, 1794, AHN 3902, in *AHAR 1896, I,* 1042–45; Gayoso to Carondelet, No. 398, Natchez, January 17, 1794, P de C 42; Gayoso to Carondelet, No. 16 res., Natchez, January 9, 1794, P de C 28; duplicate in P de C 42.

loaded with provisions for Louisiana. Gayoso feared a flour famine for Natchez and Nogales—more so since Colonel John Montgomery, a leader in the proposed expedition against Louisiana, was also rumored as intending to post himself at the mouth of the Ohio to cut off Louisiana-bound supply ships. So threatening were reports of hostile activity on the Ohio that Carondelet felt obliged, on February 21, to order all lanchones, berchas, or pirogues ascending from the capital to St. Louis and that neighborhood to be detained at Natchez in order to avoid seizure of their cargoes by the enemy.[14]

While Carondelet worried over the growing menace of invasion and Gayoso hastened to prepare Natchez and Nogales for attack, measures for defense on the upper river were also under way. As we have noted above, Ferrúsola was ordered to take *La Flecha* and patrol the river between Nogales and the Arkansas River, inspecting all descending vessels, and, above all, to be on the lookout for French agents.[15] Ferrúsola received his instructions from Gayoso on November 7, and *La Flecha* sailed from Natchez on November 9,[16] taking on provisions and additional munitions at Nogales on November 20. Leaving the latter post on the twenty-third, Ferrúsola reached the Arkansas River on December 13. There, after dispatching a pirogue with letters to commandant Delinó at Arkansas Post, he set up his cruising station at the site of the military detachment at the White River. He heard nothing

14. Gayoso to Carondelet, No. 16 res.; same to same, No. 17 res., Natchez January 15, 1794, P de C 42, and draft of reply; Delassus to Carondelet, Ste. Geneviève, December 26, 1793, P de C 207B; copy encl. in Carondelet to Las Casas, No. 104 res., New Orleans, February 9, 1794, P de C 1447; draft in P de C 2363. Draft [Carondelet] to Gayoso, New Orleans, February 21, 1794, P de C 28. Nasatir and Liljegren, *LHQ*, 21, 32–33.

15. Anyone who carried the tricolor bonnet of liberty or any other sign of the French Revolution was to be considered suspicious.

16. The crew consisted of 14 rowers, a carpenter, a seaman, and the patrón, Antonio Molina; 2 artillerymen and 4 soldiers of the guard composed the troop (Carondelet to Gayoso, New Orleans, November 27, 1793, P de C 20; Instructions to Barnó y Ferrúsola on the cruising station between Nogales and Arkansas, signed by Gayoso de Lemos, November 7, 1793; certified copy in P de C 42; draft in P de C 123).

The diary of this voyage is given below, pp. 193–231. It is in full. There is ample correspondence to cover each and every entry in Ferrúsola's diary in the Spanish archives. I have copies of many of Ferrúsola's letters. Only the barest outline of the voyage is given here.

about rumored hostilities on the upper part of the province from that commandant,[17] but on the next day, December 14, he stopped Medad Mitchell descending to New Orleans as an envoy of the Spanish agents in Philadelphia. From him Ferrúsola learned of the intended French attack scheduled for May. Shortly thereafter, he received the alarming news from Portell at New Madrid that the French were planning to attack as early as March. Feeling it his duty to depart from Gayoso's instructions in order to go to the aid of New Madrid, Ferrúsola left at dawn on the nineteenth of December. Speed was essential, for the river was rising rapidly and the invaders might arrive before March. Ferrúsola had on hand only limited rations, but he managed to add a couple of oars to his galiot and put the soldiers themselves to rowing, promising his crew double rations of meat to speed their progress—even though he knew he might have to depend on passing chalanes or hunters for supplies.

Ferrúsola reached New Madrid on January 10 and found the post in great activity. He put sixteen of his sailors to work helping with the fortifications during the day, Ferrúsola acting as inspector of the works,[18] and crossed to the opposite bank at night to keep close watch on any descending vessels that might try to slip by. Throughout the month of January, however, events remained indecisive, with the usual rumors of activities of French and Americans in the American West. Those in the militia at New Madrid worked badly together, and the Americans in particular were disposed to be surly about the whole business.

On February 5 Ferrúsola's careful search of all descending vessels was rewarded by the discovery of Pierre Pisgignoux descending on the chalan of a French émigré doctor named Cruzat de St. Martial.[19] Although Ferrúsola recognized Pisgignoux from Gayoso's

17. Gayoso notified all the post commandants on the upper river of Ferrúsola's commission and ordered them to supply him with whatever provisions, troops, or materials he requested drafts of letters of Gayoso to Delinó, November 7; to Beauregard, November 10; and Gayoso's order of November 9; all in P de C 123).

18. Ferrúsola to Gayoso, on *La Flecha* before the Fort of New Madrid, January 17, 1794, P de C 47; Portell to Carondelet, No. 226, New Madrid, January 18, 1794, P de C 28.

19. See in addition to Diary 2, below, pp. 225–31. Cruzat de St. Martial to Carondelet, New Madrid, February 8, 1794, P de C 210; Delassus de Luzières to Carondelet, New Bourbon, March 15, 1794, P de C 210; Ferrúsola to Gayoso, No. 16, Nogales, February 16, 1794, P de C 45; certified copy in P de C 42. Rousseau to Ca-

description of him, Pisgignoux protested his arrest in a torrent of injured eloquence, taking the position that the Spanish should receive him in triumph. Neither Portell nor Ferrúsola was impressed by him, but, all things considered, it seemed best to send him south on the galiot, in irons, to Nogales. Thereupon the galiot prepared for the journey downriver. At Portell's request Ferrúsola left behind seven soldiers from the Regiment of Louisiana and a gunner of the royal artillery, replacing them with men from the New Madrid regiment who seemed disinclined to defend the town. With his usual dispatch, Ferrúsola got down the river in six days and delivered his prisoner to Captain Elías Beauregard[20] at Nogales on February 16.[21] The latter had orders to forward Pisgignoux under heavy guard to New Orleans at the first opportunity.

Ferrúsola's expedition—to New Madrid, at least—had been undertaken on his own responsibility, and he had indeed given a signal demonstration of the flexibility of the galleys under reasonably favorable conditions and under strong leadership. As the center of Louisiana's defense activities shifted to the upper river, the matter of strengthening the outposts of the province became important, and the presence of the squadron at New Madrid imperative.

---

rondelet, on *La Venganza* at Nogales, June 29, 1794, P de C 210; Pisgignoux's declaration at Natchez, dated March 8, 1794, P de C 152B. The latter was enclosed in Carondelet to Alcudia, No. 29 res., New Orleans, March 20, 1794, and is translated in *AHAR 1896, 1,* 1047.

20. Don Elías Beauregard, captain in the Regiment of Louisiana, played an active part in the founding and early government of Spain's two new posts of Nogales and Barrancas de Margó. He was born in New Orleans, June 17, 1759; was a volunteer in the caribaneers in New Orleans in 1780; and took part in the siege of Mobile. In 1791 he was a member of Gayoso's expedition to the Yazoo River, where he aided in the construction of fortifications at Nogales and remained as commandant of the post when Gayoso returned to Natchez. Ygnacio Delinó relieved him of his position at Nogales in July 1794 so that he could rejoin his regiment in New Orleans. In the spring of 1795 he was summoned from the capital to join Gayoso in another expedition, this time to found San Fernando de las Barrancas. As soon as the new post was established, Gayoso commissioned Beauregard as its commandant, an office which he held until Captain Vicente Folch replaced him in September. Freed of his duties at Barrancas, Beauregard returned to his regiment in New Orleans, where he remained until the summer of 1796, when he was assigned once again to the civil command at Nogales. After the evacuation of Nogales he lived in Baton Rouge.

21. Ferrúsola expected orders to arrive soon for *La Flecha* to descend to Natchez. In March, when the squadron reached Nogales on its way to New Madrid, Ferrúsola was transferred to the command of *La Castilla,* one of the descending galleys.

Since, early in January, Carondelet decided that the danger of an attack on New Orleans by sea was over, he instituted plans to send the galleys up the river,[22] having read the over-all situation in the same sense as his subordinates. Rousseau was forthwith to take the galleys *La Venganza, La Felipa,* and *La Castilla,* the galiots *La Activa* and *La Flecha,* and the cañonera *El Rayo* all the way to New Madrid. It was the largest formal naval force ever to operate so far up the river.

22. Carondelet to Portell, muy res., New Orleans, January 2, 1794, encl. in Carondelet to Portell, New Orleans, January 19, 1794; both in P de C 21.

5   Fort San Fernando Establisehd at Barrancas de Margó

Under instructions drawn up by Carondelet in the middle of January, Rousseau was to command the squadron under severely limited conditions. Its main objective on the upper river was to lend support to the defenders of New Madrid, to prevent the enemy from capturing Spanish artillery. Rousseau was instructed not to engage the enemy unless victory was certain. If the outcome was at all doubtful, the galleys were to retreat to Nogales, taking troops and artillery from New Madrid with them. More intelligent were Rousseau's instructions to cruise to the Ohio and, with the lighter galiots, to go as far as St. Louis. Under Domingo Bouligny 150 troops were transported with the squadron—a very substantial addition to the defensive power of the upper river.[1]

With the departure of the squadron, Carondelet revised his original plan for defense of the province by moving the first point of a major armed resistance from Nogales to New Madrid: defense now depended upon the presence of the naval squadron on the upper river, as well as on active Indian aid. He thought that if the squadron should arrive in time, it would be capable of stopping any expedition that might descend the Ohio, for the enemy's boats would not be as large as the galleys, and without artillery they could not hope to pass Spain's armed war-vessels. If, however, the invaders took New Madrid before the squadron could arrive, they were to fall back to Barrancas de Margó, where Carondelet hoped

---

1. Draft of secret instructions to Rousseau [by Carondelet], New Orleans, January 15, 1794, idem dated New Orleans, January 16, 1794; both in P de C 2354; drafts in P de C 2352. Carondelet to Portell, muy res., January 2, 1794, encl. in Carondelet to Portell, New Orleans, January 19, 1794; both in P de C 21. Carondelet to Gayoso, res., New Orleans, January 22, 1794 (three different letters of same date), P de C 21; copy attached to Carondelet to Las Casas, No. 103 res., New Orleans, February 8, 1794, P de C 1447; Carondelet to Las Casas, New Orleans, March 20, 1794; copy in *AHAR 1896, I,* 1049–51.

for active Indian aid in repelling the enemy, with the galleys blocking the river. If that were not successful, Rousseau was to retreat downriver to Nogales, stopping on the way to pick up the Arkansas garrison. However, the more experienced Rousseau and Gayoso, knowing the capacities and limits of Louisiana better than did Carondelet, differed sharply with him over some features of his plan, especially the abandonment of Arkansas and Carondelet's project for defense of Lower Louisiana. In fact, Gayoso, finally disgusted with Carondelet's nervous fears, his pessimistic resignation to defeat, and his ill-considered measures for defense, wrote directly to the Duque de la Alcudia. The only measure of Carondelet's that Gayoso commended was the sending of the naval squadron to New Madrid, which had been done anyway at Gayoso's constant and repeated urgings.[2] Carondelet probably could not discriminate between fact and fancy in the many rumors that reached his ears: he accepted most of the stories at face value and consequently was kept in a continual state of worry and anxiety. Although the defects and weaknesses of Louisiana's defenses were only too clear to him, he had little notion of the enemy's forces and knew that people in the capital were sympathetic to the Jacobins.[3]

Wind, weather, and river-flood set nice limits to the game Carondelet and the enemies of Spain had to play. Because a French attack at New Orleans was blocked by adverse winds, Carondelet could concentrate toward the New Madrid and St. Louis end of the embattled line. With luck and skill, he could hope to beat off attacks until such time as the subsiding of the Ohio should reduce the pressure from that direction and the galleys could shuttle a thousand miles south to resume a defensive posture near New Orleans. While long, critical months had to be spent in the difficult passage upstream, the institution of the galleys nevertheless gave

---

2. Gayoso to Carondelet, No. 22 res., Natchez, January 31, 1794, P de C 42; No. 33 res., Natchez, February 20, 1794, P de C 28. Rousseau to Carondelet, on *La Venganza*, Natchez, February 25, 1794, P de C 209; Gayoso to Alcudia res., Natchez, February 18, 1794, AHN 3902; in *AHAR 1896, I,* 1042–45. Gayoso to Carondelet, No. 31 res., Natchez, February 20, 1794, P de C 42; same to same, February 11, 1794, P de C 28.

3. Carondelet to Las Casas, No. 105 res., New Orleans, February 27, 1794, P de C 1447; draft in P de C 152B.

the Governor General a precious and indispensable freedom of movement—at least relatively.

As an instance of such flexibility, early in February, Carondelet ordered Juan Baptista Metzinger to take the two heavy galleys *La Luisiana* and *La Victoria* to Natchez with the intent of having them added to Rousseau's squadron ascending the Mississippi. Before this move could be effected, however, Carondelet learned of threatened attacks on Nogales. It was then a simple matter to send orders to Gayoso to keep those heavy galleys at Nogales to aid in the defense of the fort, which was carried out when Metzinger reached Natchez on March 25.[4]

But it was high time for the squadron to reach the upper river. Constantly multiplying rumors of hostile armies at Vincennes and elsewhere put officials and people alike in a state of panic. Portell regarded New Madrid as good as lost if it had to depend on its own resources, but since Carondelet had now fixed that point as a major one for armed resistance to the foreign aggressors, there were outside resources. Militia and Indians at the other Illinois points, as well as men and munitions, were ordered sent to the aid of Portell at New Madrid, and most of the posts, except Ste. Geneviève, did send some men and aid. Henri Peyroux de la Coudrenière, commandant at Ste. Geneviève, felt that there was nothing to do but to capitulate and sue for terms, but he was replaced by Vallé, who rallied the populace and built a fort—he advancing the funds for it. Trudeau at St. Louis, however, maintained a stern resolution. He did not believe the rumors justified. He summoned the neighboring militias, rallied the Indian nations friendly to Spain—Kickapoos, Mascoutins, and Sacs, as well as Lorimier and the Shawnees—and even dallied with the idea of making peace with the mischievous Osages, dismissed Peyroux, and led his subjects to work

---

4. Carondelet to Las Casas, No. 104 res., February 9, 1794, P de C 1447; draft in P de C 2363. Carondelet to Gayoso, res., New Orleans, March 3, 1794, P de C 1447; draft in P de C 210.

My intention here is not to give a full discussion of the general plans of defense for all of Louisiana, but rather to tell the story and place of the naval vessels in that scheme and to narrate some of their activities, chiefly as illustrated by the diaries given below, pp. 149–326. There is a great deal of documentary evidence in the Spanish archives relating to the defense measures taken at the Spanish posts and of the quarrel between Gayoso de Lemos and Carondelet over the strategy proper to the defense of Louisiana.

on the fortifications even in a heavy snowstorm.[5] But everyone was nervous—slaveholders in particular—and all eyes turned anxiously southward, waiting for the arrival of the river navy. Upper Louisiana depended a great deal upon the aid from that source. Having left the capital in January, early in March it was reported in New Madrid to have passed Nogales, so that Portell was now able to view the defense situation in New Madrid with greater confi-

5. There is much documentation in the archives on these matters. Only a few are cited here. See Nasatir, *IJHP*, *29*, 155–232; Liljegren, *LHQ*, *22*, 3–53. The center of the defense against the projected invasion was New Madrid. See Liljegren, ibid., pp. 35–47. See also Luzières to Carondelet, Ste. Geneviève, December 28, 1793, P de C 207B; copy in Carondelet to Las Casas, No. 104 res. Trudeau to Carondelet, No. 153, St. Louis, January 15, 1794; and draft of reply, P de C 122A, encl. No. 2 in Carondelet to Las Casas, No. 105 res.; Trudeau to Carondelet, No. 166, St. Louis, March 20, 1794, P de C 125; same to same, No. 160, [St. Louis], February 2, 1794, encl. No. 1 in Carondelet to Las Casas, No. 105 res.; and many other letters.

Henri Peyroux de la Coudrenière was born in France and came to Louisiana in 1784 as interpreter for the Acadians. Shortly after, he wrote a memoir on the advantages to be gained for the Spanish crown by the settlement of Van Dieman's Land. (Oscar W. Winzerling, *Acadian Odyssey* [Baton Rouge, 1955].) On August 5, 1787, he succeeded Antonio de Oro as commandant at Ste. Geneviève and was replaced by François Vallé in 1794 because of suspicions as to his loyalty. In the previous year, 1793, Peyroux had made a trip to the United States, where he became imbued with the democratic spirit of that country and of France. On this trip he had made the acquaintance of André Micheaux, who in turn had introduced Peyroux to Genêt and had recommended him as one who could be used to aid the projected invasion of Louisiana. Upon Peyroux's return to Ste. Geneviève he openly and approvingly spoke of the American and French constitutions and advocated a policy of capitulation to the French. In the latter part of 1793 he refused to cooperate in the defense of the village of Ste. Geneviève. Peyroux maintained his residence, the garrison, and munitions in an abandoned section of the village and refused to organize the militia. He also refused to permit the inhabitants of the village to build a fort for their safety. Peyroux received a garbled report of the events taking place in New Orleans, and made public the news that a revolt had occurred in New Orleans. Trudeau suspected Peyroux and later sent him to New Orleans. Neither Carondelet nor Gayoso de Lemos were successful in proving Peyroux's disloyalty, and he returned to St. Geneviève as captain of the militia after promising Carondelet that he would move from the post as soon as possible. The Governor General continued to distrust him and in 1796 suggested to Carlos Howard that he remove Peyroux if an excuse could be found. Nevertheless, when Delassus became lieutenant governor of Upper Louisiana, Peyroux was transferred to New Madrid and remained commandant there until 1803. In May of that year he was replaced because of insubordination, and was ordered not to attempt to take part in the government of the post on the threat that, if he did, he would have to face formal charges. Peyroux then resigned from the Spanish service and went to France. (Liljegren, *LHQ*, *22*, 41–43. See also Gayoso's report, below, pp. 339–41.

dence.[6] Although the faster traveling vessels of traders and hunters —keelboats and pirogues—gave reports of the progress of the river naval flotilla, tensions increased in the upper posts. The militia concentrated at St. Louis and New Madrid wavered, and the savages, always fickle, were troublesome and expensive.

Despite the urgency and the need for speed, the squadron made progress in the teeth of acute difficulties. In a time of peril its schedule was heartbreaking to the zealous and conscientious Rousseau. It left New Orleans on January 21,[7] not reaching Natchez until February 18, after an especially arduous trip. Here Rousseau was obliged to lay over for a week, because *La Felipa* had been severely damaged in a collision with a submerged rock and had to be repaired. The crew was short-handed, as well, and although Rousseau and Gayoso endeavored strenuously to recruit a few more sailors, it was not an easy task.

On the morning of the twenty-fifth the squadron sailed for Nogales and at once ran into difficulties. Terrific storms sprang up, severely testing the timbering of the stout galleys, and *La Venganza* and *La Castilla* lost their topmasts. The crews were beaten by heavy rains, and in their floundering progress the vessels repeatedly shipped water. After nine days, however, the squadron won its way to Nogales. Supplies for the fort were unloaded and the damaged masts repaired. Since all the matchcord on the vessels was found to be ruined by water, in case of battle the artillerymen would have to use firebrands. When at Nogales the squadron was joined by *La Flecha,* Rousseau made several shifts in command of the flotilla vessels, and some unfinished benches on *La Felipa* were completed. By the morning of March 10 the squadron was at length ready to brave the current again. With the regular flotilla there went two private lanchones—one well-armed—and a large pirogue.

Leaving Nogales, the total number of vessels in the flotilla amounted to 9, the galleys' crews were complete, and the men,

6. Gayoso to Portell, Natchez, January 16, 1794, P de C 42; Portell to Gayoso, New Madrid, March 16, 1794, P de C 47.

7. I have been unable to find a diary of this expedition, although undoubtedly one must exist. I have, however, a nearly complete copy of the correspondence of Rousseau and Ferrúsola on this trip, as well as the correspondence of Gayoso and Carondelet. Since the specific references are so numerous, I have restricted myself to citing just a few in nn. 8 and 9, below.

whose number totaled 240, were well disposed and eager to meet the enemy. Rousseau felt that his strongly manned galleys should at least make as good a record as the commercial keelboats that plied the river, and he hoped to reach New Madrid in less time than it had taken the galleys to go from New Orleans to Nogales.[8]

Rousseau's luck did not greatly improve, however. Storms and rain continued to hinder the progress of the galleys from Nogales to the mouth of the Arkansas River, where they were detained for several days. While there, Rousseau received a message from Portell urging haste. He sent *La Flecha* up the Arkansas to the post to deliver the Indian presents and money that the galleys carried for that post, and asked Delinó for eight replacements for a like number of sailors in the squadron who had fallen ill; he then resumed his journey.

Once he reached Barrancas on the afternoon of April 8, he met a further delay because Rousseau had been entrusted with the delivery of the annual presents for the Chickasaw Indians. He had therefore to send two men to the Chickasaw village with news of their arrival, although Gayoso had sent word ahead asking the interpreter to be on hand at the bluffs with Chief Ugulayacabé when the squadron arrived. A long week passed, but no savages arrived. At last, on April 16, Chief Ugulayacabé arrived with his son and a few braves, the rest of the nation having been delayed by high waters. But Rousseau's supplies were running low; he could wait no longer. He entrusted the gifts to Ugulayacabé for distribution to his people, and, after ordering the squadron to assume combat formation, he fired a general salute of the artillery to impress the Indians with the power and prestige of Spain. Then he departed for New Madrid on the afternoon of the seventeenth.

While the squadron was held at Barrancas by this embarrassing delay, it received from some descending chalanes the news that the proposed Franco-American expedition had failed and was over. The French expedition from Kentucky had in reality disintegrated

---

8. Rousseau to Carondelet on *La Venganza,* Natchez, February 19, 1794, P de C 210; same to same, same place, February 25, 1794, P de C 209; same to same, n.p., n.d., [above Nogales March 10?, 1794], P de C 216A; draft [Gayoso] to Fooy, Nogales, March 9, 1794, P de C 210; Gayoso to Carondelet, No. 430, Natchez, March 13, 1794, P de C 28; official copy in Carondelet to Las Casas, No. 497, New Orleans, March 20, 1794, P de C 1443A.

FORT SAN FERNANDO ESTABLISHED

long before it reached a crisis in the minds of the rumor-clouded Spanish defenders; it was formally pronounced dead and buried by a proclamation of Jean-Antoine-Joseph Fauchet, successor to Genêt as French minister to the United States, dated March 6, forbidding Frenchmen to violate the neutrality of the States by organizing hostilities against Spain on American soil. But it was several weeks before the confirmation of this bloodless deliverance reached Spanish officialdom.[9]

Despite the increasing number of reports that the projected French expedition had failed, Rousseau continued up the river to his destination, arriving at four o'clock on the afternoon of April 26, just three months after his departure from New Orleans. It was a great occasion. The militia was drawn up in review formation; the inhabitants of the region and hundreds of savage allies swarmed to the river to see the astonishing sight of a war squadron. When Rousseau gave the signal, the full armada discharged all its artillery in a loud general salute. Not only were the Spanish adherents of the region joyous, but all others were impressed. Never before had the heavy galleys gone further up the river than Nogales, and everyone, even the officials, had thought it impossible for them to ascend that far. Instead of the six months that some people in

---

9. This news of the breakup of the projected Clark-Genêt expedition reached all the upper posts. Pertinent documentation: Rousseau to Gayoso, April 12, 1794, P de C 209; Rousseau to Carondelet, same date, P de C 210; Fauchet's proclamation, Philadelphia, March 6, 1794, encl. in Laccasagne to [Gayoso], Louisville, April 16, 1794, and draft of reply attached, P de C 209; also in P de C 2371. Luzières to Carondelet, New Bourbon, March 15, 1794, P de C 210; Trudeau to Carondelet, St. Louis, April 11, 1794, P de C 209; La Cassagne to Portell, Louisville, April 30, 1794, P de C 203; Portell to Carondelet, No. 249, New Madrid, April 27, 1794, P de C 28; Rousseau to Gayoso, New Madrid, April 27, 1794, P de C 209; Ferrúsola to Gayoso, New Madrid, April 27, 1794, P de C 47; Rousseau to Carondelet, New Madrid, April 27, 1794, P de C 220; draft [Gayoso] to Rousseau, Natchez, May 6, 1794, P de C 126; Carondelet to Las Casas, No. 116 res., New Orleans, May 10, 1794, P de C 1447; Rousseau to Carondelet, New Madrid, May 1, 1794, P de C 210; Rousseau to Gayoso, New Madrid, May 1, 1794, P de C 211.

On March 6, 1794, Fauchet canceled the plans for the expedition as well as all arrangements that had been made for it. His official notice forbade Frenchmen to violate the neutrality of the United States and recalled all commissions or authorizations that had been made (P de C 202). Fauchet's proclamation as published in a Philadelphia newspaper may be found in *AHAR 1897*, p. 629; it was also published in French and in English in the *Kentucky Gazette*, April 26 and May 3, 1794. See the accounts in James, *George Rogers Clark*; Whitaker, *Spanish-American Frontier*; Liljegren, *LHQ*, 22, 3-53.

New Orleans had predicted for the vessels to reach New Madrid, the galleys had forced the ascent within the time customary for trading vessels, and of the three months that had elapsed since the squadron had left New Orleans, only 75 days had actually been spent in river travel.

Although the immediate military crisis had evaporated, Portell was heartily glad to see the squadron. The moral effect on Spain's Indian allies and on the French and American settlers whose allegiance to Spain was suspected to be wanting in warmth was important. It had been reported even that some of New Madrid's most trusted inhabitants actually held commissions in the invading expedition, ready to reveal their political faith as soon as the French army appeared.[10]

Once the victory celebration was over, the squadron was obliged to retreat down the river by another foe—the rapidly subsiding Mississippi. The galleys could not maneuver and fight in shallow waters, and as the river channel narrowed, it would be too easy to ambush the squadron from the banks. Forty men, thought Rousseau, hidden in ambuscade, might destroy it, and it was in this sense that he wrote to Carondelet about the return of the galleys.[11]

The weeks wore away without official word until at length, on June 18, Rousseau took the squadron south on his own responsibility, leaving behind the galiot *La Flecha* under the command of Francisco Langlois to patrol the river from New Madrid to the mouth of the Ohio.[12] The descent of the galleys was for the most

---

10. Among many other letters that might also be cited, see the following from Portell: to Carondelet, New Madrid, No. 236, February 28, March 14, and March 29, 1794, P de C 28; to Gayoso de Lemos, New Madrid, March 29, May 4, and June 2, 1794, P de C 47.

11. Rousseau to Carondelet on *La Venganza* at New Madrid, May 8, 1794, P de C 210; certified copy in P de C 211.

12. *La Activa*, under the command of Francisco Langlois, was charged with two main objects: (1) to guard against surprise attack from the Ohio, and (2) to discover and capture certain men who, since the beginning of the Clark-Genêt expedition, had been spreading lies among Spain's Indian allies in an attempt to withdraw the allegiance of those savages from Spain. These orders were changed by Carondelet, and Ferrúsola was left in command of *La Activa* to cruise from New Madrid to the mouth of the Ohio, while Langlois was to be in charge of another galley to cruise on the Arkansas. See references below, p. 94, n. 13. Ferrúsola, commanding *La Activa*, after some careening in Natchez, reascended the river to patrol and cruise between Nogales and the mouth of the Arkansas.

Francisco Langlois, born in New Orleans, was a sublieutenant in the militia and

part uneventful. Although at Barrancas de Margó they met a pirogue carrying Carondelet's letter and orders for the squadron to remain at New Madrid, Rousseau felt that under the circumstances—the falling Mississippi having transcended the orders of Carondelet—he should continue the descent to Nogales and there

---

a commander in the river squadron, and saw his first service with the galleys in January 1794. At that time he replaced Duparc as second in command of the squadron and was put in charge of *La Felipa* for the galleys' first ascent to New Madrid. When the squadron descended in June, Rousseau left Langlois at New Madrid with *La Flecha* to guard the upper river. Langlois established a cruising station at the Ohio and operated from there during the remainder of 1794 and throughout spring and summer 1795. Early in 1795 he was joined by Ferrúsola, and the two officers took turns guarding the Ohio and making short trips on the upper river for the royal service. During the establishment of Fort San Fernando, Langlois made frequent trips to Barrancas to deliver food from the Illinois posts and perform various missions for Gayoso. When the formal treaty ceding Barrancas to the Spaniards was signed in June, he was there, for his name appears on the treaty. In December he was transferred to the command of *La Felipa* so that *La Flecha* could descend with the squadron for needed repairs. He was stationed at Barrancas with *La Felipa* until June 1796, when he descended to New Orleans to have the galley repaired. He remained at the capital for the rest of the year, in the fall receiving a promotion to the grade and salary of sublieutenant in the army. In 1797 he was back at New Madrid, where the census for that year lists him as a resident of the post.

In the opinion of Rousseau, Langlois was an active and intelligent officer, but this belief was not shared by all of Langlois' fellow officers. During the two years he was stationed at New Madrid, Portell developed a hearty dislike for him and more than once suggested that he be replaced. Early in 1796 he wrote Carondelet that Langlois was forcing men to serve on the galleys. He had the population around New Madrid so terrorized with his chains, clubs, and shackles that the sailors were all deserting. García accused Langlois of working for his own interests rather than for the best service of the King; and according to Langlois' story, even Gayoso was against him.

(List of subjects recommended by Carondelet for promotion, encl. in draft [Carondelet] to Prince of Peace, No. 73 res., P de C 178A; also in AHN 3886; Rousseau to Carondelet, on *La Venganza*, Nogales, June 29, 1794, P de C 210; Langlois to Lorimier, on *La Flecha* opposite mouth of the Belle Rivière, November 3, 1794, Portell Letterbook, 1793-94, P de C 2363; Portell to Carondelet, No. 433, New Madrid, February 12, 1796, P de C 215A; Folch to Carondelet, San Fernando, June 19, 1796, P de C 33; draft [Carondelet] to Degoutin, New Orleans, November 22, 1796, P de C 130; Langlois to Carondelet, No. 23, San Fernando de Barrancas, January 28, 1796, P de C 33; draft [Carondelet] to Langlois, New Orleans, March 17, 1796, P de C 130; list of inhabitants of New Madrid, their slaves, stock, and harvest for 1797, in Houck, *Spanish Régime*, 2, 393-97; Portell to Carondelet, New Madrid, May 10, 1795, P de C 33; García to Carondelet, on *La Castilla* at San Fernando, December 9, 1795, P de C 32; García to Gayoso, Campo de la Esperanza, December 17, 1795, P de C 48; Langlois to Carondelet, San Fernando des Ecores à Margot, December 23, 1795, P de C 211.)

await further instructions. They arrived on the afternoon of June 27.

Carondelet finally approved Rousseau's descent: the galleys were to remain at Nogales. A lanchón, *La Céréz,* was outfitted to accompany Auguste Chouteau's lanchón carrying supplies to the upper posts, and the galiot *La Activa,* under Ferrúsola, was ordered to patrol the river around New Madrid, with a second galley under Langlois to cruise at the Arkansas. Thus the heavy galleys *La Luisiana* and *La Victoria* were freed and ordered to descend to New Orleans under Metzinger's command.[13]

The dissolution of the Clark-Genêt expedition brought a lull in aggressive activities against Spain's Mississippi Valley possessions, but the respite was to prove short-lived. After a summer of inactivity, the fall of 1794 found the Americans renewing their push against the Mississippi. Nevertheless, Spanish officials in Upper Louisiana followed a policy of watchful caution. Although the militiamen of New Madrid, Ste. Geneviève, and St. Louis were dismissed, the Spaniards kept close tab on the activities of the Westerners. They not only had spies and confidential agents, but instructed Lorimier to keep his Indians ever ready to repulse an attack.[14] And they had *La Activa* cruising. Even the government of the United States became active in stopping these hostile actions of the restless Westerners and Frenchmen, establishing a post near the mouth of the Ohio—Fort Massac—for that purpose and to pro-

---

13. Letters of Carondelet to Gayoso, New Orleans, May 18, 1794, P de C 21; draft in P de C 47; June 2, 1794, P de C 21; July 2, 1794, P de C 21. Letters to Carondelet: from Langlois, No. 1, New Madrid, June 16, 1794, P de C 29; draft of reply dated July 8, ibid.; No. 4, New Madrid, September 19, 1794, P de C 30; from Rousseau, Nos. 17, 18, 19, all Nogales, June 29, 1794, P de C 29; unnumbered letter of same date, P de C 210.

Letters to Gayoso: from Langlois, New Madrid, July 1, 1795, P de C 210; from Rousseau, Nogales, June 27 and 29, 1794, both in P de C 209; New Madrid, June 1, 1794, P de C 209; June 2, 1794, P de C 47.

Letters from Portell to Carondelet, New Madrid, June 17 and 15, 1794, P de C 29; Portell to Gayoso, New Madrid, June 2, 1794, P de C 47.

See below, pp. 95-102.

14. Portell to Lorimier, New Madrid, June 30, 1794, in Portell Letterbook, 1793-94, P de C 2363; Portell to Carondelet, New Madrid, July 5, 1794, P de C 29; Portell to [Carondelet], New Madrid, July 15, 1794, P de C 29; Lorimier to Monsieur, Cape Girardeau, September 6, 1794, P de C 212A; Trudeau to Carondelet, No. 191, St. Louis, July 16, 1794, P de C 29; Carondelet to Trudeau, New Orleans, April 14, 1795, P de C 21.

tect the Ohio River traffic from any interference. However, Carondelet and his brother-in-law, the captain general at Havana, suspected the American establishment of a fort at the mouth of the Ohio. Luis de Las Casas ordered Carondelet to induce and aid the Chickasaws to dislodge the Americans and claim the area as their territory. This was too much for the more stable Gayoso, who wrote directly to Alcudia about it and succeeded in dissuading Carondelet from carrying out those orders.[15]

By early summer the entire river fleet, with the exception of *La Flecha*, was on the lower Mississippi, where it stayed throughout the remainder of 1794. When Rousseau's fleet had returned to Nogales from upstream on June 27, his vessels were in need of careening and repairs and his crews were tired and somewhat disgruntled. The next day he received orders from Carondelet which he did not like but dutifully set about carrying them out. For the sake of economy, the crews on his galleys were reduced; and so that two galleys always remained at Nogales, the vessels needing repairs were to go to Natchez for them one at a time.[16]

15. Among the abundant documentation see: Nasatir and Liljegren, *LHQ, 21*, reprint pp. 45 ff.; Gayoso to Alcudia, No. 1 res., Natchez, September 19, 1794, in *AHAR 1896, 1*, 1079–81; Wilkinson to Carondelet, Fort Jefferson, February 26, 1794, encl. in Carondelet to Las Casas, No. 113 res., New Orleans, May 1, 1794, P de C 2354; Portell to Carondelet, New Madrid, March 29, 1794, P de C 28; Carondelet to Las Casas, No. 118 res., New Orleans, June 28, 1794, AGS 7235; draft in P de C 152B. Carondelet to Las Casas, No. 137 res., New Orleans, June 13, 1794, P de C 2364; in Houck, *Spanish Régime, 2*, 111–14. See also documents printed on pp. 119–20, from P de C 2364 and AHN 3897. Las Casas to Minister of War, No. 815, Havana, July 19, 1794, AGS 7235; also in P de C 1484. Las Casas to Carondelet, res., Havana, August 5, 1794, in *AHAR 1896, 1*, 1082–84 (original in P de C 152B, copy in P de C 210); Carondelet to Gayoso, res., New Orleans, August 20, 1794, in *AHAR 1896, 1* 1081–82; Carondelet to Alcudia, No. 43 res., August 18, 1794, AHN 3899.

16. Rousseau had made the descent from New Madrid with the galleys *La Venganza, La Felipa*, and *La Castilla*, the galiot *La Activa*, and the cañonera *El Rayo*. Carondelet ordered *La Luisiana* and *La Victoria*, stationed at Nogales and under the command of Metzinger, to descend to New Orleans with Bouligny and the land troops that had garrisoned the squadron during its voyage to New Madrid. Rousseau's 3 galleys with their crews, reduced for sake of economy to 30 sailors and a patrón for each, were ordered to remain in Nogales to replace *La Luisiana* and *La Victoria*. If any of the 3 larger vessels needed repairs, they were to descend singly, as needed, to Natchez, only one at a time descending, always leaving 2 galiots at Nogales. (Draft [Gayoso] to Rousseau, Natchez, May 26, 1794, P de C 128; Carondelet to Gayoso, New Orleans, June 4 and 16, 1794, P de C 21; Rousseau to Carondelet, on *La Venganza* at Nogales, June 29, 1794, P de C 210; Rousseau to Gayoso, same date, P de C 209.)

Rousseau thought that his galleys should descend to New Orleans, since his men had completed a long, painful six-month voyage and needed a good rest to be in condition for their next campaign. He himself was suffering from a bad case of insomnia and feared he might become ill if he stayed in Nogales, where everyone was sick. Moreover, he feared losing many of his men, because the necessary proper care was unobtainable in Nogales. In Rousseau's opinion Natchez was a much better base for the squadron during the summer months. After *La Activa* was repaired, he ordered it, in accordance with Carondelet's instructions, to cruise between Nogales and the Arkansas and to deliver supplies requested by Delinó at Arkansas. He also urged Carondelet to purchase an excellent lanchón, built originally by Luis Vanden Bemden for Bartélemi Tardiveau, which was approved, made into *La Vigilante*, and designated for the use of Gayoso de Lemos. Rousseau then asked for and received permission to descend to Natchez with his three remaining vessels, and on the morning of July 19 he arrived in that more healthy post.[17]

In early August disturbing news from Wilkinson in Kentucky led Carondelet to order the immediate ascent of the squadron to New Madrid. Wilkinson reported that Clark and his myrmidons were reviving their schemes against Louisiana, and Carondelet, he warned, must be ready to repel an attack on any part of the province. He suggested stationing two armed lanchas at St. Louis, two at the mouth of the Ohio, and two at New Madrid, each capable of carrying six-caliber bronze cannon in its prow. To prevent an attack on Natchez, he suggested that a strong force be placed on the Mississippi near the mouth of the Arkansas, where the Spaniards, aided by the Indians, could barricade or sink enemy vessels, and that the garrison at St. Louis be increased to 300 men, that at New

---

17. Rousseau to Carondelet, Nogales, June 29, 1794, P de C 210; Rousseau to Gayoso, same date, P de C 209; Rousseau to Carondelet, No. 19, Nogales, June 29, 1794, P de C 29; Carondelet to Gayoso, New Orleans, July 7, 1794, P de C 21; Gayoso to Delinó, Natchez, September 13, 1794, P de C 42; Gayoso to Carondelet, No. 429, Natchez, March 13, 1794, P de C 28; Carondelet to Gayoso, New Orleans, June 4, 1794, P de C 21; Portell to [Carondelet], New Madrid, July 15, 1794, P de C 29; Carondelet to Rendón, New Orleans, October 16, 1794, P de C 618; draft [Rendón] to Carondelet, New Orleans, November 20, 1794, P de C 581A; Rousseau to Carondelet, No. 27, Natchez, July 19, 1794, P de C 29.

Gayoso had asked Carondelet for permission to purchase a vessel in his dispatch No. 429, dated Natchez, March 13, 1794, P de C 28.

Madrid to 200. Greatly alarmed by Wilkinson's reports, Carondelet instructed Gayoso to have the squadron careened immediately at Natchez so that it would be ready to leave for New Madrid in September. To that end he dispatched a lanchón loaded with materials necessary for careening the vessels.[18]

Carondelet's order killed all the hopes the squadron had for descending to the capital before starting another campaign. Since it was necessary for Gayoso to bolster the sailors' sagging morale, he explained to them that the honor of Spanish arms made it impossible to descend to the capital at the time. Rousseau bluntly told the men that orders forbade their sailing to New Orleans, assured them that their pay was coming, and promised them winter clothing at New Orleans prices. It is evident that this loyal officer knew his trade: the men ceased grumbling and begged their captain to secure for them a raise in pay from 15 to 20 pesos a month.

In his usual way Rousseau set faithfully to the task of trying to prepare the squadron to carry out Carondelet's orders, although he considered them quite inoperable. The squadron as a whole, he knew, could not ascend the Mississippi before the first of December, nor fight on the upper river before the middle of March. Since during October and November the river was at its lowest point, vessels as large as the galleys could not navigate. In some places the water was too shallow for the galleys to pass; in others hazardous rock chains and rubbish mounds barred their way. Not for nothing had Rousseau made careful notes, mile after mile, of river conditions; nor were his thorough, precise maps in vain.

Although Carondelet disposed of no such forces as Wilkinson had advised, he did have the galleys, and those he could expend ruthlessly. Preparations to send the squadron north were therefore steadily pressed. They were checked in August, when hurricanes stormed up the river and damaged the galleys *La Luisiana* and *La Victoria,* which were at New Orleans to transport the materials necessary for careening and repairing the fleet at Natchez. But the delay was not serious; Gayoso still believed that the galleys would be able to leave for the upper river by October. Rousseau descended with the remaining vessels to New Orleans on orders from

18. Draft [Wilkinson] to Carondelet, n.p., n.d., copy encl. in Carondelet to Alcudia, No. 43 res., New Orleans, August 18, 1794, AHN 3899.

Carondelet probably to collect the supplies necessary for his squadron's next trip upriver. While there Rousseau contracted a serious illness, which delayed the departure of galleys until nearly the middle of November.[19]

Meanwhile, reports in the upper posts made everybody jittery once more. Preparations for the defense of New Madrid were again undertaken: *La Flecha* was strengthened and cruising at the mouth of the Ohio; plans were made to arm the lanchón *La Céréz*. Trudeau alerted Lorimier to gather a reserve force of Indians to aid the Spaniards if an invading army should appear, and sent men from his St. Louis garrison to aid Portell. Toward the end of September, Portell received the welcome news of Carondelet's decision to order the galleys' reascent to New Madrid.[20]

The general situation in which Carondelet was directing the movement of the galleys was created by his fear that the New American Fort Massac on the Ohio was intended to instrument a push down the Mississippi, resuming the American idea of seizing Ecores à Margot and getting control of the river. He was acutely alarmed by the news that the Americans were not only strengthening their garrison at Fort Massac but were also preparing to build an armed lanchón with swivel guns at that point. To hold the cork in the bottle, he was desperately anxious to hurry the squadron to New Madrid again. However, since he lacked sailors to man the

19. Draft [Gayoso] to Rousseau, Natchez, August 13, 1794, P de C 128; Rousseau to Gayoso, Natchez, August 15, 1794, P de C 47, and encl. in Gayoso to Carondelet, No 540, Natchez, August 15, 1794, P de C 29; Carondelet to Alcudia, No. 43 res.; Carondelet to Gayoso, New Orleans, August 11, 1794, P de C 21; Rousseau to Carondelet, Baton Rouge, November 15, 1794, two letters, one in P de C 20, the other in P de C 211; Rousseau to Carondelet, Natchez, November 30, 1794, P de C 210.

The hurricane struck New Orleans on August 10, causing damage in Balize, Placaminas, New Orleans, and other parts of Lower Mississippi. "What is worse, however, is that the squadron of *galeras* will not be able to ascend to its cruising opposite the mouth of the Ohio and New Madrid before the last days of December." Carondelet enclosed a relación of the King's vessels and commercial vessels which suffered damage as a result of the hurricane. The "galeras *La Luisiana y La Victoria* [estában] desarboladas y baradas [sic] [*lost their masts and were grounded*]." (Carondelet to Alcudia, No. 45 res., New Orleans, August 20, 1794, AHN 3899.)

20. Trudeau to Lorimier, St. Louis, September 18, 1794, in Portell Letterbook; Portell to Carondelet, No. 340, New Madrid, September 24, 1794, P de C 32; same to same, September 25, 1794, P de C 30; Portell to Gayoso, New Madrid, October 20, 1794, P de C 47.

ships, Rousseau had gone so far as to suggest hiring colored slaves to pull the oars—a most unattractive expedient. Carondelet could, though, beg the captain general at Havana for the return of the seagoing galleys *La Leal* and *La Fina*. Another difficulty was that the indispensable Captain Rousseau continued ill. And again the shattering hurricanes struck, leaving an aftermath of damage to repair.[21]

Rousseau was able to improvise a defense with the ubiquitous galiots, however, and gave orders to Portell to that effect. *La Flecha* was already on duty; *La Activa* should go north, along with a sturdily armed lanchón. This smaller squadron should establish a cruising station somewhere near the mouth of the Ohio and cruise between New Madrid and St. Louis, keeping an eye on the ever-menacing Ohio and comforting the troubled inhabitants of the Illinois with the assurance that the might of Spain would ever protect them. The squadron was commanded to destroy and annihilate Montgomery and his men or any other armed band that dared enter the Mississippi or tried to cross to Spanish soil, regardless of whether they were on the east or west bank of the river.

This was a gallant scheme, and it received in practice a bizarre execution. After a long, slow exchange of news and instructions, Gayoso was finally enabled to transmit the proper orders to Lieutenant Ferrúsola, commander of *La Activa*, who under similar strategic circumstances had distinguished himself the year before by his initiative, energy, and resourcefulness. On November 26 Gayoso told him to be ready to leave for New Madrid within two days, there to serve under Portell's order until the squadron should arrive. The galiot at the moment needed repairs, but these were effected and supplies were loaded with Ferrúsola's customary dash. Then, however, there ensued an awkward moment: the sailors refused to head up the wintry Mississippi unless they were paid. Despite all pleas and cajolery, the sailors were obdurate: Ferrúsola had perforce to wait for the long-overdue pay to arrive. During this

21. Carondelet to Las Casas, No. 125 res., New Orleans, October 20, 1794, P de C 1447; draft in P de C 152B. Las Casas to Carondelet, Havana, December 23, 1793 [1794], P de C 152B; Carondelet to Portell, New Orleans, October 20, 1794, P de C 21; copy encl. in Carondelet to Las Casas, No. 125 res. Carondelet to Portell, New Orleans, October 27, 1794, P de C 21; draft [Carondelet] to García, New Orleans, January 20, 1795, P de C 128; resumé of orders remitted to New Madrid in 1794, signed by Macay, New Madrid, August 20, 1799, P de C 124B.

distressing interim, orders arrived from the commandant of the squadron, Rousseau, transferring Ferrúsola to the gunboat *El Rayo*. This was a surprising—and to the gallant officer, a most painful—transaction. *El Rayo* was a very small boat—hardly large enough to hold the provisions needed for the journey to New Madrid, and so slow that the sailors nicknamed it "Buey." With speed so essential and the boat so small and slow, Ferrúsola did not believe that he could properly fulfill his commission, but he resolved to do his best. He prepared *El Rayo* for the trip to New Madrid. He recruited eight oarsmen, a proel, and a patrón, laid in the indispensable stores, and then stepped back to survey the results. With the little gunboat already deep in the water, there was no place to stow beds and baggage, so Ferrúsola piled them in the only place available—the stern—and prepared to perch on this humiliating quarterdeck of sailor's duffel to command his ship. He started out and made the voyage under forced march, but even so, it took the *El Rayo* a full two months to reach New Madrid.[22]

Upon receiving Carondelet's pressing entreaties, Rousseau forced himself from a sick bed and left New Orleans for the north on November 12. On the fifteenth the flotilla passed Baton Rouge, and on the evening of the twenty-ninth arrived at Natchez, after an accident that put three holes in *La Castilla's* bottom. Repairs were extensive enough to hold them at Natchez over a week. Before he could leave to continue his voyage northward, however, Rousseau received word from Gayoso that new developments reduced the urgency of the galleys' ascent. Consequently, on Carondelet's orders, the squadron was to remain at Nogales until further notice.[23]

---

22. Carondelet to Gayoso, New Orleans, October 27, 1794, P de C 21; Gayoso to Carondelet, No. 577, Natchez, November 29, 1794, P de C 30; Gayoso to Ferrúsola, Natchez, November 29, 1794; copy encl. in Ferrúsola to Carondelet, New Madrid, March 28, 1795, P de C 32. Draft [Gayoso] to Rousseau, res., Natchez, December 10, 1794, P de C 125; Ferrúsola to Gayoso, Nogales, December 23, 1794, P de C 47; Ferrúsola to Carondelet, New Madrid, March 28, 1795, P de C 32; another on same date, P de C 31.

23. Drafts of letters from [Carondelet] to Gayoso, New Orleans, October 28, 1794, P de C 21; to Rousseau, November 12, 1794, P de C 125. Rousseau to Carondelet, Nos. 1 and 2, Baton Rouge, November 15, 1794, P de C 30; another letter of same date, P de C 211. Rousseau to Carondelet, Natchez, November 30, 1794, P de C 210; draft [Gayoso] to Rousseau, res., Natchez, December 10, 1794, P de C 125; Rousseau to Gayoso, Natchez, December 11, 1794, P de C 47.

Changed conditions in the capital and in Lower Louisiana were the reasons for Cardondelet's sudden cancellation of the squadron's ascent. Adverse news of French victories in Spain made it necessary to concentrate the defenses of the colony on the more important and populous part of the province, for Carondelet feared that the news of French victories might inspire Jacobin sympathizers to stage an insurrection in favor of France. The presence of the squadron at Nogales would tend to restrain rebellious elements in the colony, and in the event of a rebellion the galleys could aid the militia in putting it down. They could aid in case a French maritime expedition should appear to threaten the capital, and could stop a force of Americans should they attempt to descend the river.[24]

So far as the upper river was concerned, Carondelet, even in these almost extreme straits, was not willing to concede the game. The little detached force of two galiots and an armed lanchón was to contest any American expedition attempting to descend the Mississippi bound for Ecores: first, by formal protests, and if these failed, by armed force, should success be likely. If the light squadron could not hold superior forces at the Ohio line, it was to follow the invader downriver and endeavor to prevent his unloading materials for a fort—again by force, but again only in the event that success seemed certain. Otherwise, Lieutenant Langlois, in charge of the light squadron, was to summon the Chickasaw Indians and hold the enemy closely blockaded by sea and land at Ecores until the main squadron could arrive to oust them. Gayoso was given proper orders to rush to the aid of Ecores the moment he should hear the Americans were there.

Ferrúsola reached New Madrid on February 12, only to find trouble brewing and more rumors afloat that gave the Spaniards the jitters. Portell had received the apprehensive news of large American army forces: 3,000 at Greenville under General Wayne; 1500 to 2,000 at Fort Pitt, supposedly to restrain the Western insurrection; and another 2,000 ready to join the Chickasaws and

---

24. Carondelet to Gayoso, res., New Orleans, November 17, 1794, P de C 21; draft in P de C 47. The documentation for these events and for the background of Carondelet's fears, as well as the reasons for the peripatetic Governor General's abrupt changes of orders, are too abundant to cite in these notes, which are concerned only with the part played by the naval vessels on the Mississippi.

Cherokees in their war against the Creeks. Although Portell himself doubted the truth of these rumors, he did send Thomas Power, Carondelet's confidential agent, up the Ohio to ascertain the truth, prepared to strengthen Langlois' small fleet and strengthen the fortifications of New Madrid.

When Ferrúsola arrived at New Madrid, he found Langlois there overhauling *La Flecha* for a bad leak.[25] The combined squadron, detailed to watch the Ohio, did cruise up and down the mouth of the river, building a station opposite the mouth of it, and passing some miserable times during the winter. Since Ferrúsola's slow *El Rayo* could not keep up with *La Flecha*, they squeezed two more oars onto the tiny vessel and stored provisions on the lanchón. Bad weather added to the many problems faced by the guardian flotilla. Once the station was established to suit Ferrúsola, *La Flecha*, leaving the *El Rayo* to maintain the guard, cruised up river to Ste. Geneviève to pick up Captain Luis de Vilemont. Delayed somewhat, on returning to the cruising station *La Flecha* found it almost completely exhausted of provisions. Finally, in March 1795, Portell was able to inform Carondelet of some good news: Colonel Montgomery, arch-enemy of Spain, long the strenuous agitator for the seizure out of hand of the whole east bank of the Mississippi, was dead,[26] and threats of attack from Cumberland, at least for the time being, were at an end.

There was no verbal response to this lightening of the ever-present western menace, but shortly there began to drift up the river rumors of an exciting Spanish advance: the galley squadron was coming in full force, charged with the mission of settling the destiny of the bluffs at Ecores and hence the river, by establishing a strong Spanish fort there. Portell at New Madrid was impressed

---

25. Carondelet to Portell, New Orleans, November 17, 1794, P de C 21; copy in P de C 2354; draft in P de C 210. Same to same, November 22, 1794, P de C 30; Carondelet to Gayoso, res., New Orleans, November 17, 1794, P de C 21; draft in P de C 47. Portell to Carondelet, New Madrid, February 10 and March 12, 1795, P de C 31; Langlois to Lorimier, November 3, 1794; Portell Letterbook; Langlois to Gayoso, New Madrid, January 12, 1795, P de C 210; Langlois to Carondelet, Nos. 14 and 15, New Madrid, February 6, 1795, P de C 31; Ferrúsola to Carondelet, New Madrid, March 28, 1795, P de C 31.

26. Late in February, Luis de Vilemont informed Portell of Montgomery's assassination by the Indians.

yet concerned; he wrote anxiously for official word, so that he might have provisions ready for this great expedition.[27]

During the spring and summer of 1795 Langlois and Ferrúsola continued to cruise between New Madrid and the Ohio naval station, also making several trips to Ste. Geneviève. They were in the habit of bringing supplies to Ecores when Rousseau and the main squadron arrived there in April. During the summer of 1795 *La Flecha* was kept especially busy fulfilling commissions for the royal service at the order of Captain Rousseau. Both Langlois and Ferrúsola remained stationed at New Madrid until the fall of 1795.[28]

The year 1795 furnishes, fully as much as the years of major external crises, an interesting example of the galleys running the chores of empire up and down the 1200 miles of the Mississippi frontier. Throughout all the storms and bluster of the winter, a little squadron had beat slowly back and forth between New Madrid and the Ohio, ever on the alert to block the expected Western push. Now, in the spring, the greater part of the squadron was ready to accomplish Carondelet's long-matured design of taking the strategic bluffs by a coup-de-main.

The heavy galleys *La Luisiana* and *La Victoria* spent their time until March 1795 on the lower Mississippi within easy reach of the capital. Then, once the heavy galley *La Luisiana* ascended from New Orleans to Natchez bearing the annual gifts to the Indians, under Manuel García's command,[29] the gifts were to be loaded

---

27. Letters from Langlois to Carondelet: No. 14, New Madrid, February 6, 1795, P de C 31; February 25 and April 14, 1795, P de C 210. Letters from Langlois to Gayoso: New Madrid, January 12, 1795, P de C 210; April 16, 1795, P de C 211. Langlois to Carondelet, Ecores, May 15, 1795, P de C 210; Portell to Carondelet, New Madrid, March 12 and April 18, 1795, P de C 31; Ferrúsola to Carondelet, New Madrid, March 28, 1795, P de C 32; another of same date, P de C 31; Portell to Carondelet, No. 368, New Madrid, February 10, 1795, P de C 32.

28. Rousseau to Carondelet, Ecores, April 24, 1795, P de C 211; letters from Langlois to Carondelet, No. 17, New Madrid, April 14, 1795, P de C 31; No. 20, New Madrid, September 1, 1795, P de C 32; Ecores, May 15, 1795, P de C 210; Portell to Carondelet, No. 396, New Madrid, May 10, 1795, P de C 33; New Madrid, May 24, 1795, P de C 48; Ferrúsola to Carondelet, New Madrid, May 9, 1795, P de C 31; Ferrúsola to Gayoso, November 2, 1795, P de C 212A.

29. Manuel García y Muñiz was born in Puerta Real, Andalucia, about 1765. He was a pilot for merchant vessels. In October 1793 Carondelet made him a first lieutenant with rank of captain in the New Orleans militia, and appointed him sec-

onto the squadron for delivery upriver. Although García joined the squadron ascending the river at Nogales, *La Luisiana* returned to Natchez and in early May headed south at full speed: a slave insurrection was threatening at Punta Cortada.

---

ond in command of the river squadron, but he was not actually attached to it until early 1795. His appointment, signed by Carondelet, October 1, 1793, is in P de C 23. In 1794 he was based at Placaminas in command of the galley *La Leal* to guard the mouth of the Mississippi. In command of *La Fina* in January 1795, when Carondelet transferred him to *La Luisiana*, he ascended the Mississippi in March with gifts to Natchez. García was transferred by Rousseau to *La Castilla* at Nogales and made second in command of the squadron at Barrancas. There he fulfilled his duties well until a difficulty with the interpreter Benjamin Fooy led to his arrest and confinement on board *La Castilla*. As a result of the quarrel García was confined for nearly three months, but the incident apparently did not affect his record too greatly, for in January 1796, when Rousseau's ill health forced him to retire from active service, García took his place as commander of the river squadron. In February, Carondelet recommended to the Court that García be promoted to the rank and salary of lieutenant in the army in recognition of his activities against French corsairs, and requested that his appointment as squadron commander be made permanent. The Court's reply arrived the following fall, conferring on García the rank of captain in the army with lieutenant's pay. In April he left the capital to reascend to Fort San Fernando on the squadron's flagship *La Venganza*. He arrived in June and set up a permanent headquarters for the squadron on the Island of Fooy. He also established a home for his family on the island and remained there until the post's evacuation in March 1797. The entire squadron then joined Howard's expedition and proceeded to St. Louis, where García remained until the summer of 1797, when he returned to New Orleans.

García was a good officer. Gayoso considered him the best to replace Rousseau. He was intelligent but had difficulty in getting along with his fellow workers. García was active against corsairs in the Gulf of Mexico, observed the activities of the Americans in a cruise to Nogales in 1798, and attacked the English brigantine *Hero*. He was in command of a galera on the expedition against Bowles in 1800, of the goleta *Favorita* in 1808, and of the coast guard of West Florida at Pensacola. He went to Vera Cruz for supplies.

(See Appointment of García, signed by Carondelet, New Orleans, October 1, 1793, P de C 23; Instructions to Metzinger at Balize, signed by Carondelet, New Orleans, November 10, 1794, P de C 21; draft to García, New Orleans, January 20, 1793, P de C 128. Gayoso to Carondelet, San Fernando de las Barrancas, July 18, 1795, P de C 198; Gayoso to Carondelet, No. 18 res., New Madrid, September 22, 1795, P de C 32; list of subjects recommended by Carondelet for promotion, encl. in draft [Carondelet] to Prince of Peace, No. 73 res.; draft [Carondelet] to Degoutin, New Orleans, November 22, 1796, P de C 130; Rousseau to Gayoso, on *La Venganza* at San Fernando, October 7, 1795, P de C 211; Gayoso to Carondelet, San Fernando de las Barrancas, July 18, 1795, P de C 198. A full account of García's activities in 1795 and 1796, including his quarrel with Fooy, is to be found in Coughlin's "Spanish Galleys"; and further material concerning García may be found in Ernest R. Liljegren's unpublished dissertation "the Commission of Carlos Howard." See also Nasatir, *IJHP*, *28*, 337–89.)

In April 1795 her sister heavy galley, *La Victoria,* stationed at New Orleans, was sent hastily to the German Coast to sweep together reinforcements from Punta Cortada, Baton Rouge, Manchac, and other points, and to send them to the capital. There had been another flurry of seditious agitation among the unsettled Republicans of the capital, but an alarmed and vigilant governor general was determined to be in advance of such ill-thinking gentry. *La Luisiana* again ascended to her patrol station at Nogales but was put on the alert to be ready to descend the river with 500 loyal men, should the capital be plunged into the flames of revolt. No rebellion broke out, however, and *La Luisiana* once more ascended to Natchez and remained there until the fall of 1795, with the exception of a couple of trips to the capital. Probably late in the summer it was joined by *La Victoria,* which remained stationed at Natchez until the end of the year, except for occasional descents to New Orleans.[30]

The most constructive use of the war galleys in 1795 was the materialization of the rumored scheme that had come to the attention of the upper province: that of crowning the beautiful bluffs of the middle river with a fort that would seal possession of the new land in the hands of the King.[31] Barrancas de Margó, lo-

---

30. Carondelet to Gayoso, New Orleans, August 11, 1794, P de C 21; Instructions to Metzinger at Balize, signed by Carondelet, New Orleans, November 10, 1794, P de C 21; drafts of letters of [Carondelet] to Metzinger, New Orleans, March 24, 1795, P de C 28; to García, January 20, 1795, P de C 128; draft [García] to Rousseau, Natchez, March 12, 1795, P de C 128; Rousseau to Carondelet, Natchez, March 14, 1795, P de C 211; draft [Grandpré] to [Carondelet], No. 3, Natchez, April 27, 1795, P de C 33; Grandpré to Carondelet, Natchez, May 12, 1795, P de C 211; Carondelet to Grandpré, muy res., New Orleans, May 5, 1795, P de C 22; draft in P de C 211; quoted as an encl. in Grandpré to Gayoso, Natchez, May 18, 1795, P de C 211. Carondelet to Metzinger, New Orleans, May 5, 1795, P de C 22; Grandpré to Gayoso, Natchez, May 18, 1795, P de C 211; Grandpré to Carondelet, Natchez, July 16 and September 2, 1795, P de C 32.

31. The reasons for the establishment of a fort at Barrancas de Margó were: to keep the Americans out, to strengthen Spain's control of the Mississippi and defend Upper Louisiana from invasion, to shorten the lines of unprotected territory between Arkansas Post and New Madrid—321 miles of uninhabited land (mileage from Collot, *Voyage,* 2, chap. 19), to increase Spain's influence and control over the Choctaw and Chickasaw Indians, to secure Spanish commerce from American interference, and to advance Spain's intrigues with the Westerners by facilitating communications with Kentucky. (Gayoso to Carondelet, No. 6 res., Esperanza, May 23, 1795, P de C 48; see Whitaker, *Spanish-American Frontier.*) Barrancas de Margó was located 340 leagues above New Orleans, and from 40 to 50 leagues below New Madrid.

cated some 340 leagues above New Orleans and from 40 to 50 leagues below New Madrid,[32] had been early recognized as a desirable settlement site by both Spaniards and Americans.[33] It had been used since early days by Indians and whites as a point of advantage for fighting, defense, and piracy. Bernardo de Gálvez, governor general of Louisiana during the American Revolution, had complained that not a boat had come down from the Illinois country, not even a trapper's boat, without being fired upon at Barrancas de Margó and de Prud'homme, for at the time there was a detachment of British soldiers and Chickasaw Indians at that convenient control and watching-point on the river.[34] In 1784 General James Robertson and other North Carolinian land speculators considered the possibilities of a colony there, but nothing came of their plans.[35] The first real threat of an American settlement at Barrancas appeared in January 1793, causing Carondelet, in great alarm, to begin plans for establishing a Spanish post there.

The bluffs[36] were the most conspicuous feature in several hundred miles of swamp and forest. They consisted of a long stretch of high land extending for about twenty leagues in a northeasterly

---

32. Distances taken from diary of Ferrúsola on *La Flecha*, Nogales, February 16, 1794, P de C 2353. See below, pp. 220–21.

33. See plan, advertisement, and invitation to the people of Maryland for an American settlement at Chickasaw Bluffs planned for the spring of 1792, in Kinnaird, *AHAR 1945, 3*, 317–21. It is dated April 3, 1790.

34. B. Gálvez to Chester, February 20, 1778; draft and copy in P de C 2351. J. W. Caughey, "Panis Mission to Pensacola 1778," *HAHR, 10*, 480–87; D. C. Corbitt, "James Colbert and the Spanish Claim to the East Bank of the Mississippi," *MVHR*, 24, 457–82; J. W. Caughey, *Bernardo de Gálvez in Louisiana 1776–1783* (Berkeley and Los Angeles, 1934).

Miró urged that a fort be established at Barrancas de Margó (Miró to Gálvez, June 5, 1782, in Houck, *Spanish Régime, 1*, 214–18); Madame Cruzat was captured there in 1782 (Kinnaird, *AHAR 1945, 3*, 18–20, 21–34).

35. Whitaker, *Spanish-American Frontier*, p. 54.

36. Descriptions of Barrancas de Prud'homme: Gayoso to Carondelet, No. 17 res., New Madrid, September 16, 1795; No. 9 res., San Fernando, June 13, 1795; both in P de C 2364. Rousseau's description sent by Gayoso to Carondelet, No. 252, Natchez, April 4, 1793, P de C 2363; Houck, *Spanish Régime, 1*, 410–12; Holmes, *Documentos*, pp. 253–59; Holmes, "Fort Ferdinand of the Bluffs," *West Tennessee Historical Society Papers, 13*, 38 et seq.; Pope, *A Tour*, pp. 23–25; Bailey, *Journal of a Tour*, pp. 267–70; Collot, *Voyage, 2*, 20–25; Nuttall, *Journal of Travels into Arkansas Territory*, in Thwaites, *Early Western Travels, 13*, 88–89. See also the diaries below, pp. 172–74, 185–86, 216–17, 279–83.

direction along the east bank of the Mississippi, touching the river at four points. Each of these bore a different name: Barrancas de Margó, Barrancas del Medio, Barrancas de Prud'homme, and Barrancas de Farina. When Rousseau visited the bluffs in 1793 he reported that Barrancas de Margó was the only one of the four suitable for a fort, all the others possessing certain disadvantages that disqualified them.[37] There, two little streams—the Las Casas and Wolf Rivers—cut sharply in behind the highlands, affording a defense against attacks from the landward side; and the river channel suddenly narrowed below, so that batteries on the bluff completely dominated the river. It was an ideal site for a fort to protect and control the navigation of the Mississippi, Las Casas, and Carondelet Rivers.[38]

The country around Barrancas de Margó was beautiful. The soil was rich and fruitful; springs were abundant. While Cypress trees were thick in the river bottoms, walnut, oak, chestnut, sassafras, and plum made a varied and wonderful forest covering. There was but one offsetting curse in this land of enchantment—the mosquitoes. They were not an annoyance but an ordeal. They hung in thick clouds over the bluffs and in hungry crawling clusters on every victim. The bedeviled workmen and soldiers were compelled to wear a kind of leather or pelt armor to ward off these ferocious plagues and to move slowly, so encumbered in the humid atmosphere, to perform their duties.[39]

Although the plans of both the Spaniards and Americans to form a settlement at Barrancas de Margó were interrupted by the Clark-Genêt expedition, by the fall of 1794 the stage was cleared for renewed activity in that direction. The Americans were the first to act when toward the end of 1794 the Georgia legislature granted several million acres of its western lands to three land companies, including in one of the grants[40] all the territory along the Mississippi between Natchez and Chickasaw Bluffs. Carondelet in November sent a messenger to the bluffs to warn the Chickasaws of

---

37. Gayoso to Carondelet, Natchez, April 4, 1793, P de C 2363; in Houck, *Spanish Régime, 1,* 410–12.

38. Houck, *Spanish Régime, 1,* 410–12; Collot, *Voyage,* chap. 19.

39. Log of *La Flecha,* entry for March 21, 1793, below, p. 186. Rousseau to Carondelet, *La Venganza,* Nogales, June 29, 1794, P de C 210; Folch to Carondelet, San Fernando de Barrancas, June 11, 1796, P de C 33.

40. Whitaker, *Spanish-American Frontier,* p. 214; *AHAP, 5,* 395 ff.

the American plans. At that moment fear of a Jacobin insurrection in Lower Louisiana prevented Carondelet from sending the galleys any farther up the river than Nogales,[41] but by the end of January conditions in the capital had died down sufficiently to permit the squadron to continue its interrupted journey to New Madrid.

Apparently Carondelet did not believe it necessary to begin a Spanish settlement at Barrancas immediately, for he ordered Rousseau to take the squadron direct to New Madrid, stopping only long enough at Barrancas to deliver the Chickasaws' annual gift to that nation's new king. He also dispatched *La Luisiana* under Manuel García to join the squadron at Natchez with the annual presents for the Arkansas and Illinois Indians.[42] García reached Natchez on March 10, but Rousseau's departure with the fleet was delayed by bad weather, and it was not until March 14 that the main galley squadron once more began its slow trip up the winding Mississippi. *La Venganza, La Felipa, La Castilla,* the heavy galley *La Luisiana,* and the ever-present *La Activa* composed the flotilla, accompanied by many pirogues.

Within three days after the departure of the squadron, Gayoso decided that immediate action was necessary to occupy Barrancas, because he had reason to fear that the Americans, then aiding the Chickasaws in their war against the Creeks, might well seize the all-important bluffs at any moment. Therefore Gayoso dispatched a messenger to Nogales with orders for Rousseau to delay the squadron at Barrancas until more definite instructions could arrive from Carondelet. In the meantime he outlined the procedure Rousseau was to follow at Barrancas until Carondelet's orders got there. These secret orders to occupy Barrancas reached Rousseau at Nogales, where the squadron arrived on March 20, and a few hours later Gayoso's messenger came with the secret instructions. Hurried preparations, loading and unloading, took place despite drenching rain. Gayoso's instructions were of such a tenor that Rousseau thought it advisable to replace four Americans in the galley crews. *La Luisiana* returned to Natchez, and García was transferred to *La Castilla,* making him second in command of

---

41. Carondelet to Gayoso, res., New Orleans, November 17, 1794, P de C 21; draft in P de C 47.

42. Draft [Carondelet] to Rousseau, February 4, 1795, P de C 128; Rousseau to Carondelet, *La Venganza,* Natchez, February 11, 1795, P de C 211.

FORT SAN FERNANDO ESTABLISHED

the squadron. The fleet was ready by March 22 and sailed the following morning.[43]

Despite much rain, good winds enabled the galleys to reach the mouth of the Arkansas. There they awaited the arrival of Carlos de Vilemont from Arkansas fort, delivered to him the Indian presents for the Indians, and set out again for Barrancas on the morning of April 11, once Rousseau had written Carondelet that when he reached Barrancas he would, with the Chickasaws' consent, erect a fort from which, he boasted, the Americans would be unable to oust the Spaniards. He arrived at Barrancas on April 20, twenty-eight days after their departure from Nogales.[44]

Rousseau was now more than commonly alert, because he expected a possible fight at Barrancas. His instructions were careful, precise, and not a little ominous. To begin with, he was to station the galleys below the bluffs and await the Indians' arrival to receive the royal presents. This was normally no occasion for anxiety, but the Americans were known to be on the march and mischievously active among the Chickasaws. Since a strong party of Chickasaws, led by Chief Payemingo, favored the American cause and had permitted the Americans to build forts on the nation's territory, Rousseau was obliged to maintain all crews at their posts and the artillery loaded for firing whenever Indians came on board and against any surprise attack; moreover, he was never to permit any Indians on board unless they were known to be friendly. In other words, diplomacy, guile, and cajolery were to be used to influence the Spanish party among the Chickasaw Indians. When the great Chief Ugulayacabé arrived, Rousseau was to explain that he was in a great hurry to take his warships on to the Illinois but that another lanchón, loaded with further presents, was on its way accompanied by a galley, and of course he had to await its arrival. By a happy chance this would be the lanchón of John Turnbull, a trader favorably known to the Chickasaw, who, Carondelet hoped, would establish a trading post among the Indians. Further, since it was Gayoso's dip-

---

[43]. Rousseau to Carondelet, Nos. 5 and 6, Nogales, March 22, 1795, P de C 31; another of same date, P de C 211; draft [Gayoso] to Rousseau, No. 6, muy res., Natchez, March 17, 1795, P de C 211; Gayoso to Carondelet, Natchez, March 14, 1795, P de C 43; March 20, 1795, P de C 2364.

[44]. See below, p. 253. Rousseau to Carondelet, No. 8, foot of Arkansas, April 10, 1795, P de C 31; another April 10 [11], 1795, P de C 211; Rousseau to Gayoso, April 10, 1795, P de C 211.

lomatic hope that Ugulayacabé would himself be inspired to ask the Spaniards to build a fort to protect the trading post, the Spanish agent was instructed to insinuate this idea into the chief's mind. As a hopeful approach toward the grand design, Rousseau was to suggest, in the event that the natives were willing to have the squadron wait for the arrival of Turnbull and the supernumerary presents, that it would be a good idea to build a small redoubt ashore—so placed as to command the river—with a road from the point of embarkation.[45]

On the evening of April 20, as noted above, the Spanish squadron reached Barrancas de Margó, set up camp at the mouth of Las Casas River, where all approaching vessels could easily be seen, and ordered a strict alert maintained at all times and a strong guard placed to protect the camp.[46] On the twenty-first the squadron heard that the Indians were coming. Rousseau made sure that the galleys were anchored in a mutually supporting fashion and that there were heavy guards on duty at the camp ashore. He then ordered three cannon shots fired at evening as a signal of the squadron's arrival, followed by another three the next morning. Chief Ugulayacabé, accompanied by 1,000 men and women from his tribe, reached the bluffs at noon, and the presents were distributed at once. The Indians seemed well pleased with their gifts, and promptly proceeded to get drunk.

On the following afternoon Rousseau entertained Ugulayacabé and 25 of his braves on board his flagship *La Venganza*. In accordance with his instructions Rousseau approached the matter of building a fort. The Indian chief entertained Rousseau's propositions with sympathy, but he refused to commit himself until he had received a reply to his letter from the "great chief in New Orleans." Not only was he anxious to see Gayoso, who he heard was ascending from Natchez, but he also wanted to consult his nation. Sending most of his Indian entourage back home, Ugulayacabé

---

45. Rousseau to Gayoso, and Rousseau to Carondelet, April 11, 1795, P de C 211.

46. The correspondence of Rousseau relating to these events is very voluminous, as is the correspondence and documentation relative to the establishment of the Spanish post at Barrancas and Gayoso's journey upriver. It is touched on by Whitaker in *Spanish-American Frontier*. An analysis of the relevant data and a sketch of Fort San Fernando drawn from the engineer's plans and instructions are included in Coughlin's "Spanish Galleys on the Upper Mississippi," a work that has been freely drawn upon in this narrative.

and 25 of his warriors remained at the bluffs. These and other Indian guests soon reduced the squadron's provisions critically; whereupon Rousseau dispatched an armed pirogue to New Madrid for supplies earlier prepared by very secret orders sent by Gayoso, without informing even the commandant of that post that they were destined for Barrancas.

After these cautious diplomatic exchanges there ensued one of the most picturesque spectacles of the river squadron's career. Since Ugulayacabé desired Rousseau to let the Indians see the squadron sail, the Spaniard was quick to seize this opportunity for an impressive display. In mid-afternoon the galleys sailed down the river single-file to the center of the bluffs, where they assumed combat form. Then Rousseau gave the order to the flagship *La Venganza* to fire. Each galley in turn discharged a salvo, and the bluffs resounded with unaccustomed thunder. The noise brought 600 yelling Indians to the edge of the bluff, wildly shooting their guns. The galley crews stayed prudently under cover until this firing was at an end; then *La Venganza* discharged a single shot, and the whole squadron discharged a simultaneous broadside. Thereupon the galleys turned upstream to their moorings, and the Indians started shooting again, keeping it up until nightfall. Chief Ugulayacabé was extremely pleased with the elaborate ceremony, and Rousseau must have been satisfied with his impression upon the Indians of Spain's power and prestige.[47]

Shortly after, the worried commandant at New Madrid, Thomas Portell, heard that an American expedition to Barrancas was under way and that shortly a convoy of Indians and supplies bound for that point would soon reach the Mississippi. He hastened to inform the Spaniards at Barrancas. A budget of rumors all tended to this effect, and Francisco Langlois, cruising with *La Flecha* at the mouth of the Ohio, picked up some disquieting confirmatory news: the Americans were building boats at Fort Pitt to use in the coming summer for cruising on the Mississippi. Also, emanating from Fort Massac on the Ohio, came some quite precise information: 500 armed whites were leaving Cumberland for Barrancas, joined by the remnants of a detachment routed by the Creeks in an earlier movement on the bluffs. The planned attack from Cumberland

47. See esp. Rousseau to Carondelet, Ecores, April 24 and 26, 1795, the first in P de C 211, the second in P de C 198. See below, n. 48.

under General Robertson was disquieting news. Portell informed the commandants at Ste. Geneviève, St. Louis, and the Arkansas posts to prepare themselves. Portell's words sent to Rousseau also caused anxiety and required that he weigh the situation with care. Against an overland movement of hostile forces, the position under the bluffs had many disadvantages. Rousseau moved his flotilla to battle stations across the river, where they might bring their redoubtable fire-power into play on the heights of the bluffs and also offer a challenge to any force sweeping downriver.[48]

So the situation remained until the end of May, when Gayoso de Lemos arrived at Barrancas. The reports which in March had caused Gayoso de Lemos to order the squadron under Rousseau to be delayed at Barrancas had long since reached Carondelet and brought him to the same conclusion: that immediate occupation of Chickasaw Bluffs in the name of the Spanish King was necessary. He therefore appointed Gayoso de Lemos commander-in-chief of an expedition to take possession of Barrancas, authorizing him to establish there, if possible with the Chickasaws' consent, a post, stronghold, and storehouse.[49]

As the main forces of the expedition had already departed, Gayoso quickly put his affairs in order at Natchez and prepared to join them.[50] On the afternoon of April 16 he embarked in his new

---

48. Although Rousseau wrote many and frequent letters, the correspondence is too extensive to cite specifically here; see above, p. 110, n. 46. But see e.g. the documents published in Houck, *Spanish Régime*, 2, 111–18, which are Carondelet to Las Casas, No. 137 res., New Orleans, June 13, 1795, P de C 2364, and encls.; and in Houck, 2, 119–21, which are Portell to Carondelet, No. 393, New Madrid, May 8, 1795, and encls., AHN 3897; copy in P de C [31] 2364.

The threats of attack vanished soon after the arrival of Gayoso at the bluffs (Gayoso to Carondelet, San Fernando, July 18, 1795, P de C 198).

49. Carondelet to Las Casas, No. 134 res., New Orleans, May 1, 1795, AHN 3899 and P de C 2364; Gayoso to Carondelet, Natchez, March 14, P de C 47; and March 20, P de C 2365. Carondelet to Alcudia, No. 53 res., New Orleans, June 10, 1795, AHN 3899; Orders of Carondelet to Gayoso, New Orleans, April 15, 1795, P de C 128; Rendón to Gardoqui, No. 10, New Orleans, June 17, 1795, Sto. Dom. 87-1-22 (old numbering); draft in P de C 38; copy in MHS, Papers from Spain, No. 88a. Rendón in his letter No. 53 to Gardoqui, New Orleans, June 15, 1795, P de C 638, tells the need for having the galleys prepared, and he asked the Viceroy of Mexico for more money for defense. He wrote to Branciforte on May 30.

50. Gayoso's correspondence on his trip is voluminous and corroborates his journal. See above, p. 110, n. 46.

galiot *La Vigilante,* accompanied by the bercha of Captain Elías Beauregard, recently appointed by Carondelet to take command of the new post at Barrancas, and a *berchita* named *Betty*. After stopping for four days at Nogales to take on ammunition and materials for building a fort, they left, taking with them some additional soldiers and the bercha *El Mosquito,* which carried Lieutenant Juan María Perchet, an engineer commissioned by Carondelet to draw up plans for the fort.[51] On May 9 Gayoso was at the confluence of the Arkansas and White Rivers, conferring with Carlos de Vilemont, and when, on the afternoon of May 20, he reached Barrancas, he promptly incorporated his small flotilla into the squadron moored on the west bank of the river at a spot which Gayoso christened El Campo de la Esperanza.

From the moment of the arrival of Gayoso de Lemos, matters progressed and indeed were flourishing for the Spaniards. No more was heard of American threats to seize the bluffs by main force,[52] and negotiations between the courtly Gayoso and the savage chief Ugulayacabé proceeded in a manner satisfactory to Spain. Ugulayacabé could not consent to a formal treaty of concession of Barrancas de Margó without calling the village chiefs together for consultation, but to begin the construction of a fort before signing a formal treaty was permitted. He even suggested, with a certain uneasiness, that it should be a strong one, for he feared that the Americans would deal harshly with those Chickasaws who did not follow the lead of Payemingo. In addition to these negotiations, grounds were cleared for a fort, and a road was constructed from the disembarcation point at the mouth of the Las Casas River to the site of the projected fort.

May 30, 1795, marked the high-water point of Spanish activity on the imperial river. On that date sufficient work had been done

---

51. On March 23, 1795, Carondelet wrote Beauregard (draft of letter is in Bancroft Library) that he had decided to give him command of the troops and fort, which "I have decided to be built at Ecores à Margot by the engineer Perchet. You will avert any surprise attack on the part of the Americans now settled at Muscle Shoals on the Tennessee or on the part of the Chickasaws who follow Payemingo who is a chief entirely devoted to the American cause. Instructions are being sent to Rousseau." Perchet was appointed by Carondelet in February. (Carondelet to Gayoso, New Orleans, February 1, 1795, P de C 22.)

52. Gayoso to Carondelet, New Orleans, July 18, 1795, P de C 198.

so that Gayoso felt it proper to take formal possession in the name of the King.[53] By then enough work had been done so that the temporary camp across the river could be formally moved to the site of the new fort. Early in the morning the men of the Regiment of Louisiana embarked on *La Vigilante, La Activa, La Venganza,* and Beauregard's bercha, followed by the officers of the squadron. They weighed anchor across the river, unloaded the artillery, and mounted it on top of the bluff. At that point Gayoso formed his officers and men in a column and marched to the site of the new fort. On the river the squadron divided into two parts, one on either bank in front of the new post. Gayoso's personal galiot, *La Vigilante,* ranged itself in front of the flagstaff, the flag of Spain was drawn up, and Gayoso and his officers saluted it with a cannon shot, echoed by fifteen shots from each vessel in the squadron. The battery of the new post answered with the same salute, the men in the squadron shouted, and the ceremony was ended with three general volleys from the infantry. This act of formal possession occurring on the name day of the Príncipe de Asturias, the new fort was christened San Fernando de las Barrancas in his honor. After further formal negotiations, a solemn treaty ceding an enclave in the dominions of the Chickasaws to Spain was signed on June 20 with impressive ceremonies.[54] Once Gayoso formally lighted his pipe and passed it to the chiefs, all was complete save for the presentation of gifts to the Indians in payment for the cession.

53. See below, diary, pp. 259–60. Gayoso to Alcudia, res., New Madrid, September 5, 1795, AHN 3902; draft in P de C 128. The date of the formal cession is also given in draft [Carondelet] to Rendón, New Orleans, June 15, 1795, P de C 31. The treaty with the Chickasaws and a sketch of the grant is given in Gayoso's letter of September 5, 1795. See Nasatir and Liljegren, *LHQ, 21,* 52–53.

54. See diary entries for June 13, 14, and 20, below, pp. 259–66. Gayoso to Carondelet, Esperanza, May 26, 1795, P de C 31; June 18, 1795, P de C 43. Gayoso to Alcudia, res., New Madrid, September 5, 1795, AHN 3902.

Gayoso notified Beauregard officially of his command of the post on the day after signing the formal treaty, but Beauregard was to remain for a while under the orders of Gayoso. On July 25, 1795, Gayoso drew up instructions for Beauregard. See diary entry for May 31, below, p. 260, and Beauregard to Carondelet, No. 1, Barrancas, June 1, 1795, P de C 32. A copy of Gayoso's instructions for the first commandant of Barrancas, Elías Beauregard, was enclosed in Gayoso's letter, No. 17 res., New Madrid, September 16, 1795, P de C 2364; trans. in large part by J. D. L. Holmes in "First Laws of Memphis," *WTHSP, 9* (1961), 95–104. The instructions or law dated July 25, 1795, are in P de C 52.

FORT SAN FERNANDO ESTABLISHED

The bulk of the presents, together with funds for payment of the men of the expeditions and additional provisions and building materials for the post at Barrancas, were to be brought up from Natchez on the lanchón *La Céréz,* which had left Natchez early in May with orders to proceed as rapidly as possible to Barrancas. Affairs of the greatest moment hung on the expedition of the little vessel, but the patrón of the *La Céréz* was apparently a raw hand and knew little of navigation on the Mississippi. The poorly handled vessel made painfully slow progress, and just 25 leagues above Nogales sprang a leak and began shipping water so badly that it had to return to Nogales for repairs. As a result of all these delaying factors, the lanchón was unable to reach Barrancas before early July.

Gayoso, who expected the *La Cérez* to appear about the first of June, was greatly disturbed by its delay. He sent a scouting pirogue downriver to look for her. Supplies were running uncomfortably low, but luckily a passing American chalán was loaded with hams and bacon, which were bought by Gayoso at a high price.[55] After the pirogues had returned without word of the missing vessel, the Indians became restless, and ugly rumors began to circulate that the Spaniards had treacherously called the Chickasaws together only so that the Creeks might burn and harry their villages stripped of their braves. Gayoso feared not only that the Americans might take advantage of the situation but that a disastrous accident had overtaken the longed-for vessel, with grave consequences. As for his Indian protégés, they had lost confidence in him, but were loathe to return to their villages emptyhanded.

Since the well-known trader Manuel Lisa[56] was descending to New Orleans with letters, Gayoso de Lemos charged him with an urgent plea to Carondelet to dispatch another vessel posthaste if no trace of *La Céréz* could be found. Gayoso instructed Commandant Carlos de Vilemont at Arkansas to watch closely for news of the lanchón. He then ordered Langlois to take *La Flecha* down the Mississippi as far as the White River to look for the missing boat.

---

55. Dairy of Gayoso's expedition, below, pp. 264-70. Gayoso to Carondelet, No. 1, July 19, 1795, dated June 12; No. 12, dated June 24, 1795; both in P de C 43.

56. See Nasatir edn. of W. B. Douglas, *Manuel Lisa* (New York, 1964); Gayoso to Carondelet, New Orleans, June 24, 1795, P de C 43.

Finally, they discovered it about eight leagues above the White River, leaking badly, but, with the assistance of Langlois' men, *La Céréz* succeeded in reaching Barrancas on July 6. Flooding had damaged much of the goods in transit; all the garments, for instance, were so water-soaked that they were falling apart. Fortunately, enough remained to distribute among the savages, and tempers improved. Gayoso judiciously reserved the firewater until the day of the Indians' departure, July 11.[57]

After the belated arrival of the hapless *La Céréz*, work at the new post went on with no further difficulties than were furnished by the Spaniards' disinclination to work steadily at the disciplined labor of construction, as well as, from Gayoso's standpoint, the presence of a lazy and incompetent engineer, Juan María Perchet, whom Gayoso disliked. Nevertheless, the fort was completed before the end of November.[58]

Because of the proximity of Barrancas de Margó to the Americans at Fort Massac and Muscle Shoals, Carondelet thought Fort San Fernando should be strongly garrisoned. In addition to having a large permanent garrison to protect San Fernando, Carondelet figured that the militias of Arkansas Post and New Madrid should be used as reserves in the event of an American attack. Men were sent up from Natchez when an attack was feared; cannon were sent from New Madrid; and a protective battery was projected by Carondelet across the river at Campo de la Esperanza but did not materialize. Moreover, a small squadron of galleys to patrol the river was to be established permanently at San Fernando de las Barrancas. New Madrid, located 44 leagues above Barrancas, was the post best suited to serve the new fort as a base. But relations among Portell, Rousseau, and Vicente Folch,[59] who replaced Beauregard as commandant at San Fernando in September, were not always

---

57. Diary entry for July 6, below, p. 270; Gayoso to Carondelet, No. 7, Barrancas, July 19, 1795, P de C 43.

58. Rousseau to Carondelet, Ecores, August 22, October 7 and 12, and November 25, 1795, all in P de C 211; Gayoso to Carondelet, Barrancas, July 18, 1795, P de C 198; New Madrid, September 12 and 22, 1795, P de C 32; September 27 and December 3, 1795, P de C 43.

59. Vicente Folch y Juan was born of noble parents in Catalonia in the year 1755. At sixteen he was commissioned a sublieutenant in the army, and, after participating in several campaigns, he was ordered to America in 1780 to serve with the army of Don Victorio de Nava. At the end of the war his uncle, Esteban Miró, secured an appointment for him as commandant of Mobile. He was promoted to a full lieutenant in 1784 and received his captaincy two years later. In 1794 he was em-

good, and the latter two men lodged many complaints against the commandant of New Madrid. While the Barrancas fort was able to engage in some truck gardening, Turnbull and his projected trading post was forgotten by Carondelet, who commissioned Panton, Leslie and Company to establish a warehouse at Barrancas, despite Gayoso's disapproval.[60]

---

ployed in reconnoitering Tampa Bay, while early spring of 1795 found him at Balize in command of the river galleys there.

On July 28, 1795, Carondelet appointed Folch commandant of the post of San Fernando de las Barrancas. He officially took over the command from Beauregard on September 17, and before very long trouble began. Apparently he was not able to get along with any of his fellow officers except Rousseau, who liked him so much he thought he could spend a lifetime with him without a single difficulty. Gayoso held a different opinion. He was uneasy over Folch's extravagance, felt that his whims were unlimited, and reported that he treated Portell badly and found fault with Fooy. His quarrel with Portell lasted until he was transferred from Barrancas. Gayoso wrote Carondelet that Folch wished to reform all the workers, lamented his lack of money, and wanted chickens and young pigeons as well as comfortable lodgings; in short, he wanted San Fernando to be New Orleans, at a time when the post was just being established under great difficulties.

In addition to the problems with his fellow officers, Folch found himself beset with many other annoyances at San Fernando. Chief among his complaints was the great deluge of mosquitoes that haunted the bluffs. Consequently, when Degoutin arrived at the end of June 1796 to relieve him, Folch willingly relinquished his command and left immediately, glad to be rid of the place at last. Probably soon after his return to New Orleans, he was assigned to the command of Pensacola, where he remained until 1811, rising to a position of great importance in the government of West Florida.

(See Folch to Carondelet, Balize, March 25, 1795, P de C 128; Gayoso to Carondelet, New Madrid, December 3, 1795, P de C 43; *Nombramiento* of Vicente Folch as commandant of San Fernando de las Barrancas, signed by Carondelet, New Orleans, July 28, 1795, P de C 1550; Beauregard to Gayoso, No. 19, Barrancas, September 18, 1795, P de C 128; Beauregard to Carondelet, New Orleans, October 19, 1795, P de C 32, and encl. signed by Folch, Barrancas, September 17, 1795; Rousseau to Gayoso on *La Venganza*, at San Fernando des Ecores à Margot, October 31, 1795, P de C 211; Gayoso to Carondelet, New Madrid, December 3, 1795, P de C 443; Folch to Gayoso, San Fernando, October 30, 1795; copy certified by Gayoso in P de C 43. Portell to Carondelet, No. 433, New Madrid, February 12, 1796, P de C 33; Folch to Carondelet, San Fernando, June 7, 1796, P de C 33; Folch to Carondelet, San Fernando, June 11 and June 19, 1796, P de C 33; Ferrúsola to Vallé, Barrancas, July 7, 1796, in MHS Vallé Collection, No. 6; Whitaker, *Documents Relating to the Commercial Policy of Spain in the Floridas*, p. 246, n. 203. For a full account of Folch's later life see I. J. Cox, *The West Florida Controversy, 1798–1813* [Baltimore, 1918].)

60. These events and matters are discussed in full by Frances Coughlin in her "Spanish Galleys," where complete and specific citations to the voluminous documentation are given. See also Holmes, *WTHSP, 13*, 38–54; see esp. pp. 47–53. Holmes does not discuss Gayoso's attempts to appoint and grant trading rights to Turnbull.

With the founding of Fort San Fernando de las Barrancas, Spain reached the peak of her power on the Mississippi River. Not only did the post successfully bar the Americans from establishing themselves on the east bank of the river anywhere below the mouth of the Ohio, but it also assured to Spain continued control of the navigation of the Mississippi River. The Spaniards' triumph was to prove short-lived, however, for scarcely two years after its establishment, Fort San Fernando de las Barrancas was evacuated in accordance with the terms of the Treaty of San Lorenzo el Real, and Barrancas de Margó passed technically into the control of the United States—although it was not dismantled until 1797.[61]

Before leaving Barrancas, Gayoso de Lemos designated three war vessels to be assigned to the permanent feature of the defense of the newly established fort. The others of the squadron were to descend to New Orleans for careening. Gayoso chose the galley *La Felipa,* commanded by Langlois; the galiot *La Flecha,* commanded by Ferrúsola; and the cañonera *El Rayo,* commanded by sub-lieutenant Roberto Macay. The latter was a member of the New Madrid militia, and since, as patrón of the lanchón *Príncipe de Asturias,* which had been delivering supplies to Barrancas regularly, he had proved himself active and intelligent, Gayoso had brought him into the squadron to command the cañonera under Langlois' orders.[62]

---

61. See Whitaker, *Spanish-American Frontier,* his *Mississippi Question,* and more esp. Liljegren, *LHQ,* 22, 42–53. Liljegren's "The Commission of Lieutenant Colonel Carlos Howard" deals in full with these matters.

62. See below, pp. 273–77. Gayoso to Carondelet, Barrancas, July 18, 1795, P de C 198; August 13, 1795, P de C 43. Carondelet to Gayoso, New Orleans, October 26, 1795, P de C 22; Rousseau to Carondelet, Ecores, August 22, 1795, P de C 211.

6 Intrigue with the Kentuckians

So far as the hard-pressed defenders of the great river could see, they had, with exiguous means—thanks chiefly to the river fleet—secured the navigation of the Mississippi and perhaps the destiny of a continent. Now Gayoso de Lemos addressed himself to greater pawns in the great game of chess on the international scene and began to exploit diplomatically the position the galleys had won. When Carondelet appointed Gayoso de Lemos commander-in-chief of the expedition to take possession of Barrancas de Margó, he also gave him permission to extend his journey up the Mississippi to include a military reconnaissance of New Madrid and the Spanish Illinois posts. His real objective, however, was not to make a military tour—although his presence did create a favorable impression of Spain's power and prestige among the inhabitants—but to contact certain American agents from Kentucky and discuss with them the possibility of separating the American West from the rest of the United States, seeking the protection of Spain as the price of the river highway.

Miró's and Carondelet's plans of defense looked to the establishment of an independent American West, attached to the interests of Spain through the concession of rights of navigation on the Mississippi. In this it also was but a continuation of the intrigues of Wilkinson with the Spanish authorities in Louisana. First begun in 1787, the intrigue had lapsed toward the end of 1791, when Carondelet replaced Miró. From 1791 to 1793 Wilkinson's correspondence with the Spaniards was intermittent, but toward the end of February 1794 he informed Carondelet that the time was ripe to reopen negotiations for the separation of Kentucky from the Union. Despite the failure of the Clark-Genêt expedition, Wilkinson reported that the agitation it had stirred up had left the Westerners restless, dissatisfied, and more determined than ever to secure the navigation of the Mississippi by whatever means necessary. Pointing out how the Westerners' dissatisfaction could be used to further the schemes of Spanish intrigue in the West, he offered his services to persuade the people that their best interest lay in secession from the Union and an independent agreement with Spain. In return he first requested an increase in his annual pension, and in further correspondence he asked for still larger sums, as well as a considerable amount of money with which to secure support and assistance for the intrigue from other prominent Kentuckians.[1]

Wilkinson's solution of the ever-present problem was welcomed by Carondelet and fitted into his schemes and plans. Furthermore, proof of the strength of the secessionist sentiment in Kentucky came to him from other sources. Harry Innes, judge of the Federal court in Kentucky, wrote Gayoso on February 14 that free navigation of the Mississippi had become essential to the inhabitants of the West and that they were determined to have it. If Spain would make some definite and satisfactory proposals on the matter to the Westerners, he was sure that they would be "supported by every influential character" in Kentucky. Gayoso, interpreting this as an invitation to overtures for the support of secession in Kentucky, forwarded the letter to Carondelet with an urgent request that he be sent to Philadelphia, "where he could take advantage of this unique opportunity and gather together all the threads of the Spanish intrigue in the United States."[2]

Carondelet, who regarded the letter as important proof of the temper of the people of Kentucky, remitted it immediately to the Spanish Court without mentioning Gayoso's mission to Philadelphia. Carondelet was not one to have a subordinate grab the

---

1. Wilkinson to Carondelet, Fort Jefferson, February 26, 1794, trans. encl. in Carondelet to Las Casas, No. 113 res., New Orleans, May 1, 1794, P de C 2354; [Wilkinson] to Carondelet, Fort Washington, June 20, 1794; copy in Carondelet to Alcudia, No. 43 res., New Orleans, August 18, 1794, AHN 3899.

2. Henry Innes to Gayoso, Kentucky, February 14, 1794, certified copy encl. in Carondelet to Alcudia, No. 36 res., New Orleans, June 3, 1794, AHN 3899; printed and discussed in A. P. Whitaker, "Harry Innes and the Spanish Intrigue 1794-1795," *MVHR, 15,* (1928), 238. See also Whitaker, *Spanish-American Frontier,* chap. 13, for a discussion of this matter, which is part of Wilkinson's intrigue. The correspondence on these events is abundant. See also T. R. Hay and M. R. Werner, *The Admirable Trumpeter, a Biography of General James Wilkinson* (New York, 1941), chap. 6, and other biographies of Wilkinson; Bemis, *Pinkney's Treaty,* pp. 233, 302-07.

prestige and glory. Meantime, Gayoso replied to Innes to the effect that Kentucky should secure its independence before negotiating a treaty with Spain. This was not what Innes had looked for, naturally. Carondelet also received similar proofs of secessionist sentiment in Kentucky from other influential Kentuckians: the French merchant Michel Lacassagne, Judge Benjamin Sebastian, Judge George Nicholas, merchant William Murray, and others interested in negotiating with Spain for free navigation of the Mississippi.

Urged on by such testimonials and interest, Carondelet turned to the highest authority, the Spanish minister of state, Manuel de Godoy, and in a series of letters in the spring and summer of 1794 urged him to accept the intrigue for the separation of Kentucky as the principal point of Spain's policy with the Americans. Carondelet believed that Spain had but two choices if she wished to preserve Louisiana and the Floridas. The first was strengthening the military defenses of the colony by repairing and building forts, increasing the troops, and stirring up the Indians against the American frontier—a program that would necessarily entail huge expenditures of money. The second was the separation of Kentucky from the United States and its attachment to Spain through a commercial treaty granting free navigation of the Mississippi to the American West. This, too, would entail heavy outlays of money, expenditures for pensions, as well as sending munitions and other supplies, but they would not equal in amounts the required expenditures to fulfill the first course.

Carondelet believed that an independent West would forever end all threats of American invasion, and wanted to take advantage of the opportunity to put a feather in his cap of glory and prestige, perhaps getting a promotion to boot. He felt not only that the welfare of Louisiana, and perhaps her preservation, depended upon making New Orleans a free port, but that reducing tariffs at New Orleans and opening its trade to all friendly nations would economically aid Louisiana, even increase the revenues of hard pressed Spain, and encourage immigration to Louisiana. Morever, Louisiana, once filled with a strong and loyal population, would serve as a living barrier against foreign aggression.[3]

3. Carondelet to Alcudia, No. 31 res., New Orleans, April 7, 1794, AHN 3899; No. 34 res., New Orleans, May 1, 1794, AHN 3899; draft in P de C 178A; No. 36 res., New

In February 1795[4] Godoy informed Carondelet of the double and somewhat inconsistent results of a great debate held in the Spanish Council of State—the highest policy-forming body in the Spanish government, under the King—over whether to reopen negotiations with the United States with regard to the Spanish-American boundary or to support Carondelet's bold alternative of holding the river in a vise, as a means of splitting the New Republic into two rival powers, with the West under Spanish control. It was agreed in Council to reopen the fateful negotiations but at the same time to continue secret negotiations with leading Kentuckians, with a view to attaching them to the Spanish interests. And it was in February that the great forward movement of the galleys was initiated.

As early as April 1794 Carondelet requested Godoy's authorization to send an agent to Kentucky or New Madrid to open negotiations with the Westerners, repeating the request in June and again in December.[5] Colonel Gayoso de Lemos was his choice to represent Spain, for he felt that Gayoso's political talents, his perfect command of English, and his acquaintance with leading citizens of the West, together with his political and mercantile relationships with the country, gave him the proper background to treat successfully with the Kentuckians. A further reason was that Gayoso could find a plausible excuse to conceal the real motive for his voyage to New Madrid. Godoy received the suggestion favorably and authorized Gayoso to begin negotiations.

Immediately upon receiving the authorization Carondelet put

Orleans, June 3, 1794, AHN 3899. Carondelet to Las Casas, No. 109 res., New Orleans, April 7, 1794, P de C 2354; copy encl. in Carondelet to Alcudia, No. 31 res.; parts printed in Houck, *Spanish Régime*, 2, 23–25. Carondelet to Las Casas, No. 113 res., New Orleans, May 1, 1794, P de C 2354; draft in P de C 152B.

Carondelet's letters reached Spain in July 1794, just after the Council of State had decided to reopen negotiations with the United States on the question of the Spanish-American boundary (Nasatir and Liljegren, *LHQ, 21,* 42 ff; Whitaker, *Spanish-American Frontier*, p. 198; Bemis, *Pinckney's Treaty,* p. 343).

4. Alcudia to Carondelet, February 21, 1795, quoted in Carondelet to Gayoso, res., New Orleans, July 18, 1795, P de C 22; draft, muy res., in P de C 48. Carondelet to Alcudia, No. 67 res., New Orleans, January 9, 1796, AHN 3886; draft in P de C 133. See Nasatir and Liljegren, *LHQ, 21,* 42–50.

5. Carondelet to Alcudia, Nos. 31 res. and 36 res.; No. 50 res., New Orleans, December 28, 1794, AHN 3886, and draft of reply attached; Alcudia to Carondelet, February 21, 1795, quoted in Carondelet to Gayoso, res., New Orleans, July 18, 1795, P de C 22; draft, muy res., in P de C 48.

the wheels of intrigue in motion. On July 16 Carondelet wrote Wilkinson that he was sending Gayoso to New Madrid to treat secretly with agents of Kentucky concerning the plan of separation. Two days later he dispatched orders to Gayoso at Barrancas to proceed to New Madrid. He sent the cipher letter to Wilkinson through Manuel Lisa, as well as instructions to Gayoso—really a list of restrictions and conditions for negotiating a commercial treaty with the Kentuckians. Although a duplicate of the letter to Wilkinson was sent by sea to New York and overland to Cincinnati, Gayoso was already in New Madrid when he received the news and letters.[6]

In August, Gayoso could regard the fort at Barrancas as a *fait accompli;* on the thirteenth he was prepared to leave on a cruise upriver ostensibly to inspect the Illinois posts but also to consummate the intrigue with favorably disposed Kentuckians. The voyage, begun with formality, did not prove to be a smooth or enjoyable cruise. Leaving with his personal and rather elegant galiot *La Vigilante* and accompanied by *La Flecha,* he ran into very strong currents and strong, unfavorable winds, which slowed the ascent to New Madrid. Further delay was caused at the Point of Ciruelas, when both galiots struck bottom and had to be pulled out. Not until nine-thirty on the morning of August 23 did Gayoso reach Fort Céleste, escorted by Portell and Ferrúsola, who had met him with the cañonera *El Rayo* half a league below New Madrid. All the officers of the town militia were assembled on the dock to greet him, and, as he disembarked, the fort fired a salute that was returned by *La Vigilante.*[7]

Gayoso had been instructed to dispatch letters to Spanish sympathizers in Kentucky, inviting them to discuss with him the terms of a treaty of commerce and navigation. But aware of, and

---

6. Letter unsigned and unaddressed [Carondelet to Wilkinson], New Orleans, n.d., English copy in P de C 2375; Spanish draft in P de C 129; copy with rubric encl. in Carondelet to Gayoso, res., New Orleans, July 18, 1796, P de C 22. Copy of Carondelet to C. W. [Wilkinson], New Orleans, July 1, 1795, encl. in Carondelet to Gayoso, res., New Orleans, July 18, 1795, P de C 22; draft, muy res., in P de C 48. Carondelet to Alcudia, No. 61 res., New Orleans, October 4, 1795, AHN 3899; draft in P de C 178A.

7. See below, pp. 278–85. Lisa did not arrive as quickly as had been thought. Gayoso, in accordance with his instructions, did send the cipher letter, which he had received in the meantime, on to Wilkinson by Thomas Power.

concerned by, Gayoso's daring temperament and flair for taking risks, Carondelet put precise restrictions on his powers, preparing for Gayoso's guidance a list of conditions that should govern the negotiations of any commercial treaty with the Kentuckians. Gayoso already was in New Madrid when Carondelet's letter reached him, and since Carondelet, a thousand miles to the south, was eager to keep his fingers on the pulse of the negotiations, an infinitely tedious three-way correspondence was begun. Canoes and pirogues bore Gayoso's repeated requests for information and advice with comparative speed to the capital; pirogue and plodding bercha worked the replies upstream months later; and in the meantime a confidential agent, Power, slipped off by canoe and backwoods trail to find General Wilkinson and other interested parties. Long weeks wore away into long months.

In October the bercha of Manuel Lisa[8] arrived finally at New Madrid, but though important instructions were to have been sent by him, he bore none. Once more Gayoso, irritated and impatient, committed a plea for essential instructions from the dilatory capital to the paddles and the soldier-guard of a pirogue. Once more he settled down to wait.[9] Instructions came not by Lisa but in an enclosed letter dated October 31, 1795, and Carondelet warned Gayoso not to deviate from them.[10]

There were in that same month uneasy indications that history might be in advance of him.[11] Lieutenant William Clark, brother

8. See Nasatir edn. of Douglas, *Manuel Lisa,* Introd.
9. Gayoso to Carondelet, New Madrid, October 2 and 3, 1795, P de C 211; same to same, No. 21 res., October 3, 1795, P de C 2364; draft in P de C 128.
10. Carondelet's instructions were sent October 31, but it was some time later before they reached New Madrid (Carondelet to Gayoso, res., New Orleans, October 31, 1795, P de C 22; draft in P de C 48).
11. While at New Madrid, Gayoso was informed of the arrival and activities of André Micheaux and Pentraux. He ordered both to be arrested. Despite assurances from Trudeau, Gayoso's suspicions of Frenchmen were profound and disturbing. Bonnevie was captured and sent to New Orleans. See Vallé to [Gayoso], Ste. Geneviève, September 14, 1795, P de C 211; draft [Gayoso] to Vallé, New Madrid, [September] 1795, P de C 130; Gayoso to Carondelet, No. 11, New Madrid, September 25, 1795, P de C 43; Gayoso to Trudeau, muy res., New Madrid, September 24, 1795, P de C 22; Trudeau to Gayoso, St. Louis, October 4, 1795 (2 letters), P de C 48; Trudeau to [Carondelet], St. Louis, October 26, 1795, P de C 211; Gayoso to Carondelet, No. 19 res., New Madrid, September 26, 1795, P de C 2364; draft in P de C 226A; Luzières to Gayoso, New Bourbon, October 2, 1795, P de C 212A; Bonnevie to Luzières, Fort Massac, August 27, 1795; certified copy in Luzières

of the notorious George Rogers Clark, arrived and delivered to Gayoso a sealed letter from his superior, General Wayne, commander of the American forces in the West. General Wayne's letter was to the effect that he was informed that several hundred Spanish troops, supported by a number of galleys, had erected a fort at Chickasaw Bluffs, on the east bank of the Mississippi. The General could hardly believe that such an unwarranted aggression against the lands of the United States could be true, particularly since the two nations were at peace. If, however, this report were true, he felt it his duty to inquire by what principles and authority the Spaniards were thus usurping and justifying themselves on American soil.

There was no mistaking the tenor of this very courtly inquiry. Gayoso answered with suave evasions,[12] warm with protestations of affection for the United States and of the most vehement disinterest in any legitimate possession of those States. He also kindly distributed fresh rations to the crew of the American galley, and invited Lieutenant Clark to dinner, together with Portell, commandant of New Madrid. Under Gayoso's genial ministrations the young lieutenant was led to declare none but the most cordial and reassuring sentiments about the Spanish possession of the river.[13]

Gayoso immediately sent word of this untoward inquiry from the American General to New Orleans, but Carondelet brushed it aside as of minor importance.[14] And in the excitement of high intrigue and other pressing matters, the squadron itself fell into the background of the statesman's attention. Yet on his request, Rousseau wrote a report on the state of the war vessels, which was very

---

to Gayoso, October 2, 1795, P de C 212A. Gayoso to Carondelet, New Madrid, October 2 and 3, 1795, P de C 211; September 27, 1795, P de C 43. The correspondence on these matters is voluminous; see Liljegren, *LHQ*, 22, 3-53.

12. Twice before, the Spaniards had erected forts on territory which was in dispute with the United States: at Fort Nogales at the mouth of the Yazoo River, and at Confederación on the Tombigbee. But this was the first time any word of protest had been received from a responsible representative of the Federal government.

13. The documentation on this event is fairly full. Among other documents see Gayoso to Carondelet, No. 21 res., New Madrid, October 3, 1795, P de C 2364; draft in P de C 128. Wayne's letter is printed in *AHAR 1896, 1,* 1091-92, and Gayoso's letter in ibid., 1093-94.

14. Gayoso urged the transfer of negotiations with the Kentuckians to Philadelphia and said that he would like to be sent there to carry out the negotiations. Carondelet failed to relay this information and request.

gloomy indeed. They had deteriorated rapidly, and if they did not receive a complete overhauling, they would be unable to navigate by spring. The bottom planks were rotting and the exposed seams split; the winter awnings were worn out; all the rigging was over a year old, there was no matchcord, and the limited supply of tow, tar, and tarred cloth was exhausted. It was even necessary to resort to putty to stuff the seams of *La Activa* whenever the galiot ran low in the water. The crews were incomplete and the vessels were no longer garrisoned with land troops. Rousseau declared roundly that his splendid squadron would be worthless as a fighting unit in the winter, and useless to Fort San Fernando until they could be repaired.

Gayoso agreed to let the galleys *La Venganza* and *La Castilla* descend to Natchez or New Orleans for careening, and in order to maintain the maximum of naval strength at the critical point, he ordered in exchange the prompt dispatch of one or the other of the heavy galleys—*La Luisiana* or *La Victoria*—loaded with supplies to repair the ravages of river service at Barrancas. Rousseau, Gayoso assured him, should have orders to take the two galleys south immediately.[15] But the orders, which were to come within a few days, did not arrive. Rousseau remonstrated again and again that the fleet was falling apart; still there was no word from the north. Gayoso was off on a formal round of visits to St. Louis[16] and the

---

15. Among other problems relating to the galleys, Gayoso had to judge the quarrel which broke out between García and Benjamin Fooy.

16. By his tour of the Illinois posts, Gayoso hoped to:

  (1) Impress the inhabitants with Spain's power and prestige. The inhabitants were mainly French, hence Gayoso's trip was in part a goodwill tour.
  (2) Impress and flatter the Indians in the district in order to attach them more closely to the interests of Spain.
  (3) Inspect the defenses of the posts.
  (4) Confer with Governor St. Clair, who was in Cahokia, in order to preside over the court there, and sound him out and try to influence him with ideas favorable to Spain.

Vallé to [Gayoso], Ste. Geneviève, September 14, 1795, P de C 211; draft [Gayoso] to Vallé, New Madrid, [September], 1795, P de C 130; Gayoso to Carondelet, No. 11, New Madrid, September 25, 1795, P de C 43; draft in P de C 32. Gayoso to Carondelet, New Madrid, October 2 and 3, 1795, P de C 211; Gayoso to Carondelet, New Madrid, October 6, 1795, P de C 32. See Gayoso's diary, below, pp. 291–313, and his report on his trip also given below, pp. 331–41.

neighboring settlements;[17] the delaying squadron slipped his mind; and it was not until after Gayoso's return to New Madrid that Rousseau received further word from him regarding the galley's destination.

Perhaps the distractions of the life of this Spanish pro-consul, moving in a formal progress through his wilderness domains, occasioned the oversight. At Cape Girardeau, Gayoso charmed a band of Abenaquis assembled to greet him with a flattering speech, in which he advised them to live in peace and quiet on their lands. At the end of the speech he presented them with a little tobacco, a barrel of whiskey, and four white porcelain necklaces. Louis Lorimier, the astute if illiterate trader who was the ruling power among the savages of the district, said that he would repeat Gayoso's speech to those Indian nations that had already left on their winter hunt; it would attach them, he was sure, more strongly to Spain's interest. Whether they should also have porcelain necklaces is not clear from the account given.[18]

Leaving Lorimier and Cape Girardeau, Gayoso and his party arrived at Ste. Geneviève on October 24, where a royal welcome had been prepared for the Spanish notable. Horsemen stationed several leagues down the river gave notice of the galley's approach, and the militia of the post was drawn up in review formation when *La Vigilante* pulled into view. After a visit of nearly three days Gayoso proceeded to St. Louis, where he again was received with military honors from the guns of Fort St. Charles.[19]

17. Gayoso left New Madrid on October 6, on *La Vigilante*, accompanied by the cañonera *El Rayo* under Ferrúsola's command.

18. Gayoso had left New Madrid on October 6 and was at Cape Girardeau on October 18.

19. Gayoso dispatched the galiot up the Mississippi and Missouri to St. Charles, while he, accompanied by Trudeau, Auguste Chouteau, and Benito Vasquez, went overland via Marais des Liards and San Fernando de Florissante. They celebrated St. Charles' Day (November 4) at St. Charles. From there the party sailed on *La Vigilante* down the Missouri and up the Mississippi, reconnoitering the mouth of the Illinois River, and returned downriver to St. Louis. Gayoso crossed over to Cahokia for one day. On November 10 he embarked at St. Louis for New Madrid. At the Gabury River, Gayoso, who in the meantime had had news of the return of Power from Kentucky, went overland to Ste. Geneviève. There he visited the salt mines and New Bourbon, spent a day in Kaskaskia, and returned to his vessel. Continuing his descent, he arrived at New Madrid at 2 A.M. of the morning of November 23. He immediately drew up and dispatched to Carondelet a report of his trip (Gayoso to

He spent several days in the area of St. Louis, the capital of Upper Louisiana (or Spanish Illinois) in company with the affable and popular lieutenant governor, Zenon Trudeau. They visited the settlement of St. Charles on the Missouri, *La Vigilante* ascending by river and Gayoso going overland by horseback. They were royally entertained, and visited on *La Vigilante* as far as the mouth of the Illinois River. Gayoso crossed the Mississippi and lunched with the Americans in Cahokia. Drifting down the river, he made several stops, and at the mouth of the Ohio was joined by the cañonera *El Rayo* and Lisa's bercha. Once he reached New Madrid on November 24, Gayoso immediately wrote a lengthy letter summarizing his trip to the Illinois.[20]

At New Madrid there were long, cloudy, contradictory epistles from the wily Wilkinson to digest and to comment on in a covering letter to Carondelet, as well as a rendezvous to arrange by confidential messenger with emissaries from Kentucky. Meanwhile, Rousseau was desperately trying to get in touch with some official quarter that would recognize the plight of the galleys, ironically allowed to rot away in neglect on the very farthest shore of their triumph, and which, their captain informed Carondelet, could not survive the winter at Barrancas. At the very least he begged for authoritative word as to whether they must winter in the north or not.

On December 2 Gayoso proposed an order authorizing *La Venganza, La Castilla, La Flecha,* and *La Activa* to descend to the capital for repairs, leaving *La Felipa* and *El Rayo* to defend San Fernando, but at just that moment the wind from the Cumberland blew cold again. Rumor had it that an attack on Fort San Fernando was being mounted, and although this did not appear too likely, Gayoso felt it wise to hold the galleys at the bluffs: their presence might produce a good effect on the Yankees in case they should appear with a parliamentary flag. Meanwhile, the sorely tried commander, Rousseau, ordered his squadron into battle stations on the other side of the river, to prevent a surprise attack,

---

Carondelet, New Madrid, November 24, 1795, P de C 2364; given in full below, pp. 331–41. See also Gayoso's diary of his trip, below, pp. 291–313.

20. See below, pp. 291–313. Gayoso to Carondelet, September 24, 1795, P de C 2364; given in full below, pp. 331–41.

knowing well, however, that the galleys would be of little use against an attack from the landward side of the fort, because the angle of fire of the warships was too flat to cover the bluffs. Unfortunately, no one paid much attention to the shrewd sense of the tough and patient sailor man.

Gayoso apparently was convinced that diplomacy was now sufficient to defend the Spanish realm in the great valley, for he left New Madrid for the mouth of the Ohio, prudently endeavoring to cover his strangely protracted delay in the inhospitable north with a pretense of work on the Ohio naval station.[21] While he impatiently scanned the Ohio for some sign of the expectant Western intrigants, Fort San Fernando received a visit of another description. Lieutenant Colonel John McKee was brought into the fort blindfolded, under a parliamentary flag, to deliver a letter from Governor William Blount bluntly declaring that the Spanish post at Chickasaw Bluffs was an encroachment upon the territorial rights of the United States, and requesting the Spaniards to withdraw and to demolish the fort and any other military works there erected.[22] Folch received him, gave him a polite but evasive answer, and told him that he would forward the letter to his superiors, who would answer directly to Knoxville. A day after McKee's departure, the long-delayed permission for the squadron to descend was received from Carondelet, and *La Flecha*, commanded by Bouligny, departed on December 22, a day ahead of the main fleet under Rousseau's command. Thus *La Venganza, La Castilla, La Activa,* and *La Flecha* left Barrancas. Three days later Gayoso's orders for the descent of the galleys arrived, but Bouligny with *La Flecha* was ordered to remain a while longer. How happy

21. With the many incidents in the intrigues that caused Gayoso's hurrying to the Ohio naval cruising station we are not concerned here. The documentation is full. However, the diaries below give an ample account of the highlights of the story —e.g. Gayoso's meeting with Micheaux. See Gayarré, *History of Louisiana, 3,* 359–66; Jacobs, *Tarnished Warrior;* Hay and Werner, *Admirable Trumpeter;* Serrano y Sanz, *El Brigadier Jaime Wilkinson;* L. Kinnaird, "American Penetration into Spanish Territory 1776–1803," unpublished doctoral dissertation (University of California, 1928). Frances Coughlin deals with these events in detail in her "Spanish Galleys on the Upper Mississippi."

22. The documentation on these events is quite extensive. Carondelet's order for the galleys to descend was issued on December 19.

the squadron was to have already been on its way can only be imagined.[23]

History was poised for a moment in a beautiful ironic tableau on the Mississippi. While in far-off New Orleans and at the Ohio, Spanish statesmen waited with high hearts for the consummation of a great design, at the same moment the future, blindfolded, knocked imperiously at the gates of the most arrogant of the Spanish bastions, and told them rudely to be gone. At the foot of the bluffs the dauntless little squadron whose sufferings and sweat had maintained the Spanish dream rotted helplessly away. It was ironic also that the very day that McKee appeared at San Fernando with Governor Blount's forthright eviction notice, Power, accompanied by Benjamin Sebastian, the long awaited agent of the Kentuckians, finally floated down the Ohio River on a flatboat. Gayoso took him aboard with the greatest satisfaction, but heavy storms blinded the river, and only after several days could they proceed the short distance to New Madrid, where they arrived in the midst of a snowstorm.

Since Sebastian and Gayoso soon discovered that they could come to terms only in New Orleans, where the Governor General could decide moot points, in early January the diplomats sailed south, making excellent if perilous progress on the winter floods. With only a minimum of respite at Natchez to enjoy the charming hospitality of the commandant's celebrated home, they proceeded to New Orleans. Once there, the Kentuckian and the Spaniards began their conference and negotiations. However, before they could make much headway, thus before any agreement could be reached, the Governor General received the royal order of October 28 advising him of the signing of the Treaty of San Lorenzo el Real. By the terms of that treaty, all the disputed east bank was gone at a

23. Gayoso, still at the mouth of the Ohio, had interviewed Micheaux, and now being confident that Fort San Fernando was quite secure, he at length gave his consent for the battered squadron at Barrancas to withdraw from the stormbound north and descend to New Orleans. On December 19 Carondelet's orders for the descent of the squadron arrived. Most of the squadron had already left for New Orleans. Gayoso was by December 23 convinced that no American descent upon Barrancas was being planned in Cumberland. His orders for the fleet to descend to New Orleans arrived at Barrancas after the fleet had departed. *La Venganza, La Castilla, La Activa,* and *La Flecha* descended, satisfied by then that the Americans in Cumberland were planning no attack on Barrancas. *La Felipa* and *El Rayo,* according to Gayoso's orders, were to remain at San Fernando de Barrancas.

stroke—even Natchez, Gayoso's cherished domain, and with it, as a matter of course, the free navigation of the Mississippi. The squadron's occupation was gone.[24]

If the provisions of the treaty had gone into effect immediately, the intrigue would have ended completely at that point. However, for various reasons and excuses, chiefly Blount's conspiracies, the Spaniards delayed its execution for nearly two and a half years, while Carondelet, unwilling to abandon his favorite project as long as there was the slightest hope of success, continued his contacts with the Kentuckians. In the spring of 1797 he made one final effort to bring about the separation of the Western country from the United States, but by that time Wilkinson received his overtures coldly and dismissed his plan as a chimerical project, impossible of success. The intrigues failed primarily because the Treaty of San Lorenzo gave the Westerners everything they wanted without separation.

There were many reasons why the Spanish Council of State rejected the intrigue in favor of a treaty with the United States. Godoy believed that an alliance with the States was necessary not only to prevent the formation of an Anglo-American agreement that might be detrimental to Spain but, indeed, to preserve the Spanish empire; and later events proved this to be a help to Spain when war broke out between Spain and England. Then again, the conservative members of the Court found Carondelet's far-sighted economic policy, upon which the success of the intrigue depended, much too progressive for them to accept. Perhaps, too, they felt that the Spanish treasury was unable to bear the great expense that intrigue and revolution entailed.

24. Bemis, *Pinckney's Treaty*; Whitaker, *Spanish-American Frontier*; and many other books deal with the treaty.

7 The Fleet Leaves the Upper River

Throughout 1796 and until March 1797 most of the river squadron was based at Fort San Fernando de las Barrancas. Late in the fall of 1795 the two *grandes galeras, La Luisiana* and *La Victoria,* were ordered to Barrancas, to replace the vessels that were due to descend for repairs. On November 30 *La Luisiana,* under Metzinger, was the first to leave New Orleans, but the fierce winter weather, with its gales and snowstorms, prevented his reaching the destination until mid-March 1796.[1] In January 1796 *La Victoria,* loaded with supplies and provisions for the outposts on the upper river, and under Bernardo Molina, left New Orleans, and, despite Rousseau's allegation that grandes galeras were too large to navigate the upper river, he reached Barrancas in April.[2]

1. Due to bad winds and snow it was a slow voyage, and Metzinger could not travel on for 16 days ("Notice of days on which we could not journey," signed by Metzinger, P de C 48, encl. in Metzinger to Gayoso, March 11, 1796, P de C 48). There is an incomplete diary of Carlos Dehault Delassus' trip up the Mississippi to take command of New Madrid beginning March 8, 1796 (last entry is May 15), in the MHS. His crew consisted of 14 rowers and a captain, with Vanden Bemden and Tardiveau as traveling companions.

2. Carondelet to Grandpré, New Orleans, December 18, 1795, P de C 22; draft [Carondelet] to Vilemont, New Orleans, December 21, 1795, P de C 22; Grandpré to Delinó, Natchez, January 10, 1796, P de C 129; Metzinger to Carondelet, on *La Luisiana,* January 13, 1796, P de C 33; Metzinger to Delinó, on *La Luisiana,* January 23, 1796, P de C 130; Metzinger, to Delinó, before the Yazoo River, January 30, 1796, P de C 130; Grandpré to Carondelet, No. 126, Natchez, February 18, 1796, P de C 33; Metzinger to Carondelet, on *La Luisiana,* February 21, 1796, P de C 33; Vilemont to Carondelet, No. 34, Arkansas, February 29, 1796, P de C 33; Grandpré to Carondelet, Natchez, February 29, 1796, P de C 208A; Metzinger to Gayoso, on *La Luisiana,* March 11, 1796, P de C 48; draft [Gayoso] to Carondelet, New Orleans, March 30, 1796, P de C 48; Grandpré to Carondelet, Natchez, February 5, 1796, P de C 212B.

Carondelet to Portell, New Orleans, January 20, 1796, P de C 24; draft in P de C 211; printed in Clark, *Proofs,* p. 33, Notes. Draft [Carondelet] to Rendón, res., New Orleans, December 29, 1795, P de C 211; resumé of orders remitted to New Madrid in 1796, made by Roberto Macay, New Madrid, August 20, 1799, P de C 129; Molina to Carondelet on *La Victoria,* Natchez, February 7, 1796, P de C 33; draft

Meanwhile, Rousseau had taken the warships down from Barrancas in December. Leaving the two galiots *La Flecha* and *La Activa* in Natchez for repairs, he continued to New Orleans on *La Venganza*. Like other officers, including Gayoso, the hardships that Rousseau had undergone during the previous long years on the river had by now told on his health. Therefore, having requested Carondelet to exempt him from further duty on the galleys until he should recover, the Governor General appointed his second in command, Manuel García, as commander of the river fleet.[3]

During that time repairs were undertaken on the battered ships. Although *La Activa* met with an unfortunate accident which took her out of service, *La Flecha* was finally repaired and went up to Barrancas, where she arrived on May 19, and *La Venganza*, repaired in New Orleans and loaded with supplies and the annual presents for the Arkansas and Chickasaw Indians, sailed upriver, made her deliveries, and arrived at Barrancas on June 12.[4] Here García found practically all the vessels of the squadron: the galleys *La Luisiana, La Victoria,* and *La Felipa,* the galiot *La Flecha,* and the cañonera *El Rayo.*[5] Since the fleet was to be headquartered at Barrancas for the remainder of the year, García set up his permanent headquarters for the naval forces on the Island of Fooy. Here they remained until December, when cold weather

---

[Carondelet] to Rendón, March 23, 1796, P de C 89; Ferrúsola to Carondelet, on *El Rayo,* Barrancas, March 21, 1796, P de C 33; Ferrúsola to Carondelet, Barrancas, April 10, 1796, P de C 33.

3. Carondelet to Grandpré, New Orleans, January 14, 1796, P de C 48; Rousseau to Carondelet, on *La Venganza,* October 12, 1795, P de C 211; same to same, on *La Venganza* at Barrancas, December 8, 1795, P de C 211; same to same, New Orleans, January 18, 1796, P de C 33. List of subjects recommended by Carondelet for promotion enclosed in draft [Carondelet] to Prince of Peace, No. 73 res.; Gayoso to Carondelet, New Madrid, September 27, 1795, P de C 43; same to same on *La Vigilante,* 6 leagues above New Madrid, December 10, 1795, P de C 43.

4. García to Carondelet, *La Venganza* at Barrancas, July 3, 1796, P de C 34. García tells of his trip in this letter; despite all, he took 55 days and was faster than Chouteau's boat. The galeota *La Flecha* "arrived here yesterday from St. Louis."

5. García sent Carondelet the list of the sailors, patrones, proels, and crews garrisoning *La Venganza, La Luisiana, La Victoria, El Rayo,* and *La Flecha,* dated August 24, 1796, encl. in García to Carondelet, No. 67, on *La Venganza* at San Fernando, August 24, 1796, P de C 33.

and the inundation of the island forced García to move the galleys across the river to Campo de la Esperanza.[6]

Shortly after García's arrival at Barrancas, he received orders from Carondelet to return *La Luisiana,* commanded by Metzinger, and *La Victoria* to the capital, where they were to be disarmed in the interest of greater economy. But since *La Felipa,* commanded by Langlois, was in such bad state of disrepair, it was decided to send her with *La Luisiana* to New Orleans and to retain *La Victoria* for transport duty. Two days after leaving Barrancas, however, the vessels met the new commander of San Fernando, José Deville Degoutin, ascending to replace the disgruntled Vicente Folch, with countermanding Carondelet orders to retain the vessels at Barrancas. But *La Felipa* experienced so much leaking that she failed to make the grade and hence was turned around and limped to New Orleans. García utilized some of his time in instructing the French General Victor Collot in the navigation of the river—an art the Frenchman found very difficult to master.[7]

Early in August a rumor reached San Fernando from Vincennes that England and the United States were about to declare war on Spain. García and Degoutin at once ordered *La Flecha* back to its former cruising station at the mouth of the Ohio, so that it could prevent any bands of foreigners from entering Louisiana at that point. With *La Flecha* badly in need of repairs, its bottom torn and its cabin falling apart, García ordered it calked and renovated at once, and it was ready to sail by September 1. By then, however, food was so needed at Barrancas that *La Flecha* was sent to Ste. Geneviève for provisions, and a canoe and five men were sent to New Madrid to be used in a cruising operation at the

---

6. García to Gayoso, Barrancas, June 16, 1796, P de C 48; García to Gayoso, Barrancas, August 12, 1796, P de C 50; García to Carondelet, San Fernando, August 12, 1796, P de C 33; García to Gayoso, Barrancas, September 5, 1796, and Esperanza, December 17, 1796, P de C 48; García to Carondelet, No. 86, on *La Venganza* at Esperanza, December 16, 1796, P de C 34.

García's correspondence is voluminous. I have a collection of his letters relating to this period of his career.

7. I have collected the full correspondence relating to Collot's voyage on the Mississippi; it is very extensive. My former student Lloydine Martin has written a master's thesis on "George Victor Collot in the Mississippi Valley" (University of California, Berkeley, 1935). See Collot, *Voyage in North America.*

mouth of the Ohio. Commandant Carlos Delassus[8] at New Madrid declared that small outfit useless, and in any case the threatened rumors had not been realized. Nevertheless, transporting supplies from the Illinois to support San Fernando kept *La Flecha* constantly on the river as a transport from June till December. So also was *El Rayo* used until July, when it was grounded for repairs. But the repairs were not begun until October, and it was November before the gunboat was ready for active service.

Early in November, García received orders to station Metzinger with *La Flecha* three leagues above New Madrid to inspect descending vessels, to stop all Frenchmen who did not have a Spanish passport, and to intercept and arrest the Jacobin La Chaise, who had recently caused a Negro uprising in Louisiana. As *La Flecha* was in Illinois when García received the order, he told Metzinger with *El Rayo* to engage in that patrol until the galiot's return. Metzinger departed November 18. Later *La Flecha* returned and did replace the gunboat, while *El Rayo*, now under Molina, was used to transport provisions from Illinois.

8. Carlos Dehault Delassus de Luzières, son of Pierre Dehault Delassus de Luzières, entered the Spanish service as second lieutenant of the fifth battalion of royal guards of the Waloon infantry. He was a good military man and was breveted a lieutenant colonel. The King promoted him to colonel of infantry on October 5, 1799 (P de C 2367). In order to be near his family, who had fled from France (Carondelet had given his father the command of a new post at New Bourbon), he petitioned Madrid on July 5, 1794, to be transferred to Louisiana. In August 1794 Carlos Dehault Delassus was transferred to the Louisiana regiment and received his passport. Carondelet appointed him to replace Portell as commandant of New Madrid in 1796. (Houck, *History of Missouri, 2, 135-37; documents in Houck, Spanish Régime, 2,* 239-44.) Delassus was a busy, brave, efficient, and trusted official, loyal to Spain. He was made lieutenant governor of Upper Louisiana (Spanish Illinois Country) in 1799, replacing Zenon Trudeau, and took a major part in its defense. (Gayoso to Delassus, New Orleans, February 27, 1799, MHS.) Delassus was the last Spanish lieutenant governor of Upper Louisiana, transferring the territory to Stoddard in 1804, and supervising the Spanish evacuation of the area. In the MHS are incomplete diaries in Delassus' handwriting of both his trip up the Mississippi in 1796 and his voyage down the river on board *La Esperanza,* November 6, 1804– January 17, 1805. On December 27, 1804, he wrote Fooy from Campo de la Esperanza (letter in MHS, Pierre Chouteau Collection, No. 180). There are many Delassus letters and documents printed in Houck, *Spanish Régime;* F. Billon, *Annals of St. Louis in Its Early Days* (St. Louis, 1886); Nasatir, *Before Lewis and Clark;* and there is a Delassus Collection of manuscripts in the MHS. I have a large collection of letters and documents by and concerning Delassus while he was in Upper Louisiana—largely from the archives of Spain.

In the meantime Carondelet was making plans at New Orleans for the evacuation of Fort San Fernando. In November he appointed Lieutenant Colonel Carlos Howard military commander of Upper Louisiana[9] and commissioned him to evacuate San Fernando[10] and to transfer the men and munitions to St. Louis, which he was to fortify against the possibility of an English attack from Canada. Sedition was thought to be rife, and although France was no longer fostering an uprising in Louisiana, the people retained the revolutionary precepts. General Collot had made his well-known circuit, offering evidence of what was the Blount's conspiracy divulging the defenselessness of the Spanish possessions in the Mississippi Valley. Further, it was common knowledge that British and American statesmen were contemplating using unrest in the Spanish colonies to their own advantage. Carondelet envisaged Upper Louisiana as an independent state that the Americans and British would help to maintain. Thus all the lucrative fur trade would be diverted to Montreal and New York. To add to his distress, he learned that La Chaise was returning to Louisiana to effect another uprising of the slaves.

Sedition, however, was not the only problem confronting Carondelet on this remote frontier. Not only was war with England imminent, but Collot and others had brought rumors of a conquest of

---

9. Carondelet's instructions to Howard are dated New Orleans, November 26, 1796; original in P de C 2364; trans. in MHS *Collections, 3,* 71–91, and in Houck, *Spanish Régime, 2,* 123–32. For a full account see Liljegren, "Carlos Howard"; see also Liljegren *LHQ, 22,* 47–52. I have a full collection of Howard letters and other documentary materials relating to Howard's activities on this venture. A few are printed in Nasatir, *Before Lewis and Clark,* and Nasatir, *IJHP, 28,* 337–89.

Carondelet notified Trudeau of Howard's appointment on November 27, 1796, and notified Delassus on same date. Letters in P de C 2364, printed in Houck, *Spanish Régime, 2,* 122. See also Carondelet to Prince of Peace, No. 85 res., New Orleans, December 1, 1796, AHN 3900; same to Las Casas, No. 85, same date; draft in P de C 178B.

St. Louis expected an attack in 1797. Carondelet wrote Trudeau on November 22, 1796 (P de C 23), that war with Spain was certain; and on December 20, 1796, he wrote Howard (draft in P de C 129) officially notifying him of war having been declared between Spain and England.

10. García to Carondelet, Barrancas, March 6, 1797, P de C 35. "Yesterday we began to destroy the *casas fuertes* of the bastions in order to situate them in El Campo de la Esperanza"; they used the galleys in removing the torn-down fort's materials across the river. The story of the dismantling and evacuation of Barrancas is told in Liljegren, "Carlos Howard."

the province from Canada.[11] The British had taken advantage of their alliance with Spain to penetrate far into Spanish territory in search of furs, establishing a fort among the Mandans on the Upper Missouri, and the Spanish Court had sent orders to drive the unlicensed traders from the Missouri Valley.[12] With these problems in mind, the Governor General sent an Irish Catholic to lead a military expedition to the Illinois. Lieutenant Colonel Carlos Howard was chosen for the mission and given wide latitude and freedom of action. In a lengthy letter of instructions he was ordered, among other things, to evacuate Fort San Fernando de Barrancas, put the town of St. Louis in a respectable state of defense, quell the sedition, break up the Jacobin club, send the leaders of it to New Orleans for trial and punishment, and drive the English out of the Upper Missouri.

At the end of November, once preparations were made for the expedition, Howard left New Orleans on *La Felipa*. At Natchez he was to transfer to *La Activa,* but, after consulting with Gayoso, he decided to take both vessels with him on his expedition. Although he left Natchez on January 12, the progress of the expedition was considerably slowed by the rapidly falling waters of the Mississippi. When he finally reached Barrancas in early March, he immediately ordered the demolition and evacuation of Fort San Fernando and then left by land for New Madrid. Everything of value was salvaged from San Fernando, including old iron, lumber, and nails. Some of the salvaged material was used to construct a stockade in the squadron's camp at Esperanza, with the remainder, including artillery, loaded on the galleys and transported to St. Louis. By March 20 the evacuation of Barrancas was complete, and the

---

11. Carondelet to Santa Clara, No. 1 res., New Orleans, April 22, 1797, P de C 1502B. He learned from letters sent by Irujo on March 13 on the advice of a planned attack on Louisiana from Canada, and sent an engineer to strengthen St. Louis. See Liljegren, "Carlos Howard," where full story is given, and for a short summary, Liljegren, *LHQ,* 22, 47–53. See also James B. Musick, *St. Louis as a Fortified Town* (St. Louis, 1941).

Sent with Howard were 4 galeras, 2 galeotas, 1 lancha cañonera, artillery, munitions, 130 troops, and engineer Vanden Bemden. Carondelet suspended the evacuation of other Spanish posts ceded to the United States in Pinckney's Treaty. He said that if St. Louis fell, the British would be masters of Upper Louisiana—that is, the Missouri as far as California, and the Mississippi as far as Nogales. He asked for the *situado* and reinforcements.

12. See Nasatir, *Before Lewis and Clark,* for story and documents.

squadron left to join Howard in New Madrid, where they arrived early in April. *La Luisiana* having joined the squadron, Howard ordered *La Victoria* to return to New Orleans. Since it was the heaviest and most cumbersome vessel of all, he feared it would be unable to navigate in the strong currents of the river above New Madrid. On April 12, with the squadron composed of the galleys *La Venganza, La Felipa,* and *La Luisiana,* the galiot *La Activa,* the cañonera *El Rayo,* and a private bercha, he left New Madrid and on April 27 arrived at St. Louis. The number and size of the vessels made such a great impression on the inhabitants of the town that they named the memorable year the "Année des galères."

The entire squadron remained there until the end of July, while Howard carried out his instructions to fortify the post against the threat of British attack. During that time the two galiots *La Flecha* and *La Activa* alternated at cruising before the mouth of the Des Moines River under orders to arrest all traders found operating in Spanish territory without a license. By the first of August, Howard had completed his commission and was ready to return to the capital. With him went García and the three galleys in the squadron, while the two galiots were left at St. Louis to furnish naval support to the post and to continue their patrolling against the encroachments of foreign traders, especially the British.[13]

With Fort San Fernando de las Barrancas evacuated, the first major point of resistance in the defense of the colony against an invasion from the upper river was removed. Since Nogales and

---

13. See Liljegren "Carlos Howard," and among many others the following letters: Carondelet to Gayoso, New Orleans, November 21, 1796, P de C 24; draft of same to same, November 22, 1796, in P de C 23; Gayoso to Carondelet, No. 728, Natchez, January 11, 1797, P de C 35; García to Carondelet, No. 90, Esperanza, January 20, 1797, P de C 35; Francisco Borras to Degoutin, on *La Luisiana,* January 21, 1797, P de C 35; Degoutin to Carondelet, No. 45, Barrancas, January 22, 1797, P de C 35; García to Carondelet, No. 94, on *La Venganza* at Esperanza, January 26, 1797, P de C 35; same to same, on *La Venganza,* Nos. 15 and 16, at New Madrid, April 18, 1797, and Nos. 17–22, at St. Louis; all in P de C 628. Howard to Carondelet, New Madrid, April 7, 1797, P de C 35; Augustín Grande to Carondelet, Esperanza, April 7, 1797, P de C 35; Delassus to Gayoso, New Madrid, April 21, 1797, P de C 48; Gilberto Guillemard and Perchet to Carondelet, Nogales, May 18, 1797, P de C 35; resumé of orders remitted to New Madrid in 1796, signed by Macay, New Madrid, August 20, 1799, P de C 129; letter of Metzinger [to ?], on *La Luisiana* at St. Louis, June 28, 1797, P de C 628. A number of Howard letters are printed in Nasatir, *Before Lewis and Clark,* 2; and in Nasatir, *IJHP 28,* 337–89.

Natchez were also relinquished to the Americans by the Treaty of San Lorenzo el Real—actually in 1798—the focal point of Louisiana's defense shifted to the lower part of the province, to New Orleans and Placaminas.[14]

Despite the fact that St. Louis was regarded by Collot[15] as one of the essential points for the defense of Louisiana, the Spaniards could afford only to fortify the post against Indian attacks and small bands of whites unequipped with artillery. A defensive system adequate to defeat a regular corps equipped with artillery would require fortifications that the Spaniards had neither the money, time, nor men to build. It would also require maintenance of a large naval force on the upper river, and St. Louis was too far north to serve as a permanent year-round naval base for vessels as large as galleys. Consequently, the center of activity for the squadron shifted to Lower Louisiana, and after the summer of 1797 the galleys were rarely seen on the upper river, although the galiots continued to cruise in or near the Illinois district until the retrocession of the province to France and the United States.[16]

Among Howard's other assignments were those of destroying the British fort among the Mandans, suppressing English trade in the Upper Mississippi Valley, and even fomenting revolution in Canada. To start with, he actually sent men and spies out to Prairie du Chien, Chicago, Canada, and Philadelphia. A galiot was sent up the Mississippi, an outpost established at the mouth of the Illinois River, and another gunboat started for Prairie du Chien. Since St. Louis was the key to the control of the entire Mississippi Valley, all officials from Carondelet down knew that the fall of St. Louis

14. Carondelet suspended the evacuation of the posts on account of war with England and rumors of an attack on Louisiana. Carondelet's orders and proclamations of May 24 and 31, 1797, are in the Bancroft Library. See also Pedro de Nava to Godoy, No. 17, Chihuahua, September 5, 1797, AGI 37; same to same, No. 18, AGI 34.

15. On Collot's plans see Martin, "Collot"; *AHR, 10;* Musick, *St. Louis as a Fortified Town,* pp. 94 ff.

16. Gayoso to Carondelet, Natchez, October 15, 1796, P de C 43; Carondelet to Las Casas, No. 163 res., New Orleans, November 1, 1796, P de C 1447; letters from García (probably to Gayoso), Nos. 35–39, on *La Venganza* on the Lower Mississippi at New Orleans, Placaminas, Valiza, February 14, 1798, to December 9, 1799, all in P de C 628; letters of Metzinger, written on *La Luisiana* on the Lower Mississippi at Bayú San Juan, Lake Pontchartrain, New Orleans, May 18, 1798, to October 30, 1798, all in P de C 628; letters of Molina, written on *La Luisiana* on the Lower Mississippi at Bayú Chafronten [sic], Lake San Juan, June 28, 1799, to September 14, 1799, all in P de C 628; see also Liljegren, "Carlos Howard."

would presage the loss of Lower Louisiana, the loss of the Missouri Valley, and the consolidation of English power on the Pacific Coast.[17]

With the descent of Howard to New Orleans, however, the overall scene shifted shortly thereafter to Lower Louisiana, where there was crisis after crisis. Nevertheless, fears of an English attack again became acute early in 1799, and the Mississippi fleet was called into action once more. Also, since the United States had reinforced its northwestern posts against the English, the possibility of that power being turned against the Spaniards was apparent to those in St. Louis and New Orleans. Indeed, this was one object in Spain's having given in to the United States in signing the Treaty of San Lorenzo el Real. Moreover, in June it was reported that the English were circulating collars among the Indians to incite an attack.[18]

Upper Louisiana was now under the command of Carlos Dehault Delassus,[19] who, thinking he would be able to withstand an

---

17. On Howard, see Liljegren, "Carlos Howard"; Nasatir, *Before Lewis and Clark;* Nasatir, *IJHP, 28,* 337–89. Molina was ordered to cruise on the Des Moines River in *La Flecha* (Howard to Carondelet, St. Louis, May 20, 1797, P de C 35). Molina did cruise and Howard intended to send Metzinger in *La Activa* to relieve him (Howard to Carondelet, St. Louis, June 14, 1797, Bancroft Library, in Nasatir, *IJHP, 28,* reprint pp. 37–40).

18. Gayoso in his letter to Saavedra, No. 19 res., New Orleans, June 9, 1799 (AHN 3901), summarizes the conditions of the province and frontier. He encloses a list of the river squadron signed by Manuel García, New Orleans, June 14, 1799 (AGI 33). The squadron consisted of the galeras *La Leal, La Luisiana, La Venganza, La Felipa;* the *bombardera y obusera La Margarita;* the lanchas cañoneras *Aguiles, Fetis, Fulminante,* and *El Socorro;* the galiots *La Vigilante, La Activa,* and *La Flecha.* These are in condition of service. Of these *La Activa* under Roberto Macay was at New Madrid and *La Flecha* under St. Vrain was at St. Louis. "In my present situation I do not fear an attack on Lower Louisiana; I only fear some attempt against the establishments of Illinois."

See Gayoso to Santa Clara, No. 17 res., New Orleans, July 30, 1798, P de C 1502B, which also lists the naval vessels and tells of dangers to the province. The Illinois needed 1,000 men and 2 galeras, 1 bombardera, 4 cañoneras, and 2 galeotas.

Gayoso, in a letter to Santa Clara, No. 94, New Orleans, January 23, 1798 (P de C 1501A), ordered *La Vigilante* for his own use on September 26, 1797, for he needed it. See also diary of Manuel García to Roca Davion on orders of Gayoso (letter of February 27). García left New Orleans; his diary includes entries from February 28 to March 23, 1798. The diary is enclosed in García to Gayoso, New Orleans, March 29, 1798, P de C 49.

19. On Mandans, the British, and the Upper Missouri Valley activities see Nasatir, *Before Lewis and Clark.*

invasion, drew up elaborate plans for retreat from St. Louis and sent out patrols and spies. In 1800, however not only were the Canadians worried about a Spanish attack, but the English were working hard among the Indians—which may well have been considered offensive preparation by the Spaniards. Then, too, the English policy was to keep the pressure on, in order to make the other side fear attack so that it would not have time to take the offensive. *La Flecha,* commanded by Bernardo Molina, had left St. Louis on March 22, 1798, to ascend as far as Prairie du Chien and to patrol the Iowa country.[20] The same galiot, commanded by Santiago de St. Vrain, patrolled the Mississippi in 1800, 1801, and 1802,[21] but in the latter year it was forced to retreat to St. Louis

20. Diary printed in Nasatir, *IJHP, 28,* 337–89, reprint pp. 49–55; see also pp. 48–49, Trudeau to Gayoso de Lemos, No. 319, St. Louis, March 16, 1798. Howard instructed Molina to cruise on the Des Moines (Moingona) River in *La Flecha;* he left May 23 (Howard to Carondelet, St. Louis, May 30, 1797, P de C 35). Molina went upriver from St. Louis in *La Flecha,* and he "returned from Prairie du Chien a few days ago" and transferred *La Flecha* command to St. Vrain. *La Flecha* left St. Louis April 22, 1798 (Trudeau to Gayoso, No. 2, St. Louis, June 19, 1798; No. 326 of April 23, 1798; both in P de C 49). Molina to Gayoso, New Orleans, July 14, 1798, Molina, in his letter to Gayoso, New Orleans, July 14, 1798 (P de C 44), said he made the trip from St. Louis to Prairie du Chien; he left on March 22. "Continuation of Journal of Galiot *La Flecha"* by St. Vrain, May 8, 1802, P de C 2367.

21. August 10, 1801, New Orleans, "Instructions to M. García Captain of the Army and Commandant of the Squadron of Galleys of the River," encl. No. 10, in Morales to Soler, No. 7, September 30, 1801, P de C 638, "Letterbook of Intendant of Louisiana," Pt. IV.

Due to the war scare in 1797 Carondelet sent the river squadron to reinforce Carlos Howard (Carondelet to Santa Clara, New Orleans, April 22, 1797, P de C 1502B; [Carondelet] to Irujo, New Orleans, April 20, 1797, P de C 104A; Carondelet to Prince of Peace, New Orleans, April 25, 1797, draft in P de C 2365; printed with encl. in Houck, *Spanish Régime, 2,* 225–37). *La Flecha* was ordered to patrol the Upper Mississippi around the Des Moines River (Instructions of Howard to Molina, St. Louis, May 23, 1797, P de C 24; Carondelet to Howard, July 24, 1797, P de C 24; July 17, 1797, P de C 131A).

In the spring of 1798 the Governor General of Louisiana appointed Captain of Militia Santiago de St. Vrain de Lassus (younger brother of Carlos Dehault Delassus) Commander of *La Flecha* (Draft [Delassus?] to Morales, April 2, 1798, P de C 91). Change of command took place at St. Louis in June (Delassus to Casa Calvo, April 24, 1800, P de C 71B).

Due to the war scare of 1799 and the war scare of 1800–01, the galiot was again active. For the first-named scare see: draft [Captain General] to Minister of War, Havana, May 26, 1799, P de C 1750; Gayoso to Saavedra, New Orleans, June 9, 1799, AHN 3901; Mailler to Delassus, Peoria, June 9 [and] 16, 1800, and June 11, 1799, P de C 135; Delassus' Proclamation, St. Louis, July 10, 1800, P de C 135; Delassus to Casa Calvo, St. Louis, August 20, 1800, P de C 71B; Casa Calvo to Urquiza, New

because of a threatened attack by the Sioux Indians.

That all the activities of the Spaniards in the Upper Mississippi, including the valiant efforts of the warships, did not succeed in ridding Spanish-claimed territory of its foreign competitors and traders, is not to be wondered at too much, since the entire area was overridden by the well-financed and supported aggressive English traders from Canada. After all, the United States tried also to clear its territory of other than American traders and control; yet when Zebulon Montgomery Pike ascended the Mississippi in

---

Orleans, October 19, 1800, AHN 3889; in Houck, *Spanish Régime*, 2, 464–68. Casa Calvo to Cornel, New Orleans, October 19, 1800, AGS 6829. During 1799 St. Vrain was in command of *La Flecha*.

On English fears of threat of attack on Canada from Louisiana see e.g.: P. Selby to Russell, Sandwich, January 23, 1799, in *Michigan Pioneer and Historical Collections*, 25, 185–87; more conveniently in E. A. Cruikshank and F. A. Hunter, eds., *Correspondence of the Honourable Peter Russell*, 3 (3 vols. Toronto, 1932), 60–62; same to same, January 18, 1799, ibid., pp. 56–57; March 2, 1799, ibid., pp. 126–27; Russell to Selby, York, February 2, 1799, ibid., pp. 89–90; see also pp. 149–51.

In 1801 Delassus ordered St. Vrain to cruise on the Upper Mississippi (Delassus to Casa Calvo, St. Louis, April 14, 1801, P de C 72). St. Vrain left St. Louis to cruise, especially around the mouth of the Des Moines River, on April 11. Delassus enclosed his instructions to St. Vrain dated April 7, 1801, in his letter to Casa Calvo, No. 91, St. Louis, April 14, 1801 (P de C 72). Casa Calvo reported this to Intendant López y Angulo in a letter dated New Orleans, May 7, 1801, in which he tells the Intendant that the lieutenant governor of Illinois had sent the galiot *La Flecha* under St. Vrain to the Des Moines River for the purposes of restraining the Indians and obstructing the English and American traders, and for the defense of Spanish territory. The letter was enclosed in López y Angulo to Cayetano Soler, No. 90, New Orleans, July 13, 1801 (Sto. Dom. 2617). This trip of St. Vrain ordered by Delassus was approved by Casa Calvo in his letter to Delassus dated New Orleans, May 7, 1801, MHS, Pierre Chouteau Collection, Box ii, Env. VI.

In 1802 St. Vrain was ordered by Delassus to ascend the Mississippi to Prairie du Chien and to the mouth of the St. Peters (Minnesota) River if possible. Instructions were given to St. Vrain dated April 2, 1802, and he left St. Louis on April 4. St. Vrain ascended to Prairie du Chien, where he sent letters ordering the English to get out of Spanish territory to the commandant at Prairie du Chien and to the governor at Michilimackinac. These letters are enclosed with St. Vrain's journal (supplement to Journal of Galiot *La Flecha*, May 8, 1802, P de C 2367). St. Vrain's letter to the commandant of Prairie du Chien, April 28, 1802, and his letter to the governor of Michilimackinac, May 1, 1802, are enclosed with the supplement to his journal. See Delassus to Salcedo, No. 136, St. Louis, April 15, 1802, P de C 72. See also Eugenio Alvarez to J. V. Morales, No. 72, St. Louis, May 17, 1802, P de C 581B, wherein he encloses the list of expenses of *La Flecha* January 1–December, 1801.

Thus the Spanish fresh-water navy, or river squadron, was not strongly represented in Upper Louisiana after 1797, but it played an important part in the regulation of commerce, Indian affairs, and defensive measures taken for the security of the Spanish possessions in the Upper Missippi Valley area.

1805 with United States troops to perform the same function that St. Vrain, *La Flecha,* and the Spaniards had in previous years, he was no more successful than the Spaniards had been. Indeed, it was only after the War of 1812 that the Americans, then masters and owners of the territory, finally got the English out of the Upper Mississippi Valley.

EPILOGUE

Among the chief policies adopted by the Spaniards in their defense of their Mississippi frontier was the use of war vessels on the Mississippi River—a daring and novel undertaking in eighteenth-century Louisiana. Since the galleys were never put to the test of actual combat, it is difficult to evaluate their real contribution to the defense of Spain's Mississippi frontier. However, from the time of the formation of His Catholic Majesty's Light Squadron of Galleys until the execution of the Treaty of San Lorenzo el Real and later, Louisiana was constantly menaced with attack. The galleys played a major role in the Spaniards' plans for defense against these threatened aggressions, and their mere presence created a salutary effect upon the restless American frontiersmen. Since none of the attacks materialized, it may be concluded that the river squadron fulfilled its purpose of protecting Louisiana against foreign assault.

Initially, war vessels were put on the Mississippi River to protect Louisiana from the aggression of American Westerners who sought, by direct action, to settle the problems of free navigation and the boundary dispute. The river galleys were first used to lend naval support to Natchez and Nogales when those posts were threatened by American attack. Early in 1793 a galiot carrying reinforcements and munitions was dispatched to New Madrid, which was menaced by an attack from the Ohio. Later that same year plans were begun to strengthen Spain's position on the Mississippi by establishing a military post at Chickasaw Bluffs. Before the plan could be put into execution, however, the threat of a French attack from the sea demanded the presence of the squadron on the lower river. The galleys descended to Fort Placaminas and established a cruising station near the mouth of the river to guard the province from invasion by sea.

During the winter of 1793–94 with the Clark-Genêt expedition completely absorbing the attention of Spanish officials in Louisiana, the major burden of defense against the threatened Franco-American attack rested on the galleys. As soon as the possibility of a sea attack vanished, the squadron was dispatched to the upper river with reinforcements, men, and munitions. This was the first time that such large vessels had ever ascended the Mississippi as far as New Madrid, and the presence of the galleys greatly strengthened Spain's position in Upper Louisiana.

During the Clark-Genêt scare the first cruising station on the Upper Mississippi was established between Nogales and the Arkansas River. After the squadron reached New Madrid in the spring of 1794, the second and most important cruising station on the upper river was established opposite the mouth of the Ohio. When the squadron returned to Natchez for careening in the summer of 1794, a galiot remained at New Madrid to form a permanent naval station at the junction of the Ohio and Mississippi Rivers.

Early in 1795 the galleys were ordered to assist in the establishment of a military post at Barrancas de Margó, which fort gave Spain complete domination of the Mississippi and effectively prevented the Americans from establishing themselves anywhere along the east bank of the river. After the new post was established, the squadron remained to protect it from threats of American aggression; and until its evacuation in the spring of 1797, Barrancas served as a naval base for the galleys operations on the Upper Mississippi.

In the summer of 1795 Gayoso de Lemos ascended from Barrancas to New Madrid on his galiot *La Venganza* and made a military reconnaissance of Spain's Illinois posts not only to impress the inhabitants and Indians with Spanish power and prestige but to inspect the defenses of the upper posts. Warships had ascended to the mouth of the Illinois River and had entered the Missouri. Until the time of the withdrawal of Spain from its posts on the east bank above the 31st parallel, which was effected in 1798, the squadron of galleys remained on the upper river, based at San Fernando de las Barrancas until that fort's evacuation by Howard in the spring of 1797. Howard then took the squadron to St. Louis, and upon the completion of his commission in Upper Louisiana, the squadron was withdrawn to the lower river, where it remained until the end of the colonial regime in Louisiana. This was true both of the galleys and of the heavier and larger war vessels that made up the squadron. However, several of the galiots, themselves ships of war, were stationed in the upper river after 1797, and indeed cruised and patrolled the Upper Mississippi above their base at St. Louis. *La Flecha* and *La Activa* were active in that work until the end of the colonial period and the transfer of Louisiana to the United States in 1804.

DOCUMENTS

Diary of Captain of the Army Don Pedro Rousseau, commander of the squadron of galleys, upon the war galiot *La Flecha,* from Natchez to New Madrid in the year 1793 by order of Colonel of the Royal Army Don Manuel Gayoso de Lemos, military and political governor of the Plaza of Natchez.

January 5–March 25, 1793
Natchez to New Madrid and Return

Introduction[1]

The following is a nineteen-page diary, originally written in French, of Rousseau's voyage from Natchez to New Madrid and return. Found in the Bancroft Library, unsigned, it was undoubtedly written by Rousseau, since a letter of Carondelet to Portell, dated New Orleans, May 1793 (P de C 19), states that Rousseau arrived at New Madrid on *La Flecha* on March 6, 1793, the date given in the diary for the galiot's arrival there.[2]

While I have not seen the Rousseau maps, Rousseau reported that no settlements existed in the Spanish dominions between Natchez and New Madrid except those already known. His map of the Mississippi had the distances and directions of all landmarks on the river between Natchez and New Madrid accurately marked upon it, all agreeing with observed latitudes and longitudes. The map's only inaccuracy lay in the location of the mouth of the Yazoo River, which was blocked from an observer on the Mississippi by an island situated in front of it. Gayoso employed Medad Mitchell, who had proven himself a skilled map-maker at New Madrid, to make a copy of this map.[3]

Having presented three maps to Gayoso—one of the Mississippi River from Natchez to New Madrid, one of New Madrid, and one

---

1. For background material see above, pp. 59–63.
2. See also a letter from Gayoso to Carondelet, No. 252, Natchez, April 4, 1793 (P de C 2363; printed in Houck, *Spanish Régime in Missouri, 1,* 412), in which Gayoso mentions the diary of Rousseau's recent journey, which he is sending with some maps to Carondelet; a letter from Rousseau to Carondelet, Natchez, n.d. [March 27–31?] (P de C 118), in which Rousseau mentions the journal and the maps he made on his trip to New Madrid and is sending to Carondelet; and a letter from Carondelet to Gayoso, New Orleans, April 23, 1793 (P de C 19), in which Carondelet says he received the diary of the voyage to New Madrid that Pedro Rousseau made at his order.
3. Gayoso to Carondelet, Natchez, April 4, 1793, P de C 2363; in Houck, *Spanish Régime, 1,* 410–12. Gayoso to Carondelet, No. 8 res., Natchez, April 18, 1793, in ibid., 2, 4–8.

of Barrancas de Margó,[4] between the Carondelet and Las Casas Rivers—Rousseau reported that Barrancas de Margó was the only spot between Nogales and New Madrid suitable for the establishment of a fort. In April, Gayoso sent him to New Orleans to deliver Medad Mitchell and the maps to Carondelet.[5]

In P de C 2363 there is a diary written in French and signed by Pedro Rousseau (rubric). This is the one given below, beginning on January 5, with the last entry for Monday, March 25, 1793. It is contained in 32 pages bound together. Its title, given in Spanish, is as follows: "Diario del Cap^n de Ex^{to} D^n Pedro Rousseau Comand^{te} de la Esquadra de Galeras sobre la Galeota de guerra la Flecha, de Natchez a Nuevo Madrid en el año de 1793 por disposición del coronel de los Real^s Extos.D^n Manuel Gayoso de Lemos, Govern^{or} Militar y Politico de la Plaza de Natchez."

The translation given here, based upon the copy in the Bancroft Library, is a literal one. Rousseau does not write grammatically correct French. His punctuation or, rather, lack of punctuation is ever-present. Indeed, since accents and periods are almost nonexistent in the original, the translation was fairly difficult at times. In several instances he uses Spanish expressions in form but writes them in French. Feminine and masculine adjectives with the opposite gender nouns are used very frequently. In general, however, the meaning is quite clear. But to render the translation in a toofree style, as some have done, seems to me to be a mistaken procedure and gives a wrong impression not only of the document translated but of the writer.

Another translation of this diary, since I made my own, has been published in L. Kinnaird, "Spain in the Mississippi Valley," *AHAR, 4* (1945), 111–38. I have carefully checked my translation against the published one and compared it with the original document in the Bancroft Library. Further, Professor E. M. Brown has carefully checked both translations against the original. Mine differs in several details from Kinnaird's.[6]

---

4. Chickasaw Bluffs, near Memphis, Tenn., variously referred to in French and in Spanish as: Ecores à Margot, Barrancas de Margó, Ecores à Prud'homme, and San Fernando de las Barrancas. For differences and a scale sketch see J. D. L. Holmes, "San Fernando of the Bluffs," *WTHSP, 13* (1959), 39. In translation of the diaries, I have used the original spelling of the authors.

5. See above, pp. 64–65.

6. See above, pp. v–vi.

DIARY[1]

Saturday, January 6, 1793. At two o'clock in the afternoon, I[2] received the order from Don Manuel Gayoso de Lemos,[3] Governor of the Plaza of Natchez,[4] to embark on a secret expedition on the

1. The distance by river from Natchez to New Madrid in high water was 201 leagues, while at low water it was increased to 301 leagues. See below, Diary 2, p. 220–21.
2. See above, p. 32, n. 29 and p. 151.
3. For a short sketch of Gayoso de Lemos see above, p. 11, n. 12.
4. Natchez, like Nogales, was situated on the east bank of the Mississippi River, about 40 leagues below the mouth of the Yazoo River. Although geographically a part of West Florida, Natchez was important as the main base from which the squadron of galleys on the Upper Mississippi operated during the 1790s.

The first white settlement at Natchez was made by the French in 1726. In 1788 the Natchez district was chosen by Spain as the proving ground for a newly adopted policy of immigration for Louisiana and West Florida. Gayoso was sent from Spain to become governor of Natchez for the express purpose of administering the new policy. He arrived in 1789 and served as governor of the district until his appointment to the governor-generalship in 1797. Growth of the Natchez district under Gayoso was rapid. In 1787 the population was 1926; by 1792 it had more than doubled to 4300. The vast majority of the new settlers were Anglo-Americans, many of them British loyalists who had fled from the United States after the close of the Revolutionary War. The predominant religion was Protestant, despite Spain's traditional policy of excluding all but Catholics from its colonies.

The Protestant Anglo-American inhabitants of Natchez proved to be loyal and zealous subjects of the King during the period of Spanish rule. When the province was threatened by the Clark-Genêt expedition, they were quick to take up arms in its defense; and in 1793, when Louisiana was threatened with invasion by way of Balize, 300 of them traveled to New Orleans to offer their services. The success of Spanish rule in Natchez was due largely to the personality of Governor Gayoso. His mild administration, his protection of debtor planters, his open hospitality, and his polished and genial manner made him well liked by all the inhabitants and inspired loyalty in them to both himself and to Spain.

The majority of the inhabitants of Natchez were small farmers or slaveholding planters. The chief products cultivated were cotton, tobacco, and indigo. Most of the tobacco was sold to the Spanish government. The town was built on high ground about a mile from the river, and contained many fine houses and rich shops. Beyond the town stretched miles of fine plantations and farms.

Carondelet did not consider the fort at Natchez of much military importance. It was dominated on every side, and he did not think it capable of a regular defense. In his military report of 1794 he recommended that the fort be abandoned and the gov-

war galiot *La Fleche*,[5] armed with eight bronze swivel guns, a crew of eighteen men, and three soldiers of the Regiment of Louisiana. I gave over the command of my squadron to Mr.

ernor, artillery, and troops transferred to Nogales. A commandant with 30 men and a detachment of 15 dragoons were sufficient, he believed, to protect Natchez from the Indians and keep the people subordinate to the Spanish government. Gayoso, on the other hand, thought Natchez an important point in the defense of Louisiana. Although the inhabitants were loyal, their loyalty depended in large measure on Gayoso's presence, and he felt that the plaza's fortifications should be maintained at full strength. Gayoso's point of view won out, for Carondelet's recommendations were never carried out.

(Natchez has had a long history. See Gayarré, *History of Louisiana*, *1*, chap. 4; *3*, esp. p. 333; Collot, *A Journey in North America*, *2*, 57-64; Perrin du Lac, *Travels through the Two Louisianas*, pp. 83-84; Whitaker, *Mississippi Question*, pp. 61-63; Carondelet's Military Report; Gayoso to Carondelet, Barrancas, July 18, 1795, P de C 198; Leonard, "A Frontier Library," *HAHR*, *23* [1943], 24.)

5. *La Fleche* or *La Flecha* was a galiot belonging to the river squadron of vessels. *La Flecha* and *La Activa* were the 2 well-worked galiots in that fleet. *La Flecha* was constructed with a keel, mast and sails, rudder and helm, and covered deck and cabin. It was equipped with 16 oars, and in 1793 and 1794 was armed with 8 bronze swivel-guns and no cannon. When Ferrúsola took the galiot to New Madrid at the end of 1793, its crew consisted of a *patrón*, 14 rowers, a carpenter, and a *proel*. It also carried a garrison of 6 soldiers, which with Ferrúsola made a total of 24 men on board. In August 1796 only 9 sailors and a patrón were reported on the crew of *La Flecha*, but at that time it was incomplete.

La Flecha and *La Activa* were both active on the Upper Mississippi around Barrancas de Margó, New Madrid, and the Illinois country. *La Flecha* was on the Upper Mississippi as far as New Madrid early in 1792, and made two more voyages there in 1793. Early in 1794 *La Flecha* ascended again to New Madrid, and this time remained on the upper river, except for one short trip to Natchez, until well into 1797. At the end of 1795 *La Flecha* descended with *La Activa* for careening and repairs at Natchez, reascending to St. Louis in the spring of 1797. When the river squadron returned to the lower river in the summer of 1797, both galiots were left at St. Louis to furnish the post with naval support against English and American aggressions.

(See García to Gayoso, Barrancas, August 24, 1796, P de C 48; this diary and diary of Ferrúsola below, pp. 192-231; instructions to Ferrúsola in the cruising station between Nogales and Arkansas, signed by Gayoso, Natchez, November 7, 1793, copy certified by Vidal, Natchez, November 10, 1793, P de C 42; García to Carondelet, No. 67, on *La Venganza*, San Fernando, August 24, 1796, P de C 33; *relacion* of the patrón and sailors who garrison *La Flecha*, signed by Bernardo Molina, encl. in García to Carondelet, No. 67; Grand-Pré to Carondelet, Natchez, February 5, 1796, P de C 212B; Rousseau to Gayoso, on *La Venganza*, Nogales, March 9, 1791 [1792], P de C 46; draft of instructions to Rousseau [drawn up by Carondelet], New Orleans, January 16, 1794, P de C 2354; another draft in P de C 2352.)

Most of the above data has been based on numerous letters written by Spanish officials in the years 1794 to 1797 and found in the P de C. See Liljegren, "The Commission of Lieutenant-Colonel Carlos Howard"; Nasatir, *IJHP*, *29*, 155-232, esp. 174 ff.; Nasatir, ibid., *28*, 337-89.

DIARY

155

Gayoso, who took charge of it. At three o'clock I received a sealed package that was sent to me by M. Gayoso de Lemos, governor of Natchez, with orders to start.[6] At four I started out and made camp at one league's distance from Natchez.

Sunday, January 6, 1793. I started out at six o'clock in the morning. At five in the evening I camped at five leagues from Natchez. At five in the morning there came alongside a canoe from the *galères,*[7] which brought me two sacks of biscuits and a letter from the governor of Natchez.

Monday, January 7, 1793. Started out at six o'clock in the morning. Weather very cold. Camped at five in the evening at ten leagues from Natchez.

Tuesday, January 8, 1793. [Started out] at six o'clock in the morning [with] a strong wind at the prow. At five in the evening camped at one league below Bayou aux Pierres [Stony Creek].[8] Made six leagues.

Wednesday, January 9, 1793. Started out at six in the morning. Headwind to the prow. At eight o'clock the same day, across from Bayou aux Pierres, there came alongside a barge and a pirogue. They came from Illinois. Their proprietor was named Cerré.[9] He told me nothing new; that all was very peaceful above; that he was going to New Orleans loaded with peltry. At the same hour there came alongside two pirogues which had come from the Ar-

---

6. Early in January, Gayoso received Carondelet's order to send a gunboat to New Madrid.

7. *Galère* might be translated as "galley," and *galiot* or *galliote* as "galiot." The latter is smaller than the former. I have kept the French *galère,* but have translated both the French *galliot* and the Spanish *galeota* as *galiot.*

8. There are some quarries of stone near here. Thirty miles up the fork is the village of Gibsonport, Mississippi, and it is 44 miles from Natchez landing. See Cramer, *The Navigator,* p. 188; Collot, *Journey in North America,* 2, 56–57; Thomas Hutchins, *Historical Narrative and Topographical Description of Louisiana and West Florida,* printed as Appendix I in Gilbert Imlay, *A Topographical Description of the Western Territory of North America* (London, 1797), pp. 387–458; see pp. 425 f. and 458.

9. Jean Gabriel Cerré was born in Montreal, Canada on August 12, 1724, and came to Kaskaskia in 1755, where he engaged in business and thence went to St. Louis. He aided G. R. Clark and was appointed judge in Kaskaskia by Colonel John Todd. He came to St. Louis in 1779 or 1780, became a leading merchant and trader and remained so until he died on April 4, 1805. (Houck, *History of Missouri,* 2, 40, 47, 74, et seq.; Billon, *Annals of St. Louis, 1,* 452.) See Walter B. Douglas, "Jean Gabriel Cerré—A Sketch," in MHS *Collections,* 2, 58–76.

kansas, loaded with peltry and salted meat belonging to Mr. Menard,[10] who was on board, [and] who was going to New Orleans. At five in the evening camped at a half-league above Grand Gouffre [Grand Gulf].[11]

Thursday, January 10, 1793. Started out rowing at six in the morning. Wind almost calm. Camped at five o'clock below the three isles [*au bas des trois Yles*]. Made five and a half leagues. Weather very cold and foggy.

Friday, January 11, 1793. Started out at six o'clock in the morning. Weather calm. At nine in the morning a stump under the water caught our rudder and broke the iron binding. At five o'clock camped below the Yle de Nogales [Island of Nogales]. Made six and a half leagues, having used sails for three hours.

Saturday, January 12, 1793. Started out at six o'clock in the morning with a little good wind. At three in the afternoon the commandant of Nogales, Don Elie Beauregard,[12] and the storehouse keeper of said post came in a canoe to my ship. Camped at four

10. There are many Menards in Missouri. Perhaps this is Pierre Menard, fur trader, merchant, and statesman. He was born in Quebec in 1766 and moved to Vincennes about 1786, where he was employed by Vigo. In 1789 he accompanied Vigo to Carlyle, Pennsylvania, to consult with Washington concerning the protection of the frontier. Menard moved to Kaskaskia in 1791 and opened a store there in partnership with Toussaint Dubois. He was appointed to office by Arthur St. Clair, William Henry Harrison, and others. He was one of the organizers of the Missouri Fur Co., and accompanied an expedition to return the Mandan chief. He and Andrew Henry led the first expedition to the three forks of the Missouri River. Pierre Menard was elected to the legislature in 1812 and became the first lieutenant governor of Illinois. He died in Kaskaskia in 1844. (See Nasatir edn. of Douglas, *Manuel Lisa;* John Reynolds, *Pioneer History of Illinois* [Belleville, 1852]; *Chicago Historical Collections, 4* [1890]; Alvord, *Kaskaskia Records;* H. M. Chittenden, *History of the American Fur Trade of the Far West* [New York, 1902]; F. S. Philbrick, ed., *Laws of Indiana Territory* [Springfield, Ill., 1930], pp. ccli–liii.)

11. At Big Black River about fifty-four miles above Natchez landing. See Cramer, *The Navigator,* p. 188; Hutchins, in Imlay, *North America,* pp. 425 f. and 458, which gives the mileage as 45¾ miles from Natchez.

12. See above, p. 83, n. 20. On the expedition to Barrancas, Gayoso discovered a sketch of a family seal in Beauregard's possession that made him doubt the captain's loyalty. To verify his suspicions, he described the seal to Carondelet and asked him to find out if the Beauregard family possessed such a coat of arms. Apparently Gayoso's fears were groundless, for he does not mention the matter again, remarking in September that he believed Beauregard would have fulfilled his obligations if the enemy had attacked Barrancas. (See Gayoso to Miró, No. 84, Natchez, May 10, 1791, P de C 2352; Carondelet to Gayoso, New Orleans, May 7, 1794, P de C 21; Gayoso to Carondelet, No. 479, Natchez, May 19, 1794, P de C 28; *Estado en que se hallan las*

o'clock before the post of Nogales.[13] Immediately I sent an official letter to the commandant so that he would have me provided with an iron binding for the rudder, [and so] that he would give me one hundred gun cartridges and six pounds of bullets, one package of gun flints that had been forgotten when embarking at Natchez, and two ox-hides to put over the cargo because the water soaked through the covering [tarpaulin], all of which I received from him.

Monday, January 14, 1793. At ten o'clock in the morning the iron binding for my rudder was ready and put in place—ready to start. As I was about to start out, a barge arrived. I went on board to visit

---

Reales Obras de los Nogales en la Entrega de Mando de dicho por el Capitán Don Elías Beauregard al Capitán Ygnacio Delinó el 22 de Julio de 1794, P de C 126; Diary of Departure from Natchez, on *La Vigilante,* April 16, 1795, P de C 2354 [below, pp. 241–326]; Carondelet to Las Casas, No. 136 [134] res., New Orleans, May 1, 1795, AHN 3899; same letter in P de C 2354 cited as No. 134 res.; Beauregard to Gayoso, No. 19, Barrancas, September 18, 1795, P de C 128; Beauregard to Carondelet, New Orleans, October 19, 1795, P de C 32; Delinó to Carondelet, No. 39, Nogales, May 19, 1796, P de C 33; Beauregard to Carondelet, No. 1, Nogales, June 24, 1796, P de C 33; *Entrega que Haze el Capitán Don Ygnacio Delinó al dela misma clase don Elías Beauregard de la Secretaría y Papeles que existen en ella hoy día de la fecha,* Nogales, June 22, 1796, copy certified by Delinó in P de C 129; Gayoso to Carondelet, Barrancas, July 18, 1795, P de C 198; Gayoso to Carondelet, No. 18 res., New Madrid, September 22, 1795, P de C 32. A good deal of Beauregard's correspondence, especially from Nogales and Barrancas, is contained in several *legajos* in the P de C.)

13. Nogales was situated about 100 leagues below the mouth of the Arkansas River. Although by its location below the mouth of the Yazoo River, Nogales was a part of West Florida, the post played an important role in the story of the Spanish squadron of galleys that patrolled the Upper Mississippi. Nogales was a new post, established early in 1791, to prevent an American land company from occupying the territory around the mouth of the Yazoo and thus threatening Spain's entire plan of defense on the Mississippi River.

There were many early American plans for establishments in the area: the South Carolina Yazoo Co. and the intrigues of Dr. James O'Fallon involved the region. Early in 1791, under orders of Miró, Gayoso was sent up to the area of the mouth of the Yazoo to explore the surrounding country for a suitable fort site. The mouth of the Yazoo River, according to Gayoso's observations, was located in latitude 32° and 33' north latitude, and was from 80 to 100 fathoms wide. The course of the river ran almost directly northeast-southwest, thus making its point of confluence with the Mississippi a very acute angle. A large island concealed the mouth of the river and formed two entrances that were difficult to distinguish at low water. The island was once a great curve opposite the Yazoo, but the Mississippi had cut across the curve to form an island.

Gayoso picked out the location for the fort and it was constructed, although he changed his original plans for a small redoubt to a regular palisaded fort on the height, which he named Monte de Vigia. Beauregard served as commandant of the fort at Nogales until July 1794, when he was succeeded by Ygnacio Delinó, returning

it and to find out where it came from. They told me that they came from Fort Pitt; that its owners were on board; that their names were Guillaume Moore and Robert Scott. It appeared to me to be loaded with merchandise.[14] The weather was so bad that I could not start out.

Tuesday, January 15, 1793. The wind was so strong from the north that I could not start out. I have observed the latitude of the Fort of Nogales to be 32 degrees and 14 minutes, north. At ten o'clock in the evening I observed the longitude of said place to be 95 degrees, 20 minutes, meridian of London.

Wednesday, January 16, 1793. The wind having become calm, I started out at seven o'clock in the morning and continued until

---

to replace the latter in June 1796. The commandant was always in close contact with the governor of Natchez. He frequently received orders from him and often asked his advice on how to handle post affairs.

Since the post of Nogales was constructed on lands belonging to the Choctaws and Chickasaws, Gayoso had to negotiate for its cession from them, and took a year to complete the affair. Rousseau corrected the latitude and longitude of the post.

The military importance of the post and fort was apparent to both Gayoso and Carondelet. In the latter's view Nogales was the best point to stop an attack against Lower Louisiana made from the upper river. Since the current of the Mississippi as it passed Nogales swerved toward the east bank, all descending vessels were forced to pass directly beneath the batteries of the fort. Because of this fact, no enemy force descending the Mississippi could pass Nogales without first besieging and capturing the fort.

(Although the long and rather complicated story of the founding of Nogales [Walnut Hills, Vicksburg] has never been fully told in print, see Whitaker, *Spanish-American Frontier*, pp. 31, 43, 126–27; Bemis, *Pinckney's Treaty*, pp. 202–03; Collot, *Journey in North America*, 2, Chap. 21; Gayoso's Political Report and Carondelet's Military Report, both printed in Robertson, *Louisiana under Spain, France and the United States;* Stoddard, *Sketches of Louisiana;* Whitaker, *MVHR, 16,* 383–94; Parish, *MVHR, 17,* 230–63. There is a great deal of correspondence relating to the founding of Nogales in the P de C. Among many letters that could be cited are the following very few: Gayoso to Miró, No. 84, Natchez, May 10, 1791, P de C 2352; Carondelet to Gayoso, res., New Orleans, January 15, 1794, P de C 21; March 3, 1794, P de C 21; draft in P de C 210.)

14. Rousseau wrote Gayoso de Lemos on board *La Flecha* on January 15, 1793, saying that he met the flatboat from Fort Pitt, *La Amistad,* owned by Guillermo Moore and Robert Scot. He stopped them and asked for their *factura de la carga,* which the owners said they had not made. Rousseau had the boat examined and found products "que no son producción de aquel país," which therefore appeared to him as "goods prohibited by His Majesty"—"lo he detenido"—and endorsed a list of such to the governor general, but not with a letter, "as I had to continue my expedition and could not spare men to descend with him or to accompany it" (P de C 207B). At Nogales a descending American flatboat informed Rousseau that 2,000 poorly disciplined men were at Fort Pitt and that they were ready to desert.

DIARY   159

five in the afternoon, when I camped at a half-league from the Yazoo River. Good weather. Made four leagues.

Thursday, January 17, 1793. Started out at six o'clock in the morning. Weather calm. At ten o'clock in the morning passed a large isle on the western bank. Passed between the land and said isle. At three o'clock passed a small and a large isle on the same bank.[15] Camped at five o'clock. Made five and a half leagues. Good weather. Appearance of rain.

Friday, January 18, 1793. Started out at six o'clock in the morning. Good wind. Put up the sails at 10:30 in the morning. Passed four isles on the eastern bank. No water passes between said isles and the land. The battures[16] extend far out and go almost to the middle of the river, which lengthens our route quite a bit.

Saturday, January 19, 1793. Started out at six in the morning. Weather calm. At eight o'clock passed several isles on the western bank. Made the great turn. At four in the afternoon passed three isles. At five o'clock camped above the three isles.

Sunday, January 20, 1793. Started out at six in the morning. Good wind. Put up the sails. At one o'clock, passed a small isle in the middle of the river. At five in the evening camped on the isle named La Tête de Mort [Death's Head].[17] Made eight leagues. Good weather, but very cold.

Monday, January 21, 1793. Started out at six in the morning. Wind ahead. At nine o'clock the wind was so strong that I was obliged to camp on an isle on the western bank at one league from La Tête de Mort until the next day. The weather very cold and the current very strong.

Tuesday, January 22, 1793. Started out at six o'clock in the morn-

15. Some of these isles and the channel of the Mississippi are described and distances given in Cramer, *The Navigator*.

16. A *batura* in Spanish, called a batture in English, is the bottom of a sandy or rocky shallow, a river bed elevated to the surface by drought, also probably a sand bar—in other words, a sand bar or bank laid down by a river on the inner side of a turn. See C. C. Robin, *Voyages dans l'interieur de la Louisiane—1802–1806*, 2 (3 vols. Paris, 1807), 282; V. Tixier, *Travels on the Osage Prairies*, trans. Albert A. Salvan, ed. John Francis McDermott (Norman, Okla., 1940), p. 54.

17. The distance from the Arkansas River to the Yazoo is 158 miles, and from one to the other there are only two passages: the Isle à la Tête de Mort and the Isle aux Chicots, both of which are encumbered with driftwood heaped 60 feet high in some places and thus narrowing the channel of the river (Collot, *Journey in North America*, 2, 43).

ing. Sails up. Wind good and stiff. At five in the evening camped below the Isle de la Coupe [Isle of La Coupée] on the western bank. The isle is located on the same side. Made nine and a half leagues that day. Good weather. Current very strong.

Wednesday, January 23, 1793. Started out at six o'clock in the morning. At noon put to shore to prepare dinner. While we were on land, there came along the western bank 25 Chactas [Choctaws] with their wives and children and 15 horses loaded with furs, and two pirogues loaded with skins, which were drifting on the river manned by two [Indian] men and four women savages. There was among them a half-breed who spoke very good English, who told me that he had just been hunting on the western bank of the Mississippi, that he was returning to his village, which was the one wherein Mr. de la Villebeuvre resided,[18] [and] that he had crossed the river yesterday morning. I asked him if he had seen anyone since he left his village. He answered that he had not seen any white men; that ten days ago he had found a party of fifteen Chikachas with their wives, who were returning to their village, but that he had said nothing to them. They asked me to trade their skins. I answered that I was [in charge of] the King's boat and that I do not trade with anyone. They asked me for some *tafia*.[19] I told them that I did not have any. They asked me for a little bread. I gave them 24 sea biscuits, and afterward I resumed our course and left them to camp in the same place. At five o'clock in the evening I camped on the western bank, having gone twice on the eastern. Made five and a half leagues.

Thursday, January 24, 1793. Started out at six o'clock in the morning. Wind ahead. I found a great deal of current and very large battures. At noon landed to prepare dinner. At 1:30 saw two barges which were drifting from the shore. I had them put to land. They came from the Belle Rivière [Ohio River] to hunt. One

---

18. There is a great deal of Juan de la Villebeuvre's correspondence in the P de C. For some information concerning this official consult, Whitaker, *Spanish-American Frontier;* Bemis, *Pinckney's Treaty;* J. W. Caughey, *McGillivray of the Creeks* (Norman, Okla., 1938); Gayarré, *History of Louisiana, 3;* Serrano y Sanz, *Documentos históricos de la Florida y la Luisiana;* Serrano y Sanz, *España y los Indios Cherokis y Chactas.* Some few biographical and genealogical facts are given in Arthur and Kernion, *Old Families of Louisiana.*

19. Rum. See W. A. Read, *Louisiana French* (Baton Rouge, 1931), pp. 106–07.

DIARY 161

was manned by Frenchmen who had a passport from Mr. Zenon Trudeau,[20] commandant of St. Louis, Illinois. I gave them a letter for the governor of Natchez. And the other one was manned by Americans from Kentucky. They had left Kentucky three months ago and had been hunting on the Belle Rivière. They told me that before their departure the Cherokees and the Creeks had attacked the post of Cumberland, had killed several persons and burned several houses, and had withdrawn; and that in the direction of Fort Washington they had attacked a party of Americans, had killed several soldiers, had carried off 60 horses, and had taken flight with what they had taken. Bought 60 pounds of dried meat and started on. Camped at five in the evening. Made five leagues, according to my estimation.

Friday, January 25, 1793. Started out at six in the morning. The wind being good we put up the sails. At ten o'clock we passed an island on the eastern bank. At noon we saw a savage on the western bank, recognized him as an Arkansas. At four in the afternoon passed the Isle aux Chicots [Stump Island].[21] Spoke to a *chalán* that came from the Wabash loaded with dried salted meat [*viande salé* (sic)] [and that was] manned by some Americans. At the same time saw a barge which passed on the other side of the isle, and which we did not recognize. Camped at five in the evening. Made six leagues.

Saturday, January 26, 1793. Started out at six in the morning with sails and oars. At nine o'clock saw a boat that was descending the river. I made it come alongside. It was coming from Arkansas. Its master was named Bougigne. [It had a] crew of four men on board and Mr. Vaugine, *fils,* a passenger on board, with a passport, from Mr. Delinó,[22] commandant of the Arkansas, going to New

20. For Trudeau see above, p. 59, n. 2.
21. See Read, *Louisiana French,* p. 164; J. F. McDermott, *A Glossary of Mississippi Valley French 1673–1850* (St. Louis, 1941), p. 51.
22. Juan Ygnacio Delinó assumed command of the Arkansas Post in July 1790, and served there until July 1794, when he was transferred to Nogales. Carondelet apparently regarded him as a loyal and able servant, for he chose Delinó to command the Spanish settlement he intended to establish at Barrancas de Margó in the spring of 1793. As Carondelet's early plans for a post at Barrancas failed to materialize, Delinó remained at Arkansas until ordered to replace Beauregard at Nogales. When Fort San Fernando de las Barrancas was finally founded, he was in command at Nogales, and the Barrancas appointment went to his predecessor at that post, Captain Beau-

Orleans. It was loaded with furs and dried salted meat. I gave him a letter for the governor of Natchez and I started out. At the same time, passed a wonderful cypress grove [miprière],[23] at one league below the three channels, 12 leagues from the Arkansas River. At noon passed the three channels. The whole morning we had had a little rain. At five in the evening camped on a point on the eastern bank. At seven there came to our camp an Arkansas savage with two women. He told us that he was camped on the other side of the river, that he was hunting there, and that we were at six *pointes* [sic][24] from the Arkansas River. Made six and a half leagues according to my estimation.

Sunday, January 27, 1793. Started out at six o'clock. Wind was good so we used the sails. Passed between two isles on the western bank. At noon passed between six isles. Found current very strong. Did not put to land for dinner, the wind being good. At three o'clock passed an isle on the eastern bank. At six o'clock camped across from the great Ile au Bled [Wheat Island] on the western bank at two leagues from the Arkansas River. Signs of bad weather. Made seven and a half leagues.

Monday, January 28, 1793. Started out at six o'clock. Wind was strong to the prow. Very strong at noon. We made only one league. We were below the small Ile au Bled; since it seemed to us that there was some water [sic], we wanted to pass into it, but

---

regard. Delinó remained at Nogales until June 1796, when he delivered command of the post back to Beauregard. Carlos de Vilemont succeeded Delinó at Arkansas Post. (See Delinó to Miró, No. 1, Arkansas, July 22, 1790, P de C 16; Carondelet to Gayoso, New Orleans, May 7, 1794, P de C 21; Delinó to Carondelet, No. 1, Nogales, July 22, 1794, P de C 29; Delinó to Gayoso, No. 1, Nogales, July 22, 1794, P de C 47; Carondelet to Delinó, muy res., New Orleans, April 1, 1793, P de C 19; draft in P de C 208B; copy in Bancroft Library. Carondelet to Gayoso, New Orleans, May 7, 1794, P de C 21; Delinó to Carondelet, No. 39, Nogales, May 19, 1796, P de C 33; Beauregard to Carondelet, No. 1, Nogales, June 24, 1796, P de C 33. Carondelet to Delinó, New Orleans, May 7, 1794, P de C 21; same to same, May 12, 1794, P de C 21; draft in P de C 122B. Delinó to Carondelet, No. 171, Arkansas, June 14, 1794, P de C 29; same to same, No. 176, Arkansas, July 13, 1794, P de C 29; Stanley Faye, "Arkansas Post of Louisiana: Spanish Domination," *LHQ*, 27 (1944), 629–711.)

23. See note on island No. 77 in Cramer, *Navigator*, p. 177. It is a cypress forest or swamp. A *miprière* is described in Tixier, *Travels*, pp. 65–69, 89. See Collot, *Journey in North America*, 2, 43–44.

24. A wooded point of land or bend. See note on *pointe* in McDermott, *Glossary of Mississippi Valley French*, p. 123.

DIARY

when we were at the exit, we had not found water and were obliged to return below the isle. Wind still from the north and very stiff. As we were above the isle there passed two chaláns and a pirogue, which were drifting and were out of view when we were below the isle. At five o'clock in the evening camped on the eastern bank at a half-league from the mouth of the Arkansas River. The wind was very strong from the north. Weather overcast and very cold. Signs of snow.

Tuesday, January 29, 1793. Started out at six o'clock, with a strong wind from the northeast, to reach the Arkansas River. At nine o'clock entered said river, my *patrón*[25] having told me that it was impossible to continue our voyage with the iron bindings of our broken rudder. For four days we had been holding them with ropes. Therefore I decided to put into the post of Arkansas to get my rudder in shape in order to continue my voyage. At noon the weather was so bad and the wind so strong and snow was falling, that I was obliged to camp a half-league [in] from the Arkansas River. All day the wind blew and it snowed. Happy to be sheltered from the bad weather and the wind.

Wednesday, January 30, 1793. Remained incamped all day. Frightful weather, snow falling continually—two feet of snow on the ground. Very cold wind from the northeast. At four o'clock the wind shifted to the north, very strong, and everything froze.

Thursday, January 31, 1793. The weather continued to be very cold. Very strong wind from the northwest until noon, when it calmed. At once I started out. Made three pointes on the river and camped at five o'clock.

Friday, February 1, 1793. Started out at six o'clock in the morning. Weather still cold. At noon had made six pointes and arrived at the junction of the White River and the Arkansas. Followed the Arkansas River. At five o'clock camped. It is eleven pointes from the entrance of the river to that point. Since noon made six pointes on the Arkansas River. The river is very bad, full of stumps, and

25. Rousseau found that the use of *patrones* to execute his orders and to supervise operation of the artillery was not satisfactory because they were unable to see everything that happened, and were too busy running the vessel to perform the duties officially (Rousseau to Carondelet, Natchez, December 17, 1792, P de C 219; Carondelet to Gayoso, New Orleans, December 22, 1792, P de C 18; draft in P de C 2362).

[there is] a great deal of current, and the battures [are] very bad. The water is as red as in the Red River at the post of Nachitoches.

Saturday, February 2, 1793. Started out at 6:30. Bad weather with rain. Two hours later arrived at the Fort of Arkansas.[26] I went by

---

26. Arkansas Post was located about 100 leagues below New Madrid. Strictly speaking it was not on the Mississippi River, for it was located about 14 leagues inland on the left bank of the Arkansas River. The region was bordered on the north by the Illinois country (upon which it was only nominally dependent) and on the south by Natchitoches. It was drained by the Arkansas River and, according to Perrin du Lac, was noted for the fertility of the country, the beauty of the meadows, the abundance of game, and its salt springs and mines. The country around the mouth of the Arkansas River was low and usually inundated at flood time. A short distance above the mouth of the Arkansas the White River entered, and about 6 miles inland a navigable channel connected both rivers.

Arkansas Post was one of the oldest French settlements in Louisiana. In the Spanish period it consisted of a small fort bearing the impressive name of Fort Carlos III of the Arkansas, and a tiny village of some 40 to 50 houses located a little behind the fort. In 1793 Rousseau observed that above the fort there were about 30 shingle-board houses with galleries running around them, and about a dozen very pretty homes below it. Not far above the white settlement three villages of Arkansas Indians were located. Both above and below the highland on which the post was situated, the country was low and swampy.

The inhabitants of Arkansas Post were nearly all French, and their principal occupations were hunting and trading. At the end of 1791 the population of the post amounted to 116 free persons and 36 slaves, making a total of 152. During the next few years the population increased, the census of 1794 showing 335 inhabitants at Arkansas. (See above, p. 161, n. 22.)

Fort Carlos III of Arkansas, despite its grand name, was little more than an enclosure of stakes located on top of a hill overlooking the Arkansas River. It was occupied by a garrison of about 30 Spanish soldiers and was of no military value except against Indian attacks. When Delinó took possession of the fort in 1790, he reported that it no longer had a stockade and consequently its artillery had been dismounted. The buildings were useless and about to fall in the river. As there was no lodging for the troops, they had been obliged to build some cabins, which Delinó found in the same state of disrepair as the other buildings.

Apparently Delinó repaired the fort and changed its name to Fort San Estevan of the Arkansas. When Rousseau was at Arkansas Post in 1793, he described the fort as surrounded by round stakes of white oak "under shelter from the carbine." There were bastions on the east and west sides, each mounted with a 4-caliber cannon and 2 swivel guns. Inside the fort Rousseau reported a house, a barracks, and a shingle-board warehouse. When Collot visited the Arkansas Post in 1796, he described the fort as 2 ill-constructed huts surrounded by great palisades, without ditch or parapet, and armed with 4 6-pounders.

In the summer of 1791 Commandant Delinó established a permanent detachment of soldiers on an island in the mouth of the White River to keep him informed of events on the Mississippi. He considered the action indispensable for the security of the Arkansas Post. Miró approved the establishment, and Delinó ordered a small guardhouse built on the island so a detachment of 4 soldiers and a corporal could

land to ask the commandant if he had some blacksmiths. He answered that there was an old Negro. I begged him to send for him immediately in order that he might take the measure of the iron bindings of my rudder so as to make new ones and repair the old ones. Soon the Negro arrived and took the measurements. The whole day it rained and was very cold.

Sunday, February 3, 1793. Northwest wind. Stiff breeze—very cold. The Fort of Arkansas is situated in the middle of a hill [*côte*] that overlooks the Arkansas River, which may be forty-five feet in height when the river is low and six feet when it overflows. It forms a horseshoe that may be a half league on the river and extends to the north. At a half league to the north of the river there is

---

remain there the year around. Frequently official correspondence was left with the detachment to avoid the necessity of ascending the Arkansas River to deliver it to the post, a journey of several days.

(See Perrin de Lac, *Travels*, p. 83; Anna Lewis, *Along the Arkansas* [Dallas, 1932], p. 7; Stoddard, *Sketches of Louisiana*, p. 205; Berquin-Duvallon, *Vue de la Colonie* [Paris, 1803], pp. 60–61 Gayoso to Carondelet, No. 33 res., Natchez, February 20 1794, P de C 28; Collot, *Journey*, 2, chaps. 19–20; Pittman, *Present State of European Settlements*, pp. 82–83; Alliot's report printed in Robertson, *Louisiana under Spain, France and the United States*, *1*, 131; Delinó to Miró, No. 1, Arkansas, July 22, 1790, P de C 16. Census of Arkansas, October 28, 1794, P de C 2364; December 31, 1795, P de C 2364; January 10, 1792, P de C 204; December 31, 1796, P de C 2364. Carondelet to Delinó, New Orleans, May 7, 1794, P de C 21; draft in P de C 122B. Carondelet to Delinó, New Orleans, May 12, 1794, P de C 21; Carondelet to Gayoso, New Orleans, May 7, 1794, P de C 21; Gayoso to Carondelet, No. 479, Natchez, May 19, 1794, P de C 28; Delinó to Carondelet, No. 171, Arkansas, June 14, 1794, P de C 29; Delinó to Carondelet, No. 176, Arkansas, July 13, 1794, P de C 29; Delinó to Carondelet, No. 1, Nogales, July 22, 1794, P de C 29; Carondelet's Military Report; Carondelet to Las Casas, No. 101, New Orleans, February 8, 1794, encl. in Las Casas to Campo de Alange, No. 24 res., Havana, November 9, 1793, AGS 7235; Delinó to Miró, No. 61. Arkansas, December 8, 1791, P de C 17; Delinó to Miró, No. 47, Arkansas, July 12, 1791, P de C 17; Miró to Delinó, New Orleans, August 4, 1791, P de C 8; draft [Carondelet] to Delinó, New Orleans, January 7, 1792, P de C 17; Treviño to Delinó, No. 25, New Orleans, February 28, 1792, P de C 122A; Delinó to Carondelet, No. 86, Arkansas, August 8, 1792, P de C 25A; draft [Carondelet] to Delinó, New Orleans, September 19, 1792, P de C 25A.)

I have collected a great deal of correspondence of the commandants of the Arkansas Post during the later French and Spanish periods. Stanley Faye has written monographs on the Arkansas Post during the French and Spanish periods which have been published in the *LHQ*, *26* (1943), 633–731; *27* (1944) 629–716. By far the best account of the history of the Arkansas Post to 1783 is the master's thesis of my former student Marjorie Thomas (now Marjorie Thomas Paine), "Arkansas Post of Louisiana, 1682–1763" (University of California, 1943). From the Yazoo to the mouth of the Arkansas River was 158¼ miles (Hutchins, in *Imlay, Topological Description*, pp. 428, 458).

a large prairie that follows the shore [côte], which extends as far as the Illinois, according to what has been told me by the inhabitants of Arkansas. There are several inhabitants around the prairie who sow wheat there, which I have seen as very beautiful. The Fort of Arkansas is surrounded by round stakes of white oak protected against carbine shots. It has a bastion on the east and another on the west in which are mounted a cannon of four [sic] and two swivel guns. In the fort there is a house, barracks [quartier], and a warehouse covered with shingles. Above the fort there are about thirty houses, with galleries around, covered with shingles, which form two streets. Below the fort there are about a dozen quite pretty houses [or plots] of four by four arpents, where [sic] there are very beautiful fields of wheat on the highland. And below the highland all the lands are flooded. The savages appear very docile and very attached to the Spanish. There are three villages, each governed by its chief. The sun being good, I have observed the latitude of the fort with the octant—which is thirty-four degrees, six minutes, north.

Monday, February 4, 1793. The weather has become bad, with rain. At noon I fastened the iron binding of my rudder, but it has not been possible for me to start out because of the bad weather. I gave the blacksmith, who made me two new iron bindings and repaired the old, a note for ten piasters drawn on Don Francisco Arnoyo, *ministre-interventeur,* of the Plaza of Natchez. I have been obliged to leave two of my sailors at the Arkansas because of illness, and I gave them orders that when they have recovered, [they are] to come and wait for me at the entrance of the White River, where there is a detachment of three soldiers, in order to pick them up on our descent. I took in their place a Canadian named Semit.[27]

Tuesday, February 5, 1793. Rain fell all day so that I could not start out. All the grain that I had on board was found to be spoiled. I was obliged to purchase a half barrel of it, not having been able to get more, and not having any at the post. I had to pay three piasters cash for the half barrel near the post.

Wednesday, February 6, 1793. The weather being a little better, at seven in the morning I started out to descend the Arkansas River.

27. Or Somit.

At ten o'clock the rain commenced to fall so hard that I was obliged to camp six pointes below the Arkansas. At three o'clock the rain stopped. I started out. At five-thirty I camped at the fork of the two rivers. From the post of the Arkansas to the fork it is thirteen pointes. The river is very bad. Many stumps and little water when it is low.

Thursday, February 7, 1793. At six-thirty I started out on the branch of the White River; made three pointes [where] it entered the White River. We drifted down it three pointes and entered into the Mississippi. At the mouth of the White River there is an island where two soldiers and a corporal detached from the Arkansas are stationed. At ten o'clock I was on the river, and at noon I camped at a point one and a half leagues from the White River to make dinner, and to dry the clothing of my people, which was wet. As I was going to make camp, a barge, which was descending, appeared. I had it put to land. It was coming from New Madrid with a passport from the commandant of that place, loaded with peltries and salted meat going to New Orleans. Its patrón [was] named Pierre Chausson and [it had a] crew of three men. By said barge I wrote the governor of Natchez. They told me that everything was very tranquil above; that there were no signs of anything when they left.

Friday, February 8, 1793. Started out at five-thirty in the morning. Good wind. Sailed all day. Passed four islands. Camped at five-thirty. Made ten leagues.

Saturday, February 9, 1793. Started out at five-thirty. Wind to the prow. At eleven o'clock there came alongside us eleven pirogues of Chickasaw and Arkansas savages. They asked me to trade. I told them that the vessels of the King did not trade, that they ought to see by my flag and my pennant, that I was not a trader [trading vessel]. They asked me for some tafia. I told them that I did not have any. They followed me until noon, when I put to land to make dinner, asking me for bread. I gave them three dozen sea biscuits and they were all contented.

[This is] the harangue made to me by the captain of the party, named Thomas,[28] a half-breed Chickasaw encamped on the Missis-

---

28. In a letter most likely written in February [month and day lacking because the document has been torn] 1793, on board *La Flecha* on the Mississippi, Rousseau told

sippi with a party of Arkansas Indians, speaking very good English. "My Father: When we were at war this summer with the Osages, we went to the Arkansas. The chief of the whites told us that the great chief of New Orleans had ordered all the roads closed and had forbidden all the white men to take goods[29] into their villages; that the Osages were worthy of mercy;[30] that we were able to strike them without fearing anything. Ah! my Father, [are] the Osages worthy of pity? It is we and these Arkansas that you see there who are [worthy of pity] and not the Osages. We have found them [Osages] well covered with new blankets of *limbourg*[31] and of wool, and all their guns new. My Father: Goods are pouring into their [Osage] villages. (Showing me an Osage woman that he had with him): You see, my Father, this Osage woman. She tells the truth. She says that there arrived this summer at their villages ten barges or pirogues from Illinois with many white men, among whom one recognized Cadet Chouteau and the clerk, and the Negro of M. Labady, who were all there.[32] Tell me, my Father, if the whites of Illinois are Spanish or our enemies—if it is necessary to attack them when they carry the goods to Illinois, since you see

---

Gayoso that on the 20th of that month he passed Ecores à Margot and that he expected to be in New Madrid within 6 days. Enclosed with this letter he sent a copy of the harangue "which was made to me by a half-breed [*métis*] Chickasaw named Thomas speaking very good English and in which language he made the harangue." The latter was chief of a party of 25 men and was encamped 20 leagues from the Arkansas River. With him were encamped 15 Arkansas. The harangue that Rousseau encloses is practically the same as that contained in Rousseau's diary with the following addition: "The métis named Thomas speaks very good English. It is in that language that he made his speech to me. There were with him 25 Chickasaws, as many more women, and many children. My dear Governor, you will perhaps have some difficulty in reading this, but it was very cold when I was writing, but I did not want to miss this opportunity" [end of document]. The letter and enclosure are in P de C 209. I have used this copy in editing the text.

29. *Butin* is the word used by Rousseau. French dictionaries give the meaning of this word as "booty"—e.g. Emile Littré, *Dictionnaire de la langue française* (Paris, 1873). Perhaps the Indians thought of the goods being given the Osage Indians in the sense of booty. However, see McDermott, *Glossary*, p. 36, and Read, *Louisiana French*, p. 16, where the word is translated as "baggage, merchandise, property of any sort." The Americans in the southern parts of the republic have translated the word literally as "plunder."

30. In the copy in P de C 209, it says, "And the Osages are worthy of pity,— that we could strike them without fearing anything."

31. A kind of coarse cloth.

32. P de C 209 copy says, "who are there every year."

they carry to our enemies the wherewithal to kill us. You see that they take guns, powder, and bullets to the Osages and buy from them all this merchandise which they steal from the Spaniards and red men on the rivers and that they kill all the whites of Natchitoches and Arkansas and all the red men of this region, who cannot hunt without being killed or plundered by the Osages. You see the Arkansas, who cannot go hunting on the prairies without having their throats cut by the Osages. They as well as we are obliged to hunt roebuck on the Mississippi, while the Osages make themselves masters of all the hunting country. The Osages, my Father, are at war with all men, white and red, steal the horses, and kill all the white men they find. The white men of Illinois carry goods to them. Ah! my Father, if the Osages had only their arrows and they were not given any merchandise, we could soon finish them. As for peace, we cannot hope for it with them. They have always deceived those with whom they have made it and will never have any lasting peace. They have never given a good word to other men.

"Ah! my Father, if the great chief of New Orleans had all those who carry goods to the Osages killed, there would be no one to carry it, and a year later one could hope that [with] their maize, once in flour or milk [sic], we could go to strike their village, because at that time all the Osages are on their hunt. We could destroy all their maize and make their women and children prisoners, as well as their old men, and we could place ourselves on the roads by which they would return to their villages, and we could destroy them all, and those who escaped would die from hunger or would be killed by some other red men."

He sat down on the sand, made a circle, and afterward continued his speech. "My Father, you see this circle which I have just made there; well! the Osages are in the center of it and are surrounded by white and red men, and we let them kill us and steal our horses, and we leave them alone. If a red man of any other nation kills another, we demand his head, and if he steals a horse, he is punished by his chief. I pray you, my Father, carry these words to your great chief so that he might stop the white men of Illinois from carrying goods to the Osages to kill us with. When we went to attack them, they killed two men whom we mourn still. You see my Father, it is we who are deserving of pity and not the Osages, as the chief of the Arkansas had told us. You see, my Father, all these women and children who are here. It is so that they will not die of hunger in the village, for we have raised scarcely any maize this year. We have lost nearly all our horses, which prevents us from going further to hunt. We are forced to hunt our deer on the Mississippi."[33]

After he had ended his speech he asked me for a little gunpowder. I gave him six gun cartridges that I had on hand. Since my company had finished dinner, I set out. They remained on land. On putting off, they saluted me with seven musket shots. I replied to them with seven shots from the swivel guns. At half past five I encamped on the point of an island on the east bank. Made five leagues. One hour after we had camped, the sentinel cried that some savages were coming. We prepared to receive them if they had evil intentions, but we saw that there were only eight [in number] and without arms. On arriving they gave me their hands. We recognized them as Chickasaws. One who spoke a little English told me that they were encamped on the other end of the island; that they had seen our fire and had come to see what it was. They asked for something to eat. I gave them six sea biscuits. They remained with us nearly an hour, and afterward they shook hands with us and went away. Kept good watch all night, not trusting them. The weather disagreeable.

Sunday, February 10, 1793. Started out at five-thirty in the morning. The wind to the prow. At ten o'clock passed the Ile de l'Ermitage [Island of the Hermitage]. At eleven o'clock forced to camp, being unable to sail on account of the force of the wind. Remained in camp all day. Made three leagues in the morning.

---

33. This was during the period of stress with the Osage Indians, against whom war was declared by the Spanish government. This incident tells of the difficulties which the Spanish government had in dealing with them. Control of the Osage Indians, as well as regulation and licensing of traders to them, took place at St. Louis. However, whenever Spain had difficulties in controlling them there, the Osages would appear at Arkansas Post and beg for presents and gifts or steal and harass that post as well. In other words, the merchants and traders at Arkansas Post were always having trouble with their counterparts at St. Louis over trade with the Osage Indians. The complete story and full documentation is given in my as yet unpublished "Imperial Osage: Documentary History of the Osage Indians." The reference to Chouteau is to Pierre Chouteau and to Sylvester Labbadie. This complaint led to a full questioning of Labbadie relative to this matter.

Monday, February 11, 1793. Started out at half past five. Wind being good, we put up the sails. Did not put into land at noon. At four in the afternoon spoke [sic] with a barge loaded with salted meat which came from the Belle Rivière. At 5:30 camped on the eastern bank. Made 6½ leagues. Weather cloudy with some rain, and very cold.

Tuesday, February 12, 1793. All night long rain turning into ice fell. Wind very strong from the northeast, making it very cold. We were not able to start until noon, when the wind had calmed a little and the weather turned rather fair. While we were on land there passed along the other bank a barge that was drifting with the river. At three o'clock we landed on an island on the western shore. At five o'clock camped on the upper point of said isle. Made three leagues.

Wednesday, February 13, 1793. Started out at 5:30. Wind calm. Weather very cold. At 10 o'clock passed the small prairie where there was an abandoned house. It seemed to me that maize had been grown there. This prairie is on the western shore. It does not become flooded [*elle ne noye point*]. It stretches along the river for a quarter of a league and extends back into the land. At 11 o'clock passed the entrance of the St. Francis River. At the entrance there is an island that forms two entrances to the river. At five o'clock in the evening camped at three leagues from the St. Francis. The river rose two feet in 24 hours. Very strong current. The river still carries ice in it all the time, which makes it very cold.

Thursday, February 14, 1793. Started out at five in the morning— under sail—good stiff wind. At ten o'clock passed on the land side of the *Ile du Grand Conseil* [Council Island],[34] which shortened our route by four leagues. Said batture has five leagues to go around when the river is very low. At noon a barge passed, which was drifting down the river. I yelled to it to put to shore, but the current was so strong that it could not make land. I did not go out to it, because it would have been necessary for me to lose too much ground [time]. I asked him where he came from. He answered that he came from Kentucky, that he was loaded with tobacco, that the name of the owner of the barge was Brouyain. There is lots of ice

---

34. See Cramer, *Navigator*, p. 170. An Indian Council was held there.

and wood floating in the water all the time. At 5:30 camped on an isle. Appearances of bad weather. Made 9 leagues. Very bad weather all night, with thunder and hail.

Friday, February 15, 1793. The weather continues bad. Started out at 10 o'clock. At noon passed the rapids, which were so strong that with all the oars and the sail and a stiff wind, we had difficulty passing. The whole boat trembled. At two o'clock the weather became so bad that I was obliged to camp in the shelter of an isle. Made three leagues. At midnight the weather was terrible due to the force of the wind and the rain, and the land that was on the other bank was sliding into the river.

Saturday, February 16, 1793. We were not able to make a start the entire day because of the very strong wind and rain. The river rose four feet straight up in 24 hours. The river is still full of ice and it is very cold.

Sunday, February 17, 1793. At six in the morning the weather calmed and we started out. Sky still covered with clouds. The wind was over the prow. At 10 o'clock we passed between an isle and the western bank. At three we passed between an isle and the eastern bank. At 5:30 [we] camped on the upper point of said isle. There was still ice drifting. Made 5½ leagues during the day. Weather still overcast.

Monday, February 18, 1793. Started out at 5:30 in the morning. Wind very strong to the prow, with some mist. At 10 o'clock passed on the inside of an island on the east bank. The river carried a great deal of wood. At 5 o'clock camped on the point of an isle that is in the middle of the river. Made 4 leagues. All night it rained and thundered. The river rose two feet.

Tuesday, February 19, 1793 All day the weather was terrible, with rain and thunder. Remained camped all day without being able to start. The river rose two feet in 24 hours. Very strong current.

Wednesday, February 20, 1793. Started out at 5:30, the weather having become fine. Passed on the right of the isle on which we were camped. At eight o'clock saw the beginning of Ecores à Margot [Chickasaw Bluffs],[35] below which there is a bayou or small river that runs into the land, separating the low land from the

---

35. On Chickasaw Bluffs see Cramer, *Navigator*, pp. 164–68. There are also many descriptions in Collot, Thomas Ashe, *Travels in America Performed in the Year 1806* (London, 1809), Stoddard, etc. See also Gayoso's diary below, pp. 216–17, 279–83, and

DIARY

high land. At nine o'clock we were at the point of the isle. To the left of the isle there is another isle. At the same time saw three barges that were drifting. I yelled to them to put to land. They did on the bluffs. I crossed to them. Two were loaded with flour coming from Cumberland, and the other was loaded with salted meat coming from Kentucky, all three going to New Orleans. Needing some meat for my crew, I purchased from him a hundred pounds of bacon for ten *piastres gourdes*,[36] which I paid in cash. And I gave the master of the barge a letter for the governor of Natchez. They told me that there was no news from above nor from the United States of America. At ten o'clock I continued on my way. The wind being good, I put up the sail. At 11 o'clock I was passing the middle of Ecores à Margot. At noon I was past the river at Margot, which is the end of said Ecores à Margot. At one o'clock the wind calmed. I put to land on an isle to prepare dinner. Started at three o'clock. Passed several isles. At 5:30 camped on an isle in the middle of the river. All night the weather was fine. Made 6 leagues.

Thursday, February 21, 1793. Started out at 5:30. Calm weather. Passed several isles in the middle of the river. At noon put in to shore for dinner. Started again at 2 o'clock. At 5:30 camped above the Thousand Islands on the last isle, a place that bears this name because of the number of isles that are found on a point of the eastern shore. Made five leagues during the day. Good weather, wind calm. In the evening caught a brill[37] that two men could not carry because of its enormous size.

Friday, February 22, 1793. Started out at 5:30 in the morning. Wind good—a little stiff; put up the sail. At 10 o'clock passed several isles on the western bank. At noon put in to land for dinner. At two o'clock started. At 3 o'clock passed several isles on the western shore. At 5:30 camped below the Ysle du Diable [Devil's Island], which is so named because of the force of the current that one finds there in passing it and the number of stumps that are found there. Made 6 leagues.

---

above, pp. 34–35. Rousseau spells Ecores without the final *e*. For the variant spellings and languages used, see p. 152, n. 4.

36. A piaster is a dollar, as is also a *piastre gourde*. Gourde was a West Indian coin equal to five livres or one dollar, and also known as a piastre gourde. See McDermott, *Glossary*, pp. 81–82, 95, 116; Read, *Louisiana French*, pp. 41, 150.

37. *Barbue* or catfish. See Read, pp. 4–5.

Saturday, February 23, 1793. Started out at 5:30 in the morning. At 9:30 passed the Ysle du Diable.[38] Fell [*tombé*] to a half-league from the second bluffs, which are very high and are named Ecores à Prud'homme [Prud'homme Bluffs]. The wind began to blow—good and stiff, from the south. Put up the sail. At 12:30 we had passed the third bluffs, which are very high, and the river there is very narrow. It was three leagues from the second to the third bluffs. Did not put in to land for dinner, the wind being good. At four o'clock passed a large isle in the middle of the river. At 5:30 camped above the fourth bluffs, a distance of three leagues from the third, which one finds on the river after having passed Ecores à Margot. Overcast weather. Signs of rain and bad weather. We moored very securely in a bayou at the end of the fourth bluffs. Made nine leagues.[39]

Sunday, February 24, 1793. Throughout the night we had bad weather, with rain. The rain continued all day, with strong, fresh wind from the northeast. We could not start. Remained camped all day. The river rose two feet in 24 hours. The river flows very rapidly—carrying lots of detritus in it. I went ashore in spite of the rain to see the land of the bluffs. It is very level at three arpents from the river and it seemed to me to be very good. The trees are walnut, white and red oaks, pecan trees [*pacaniés*],[40] and other woods that I do not know.

Monday, February 25, 1793. All night there was bad weather. Sleet and snow fell. Strong, stiff winds from the northeast with thunder. All day the rain fell heavily. It was not possible for us to start out. Remained camped.

Tuesday, February 26, 1793. It rained all night and all day. It was not possible for us to start out. Remained camped. The river rose three feet straight up in 48 hours.[41] The day before, one of my men

---

38. Devil's Island stands nearly in the middle of the river, which turns suddenly to the left and forms a left hand point so curious as to have obtained for it the name of the Devil's elbow (Cramer, *Navigator*, p. 167). A short distance from there is the "Devil's race ground" (see ibid., p. 165).

39. See Rousseau to Carondelet, on *La Flecha* on the Mississippi, February 27, 1793, P de C 209.

40. See Read, *Louisiana French*, pp. 99–100. For a description of the tree and its fruit see Pierre F. X. Charlevoix, *Letters to the Duchess of Lesidiguières* (London, 1763), pp. 293–94; and A. S. Le Page du Pratz, *Histoire de la Louisiane*, 2 (3 vols. Paris, 1758), 26.

41. Original text says twice 24 hours.

asked me to go hunting in order to kill a deer, and he has not yet returned. I sent two men into the woods to see if they could find him, and I had several gun shots fired and swivel guns fired to see if he would reply, but we heard nothing. The men I sent have returned and did not find him or see his tracks.

Wednesday, February 27, 1793. The weather is fine. Again I sent some men into the woods and had several swivel gun shots fired, but he did not reply to us. At noon my men returned from the woods, telling me that they had seen nothing. At the camp I left him provisions for several days in a handkerchief hung from a tree, so that in case he returns to the same camp, he will be able to go to a savage camp, which we left at two leagues below where we were.[42] Started out at noon. The wind being at the prow, I made 3 leagues. I saw three chaláns tied up to the western bank. As the sun was setting, I crossed and camped with them. I found that they all belonged to a Mr. du Paw,[43] [and were] loaded with tobacco and salted meat going to New Orleans. The proprietor had a passport from the Baron de Carondelet, governor general of this province; with him were several French families descending from Gallipolis in America to establish themselves in this province. I gave to Mr. du Paw, owner of the chaláns, a letter for the governor of the Natchez, in which was enclosed a copy of the speech that was made to me by the Chickasaw half-breed.[44] I asked the proprietor of the chaláns that if he saw a man on the bank of the river, to send for him, and I told him that I had lost a man who had been hunting. The people on the two barges told me nothing new.

Thursday, February 28, 1793. At six o'clock in the morning the chaláns started down the river and I started out—with a good, stiff wind over the prow and very cold. The banks of the river were all frozen. At 10 o'clock the wind was so strong that I was obliged to put into land, not being able to continue. At four o'clock the wind calmed a little, and I started out, and at six o'clock in the evening I camped on the second Canadian Island. Made 3 leagues.

Friday, March 1, 1793. Started out at six o'clock in the morning. The weather was overcast, the wind calm, but [there were]

---

42. See entries for March 20 and March 22, below, pp. 185–86.
43. Charles De Pauw? See above, p. 75, n. 2.
44. See above, p. 167, n. 28.

signs of snow, which makes it very cold. At noon prepared dinner at the entrance of the Bayonne River on the western bank. At six o'clock camped above the Iles aux Canadienes [Canadian Islands],[45] which number seven. Made 6 leagues.

Saturday, March 2, 1793. Rained all night until 8 o'clock [in the morning], when the weather became fine. I started out, the wind calm. At noon I put ashore to prepare dinner. While we were at dinner, a pirogue passed on the other side, [but] the river being so wide, we were not able to speak to it. At 2 o'clock started out; weather calm. At 6 o'clock camped on the western bank. Made 5 leagues. Passed three isles on the same shore—passed between them and the shore.

Sunday, March 3, 1793. At two o'clock in the morning there was a terrible landslide [dèbouli]. The trees were falling on all sides, which obliged us to break camp and to travel half a league in the night. We tied up to some willow trees,[46] awaiting daybreak. The Mississippi is beginning to overflow everywhere. At 5:30 started out. Passed two isles on the eastern bank. At noon put ashore for dinner. Started out at 2 o'clock. Since the wind was good, we put up the sail. At 6:30 camped on a *petite prairie* [small meadow],[47] 10 leagues from New Madrid. The land is very high and not under water. It may be eight arpents in circumference, and the woods round about are oak trees. Since it was late when I arrived, I could not see it well. I am leaving that for my return. Made six leagues. My men set fire to the prairie in the morning upon leaving. In an instant it was all on fire.

Monday, March 4, 1793. Started out at six in the morning. Weather overcast. Appearances of bad weather. At noon the weather was very bad, with a great deal of rain. I put ashore on the land side of an isle, and camped on the eastern bank. All day rain fell. At 6 in the evening the wind shifted to the north; strong, stiff. Made three leagues during the morning. Found the current very strong.

Tuesday, March 5, 1793. Started out at 6 o'clock in the morning.

---

45. Possibly called Canadian Reach (Cramer, *Navigator*, pp. 163–64). Called Canadian Isles on Collot's map, Atlas, plate 25.
46. "A de sols," possibly meaning *saules* or willow trees.
47. See Cramer, *Navigator*, p. 163.

Very strong wind to the prow. Weather clear. At 10 o'clock, as we were passing an isle on the western shore, two chaláns that were drifting passed in the cove [Anse],[48] but they were too far away to speak to them. At 6:30 o'clock camped on an isle on the western shore. Made four leagues. Good weather; wind calm.

Wednesday, March 6, 1793. Started out at six o'clock. Weather fine; good wind; used the sail. At eight o'clock saw the Fort of New Madrid in the distance—about a league and a half. At 10 o'clock anchored before said fort.[49] I sent the packet [*pacquet*] from the

---

48. An *anse* is a cove or little bay. "Fortier found *anse* used in Louisiana for the prairie advancing in a wood like a small bay" (quoted in McDermott, *Glossary*, p. 14).

49. New Madrid is located about 12 leagues below the mouth of the Ohio River, on the west bank of the Mississippi River, in the present state of Missouri. It was one of the most important military outposts in Upper Louisiana. The position of New Madrid made it naturally the guardian of Spanish possessions against the entrance of aggressive and restless Americans from the Ohio. The post, known to early hunters and traders as l'Anse à la Graisse, was situated in the hollow of a great bend in the Mississippi about 300 leagues above New Orleans. Just opposite it in the river, a "long salient point" made the channel very narrow at low water and forced all ascending or descending vessels to pass close to the west side of the river. As the west bank was higher at New Madrid than the bank on the opposite shore, the town was not often subject to floods. However, the west bank was very unstable, and the river hit it in such away that it was being washed away, thus putting the town and fort in danger of eventual destruction. Each year the river carried off from 100 to 200 yards of the west bank.

Long before any settlement existed at l'Anse à la Graisse, the landing served as an annual meeting place for white and Indian hunters and traders. In 1783 a trading post was established there by the Le Sieur brothers, but the settlement had no military or civil commandant. Colonel George Morgan founded a settlement there which was not liked by Miró, who dispatched Foucher there to establish Fort Céleste. In 1791 Thomas Portell became commandant and served until the summer of 1796, when Carlos Dehault Delassus took over. The population of New Madrid consisted of 311 whites in 1792; the census of 1795 gave it as 535, comprising 179 families, of whom 123 were Catholic and 51 Protestant. New Madrid housed many foreigners, and the Spanish government was quite suspicious of a number of them.

The location of New Madrid gave it importance as a commercial point of entry. All boats going up or down the Mississippi had to stop there and declare their cargoes, destinations, and passports. Special instructions were frequently given to the commandants of New Madrid. Its location also gave the post a key position in the Spanish plan for the defense of Upper Louisiana. Thus, comparatively speaking, the government centered strong fortifications and garrisons there.

With the founding of Barrancas in 1795, Carondelet decided that Fort Céleste at New Madrid should be moved to a better location, since the river was slowly destroying it; in the meantime the fort at Barrancas would take the place of the one at New Madrid for the defense of Upper Louisiana. This was never done, however, and

governor general of this province and those of the governor of Natchez to the commandant, Dn Thomas Portell,[50] and informed him of my mission, and sent him the three soldiers who were coming to complete his garrison and who had been put aboard at Natchez. Found at the *embarcadero* of said fort a schooner of about 55 tons, without a mast, which came from the Belle Rivière loaded with maize belonging to Dr. Water, an inhabitant of said post, who was going to put a mast on it in order to descend to New Orleans next April. There was an American barge loaded with furs coming from Cas aux [Kaskaskia], Illinois, having on board three French passengers who were coming from the United States of America [and were] going to New Orleans; [the] names of the

---

Gayoso considered it feasible only if another fort was constructed near the Ohio to replace Fort Céleste.

(Sketches are contained in Berquin-Duvallon, *Vue de la Colonie*, p. 61; Collot, *Journey*, 2, chap. 19; Houck, *History of Missouri*, 2, 102–33; Burson, *Stewardship of Don Esteban Miró*, p. 11; Stoddard, *Sketches*, 209–11; M. Savelle, *George Morgan: Colony Builder* [New York, 1932], pp. 200–28; and by same author, "Founding of New Madrid," *MVHR*, *19* [1932], 30–56; Perrin du Lac, *Travels*, p. 82; Carondelet's Military Report; *Estado Militar* of New Madrid, December 2, 1797, P de C 217. There is a great deal of correspondence of the commandants of New Madrid in P de C. See also Liljegren, *LHQ*, *22*, 46–97.)

50. In September 1791 Don Thomas Portell arrived in New Madrid to take over the command of the post from Pedro Foucher. (For a sketch of Portell see above, p. 56, n. 65.) Although New Madrid showed little increase in population or prosperity under his rule, his superiors did not blame the situation entirely on him. Trudeau, who liked Portell, explained the lack of population by the fact that the numerous threats of American attack made the Spaniards so suspicious of the Americans that many were afraid to settle in New Madrid. Gayoso attributed the post's lack of prosperity to Portell's presence but did not believe he was at fault. The fact that he spoke no English and so had to rely on an interpreter was a great disadvantage, which frequently caused misunderstandings to arise. The uncertainty of the times aggravated the situation by obliging him to be distrustful of the residents in his own district as well as of all Americans from the Western states. As a result of these circumstances, Portell earned a bad reputation in New Madrid and Western America, retarding the town's development. A contemporary inhabitant of New Madrid describes Portell as a "man of distinguished merit equally in the military and in the cabinet, and who was superior to his position . . . if he failed, it was because he did not place himself on a level with the people he had to govern." (See Houck, *History of Missouri*, 2, 131–32; Nasatir and Liljegren, *LHQ*, *21*, reprint p. 35, n. 75; Whitaker, *Mississippi Question*, pp. 169–70; Delassus to Carondelet, New Madrid, August 12, 1796, P de C 212A; Trudeau to [Carondelet], St. Louis October 26, 1795, P de C 211; Gayoso to Carondelet, on *La Vigilante*, 6 leagues above New Madrid, December 10, 1795, P de C 43. There is a great deal of Portell correspondence in the P de C.)

three Frenchmen were the Chevalier de Luzières,[51] of the Comté d'Allegène [Allegheny County]; Mr. Barthélemi Tardiveau,[52] of Kaskaskia, Illinois; Guy Bryan, merchant of Philadelphia,[53] [and] Pierre Audrain, of Fort Pitt, all in the States of America.

Thursday, March 7, 1793. All day it rained and sleeted. Very cold weather; very strong wind from the northeast. At 10 o'clock in the evening snow fell heavily.

Friday, March 8, 1793. The weather is very black; very strong wind from the northwest. There were six inches of snow on the ground. At noon the weather turned fine, and it continued all the rest of the day, but was very cold.

Saturday, March 9, 1793. The weather is fine and calmer. I had unloaded the two cannons of eight [sic] and all the war materials I had for this post[54] and which I turned over to the commandant.

51. Pierre Charles Dehault Delassus de Luzières, a Knight of the Grand Cross of the Order of St. Michael, was a rich French aristocrat from Flanders who was forced by the French Revolution to flee with his family to the United States. He settled first at Gallipolis with a number of other royalists, but early in 1793 Bartélemi Tardiveau interested him in a scheme to induce the dissatisfied settlers at Gallipolis to move into Spanish Louisiana. Chosen by the other settlers to look into the matter, he went to New Orleans in April to discuss plans with Carondelet for establishing a colony of French royalists in Illinois. New Bourbon was the result, and Luzières was appointed civil and military commandant of the new settlement, a post he held throughout the remainder of the Spanish period in Louisiana. Luzière's son, Carlos Dehault Delassus, served as commandant of New Madrid from 1796 to 1799, when he was appointed lieutenant governor of Upper Louisiana and transferred to St. Louis. Another son, Delassus de St. Vrain, served in the galiots on the waters of the Upper Mississippi. (There is a great deal of Luzières' correspondence in the P de C, and I have some in my collection. See Houck, *History of Missouri, 1,* 331, 363–64; *2,* 135–37; some documents in Houck, *Spanish Régime in Missouri;* Trudeau's Report to Gayoso, January 15, 1798; petition of Luzières, New Bourbon, September 20, 1797, P de C 214; *LHQ, 30* (1947), 359–62.

52. For a sketch of Tardiveau, see above p. 40, n. 44.

53. Guy Bryan, merchant of Illinois, was an uncle of William Morrison. The uncle and nephew were partners in a business that extended from Philadelphia to the Rocky Mountains. Bryan remained in the east while Morrison ran the stores in Kaskaskia and Cahokia. Wholesale providers for the Indian trade and for all the nearby settlements across the Mississippi, they shipped to the east and south the furs, lead, and flour of Illinois and Missouri (Philbrick, *Laws of Indiana Territory,* p. cclxvi.)

54. Portell to Carondelet, No. 119, New Madrid, March 16, 1793, P de C 26; Portell to Carondelet, No. 120, New Madrid, March 16, 1793, P de C 26; Portell to Gayoso, New Madrid, March 16, 1793, P de C 47; Carondelet to Portell, New Orleans, May [?], 1793, P de C 19. Portell writing to Carondelet from New Madrid on March 16, 1793, says that he was enclosing the list of arms, etc., delivered to him by

At noon I observed the height of the sun. I found that by my observation the Fort of New Madrid is in latitude 36 degrees, 8 minutes, north, and its longitude 93 degrees, 15 minutes, having corrected the distance from the horizon. The barge from Kaskaskia has started drifting toward New Orleans.

Sunday, March 10, 1793. Overcast weather with rain. Good stiff wind from the northeast. The commandant passed in review the militia of his post, which numbered 130 men in the infantry and 20 for cannoneers. He had recognized a captain, a lieutenant, and a sublieutenant to whom I had brought commissions from the governor general of this province, the Baron de Carondelet. The commandant and the captain of militia told me that they still lacked many men who had not yet returned from trading; and that in this post they could make up a group of 180 men. They are all French and German with the exception of about 20 Americans, English, and Irish. All day the rain fell; the weather is very bad and very cold, the wind very strong.

Monday, March 11, 1793. The weather is quite good but very cold. At ten o'clock in the morning the commandant had the chiefs of the Loups come in order to talk with them about the barge which some of their nation had destroyed at Ecores à Margot. They replied that they would send for them immediately, that they would turn them over to said commandant, and that he could do with them what he pleased, but that surely they had taken them for some Americans, because they did not believe that there was one man in their nation who wanted to do harm to the Spanish or to the French; that every day they said to their young men that we were all their brothers and that they had no other father than the King of Spain. They told us also that their entire nation was going to come this summer to form a village at the Grand Prairie, at a distance of six leagues from New Madrid; that they were [in numbers] about 800 or 900 warriors and many women and children. The same day I rode on horseback with the commandant to

---

the patrón of the galiot *La Flecha* under the command of Rousseau. He also received the other things delivered. (P de C 47.)

Carondelet's plan was to have Rousseau ascend to New Madrid to deliver munitions and men. They were to be taken from Natchez and could be replaced by Carondelet from New Orleans. (Carondelet to Gayoso, res., New Orleans, December 22, 1792, P de C 18; draft P de C 2362.)

see the surrounding country of New Madrid. A quarter of a league from the fort there is a prairie that extends above to the Illinois and below to the St. Francis River, which may be about one league in width at that place and empties into a very wide lake named Ste. Marie, and on the other side of the lake it is still prairie. On leaving the fort and the site of the town of New Madrid, where there are several houses built that are beginning to form streets, [and] entering the prairie, one finds a small Cherokee village of three families and [which] have their chief with them, who is called L'Ours Maigre [Lean Bear]. On the edge of the prairie there are several inhabitants at six arpents distance from each other. The soil of the prairie is very good and black. It is necessary to dig five feet to find sand. Wheat grows there very well. Maize, potatoes, and oats grow there very well. The whole prairie is at present covered with strawberry plants. The whole prairie is covered with wild plum and apple trees and other wild fruits of the country. The animals of the prairie are very fat. On Lake Ste. Marie there is a superb cypress grove from which one can get many cypress trees for building, but cypress is not good to make stakes for the enclosures. The inhabitants enclose their sown fields with stakes of sassafras and of oak and white ash, but they [the stakes] do not last.

Tuesday, March 12, 1793. Wind from the northwest; weather clear. The savage chiefs of the Chawanons [Shawnees], Loups, Cherokees, and Watawa [Ottawa] had the interpreter tell me that they wished to go with me on the Mississippi in the galiot *La Fleche.* At two o'clock in the afternoon they embarked with the commandant of New Madrid, Dn Thomas Portell. I saluted them with seven swivel gun shots, which seemed to me to please them very much. I went up one league above New Madrid and descended on the other side through the channel on the isle that is opposite New Madrid, and came out at a half league below the fort of New Madrid, outside the range of cannon. There is plenty of water [in this channel] to float any kind of vessel, however large it may be, but when the river is low, the channel remains dry. There is at present in said channel 30 feet of water. Several barges, chaláns, and conveyances [*voitures*] have already passed there which did not stop at New Madrid, because they enter[ed] the channel without being seen, since one cannot see the entrance from

New Madrid, and when they are below it, they are already too far away and descend without anyone knowing whence they come or who they are. At New Madrid it would be very easy to close up that passage in the middle of said isle. There is in the channel another little isle where the passage on each side is not more than 30 to 40 feet wide, which becomes entirely dry when the river is low. I believe that one could easily close up that passage by planting some willows or vines at a certain distance from each other, which would stop the wood [driftwood] and within a short time would form a considerable obstacle, so that it would be impossible to pass there even with pirogues. There is another short cut higher up, but it is entirely stopped up by detritus, and one cannot even pass with pirogues. Said short cut comes out below said isle and enters at a half-league higher up. On the eastern shore opposite the point above said isle, there is another short cut, which comes out four leagues up the river. At six o'clock in the evening we were back in New Madrid. I saluted the savage chiefs again with seven more swivel gun shots to prove to them the pleasure they had given me by having come to go along with me on the ship of my great King.

Wednesday, March 13, 1793. Fine weather. I am preparing to descend. At ten o'clock in the morning, being at the home of the commandant, the chief of the Chawanons [Shawnees], with the notables[55] of his village, came to speak with said commandant. One who spoke good English spoke to me and seemed to me to testify that they would like to have among them one of their people who knew how to speak Spanish in order not to be deceived every day by white men who trick them, never reporting to them things as they are or the same words that their Spanish Father tells them to say to them; that at the time of the English, there was one of their nation who spoke and wrote English, and when the King of England wanted to send some message to them, he wrote them, and then this one, who could read English, read it to all their nation; and when they wanted to send their messages to the King of England, he wrote them and in that way they knew that was the truth. But when it is necessary that the messages pass through the mouths of interpreters, who often tell them what they want to and who often do not report the same words that their chiefs want said to their Father, that prevents their Father knowing what their inten-

---

55. The *considérés* or principal men, below the great chiefs, of the Indian tribe.

DIARY 183

tions are toward the Spaniards. I replied to him that if they wanted to give me a young notable, I would take him to my great chief at New Orleans, who would regard him as his son, and that he would have him taught to speak our language and afterward he would return to their village. They began to reflect for a moment, and the oldest man said to me: "My Brother, if you are willing not to depart for three days, he would go to where the great chief was, and the great chief and all the notables who were at sixteen leagues above, at the mouth of the Belle Rivière, would decide [whether] to send the young man, and if they did not decide to send him, he would be back in three days"; and he begged me very much to wait those three days. I promised him and he left immediately. The other remained at New Madrid awaiting his return.

Thursday, March 14, 1793. All day the weather was quite good; cold wind. Nothing remarkable happened.

Fort Céleste of New Madrid is square, with four bastions, which are northeast and southwest. Two bastions that are built on the river have two cannon of six [sic], one of four, and two swivel guns each. The two rear bastions have a cannon of four [sic] and one swivel gun. To lodge the commandant, the fort has a house inside it which is 50 feet long and 20 feet wide, [with] a gallery of 10 feet in width on three sides. There are quarters 80 feet long and 20 feet wide, in which there is a storehouse for the belongings of the artillery; a storehouse for provisions, 40 feet in length and 20 feet in width, *pièce sur pièce*;[56] a powder house 10 feet square, pièce sur pièce; a hospital 20 feet in length and 12 in width, pièce sur pièce; a prison 16 feet long and 11 feet wide, divided into two, pièce sur pièce; a bakery 15 feet long and 12 feet wide, pièce sur pièce; a guard house 16 feet long and 11 feet wide, pièce sur pièce; [and] an outhouse 10 feet long and 5 feet wide. The fort is 2312 feet in circumference, surrounded by stakes 5 inches thick and a moat 15 feet wide and 6 feet deep, over which there is a bridge 13 feet wide, with two railings [and] one parapet surrounded with stakes two inches thick in front of the fort. The fort is 250 feet from the Mississippi. The land has [been] washed

56. I am not certain of the exact meaning of *pièce sur pièce*, which is repeated here several times in the document, and the translation of which is ignored in Kinnaird's translation. Probably it means "next to each other"; perhaps "horizontal logs."

down a great deal since the fort was built, but I have been told that for some time it has not been washing away any further.

Friday, March 15, 1793. Very bad weather with rain; wind from the south—very strong. At 10 o'clock in the morning a barge arrived from Poste Vincennes on the Wabash River. It brought us no news, [except] that all was very quiet in the general quarter of the Americans, and that the Americans were making every effort to make peace with the savages. The same men from the barge told us that they would not succeed and that the savages are killing all the Americans they find on the Belle Rivière. They told us that the Americans were determined to march against the savages this summer, if they did not succeed in making peace with them. They do not seem to fear them and are preparing to receive them.

Saturday, March 16, 1793. Bad weather with much rain; wind very strong from the south. I have put my provisions on board and am prepared to leave when the savages arrive. All day the same weather —much rain.

Sunday, March 17, 1793. Bad weather, much rain and wind from the south—very strong. Expecting the savages at any moment, in order to start to drift down to Natchez. At noon the weather was very bad, with rain and hail. At midnight the wind changed to the north—very stiff—and snow fell until Monday morning.

Monday, March 18, 1793. Strong wind from the north. The weather has turned fine. Still awaiting the savages and determined to leave tomorrow if they do not arrive, because they had promised us to bring him [by] last Saturday, which makes us realize that they have not decided to send the young man of whom they spoke; but to show them that I was waiting for them, I have remained three days longer than I had promised to wait for them, being ready to start.

Tuesday, March 19, 1793. Good weather, wind from the south, a little fresh. Seeing that the savages had not arrived, I sent for the interpreter in order to find out what I should expect. He answered that perhaps they had been farther away, hunting, and that they would still be several days in returning, because, since the water was high, they would not find them immediately. At once I decided to leave and agreed with Dn Thomas Portell, commandant of said post,[57] that if they had the same intention when they returned to

---

57. Line missing in Kinnaird translation.

New Madrid, to send them by a boat which is to leave within 20 days for New Orleans. Immediately, I fired a swivel gun and called my crew and took leave of the commandant. He gave me a packet for the governor general and one for the governor of Natchez and for a man named Medard Mitchell,[58] of the American nation, to turn over to the governor general together with a map by the said Medard Mitchell of the waters of the Mississippi. At half-past eight I started out. At noon I was at the small meadow. Having been ashore, I found that the land was still two and a half feet higher than the river. The land is high for a half-league above and a league lower down the river. There is a place there to form a fine establishment. At one league inland from the prairie there is a bayou that empties into the St. Francis River, and [its] upper part goes almost to New Madrid. The lands on the other side of the bayou are all little hills and are never under water, according to what the hunters of New Madrid who are there every day told me. One could make fine establishments there, and in a short space of time one could get to the Arkansas. At two o'clock we started to drift down the river; again [I] took note of all the points and the isles to make a map of the river.[59] At seven o'clock in the evening anchored at one of the Canadian Islands, not finding any land, [it] all being covered with water since we left the Little Prairie.[60] Made 23 leagues during the day.

Wednesday, March 20, 1793. Started out at five o'clock in the morning. At nine o'clock passed Ecores à Farines [Flour Bluffs]. Put ashore at the place where we lost the man to see if he had returned. We did not find the biscuits that we had left on a tree in a handkerchief, which makes me believe that he returned and may have made a *cageux*[61] or may have been taken by the vessels that descend the river.[62] At 11 o'clock passed Ecores à Prud'homme. At noon passed those of the middle, noting always the points and the isles and their distances. At seven o'clock in the evening anchored to some willows, not being able to find land, since it was all under water on both sides. We have seen no land except at the bluffs. Made 24 leagues during the day. Wind from the south, somewhat fresh; good weather.

58. See above, p. 64, n. 10.
59. See Rousseau to Carondelet, Natchez, n.d. [March 27–31?], P de C 118.
60. See Cramer, *Navigator*, p. 163; Ashe, *Travels in America*, p. 268.
61. A raft; see McDermott, *Glossary*, p. 41.
62. See entries for February 27, above, p. 175, and for March 22, below, p. 186.

Thursday, March 21, 1793. Started out at five in the morning. Put to shore at seven o'clock at the entrance of the river of Ecores à Margot. Immediately I went on land with six men to hunt. I found almost at the entrance of the River à Margot a superb place to build a fortification.[63] The land [is] 50 feet in elevation and will not wash away. There is a small batture below which protects the entrance of the river and the *battre* [sic] below and above on the Mississippi. There are two huge trees, on one of which is written "de soi [sic] Taimo a Kin,[64] April 9, 1791," and on the other, "Tomas April 9, 1791." I went over all the land for one league around. One cannot see any finer lands, with small hills in some places, and very level in other places. On the river there are many cypress trees for building. Plum trees, hazelnut trees, and chestnut trees are very plentiful. There are many ash trees, many oaks, walnuts, sassafras, and many other trees. There are many springs, and further inland the land is very good, it seemed to me. At 10:30 I was back on board again. Immediately, I started out. At 11 o'clock passed the river, below Ecores à Margot, which is located at the beginning of the bluffs. It is very navigable, and by it one can go in a short time to the other river. At four o'clock passed the Batture du Conseil [Council Shoals]. At 6:30 passed the St. Francis River. All the land since [we passed] Ecores à Margot [is] under water. We have not found any land except at the Little Prairie—one league below the St. Francis River, where we camped. The land [at that point] was still three feet above the river. According to what I had seen, it seemed to me that it would never be under water. Made 35 leagues during the day.

Friday, March 22, 1793. Started out at five o'clock in the morning; fine, fresh wind over the prow. At nine o'clock passed the Hermi-

---

63. In a letter to Carondelet dated April 4, 1793, Gayoso described the bluffs as consisting of a long stretch of highlands stretching for about 20 leagues in a northeasterly direction along the east bank of the Mississippi River, touching it at 4 points: (1) Barrancas de Margó—the best one for a fort, said Rousseau in 1793; (2) Barrancas del Medio—too high and rugged for a fort, exposed to land attack; (3) Barrancas de Prud'homme—uneven terrain, soil loose, not good militarily; and (4) Barrancas de Farina. All of these bluffs lay in a north-south line which, measured from point to point, covered a distance of 10 leagues, though by water it was nearer to 20.

See P de C 2363; in Houck, *Spanish Régime, 1,* 410–12. Gayoso to Carondelet, No. 9 res., June 13, 1796 [?], P de C 2364; same to same, New Madrid, August 26, 1795, P de C 32.

64. Or Jaime a Kim.

DIARY

tage. At noon the rain began to fall. From the prairie to the White River the land on both sides was under water. Put ashore at five o'clock in the evening on an isle in the mouth of the White River. Delivered to the sergeant of the detachment of the Arkansas the letters for his commandant, which had been given me by Dn Thomas Portell, commandant of New Madrid. Said sergeant told me that a barge which was descending had found the man I had lost at the bluffs,[65] and that the two I had left sick at the Arkansas had left with the same barge. Immediately, I started on. At seven o'clock [was] anchored to some willows, not being able to find land on which to camp. Made 28 leagues.

Saturday, March 23, 1793. Started out at five o'clock in the morning. At seven o'clock passed the mouth of the Arkansas River. At noon passed the three channels, at eight leagues from the Arkansas. At two o'clock passed the channels at twelve leagues. At three o'clock passed a superb cypress grove on the western shore. Afterward passed land, one league and a half long, very high, which was three feet above the water. Put to shore to see whether the land would be inundated at high water. There do not seem to be any marks on the trees to indicate that the land had ever been under water. The reeds prevented me from entering the depths [penetrating inland]. Started out immediately, and right away passed the Ile au[x] Chicots. Below the isle on the eastern bank there is one league of land that is not submerged. It is not quite as high as the first. At seven o'clock anchored to some willows on the western shore. We have not found any land except in the places mentioned. Made 27 leagues during the day. The wind still ahead and fresh. In the night the weather was terrible, [with] wind and rain. The waves and the wind were so strong that I was obliged to cross [the river] in order to shelter myself from the wind and the waves. Crossed at midnight; anchored to some willow trees; no land.

Sunday, March 24, 1793. At six o'clock in the morning the wind was good, almost calm. At noon passed the Ile de la Tête des Morts. At two o'clock passed three isles on the western shore. At four o'clock passed four isles on the eastern shore. At six o'clock passed a large and a small isle on the western shore. At 6:30 passed six isles on the same shore. At seven o'clock put ashore on a hillock of land on the western shore, but the land all around was submerged.

---

65. See entries for February 27, above, and March 20, below.

The lands that I passed all day on both sides were submerged. Made 38 leagues.

Sunday [Monday], *March 25, 1793*. Started out at five o'clock in the morning. Wind over the prow. At seven o'clock passed on the land side of a large isle on the western shore. On terra firma there is a league of land that does not become flooded at three leagues from the Yazoo River. At seven o'clock passed the Yazoo River. At 8:30 arrived at the Fort of Nogales. Not having found any letters from my chiefs, I started for Natchez; noted all the isles and the points. At seven o'clock in the evening passed the Grand Gouffre; at 10 o'clock the small one. The moon [was] very bright, which favored my observation. At midnight such a thick mist [fog] arose that I was obliged to anchor to some willow trees until daybreak, when I started out. At six o'clock in the morning anchored at Natchez. I went immediately to the governor of the plaza, to whom I gave an account of my mission and delivered to him the packet which had been given me by the commandant of New Madrid, Dn Thomas Portell.[66]

Pedro Rousseau
[rubric][67]

66. End of unsigned copy in the Bancroft Library from which this translation was made. The copy in P de C contains the signature of Pedro Rousseau.

67. Rousseau traveled by day only. He observed and sketched the entire river from New Madrid to Natchez and marked the distances between all landmarks along the way (Rousseau to Carondelet, Natchez, n.d. [March 27–31?, 1793], P de C 118.) Then distances were well known. (See Cramer, *Navigator;* Harry Toulmin, *The Western Country in 1793,* ed. M. Tinling and G. Davies [San Marino, 1948], p. 116.)

From his observations Rousseau drew up 3 maps, which he presented to Gayoso. The first covered the Mississippi River from Natchez to New Madrid, the second was of New Madrid, while the third included all of Barrancas de Margó between the Carondelet and Las Casas Rivers. His maps were accurate, with the only inaccuracy in the location of the mouth of the Yazoo River, which was blocked from an observer on the Mississippi by an island situated in front of it. Gayoso employed Medad Mitchell, who had proved himself a skilled map-maker at New Madrid, to make a copy of Rousseau's map of the Mississippi. (Gayoso to Carondelet, Natchez, April 4, 1793, P de C 2363; in Houck, *Spanish Régime, 1,* 410–12. Gayoso to Carondelet, No. 8 res., Natchez, April 18, 1793, P de C 2363; in Houck, *Spanish Régime, 2,* 4–8.)

Rousseau reported that Barrancas de Margó was the only spot between Nogales and New Madrid suitable for the establishment of a fort. In April, Gayoso sent Rousseau to New Orleans to deliver Medad Mitchell and the maps to Carondelet. (See Gayoso to Carondelet, No. 8 res.; and above, pp. 64–65; 151–52.)

2

Diary of Juan Barnó y Ferrúsola, covering an expedition from Natchez to New Madrid and back to Nogales.

November 9, 1793, to February 16, 1794

Introduction[1]

On November 9, 1793, Juan Barnó y Ferrúsola[2] left Natchez with *La Flecha* to cruise between Nogales and the Arkansas River. He was ordered to embark from Natchez with provisions for one month, pick up more supplies at Nogales, and then proceed by regular marches to his cruising station at the confluence of the Arkansas River. He was to remain there until provisions for no more than fifteen days were left, then return to Nogales, renew his supplies, and reascend. His instructions were to travel only during the daytime, camping each night at sunset at a spot where the river had but one channel. Four armed guards were to be posted at the camp, and a pirogue with two armed men sent across the river to watch for unusual occurrences on the opposite bank. The guards were to be changed every quarter and were to "pass the word" every fifteen minutes to assure greater vigilance.

Ferrúsola's commission was to inspect every vessel that descended the Mississippi for seditious materials and suspicious persons. All sealed letters and books dealing with law or constitutions were to be sent to Natchez in a sealed box on the vessel that was carrying them if it did not seem suspicious. Otherwise, Ferrúsola was to deliver the box to the commandant of Nogales himself. Moreover, he was to consider every Frenchman suspicious but was to watch particularly for La Chaise, De Pauw, and Pisgignoux.

Ferrúsola was also instructed to examine all passports, including those of Americans, showing the latter the utmost consideration as long as they cooperated with him. If he discovered suspicious characters—that is, all those who carried the tricolor bonnet of liberty or any other sign of the French Revolution—he was to put them in irons, tie their elbows together, lock them in the ship's cabin, and then deliver them at once to the commandant at No-

---

1. For background material see above, pp. 76–84.
2. For sketch of Ferrúsola see above, p. 76, n. 5.

gales. In the event that he met a vessel manned by Frenchmen, he was to assume battle position, and if the French showed the slightest resistance, he was to overcome them and send them to Nogales. If several vessels descended with forces superior to his, Ferrúsola was to retire immediately to Nogales to warn the commandant of the enemy's approach.[3] Gayoso notified all the post commandants on the upper river of Ferrúsola's commission and ordered them to supply him with whatever provisions, troops, or materials he requested.[4]

Ferrúsola immediately prepared to execute the instruction with the galiot *La Flecha,* but on his arrival at the Arkansas he received word from Portell that New Madrid was in imminent danger of attack. Disregarding his original instructions, he hastened up the river to reinforce the threatened post, arriving early in January. While there, he apprehended a suspicious Frenchman named Pisgignoux and took him down to Nogales as a prisoner in the middle of February. The story of the trip is detailed in the diary below, pages 193–231.

Ferrúsola wrote in Spanish but thought in French and Italian, or such is the impression given by his sentences. The diary is written in a clear hand and is signed twice by Ferrúsola. Quite often his words, styles, and spelling are those used only by one familiar with Andalusian speech and usages. There are many gallicisms as well. Ferrúsola's diary of 42 pages here printed in translation is from P de C 2353. It has recently been printed in Spanish in Holmes, *Documentos,* pages 75–130. There are a number of slight differences in my copy and reading from the same source that Holmes uses. I have also differed from him in sentence structure. Moreover, in a number of instances he corrected the original text.

   3. Instructions to Barnó y Ferrúsola in the cruising station between Nogales and Arkansas, signed by Gayoso, November 7, 1793, certified copy in P de C 42; draft in P de C 123. See above, pp. 76–77, 81.
   4. Draft of an order signed by Gayoso, Natchez, November 9, 1793; drafts [Gayoso] to Delinó, Natchez, November 7, 1793; to Beauregard, Natchez, November 10, 1793; all in P de C 123.

DIARY

Juan Barnó y Ferrúsola. On board His Majesty's galiot *La Flecha*, at the wharf of the post of Nogales. February 16, 1794.[1]

Diary of the departure from the Plaza of Natchez for the cruise that I am going to make from the post of Nogales to that of Arkansas, in His Majesty's galiot *La Flecha*, armed with eight bronze swivel guns, eight guns with their bayonets and ammunition, fourteen oarsmen, a carpenter, a seaman [*proel*], and the *patrón*, Antonio Molina,[2] with two artillerymen and four soldiers of the guard infantry, according to the secret instructions that Señor Don Manuel Gayoso de Lemos, governor of said Plaza has given me today, the ninth of November 1793.[3]

November 9, 1793. At five o'clock this afternoon, in the presence of said governor and other officials, I departed from this wharf with a fresh southeast wind. After a short while we hoisted the sails. At six we made camp at the head of the batture above Natchez. Night fell with cloudy skies, and the same wind continued until twelve.

November 10, 1793. From twelve till two in the morning, the wind southeast, and suddenly [it] changed to east by south, with heavy rain that lasted until six o'clock, at which time it changed to a cold north wind. We set out, but as it got cold we were obliged to land. At three in the afternoon it calmed down a bit and we again

1. See above p. 76, n. 5 and below, p. 231.
2. Antonio Molina was *patrón* of *La Felipa*, which had carried presents to the Indians at Nogales in 1793 (Beauregard to Gayoso, No. 318, Nogales, July 9, 1793, P de C 47). He was an officer on the Commission of Limits under Casa Calvo in 1805. Documents referring to that commission are in P de C, legs. 70B, 142A, 225B. He is not to be confused with the better known Bernardo Molina, patrón and commandant of various *galeras* from 1795 on. The latter's *asiento* is in P de C 538A.
3. Instructions to Ferrúsola dated November 7, certified copy in P de C 42; draft in P de C 123. See also Carondelet to Gayoso, New Orleans, November 27, 1793, P de C 20.

left and went two leagues from Natchez, where we slept. Night fell, with clear horizons and with the same wind, only weaker. At 9 o'clock, on the other side of the river, Mr. Macarty,[4] with his boat drifting, passed close to the other shore. He was called by his name and was understood to be talking to his Negroes. Seeing that he did not come, I again called him, telling him that I had a paper to give him from the governor of the Plaza of Natchez. He then pretended to begin crossing, but when he reached the strongest part of the current, he had them row at full speed. Seeing this, I boarded a boat and began to drift down to catch him, and during the whole time I was calling to him, but he refused to answer. Having pursued him for more than a league and being sure by his voice that it was he, I returned to the galiot because of not being able to abandon it, realizing that the governor would not approve my chasing him into Natchez.

November 11, 1793. At midnight the wind changed to the north. At six o'clock the weather cleared and the wind changed to a weak northeast wind. We sailed away, but the wind having become stronger at 8 o'clock, we tied up again. At ten the wind changed again to a fresher north one. At twelve o'clock, the wind unchanged. All the rest of the day we did not travel because of this wind. Night fell, with the horizons being squally, and [they] continued to be so until twelve.

November 12, 1793. From midnight till six in the morning, fresh north wind with rain. All this day it has continued, but somewhat weaker. We went to sleep six leagues from Natchez. Night fell, with clear horizons and the wind unchanged.

4. Agustín Macarty was born in New Orleans about 1773 and began his service as a cadet on March 1, 1786. He was sublieutenant of the 6th company of the 1st battalion of the fixed Regiment of Louisiana. In 1793 he commanded a detachment on Bayou Pierre. Concerning the incident mentioned in the diary, Gayoso wrote Barnó y Ferrúsola on November 11, 1793, that Agustín Macarty had arrived here without his being recognized by Barnó y Ferrúsola. That was a bad beginning "for the good duty which I had hoped for from you." Gayoso trusted that the incident "will make you more vigilant" and that such occasions, which I regret very much, would not happen again." He added: "Since your commission is of such great importance and such an honor, I of course have no reason to relieve you of it." Barnó y Ferrúsola replied in his letter No. 1 from Nogales on November 23, 1793: "In the future and when I have concluded my expedition Your Excellency will be very satisfied with my conduct and vigilance, and then I will have the honor to present you with my diary" and you will see that "las faltas no han sido que por desgracia." (Both letters in P de C 47.)

DIARY   195

November 13, 1793. From midnight till six o'clock, when we unmoored, wind north ¼ northwest, weak. At seven I talked with two whites in a small pirogue that had departed from Natchez six days before to sell whiskey, sugar, and coffee at Coles Creek,[5] and who were returning to said plaza because of not having sold anything. At eight o'clock, a northwest wind, weak. A pirogue coming from Illinois drew up alongside; it was loaded with peltry and apples. Its patrón and owner, Mr. Martin, was on board, with two white rowers and a free Negro. I examined his passport. I asked if he had a letter or paper, and I found nothing on him.

The second sergeant of the Louisiana regiment, Manuel Ferreyra,[6] who is going in search of his discharge [*licencia*] was also there. At twelve o'clock, the same fresh wind, for which reason we have traveled only three leagues, and we are nine leagues from Natchez. Night fell, with clear horizons, very cold and the same wind.

November 14, 1793. From twelve o'clock at night till six in the morning the same wind was blowing. At eleven it changed to the southeast, quite weak. And we went to sleep above the batture of the Pequeño Golfo [Small Gulf].[7] Night fell, with clear horizons and the same wind.

The Event

Realizing that the boat we were towing hindered us so much from taking advantage of the little wind to make any headway against the current of the Pequeño Golfo, [at eleven o'clock this morning] I ordered the carpenter and the sailor Gañón to take it, and to take rifles to see if they could kill something at the batture. At two in the afternoon, having ascended the current, I heard many shouts on the other shore; I commanded that the galiot cross, considering that some misfortune might have happened to the men in the boat. I found the master carpenter disconsolate, saying that they had drawn the boat onto the island, on the sand, and that since the sand was treacherous, they lost control of the boat and it had sunk, and that if the sailor passing over the entanglement

5. A considerable creek at a big bend in the river (10 miles by water and 1½ miles by land), 21 miles from Natchez (Cramer, *Navigator*, p. 190).
6. Or Terreyna.
7. Or Petit-gulf; see Cramer, *Navigator*, p. 188. The distance from Natchez to Petit Gouffre was 31½ miles (Hutchins, *Historical Narrative*, pp. 425, 458).

[*embarada*] above the head of the island, trying to cross a channel of water, thinking it was not deep, had not taken hold of a pole of wood in order to take hold of it, he would have drowned. [The carpenter told us] that we should go quickly and give him aid, for he was holding onto it in the water, and that he does not know how to swim. I sent some people and they took him out. They went around the island and found that the boat had already passed. The boat had in it a mariner's overcoat, a hammer, a *utarda*,[8] and a duck.

November 15, 1793. From midnight till six, when we set sail, light variable winds to the east. At eight the wind changed to a very weak southeast wind. I went to eat at Bayou Pierre [Stony Creek].[9] I went to ask Me. Richars if she had a small pirogue for sale. She told me she had none; I then entered the bayou, where I found a *chalán* [flatboat][10] partly destroyed. I returned to the dwelling, and asked the woman to whom it belonged. She answered that it belonged to an Englishman named Vitli [Billy], who had gone away with Colonel Brain [Bruin][11] to New Orleans. I asked her if she thought the owner would care if I took four boards from it, paying her for them, now that it was useless. She answered that she believed I would be doing him a favor, because the Indians were burning all of them, [and] that when he returned he might not find it at all. Because of her answer, I told her I would take four, and that she should tell the owner when he returned, and that he should write down what I should pay for them; that I would pay for them on my return from my voyage; otherwise that he should present himself to the secretary of the governor of the

---

8. Possibly a goose. *Outarde* in French means a Canada goose.

9. Bayoux aux Pierres; see Cramer, *Navigator*, p. 188, and above, p. 155, n. 8. It has been described as 3 large rivulets 10 miles below Big Black River (Collot, *Journey in North America*, 2, 55, 56). Five miles below Stony River in the middle of the Mississippi are 2 islands called Las Islas du Bayou de Pierre (Stony Creek Islands). They form 3 passages, only one of which is navigable (ibid.). The other 2 are stopped up by driftwood. Collot says the islands are 28 miles above Natchez (*Journey*, 2, 57).

10. See above, p. 51.

11. Colonel Peter Bryan Bruin settled in the Natchez district and became one of the leaders of that community. His residence was 11 miles below Grand Gulf at Bayou Pierre. For a short sketch of Bruin see Whitaker, *Mississippi Question*, p. 281, n. 28; Miró to Valdez, No. 89, New Orleans, June 18, 1789, AHN 3888; printed in *ETHSP*, 20 (1948), 113–14. See also short sketch in Holmes, *Documentos*, p. 81.

DIARY   197

Plaza of Natchez, who would pay for them; [and] that for that purpose I was writing him. I ordered the master carpenter to go and choose them, and I ordered them brought aboard, and during the days I shall be at Nogales gathering provisions (as the instructions forewarn me),[12] I'll have a boat made.

At two o'clock we departed with a very light southeast wind, and I went to sleep at the lower point of the Gran Golfo [Grand Gulf].[13] Night fell, with cloudy horizons.

November 16, 1793. From midnight until one o'clock in the afternoon a fresh south wind blew, with much rain. At the latter time the wind changed to a strong north ¼ northeast one; and it continued to rain all day, which prevented our traveling. Night fell, with overcast horizons.

November 17, 1793. From midnight till six o'clock in the morning it was calm with rain. At that time it stopped, and the wind changed to a light north one. We sailed. At one o'clock it changed to a south wind. At that time I examined a passport of a *bercha* that was coming from St. Louis, Illinois, loaded with peltry. Its owner, Mr. Genjambre[14] (who states that he is to settle in New Orleans with his family), and four rowers and its patrón, all white Creoles of Illinois, were on board the vessel. I examined their trunks and the boxes of the sailors, and I found no letters or papers. He states that the commandant at Nogales took them from him, for which reason we continued on our way and went to sleep above the Gran Golfo. Night fell, with clear horizons.

November 18, 1793. From midnight till six o'clock in the morning, a light variable south wind. The sky is clear. At the latter hour we left. At eight o'clock the wind changed to a light westerly one. We continued sailing and went to sleep at the upper head of the last island of the three mouths or islands. Night fell, with clear horizons.

   12. See instructions to Barnó y Ferrúsola cited above, p. 192, n. 3.
   13. See above, p. 156, n. 11. The Grand Gulf is at the Big Black River, 39 miles below Nogales (Cramer, *Navigator*, p. 188). For another compilation of mileage see Imlay, *Topographical Description of the Western Territory of North America*, App. I, pp. 387–458, containing Hutchins, *Historical Narrative and Topographical Description of Louisiana and West Florida*, pp. 425–29. See also Ashe, *Travels in America*, pp. 285–86; Francis Baily, *Journal of a Tour in the Unsettled Parts of North America in 1796 and 1797* (London, 1856), pp. 277–78.
   14. Gingenbre. See Houck, *History of Missouri*, 2, 55.

November 19, 1793. From midnight till twelve noon, fresh southeast wind with heavy rain, which has prevented our sailing; nevertheless I desired to take advantage of the good wind. We set sail and went to retire one league from Nogales because of having had the good fortune of the wind changing to a south-southeast at two o'clock. Night fell, with cloudy horizons [and] light rain.

November 20, 1793. From midnight till six o'clock in the morning, when I left, light south-southeast wind, without rain. At seven-thirty I arrived at Nogales;[15] I showed the instructions to that commander. At nightfall I sent the boat to the other side. At six the word had begun to be circulated. Night fell, with cloudy skies. Today the construction of the boat was started.[16]

Note

From the Plaza of Natchez to the post of Nogales, as the river is low, it appears to be forty-eight leagues, but when the river is high, it is only thirty-five leagues.[17]

November 21, 1793. This day there is no news. The provisions and fetters[18] are being made. At night the word was given, and there was no news in the guard.[19]

November 22, 1793. The same as the day before; the guard continues as usual and the boat was finished.

November 23, 1793. At two in the afternoon we departed from the wharf of this post with a north-northwest wind. I have exchanged soldiers Joseph Ferrer and Tiburcio Sebilla, because of their being ill, for those in the same corps named Juan Azabal and Josef Agulera. I have taken a month's ration, a barrel, and a half sackful of *gru*.[20] I have borrowed a swivel gun, twenty-five bullets and grape-

---

15. See Ferrúsola to [Gayoso], No. 1, on *La Flecha* at Nogales, November 20, 1793, P de C 41 [47?]. In this letter he tells the governor that he arrived at Nogales at 7:30. Ferrúsola's letters Nos. 1, 2, 3, from Nogales, all dated November 29, 1793, are in P de C 47.

16. See entry for November 15, above, p. 196.

17. See Ferrúsola's table of distances in his entry for January 10, 1794, below, p. 220. There it is stated that it was 40 leagues.

18. *Prisiones*—shackles, fetters, chains. See Ferrúsola's instructions cited above, p. 192, n. 3, and which are summarized above, pp. 191–92.

19. This means that the guard was maintained and nothing unusual occurred.

20. "Un barril y medio saco de gru," or hominy. See McDermott, *Glossary of Mississippi Valley French*, p. 84.

shot[21] for it, five hundred musket cartridges with bullets, an engineer's chain, and two pairs of fetters[22]. We went to sleep a league and a half above said post. Night fell, with clear horizons. At six o'clock the word was given, and in the guard there was nothing unusual.

November 24, 1793. From midnight till six o'clock in the morning, when we departed, rowing, nothing new. At nine the wind changed to southeast, which favors us. It has continued all day. We went to sleep eight leagues from Nogales. Night fell, with clear horizons. At six the word was given, and in the guard there was no news.

November 25, 1793. From midnight till six o'clock in the morning, when we departed, rowing, little wind, nothing new. All day it continued calm [and we had to row]. At five-thirty in the afternoon I saw a pirogue and smoke on the other side, I went to examine it and found that it was Choctaw Chief Chafale, who was hunting. Today we are thirteen leagues from Nogales. Night fell, with clear horizons. At six the word was taken, and in the guard there has been no news.

November 26, 1793. From midnight till six o'clock in the morning, when we left, rowing, nothing new. It was calm and drizzling. At nine the wind, shifting to the southeast, began to calm a little. It has continued so all day long. We traveled six more leagues, and we are nineteen leagues away from Nogales. Night fell, with squally horizons. At six the word was taken, and in the guard there has been no news.

November 27, 1793. From midnight till six o'clock in the morning, when we departed, rowing, nothing new. Wind to the south and the horizon very cloudy. At eight o'clock it calmed down and began to rain. At nine, because of the heaviness of the rain, I was forced to land, and at this point a pirogue was seen on the other shore. I commanded it to cross over, and found that it was one returning from the hunt with a passport from the commandant of New Madrid [The pirogue carried] its owner, Antonio Tartell, and an enlisted man [*enganchado*][22] [named] Cristoval de Rojas, both Spaniards, and one Creole from New Orleans. I investigated to see if he had some letters, but he had none. All day the rain con-

21. *Metralla.*
22. See *engagé* in McDermott, *Glossary,* p. 73.

tinued, for which reason we have not left. At six the word was given, and in the guard there has been no news. We are twenty-one leagues from Nogales.[23]

November 28, 1793. From midnight till noon, rain. At this hour I enlisted Cristoval de Rojas[24] with a rank of sailor, because he knows the upper river very well, and with the obligation to go hunting for me when I command him to do so. And since he has no ration, I must feed him until the governor may decide if he is to remain as such; and if he does not approve, I must pay him at the rate of eleven pesos a month. At two o'clock it stopped raining and the wind changed to the south. We untied and set sail. At three the wind changed to southwest, and at the turn where we were, we lowered the sail and continued rowing, in spite of a little rain. We went to sleep twenty-four leagues from Nogales. At eight o'clock in the evening the sailor Miguel Mas was near the fire with others, complaining because he had to stand guard, [saying] that this was badly ordered, because he knew the ordinances of the navy. The patrón, who had heard him, told him to keep quiet and that he should do what he was ordered. He answered that henceforth he would do nothing. The patrón again told him to keep quiet and to take care that he [the patrón] should not go to where Miguel was. Miguel answered, "What do I care if you do come here." The patrón became angry at such a reply, and having in his hand no staff other than his saber, he struck him twice with the flat of it. With this he [Miguel] shut up and went to his tent. After a short time [had passed and] without being seen by anyone, he deserted and was not missed until eleven o'clock, when he was to stand guard, which someone else carried out for him.[25] The rest of the night passed with nothing unusual transpiring.

November 29, 1793. All last night and this day, rain, west wind. The entire day was spent searching for Miguel Mas, and he was not found. I sent the boat to the camp of the Choctaw Chief Ytelagana,[26] which was three leagues below ours on the opposite side of

---

23. On November 28, 1793, Ferrúsola wrote a letter saying he was at 19 leagues above Nogales and that he was taking all vigilance and care to observe and watch.

24. Rojas was used on other expeditions of Barnó y Ferrúsola. See Barnó y Ferrúsola to Gayoso, Natchez, Nov. 11, 1794, P de C 47.

25. See Barnó y Ferrúsola's letter to Gayoso written on Nov. 28, 1793, P de C 47.

26. Or Itelaghana.

the river, to see if he was there, and he was not found there. This chief has promised me to look for him and that he would bring him aboard if he should find him, even if I am twenty-five leagues further up the river. I promised him a small barrel of *aguardiente* [a kind of rum] and a shirt for his work. At six the word was taken, and there was no news from the guard.

November 30, 1793. It ceased raining at midnight, wind to the north. At daybreak I ordered two shots fired to see if the sailor Miguel Mas would return, in case he might have gotten lost in the forest; but seeing that[27] he did not appear after two more shots were fired, we rowed away. I ordered the mariner whom I [had] engaged on the 28th[28] to eat with the rest in place of Mas, who deserted, and thus he was engaged from that day.[29] The rest of the day the same wind continued, and we are twenty-seven leagues from Nogales, before entering [at the entrance of] the Grapein Island,[30] where I can well observe the freshets.[31] At six o'clock the word was taken, and in the guard there was no news.

December 1, 1793. Nothing unusual occurred from midnight till ten o'clock in the morning. At that time we left, not being able to do so earlier because of the heavy fog, but, however, we were always very vigilant and passing the word [*passando la palabra*]. Light north wind. We went up by the Mississippi and [along] Grapein Island, and the boat went on the inner side. I went to sleep at the head of the Island of La Cabeza de los Muertos [Death's Head].[32] The channel that this island has does not have water when the river is low. We are thirty-two leagues from Nogales. Night fell, with clear horizons. At six the word was taken, and in the guard there was no news.

27. Ferrúsola appears to have desired to enter here the hour of the day up to which time they waited, but no specific hour appears in the original. See his letter No. 5 to Gayoso, written 24 leagues above Nogales, November 30, 1793, P de C 47.

28. Cristoval de Rojas. See also Barnó y Ferrúsola to Gayoso, Natchez, November 11, 1793.

29. Ferrúsola to Gayoso, on *La Flecha*, 19 leagues above Nogales, November 28, 1793, P de C 47, and Ferrúsola to Gayoso, Natchez, August 11, 1794, P de C 47. In his letter No. 4, dated November 28, 1793, at 24 leagues above Nogales, Ferrúsola speaks of his trouble on board and of the desertion.

30. A letter of [Ferrúsola to Gayoso?] No. 5 dated November 30, saying that they were 24 leagues above Nogales, is in P de C 47.

31. *Las avenidas* or arrivals.

32. Or Ile de la Tête des Morts.

December 2, 1793. From midnight till six o'clock in the morning, when we left, rowing, there were no occurrences. Light variable winds to the east. At eleven-thirty we passed through the Mississippi and the boat [passed] on the outside of the small barren Islote de la Batura de la Coupé. At sunset we landed, being thirty-six leagues from Nogales. Night fell, with squally horizons. At six the word was taken, and there has been no news from the watch.

December 3, 1793. All last night it rained. At four o'clock in the morning the wind changed to the west. At eight o'clock the same wind and rain continued. At noon the same. At five o'clock in the afternoon the rain ceased and the wind changed to a north one. At six o'clock it cleared up, and the word was given, and the guard reported no incidents.

December 4, 1793. From midnight till six o'clock in the morning, when we left, rowing, no occurrences. Wind, light, south. At nine o'clock it changed to the southeast. We hoisted the sails. At twelve o'clock, the wind having calmed, I ordered rowing. At two we ascended Rascins [or Prascins] Island. The boat has been unable to penetrate within because of the channel not having water. At four we began to ascend Gouble Island, the boat penetrating within.[33] At sunset we landed. This day, without cooking [without stopping to eat],[34] we traveled ten leagues and are forty-six leagues from Nogales. At six o'clock the word was taken, and there was no news from the watch. Night fell, with clear horizon.

December 5, 1793. From midnight till six o'clock in the morning, when we left, nothing unusual occurred. Light southeast wind and cloudy. At eight o'clock the same wind continue[d]. At twelve, the same. At two we began to ascend the Yslote Chicó [Small Chicó Isle], and the boat stopped within it. I [we] went to sleep above this island. Today, with oars and using the sails a little, we have traveled eight leagues and are at fifty-four leagues from Nogales. Night fell, with squally horizons. At six the word was given, and there has been nothing unusual happening in the guard.

December 6, 1793. From midnight till four o'clock in the morning, strong southeast wind. At six o'clock we started out rowing. Without unusual incident. Drizzling. At seven, when the rain became

---

33. This means between the island and the shore.
34. "Sin haber hecho de comer."

DIARY 203

heavy, I ordered putting to land opposite the Gran Isla Chicó [Chicó Island].[35] All day the rain continued. Night fell, with squally horizons. At six the word was given, and there has been no news in the watch.

December 7, 1793. From midnight till six o'clock, when we left, rowing, much rain, with wind to the southeast. Nothing unusual. At this hour the rain ceased and the wind changed to the north. At ten o'clock we had ascended the Gran Isla Chicó, and the boat [ascended] on the inside, where it is said there are so many stumps that it is impossible for a big boat to pass, which has delayed it a long time, making me suspect that some misfortune had befallen it. Notwithstanding this delay and the contrary wind, today we traveled, by poling, four leagues, and we are fifty-eight leagues from Nogales. Night fell, with clear horizons. At six the word was given, and there has been no news in the watch.

December 8, 1793. From midnight until six o'clock, when we started out, rowing, there have been no occurrences. North-northwest light wind. Last night a thick frost formed. At seven-thirty, while passing the *Seneaux*[36] of twelve leagues, we met the boat of Mr. Verdom,[37] coming from St. Louis with a passport from that commandant, which I examined. I took all the letters that it and the enlisted men had, which I sealed in a small box [and] which I sent by the boat to the governor[38] of Natchez, as well as a box and clothing and an inventory that belonged to the sailor Miguel Mas, who deserted.[39] At one o'clock in the afternoon we met the boat belonging to the patrón Tropé, which also was coming from St. Louis with a passport from that commandant, which I have examined and investigated. I have also taken all his letters and those of the enlisted men, as well as those that Madame Peyroux, wife of the commandant of Sainte Geneviève, had, all of which I have placed together in a box, which, sealed with another remittance

35. *Chicots*, in French, means stumps. See McDermott, *Glossary*, p. 51.
36. *Seneaux*, in old French, means signs or signposts. Possibly it might mean channels.
37. Or Verdon. See Houck, *Spanish Régime* and *History of Missouri*, and consult indexes; Nasatir, *Before Lewis and Clark*, 2, 722.
38. Barnó y Ferrúsola's letters, Nos. 6 and 7, dated December 8, 12 leagues below the Arkansas, and No. 8, written 10 leagues below the Arkansas, are in P de C 47. He tells the governor he is examining the boats that are descending the river.
39. See entry for November 28, above, p. 200.

dispatch, I have sent by the same Tropé to said governor. Given these delays, today we have only traveled three leagues or just the Seneaux of twelve leagues within which the boat passed. We are sixty-one leagues from Nogales. Night fell, with clear horizons. At six the word was taken, and no incidents have been reported from the guard.

December 9, 1793. From midnight till six o'clock in the morning, when we left, rowing, nothing unusual occurred. Light north wind. At one o'clock we had traveled up the Seneaux of nine leagues, the boat going through the inside channel. At four o'clock, because of not being able to sail during the day, we landed opposite the Seneaux of six leagues in order to survey the tributaries[40] of the Mississippi. Today we have made four leagues and we are sixty-five leagues from Nogales. Night fell, with clear horizons. At six the word was given, and no news has come from the watch.

December 10, 1793. At midnight the wind changed to a very strong south wind with rain. At 8 o'clock in the morning it continued, at ——[41] the same wind and rain. At ——[42] the rain ceased and the wind changed to the north. We cannot leave because it is too late, and because we have to ascend the Seneaux for six leagues, and because the boat must go inland, and because we now have a good place to survey the tributaries[43] of the Mississippi. Night fell, with clear horizons and the same wind. At six o'clock the word was given, and in the watch there were no unusual occurrences.

December 11, 1793. From twelve till six o'clock in the morning, when we left, rowing, nothing new. Wind to the north. At seven it changed to southwest. At nine it changed to west ¼ northwest, cool and gusty. At ten the northwest wind became so strong that it forced us to tie up and fasten the boat securely. The wind increased until six o'clock in the afternoon. Nothwithstanding this, taking advantage of the light wind in the morning, we sailed up the Seneaux for six leagues, and the boat went through the channel. At this time the word was given, and no news has come from the watch. This day we have traveled only two leagues, and we are sixty-seven leagues from Nogales. Night fell, with clear horizons.

40. To reconnoiter the coming and going of vessels in the Mississippi River.
41. No hour given.
42. No hour given.
43. See above, n. 40.

December 12, 1793. From midnight till six o'clock, when we rowed away, nothing unusual occurred. Very cold northwest wind. At eight o'clock a pirogue came alongside. On board was an Englishman named Arce Price, inhabitant of Natchez, who was coming alone from Arkansas, hunting with a license from that commandant. He had no papers whatever except some letters, which I made into a parcel and directed to the governor of Natchez. I have written him a friendly letter. At ten o'clock the same wind. At twelve o'clock it still continues, and we have started to pass by the Gran Isla au Bled [Wheat Island] through the principle channel, the boat passing within. At two o'clock we were past it, and at sunset we made camp, having traveled today only three leagues because of the contrary winds. We are seventy leagues from Nogales. Night fell, with clear horizons. At six o'clock the word was taken, and there was no news from the guard.

December 13, 1793. From midnight till six o'clock in the morning, when we rowed away, there has been nothing new. Light variable winds to the northeast. At twelve o'clock we came opposite the Arkansas River. We ate, and I have dispatched a very small pirogue that we found on the way and which I had ordered the ship's carpenter to fix, with the two sailors, Cristoval de Rojas and Juan Pontenson, whom I ordered to take a letter that the governor of Natchez gave me for the commandant of that post and who commanded me in the instructions to remit it to said gentleman, which I have accompanied with an official letter.[44] I told said sailors that I would await them at the detachment of the White River,

---

44. See Barnó y Ferrúsola to Delinó, on *La Flecha* at the mouth of the Arkansas, December 13, 1793, in which he asked Delinó for information. Delinó replied from Fort Estevan de Arkansas, December 15, 1793, warning Ferrúsola of hostile Chickasaw Indians who were hunting in the district of La Cupa, between the White and St. Francis Rivers, but Delinó's reply contained no mention of rumored hostilities on the upper river. (P de C 47; copy enclosed in Barnó y Ferrúsola to Gayoso, No. 10, on *La Flecha*, 6 leagues above mouth of Arkansas, December 16, 1793, P de C 47.) The detachment at White River, which afforded a view of the freshets of the Mississippi, was Barnó y Ferrúsola's cruising station. Gayoso notified all the post commanders on the upper river of Ferrúsola's commission and ordered them to supply him with whatever provisions, troops, or materials he requested (draft of an order signed by [Gayoso], Natchez, November 9, 1793, P de C 123; draft [Gayoso] to Beauregard, Natchez, November 10, 1793, P de C 123).

The following letters from Ferrúsola are in P de C 47: 4 leagues below the Altura de Arkansas, December 12, 1793; at mouth of Arkansas, December 13, 1793; Altura de Arkansas, December 14, 1793; No. 9, same date and place.

where I shall cruise, having been informed that it is a good place to watch the navigation of the Mississippi and to prevent the ships that come from above from going to Arkansas, in case there might be any suspicion of enemies. At sunset we camped two leagues above said river. Night fell with clear horizons. At six o'clock the word was taken, and no news was reported from the watch.

December 14, 1793. From midnight until six o'clock in the morning, when we left, rowing, there was no news. At eight o'clock a pirogue was seen on the other side of the river. The flag was hoisted. Then it acted as if ready to escape. I ordered a swivel gun shot with powder fired to force it to land. I made the crossing, and overtaking it on the windward side, I found it was a small boat that was coming from Arkansas with a white man and a Negro. I asked where they were going; they answered, to hunt. I asked for their passports and they told me that the commandant of that place had not wished to give them any. For this reason and because they tried to flee, and seeing that the Negro did not have a permit from his owner, whom they say is Madame Menar, I ordered them to go back. I took the gun from the Frenchman, made the Negro come aboard, and placed an armed soldier on board together with the white man, with orders that they stay in the prow of the boat; and I shall leave them with the White River detachment so that they may go and get a passport from its commandant if they wish to go hunting again, in order to show him that without this requirement they must not leave the post. While I was examining the boat, a pirogue descended with a certain Mr. Michel [Mitchell] and two white enlisted men [*engagés*]; all three were Americans with passports from the commandant of New Madrid. This one [Mr. Michel] states that he is an envoy or courier to our ambassador in America.[45] He told me verbally that five thousand Frenchmen are to descend in

---

45. Thomas, or Medad, Mitchell was sent to New Orleans by Jaudenes and Viar with letters for Carondelet. See Nasatir and Liljegren, *LHQ, 12,* reprint p. 32 Jaudenes and Viar to Carondelet, August 21, 1793; others encl. in Carondelet to Alcudia, No. 19 res., New Orleans, October 24, 1793, and No. 21 res., New Orleans, November 6, 1793, AHN 3898; Jaudenes and Viar to Carondelet, August 21, 1793, printed in *AHAR 1896, 1,* 999–1000, copy encl. in Carondelet to Gayoso, New Orleans, October 8, 1793, P de C 20.

Mitchell's autobiography is in P de C 208A and 2363. Mitchell arrived in New Madrid on March 27. He carried Portell's letter to Carondelet, New Madrid, December 5, 1793, P de C 27A. See also on Mitchell: Carondelet to Portell, New Orleans, April 3, 1793, P de C 19; draft in same legajo. [Mitchell] to Genêt, New York, Septem-

May.[46] He had a letter for the commandant of Nogales from the commandant of New Madrid; he had another for the commandant of Natchez, and many other private letters for that plaza and New Orleans, as well as papers. I have taken them all and put them in a small box and directed it to the governor of Natchez, accompanying an official letter for said gentleman. The letter for the commandant of Nogales I returned to him so that he may give it to him on his way down, as he has told us that it pertains to the royal service.[47] At two o'clock in the afternoon, having arrived at the detachment that exists in one of the [mouths] of the White River where I have made camp, I inquired of the corporal and the two soldiers there if they knew the white man and the Negro in the boat. They answered, yes, and that the commandant is not accustomed to giving passports to these people who go out for only a few days to hunt. Seeing that it was not their fault, I let them go. Night fell, with clear horizons. At six the word was given, and in the watch there is no news.

December 15, 1793. From midnight until six o'clock in the morning, when I departed, rowing, nothing new. Calm and very cloudy. I ascended a league behind a point where the ship is hidden and the river is very narrow. I have the advantage of seeing all that is going on on the Mississippi,[48] which I did not have to such an ex-

---

ber 16, 1793, *Archives du Ministère des Affaires Etrangères, Etats-Unis Supplément,* Vol. XXVIII, folios 78-83v; same to same, New York, September 17, 1793, ibid., folios 84-87v; Gayoso to Carondelet, No. 16 res., Natchez, December 23, 1793, P de C 27B; in *AHAR 1896, 1,* 1029-32, and AHN 3897; another original in P de C 42, and certified copy encl. in Carondelet to Las Casas, No. 100 res., New Orleans, January 24, 1794, P de C 1447.

Mitchell left New Madrid on December 5, 1793. See Portell to Carondelet, No. 220, New Madrid, December 6, 1793, P de C 27A; and Carondelet's reply, dated New Orleans, January 3, 1794, P de C 21. On Mitchell see also Portell to Carondelet, No. 129, New Madrid, March 19, 1793, P de C 26; and Carondelet's reply, New Orleans, April 3, 1793, original in P de C 19; draft in P de C 125. Draft to Jaudenes and Viar, New Orleans, March 6, 1794, P de C 104A; examination of Mitchell by Gayoso, Natchez, April 10, 1794, P de C 2363; Gayoso to Carondelet, No. 8 res., Natchez, April 18, 1793, P de C 2363; in Houck, *Spanish Régime,* 2, 4-8. Portell to Gayoso, New Madrid, December 6, 1793, P de C 47; passport and letter signed by Jaudenes and Viar, New York, October 1, 1793, AHN 3895 bis; and letter of introduction [passport?], dated New York, October 5, 1793, ibid.

46. This news caused Ferrúsola some concern, and he suggested to Gayoso that his cruise be extended to 25 leagues above New Madrid (Barnó y Ferrúsola to Gayoso, No. 9, on *La Flecha* at latitude of Arkansas River, December 14, 1793, P de C 47).

47. Barnó y Ferrúsola to Gayoso, No. 9.

48. Or reconnoitering well the *avenidas* of the Mississippi.

tent the night before. At nine o'clock it began raining. At ten a pirogue from New Madrid descended with a passport from that commandant. It was headed by the Spaniard who has been a corporal of the Regiment of Louisiana, named Manuel Perez, and two white men. He has three letters: one for the commandant of Arkansas, another for the commandant of Nogales, and a parcel for the governor of Natchez. I examined the passport and returned his letters, and I made him go immediately when he told me he was carrying mail, because the commandant of New Madrid did not have too much confidence in Mr. Michel, who is the one I met in the pirogue yesterday and who says he had been sent as an express. For the rest of the day it rained a lot. The pirogue that I sent with the mail still has not returned from Arkansas. At six o'clock the word was taken, and nothing unusual happened in the guard.

December 16, 1793. All last night and this day, copious rain; south wind with much mist, which prevents our seeing the other bank of the river, for which reason I have stationed a watch there. Night fell, with cloudy horizons, and day and night the word is passed [*pasado la palabra*].[49]

December 17, 1793. Rain still continues, mist, wind, and the watch. At six o'clock this afternoon the pirogue I sent to Arkansas returned with no news. That commandant acknowledges the receiving of mine [my letter] and sends me another for the governor of Natchez, which I shall send by the first possible occasion. At seven o'clock it ceased raining and the wind changed to a strong north one.

December 18, 1793. From midnight until three o'clock in the afternoon, very strong north wind. At this hour I received mail from the commandant of Arkansas that encloses another from the commandant of New Madrid, in which he tells him that the French are making an expedition against this province in the American states in the Ohio River and that consequently he should get ready, for they said they were to descend in March according to the news that our *chargé d'affaires*[50] in those states has communicated. As

---

49. Two letters of Barnó y Ferrúsola, December 16, Nos. 10 and 11, are dated 6 leagues above the mouth of the Arkansas (P de C 47).

50. Josef de Jaudenes and Josef de Viar were the ones referred to as Spanish *chargés d'affaires* in Philadelphia at this time. Technically, they had no diplomatic rank, but Gardoqui had left them in charge upon his departure.

a consequence of this news, I have acknowledged receipt of said letter to the aforementioned commandant, and I advised him that in the morning, notwithstanding the scarcity of provisions I was experiencing, I would sail with greatest speed to give aid to that post [New Madrid], and with this answer I sent off the messenger.[51] At six o'clock the word was taken. At ten in the evening the wind became calm. Nothing unusual was reported from the guard.

December 19, 1793. From midnight until five-thirty o'clock in the morning, when we started rowing, with our destination being New Madrid—nothing new. Light southeast wind. At eleven o'clock it began to freshen. With light variable winds we raised the sails. At two o'clock, the same wind. We went up Concorn Island, the boat going within. At four o'clock we ascended Alexandre Island. This one has three inlets [mouths]. We passed through the main channel: the boat through one and the pirogue through another. We went to sleep at the head of it. Today we traveled eight leagues, and we are fourteen leagues from the principal mouth of the Arkansas. Night fell with clear horizons, and at six o'clock the word was taken, and nothing unusual was reported from the guard.

December 20, 1793. From midnight until five-thirty in the morning, when we started rowing, nothing new. Light west wind. At seven o'clock the wind became fresher and we hoisted the sails. Until seven-thirty we had it raised, and at that time we began to ascend Cayenne Island, which was at our prow [*que nos era por la proa*], and the boat entered within. Today we have made five

---

51. Barnó y Ferrusola to Gayoso, No. 11, on *La Flecha*, 6 leagues above the Arkansas, December 18, 1793, P de C 47; Portell to [Delinó], res., New Madrid, December 6, 1793, and Delinó to Ferrúsola, res., Arkansas, December 17, 1793, both encl. in Barnó y Ferrúsola to Gayoso, No. 11; Barnó y Ferrúsola to Delinó, res., on *La Flecha*, 6 leagues above mouth of Arkansas, December 18, 1793, P de C 123; copy encl. in Barnó y Ferrúsola, No. 11.

Mitchell reported that an attack on Louisiana was forming in the Western states. Portell had received news that the attack was being planned for March. (See above, 78, 82.) Speed was essential, for the river was rising rapidly and the invaders might arrive before March. Although provisions were scarce, Ferrúsola promised his crew double meat rations to speed their progress. If his supply ran out, he planned to buy meat from passing chalanes or hunters. He notified Gayoso of the reasons for his departing from his instructions. Ferrúsola would cooperate wih Portell should New Madrid be attacked, and if no attack materialized after he reached New Madrid, Ferrúsola said he would return to Nogales and resume his original cruise until new orders arrived. (See above cited references and Barnó y Ferrúsola to Gayoso, 6 leagues above the mouth of the Arkansas, December 19, 1793, P de C 47.)

leagues, and we are nineteen leagues from the principal mouth of the Arkansas. Night fell, with clear horizons. The word was given at six o'clock, and no news was reported by the watch.

December 21, 1793. From midnight until five-thirty o'clock in the morning, when we rowed away, nothing new. Southeast wind, which is blowing against us. Last night much frost fell. At this hour we began to ascend the Isla Chat [Cat Island] by the main channel, and as it has three inlets, the boat shall go through one, the pirogue through another. At four we ascended Mitasas Island and the boat penetrated within. Because of contrary wind today we have only made three leagues and we are twenty-one leagues from the principal mouth of the Arkansas. Night fell, with clear horizons. At six o'clock word was given, and in the watch, nothing new.

December 22, 1793. From midnight until five-thirty o'clock in the morning, when we rowed away, no news. Southeast wind. Last night a heavy frost fell. At eleven o'clock we ascended the Isla Felip [Felip Island], the channel of which does not have water when the river is low. At twelve o'clock we went aboard a flatboat loaded with salted meat. We encountered three men and one woman with a passport from the commandant of New Madrid, which I examined. They were destined for New Orleans. They had no letters or papers except one for the last named plaza and another for the governor of Natchez. These I made into a parcel [*pliego*] and directed it to said governor. This day, because of the wind, we have traveled only six leagues and we are twenty-seven leagues from the principal mouth of the Arkansas. Night fell, with squally horizons. At six o'clock the word was taken, and nothing was reported by the guard.

December 23, 1793. From midnight until five-thirty in the morning, when we left, rowing, no news. Light southeast wind, with squally horizons. At eight o'clock it changed to a light south-southeast; at ten o'clock, to a rather fresh southwest wind. At eleven o'clock we met four pirogues, three of them tied together. Their owner [was] the *mestizo* [half-breed] Menar from Arkansas, accompanied by four white enlisted men returning from hunting in the Rió San Francisco [St. Francis River]. He does [did] not have a passport because he states that the commandant of Arkansas did not want to give one to those who go hunting and are residents of

DIARY

that place. At twelve o'clock the same fresh wind continued. At twelve-thirty it started raining. We continued traveling with the sails up and rowing without stopping to eat in order to take advantage of the wind. The rain continued, getting stronger, and at three o'clock I was forced to land at the small meadow of the St. Francis River. In spite of our having camped so early, we have made seven leagues, and we are thirty-four leagues from the principal mouth of the Arkansas River. Night fell, with rain. At six o'clock the word was taken. At ten o'clock the rain ceased and the weather cleared up. Nothing unusual occurred in the guard.

December 24, 1793. From midnight until five-thirty o'clock, when we rowed away, nothing new. It dawned with squally horizons and calm. At seven o'clock the wind shifted to the north and it began to clear up. At eight we started ascending the island that there is opposite the St. Francis River, and the pirogue went through the inside channel. All day the wind has continued, with a thick fog, for which reason I had the pirogue ascend the other side of the river. All day the pirogue was on watch, so that no one passed by without my notice. Today, because it is Christmas Eve, I landed earlier and let the people enjoy themselves by giving them four chickens, a little rice, and two flasks of rum. All night I have been on watch to ensure tranquility, which they considered satisfactory. We have only traveled four leagues, and we are thirty-nine leagues from the principal mouth of the Arkansas. Night fell, with clear horizons. At six o'clock the word was taken, and from the watch nothing new. At seven o'clock the horizons became cloudy.

December 25, 1793. From midnight until dawn, no news. Northeast wind. Today, because it is Christmas Day, we did not start rowing until seven o'clock. Half an hour later a gun with [safety catch], loaded with lead,[52] belonging to the enlisted man Gañón [and] which was lying on a *gallinero*[?] facing the prow, went off without any one touching it, and lodged part of its shot in the shin of the left leg of the artilleryman Joseph Chávez, and seven or eight bird shot in his right thigh. I ordered an immediate landing and the erecting of a tent in order to treat him. He was washed well with warm rum and had poultices of hot bee honey bound on his wounds. Should a ship pass, I shall send him to the Plaza of

---

52. "Cargada de plomo No. 2."

Natchez, in spite of the fact that I believe, judging by the way he received the shot, that it is not dangerous and I do not doubt that on board he will get well. Because it has become very cold, he has been placed in a cot in the cabin of the ship. Having done this, we continued our trip. Due to the contrary winds, we ascended by poling to a batture which is three leagues long. When we reached the head of said batture, because the wind became stronger, we came to land; we traveled no more, being at forty-two leagues from the principal mouth of the Arkansas River. Night fell, with clear horizons. At six o'clock the word was given, and in the watch, nothing new.

December 26, 1793. From midnight until five-thirty in the morning, when we rowed away, nothing new. Very fresh north wind, which is against us. At eight o'clock we met two pirogues that were coming from Illinois with passports. The name of one [man] is Pedro Vachard, with two whites, enlisted men, bound for Punta Cortada [Pointe Coupée]. The name of the other one, who was alone, is Amalt Guijon,[53] bound for Arkansas. All are travelers on the river and did not have letters because the commandant of New Madrid had taken them and had said that he would send them to the governor of Natchez by the patrón Felipe.[54] I examined their passports and they left. At this time I myself have treated the artilleryman Chávez, and found that his recovery was progressing and that the little holes caused by the shots are [were] beginning to form pus, and that he is much better, asking for soup and cigarettes. At nightfall we landed, and because of the strong opposing wind we have traveled only five leagues today, being forty-seven leagues from the principal mouth of the Arkansas River. Night fell, with squally skies. At six o'clock the word was taken, and nothing unusual has come from the guard.

December 27, 1793. From midnight until five-thirty in the morning, when we left, rowing, no news. Light north wind. We have begun to approach the batture of Sarpy Island, whose channel does not have water when the river is low. At seven o'clock the wind

---

53. Possibly Amable Guion.
54. Barnó y Ferrúsola's letter No. 12 is dated December 25, 1793, from 40 leagues above the mouth of the Arkansas, P de C 47. In it he said that the patrón Felipe will descend from New Madrid. Beauregard, in his letter No. 398 to Gayoso, dated Nogales, February 9, 1794, P de C 47, mentions a Felipe García as patrón of *La Activa,* bringing supplies and munitions to Nogales.

changed to a fresh northeast wind, and so cold that it prevents our continuing. At two o'clock we began to near the island of the Batura du Conseill [Council Shoals]. Today, because of the contrary wind, we have traveled only six leagues; we are fifty-four leagues from the principal mouth of the Arkansas River. The artilleryman fares so well that his wound scarcely hurts him. Night fell, with clear horizons, and the word was given at six o'clock, and no news from the guard.

December 28, 1793. From midnight till five-thirty in the morning, when we rowed away, no news. Light north wind. This night the gunner Chávez uncovered his wounded leg, and upon treating him, I found it much worse than it was yesterday, and it was completely frozen. I believe that he has contracted lockjaw, since he does not feel it at all; it is as if it were dead because of the cold weather last night. His leg had formed no more pus. At three-thirty we met José Blanco with a courier-pirogue from New Madrid. He has asked me on the part of the commandant to hasten my trip as much as possible. In view of this, tonight upon landing I shall rearrange the load, and tomorrow I shall place three more rowers on the galiot, placing two near the cargo and one at the prow, and two in the boat that follows our track, in order to remove the towline that we have.[55] They are the four soldiers from the guard, and the gunner Juan Azeytuno. I have assigned to them two *reales* and a *filete*. The carpenter Luís González has offered to follow in the pirogue for nothing. With these arrangements we shall make the trip much faster. All day, light variable winds to the south without our being able to hoist the sails, for which reason, and because of the delay and rearranging of the load, we have made only four leagues. We are fifty-eight leagues from the principal mouth of the Arkansas. All day the wound of the gunner Chávez has formed no pus,[56] and since he seems stupified,[57] I fear greatly that tonight he will die. Night fell with clear horizons. At six o'clock the word was taken, and nothing unusual occurred in the guard.

---

55. Ferrúsola rearranged the galiot's load so that 2 more oars could be added. It may be that this means that 2 more men were assigned to row the towboat. Everyone rowed including the soldiers. (See Barnó y Ferrúsola to Gayoso, on *La Flecha*, 2 leagues below Ecores de Perdom [Prud'homme], January 3, 1794, P de C 47.)

56. Or, the pus has not drained. See Barnó y Ferrúsola to Gayoso, No. 13, *La Flecha*, 73 leagues from the principal mouth of the Arkansas, December 30, 1793, P de C 47.

57. *Pasmado;* possibly lockjaw had developed.

December 29, 1793. Josef Chávez, artilleryman, died at midnight of lockjaw, and with the assistance of two witnesses, I immediately took inventory of his clothing, and this morning I had him buried in a high place five leagues below Ecores Amargó [Chickasaw Bluffs]. All day we have rowed with light variable southeast winds. At two o'clock in the afternoon we met a bercha that was coming from Illinois with salted meat. Its owner, Antonio La Chapelle, with four whites, enlisted men, all Creoles, were from that place. I examined his passport and the letters that he had for private persons. I made them into a parcel and addressed them to the governor of the Plaza of Natchez. Realizing the scarcity of provisions in which we were because of giving rations without discretion to all the people, I bought from him a *tercio* of bison meat;[58] the price upon which I agreed, in the presence of all the people, was 15 pesos cash, which I paid him. Today the four soldiers whom I have for guard duty and Juan Azeytuno, artilleryman, began rowing, earning two reales a day and *doble filete,* as all the sailors [receive]. All day today we have rowed, and because of the delays we have only traveled five leagues, and we are sixty-three leagues from the principal mouth of the Arkansas River. Night fell, with somewhat cloudy horizons. At six the word was taken, and there was no news from the guard.

December 30, 1793. From midnight until five-thirty o'clock in the morning, when we rowed away, no news. Light variable winds to the southeast. At ten o'clock we began to approach the island that exists before reaching the bluffs. The pirogue went within. At one o'clock we had passed it [the island]. The wind became cooler and we hoisted the sail. At two o'clock we came to the first bluffs. We crossed in order to prepare dinner and to await the pirogue. During this time I had the pleasure of seeing the beautiful location that there is here for building a fort, which would have a range of a league up the river and a league down. But this should be constructed an arpent inland, because the rock is not mineral although red, and [it] shakes a little, so it seems.[59] At three-thirty o'clock the pirogue arrived, we placed it within [inside] and hoisted the sail. And in spite of this delay, we have—by rowing and

---

58. "Un tercio de carne de cíbalo."
59. "Porque la piedra no es mineral, sí colorada y debuie [debule?] a lo que parece un poco."

sailing—traveled ten leagues today, and we are seventy-three leagues from the principal mouth of the Arkansas River.[60] Night fell, with cloudy horizons. At six o'clock the word was taken, and no news from the guard. Rain until eleven o'clock.

December 31, 1793. At midnight the weather began to clear up. The wind changed to a very strong north ¼ northwest, which has not permitted us to leave because it is against us. From eight o'clock until twelve the same [wind] continued, and it continued for the rest of the day, which has prevented our continuing. Night fell, with clear horizons. At six o'clock the word was taken, and no news has come from the guard.

January 1, 1794. From twelve until five-thirty in the morning, when we rowed away without any wind—nothing new. Last night a heavy frost formed. At eight o'clock we began to ascend Vilein Island. Its channel has no water when the river is low. At twelve o'clock a weak southeast wind began. In spite of this fact, we hoisted the sail. At one o'clock I went on board two big pirogues tied together, loaded with salted meat, coming from New Madrid and destined for New Orleans, with a passport from the commandant of the former, which I examined. He was bearing a letter to the commandant of Nogales, which I have included in a *pliego* [sealed packet of letters] for the governor of Natchez. I also examined other personal letters, all of which I took and [placed] in a pliego [which] I sent to the aforementioned governor. Its owner, Mr. Harbey, and two enlisted men are all whites and all Americans. At two o'clock we passed Vilein Island. At three o'clock we began to approach the Thousand Islands, and I went to sleep at the head of it [them], overlooking the Mississippi. It is [sic] a lone island, which is two leagues in length. It is called that because within it there are many small barren islands. It has only one entrance below and nine above, but when the river is low they have no water. Today, due to the large *baturas*,[61] we have traveled only six leagues, being seventy-nine leagues from the principal mouth of the Arkansas River. Night fell, with clear horizons. At six o'clock the word was given, and there has been no news from the guard.

60. Barnó y Ferrúsola's letter No. 13 of December 30, 1793, was written 73 leagues from the mouth of the Arkansas River (P de C 47).
61. See above, p. 159, n. 16.

January 2, 1794. From midnight until five-thirty, when we rowed away, calm. There has been nothing new. At six-thirty o'clock we began to approach the Isla Chicó [Chicó Island], following the river with the boat in the channel. At eight-thirty we had passed it. At eleven a weak south 1/4 southwest wind began to blow and we hoisted the sail. At one-forty-five we approached the Isla du Diable [Devil's Island],[62] opposite the bluffs, which are one league in extent and called Middle [Bluffs].[63] When the river is low, its channel has no water. At three-thirty we were beyond them and we camped two leagues further up, at the entrance of the Gran Isla aux Ecors [Great Bluffs Island]. We did not continue on because this one is so large, and in so doing we would lose our opportunity to examine the navigation of its channel,[64] which is very wide and has water. The people have not eaten today.[65] We have traveled seven leagues, being eighty-six leagues from the principal mouth of the Arkansas River. Night fell, with somewhat cloudy skies. At six o'clock the word was given, and there has been no news from the guards.

January 3, 1794. From midnight until seven-thirty in the morning there was much rain. At this hour, without news, we rowed away. Calm. We began to pass the Gran Isla aux Ecors on the outside, and the pirogue went inside. At ten o'clock we met Madame Portell, who was descending to New Orleans. Her husband, who is the commandant of the post of New Madrid,[66] sent her there because he has definite news that the Frenchmen [*Franceses de la Convención*] are going to attack it. In view of the news, I am hurrying still more to give him aid. I have not wished to write to the governor of Natchez in order not to lose time, but I wrote to him while the ship was sailing,[67] in order to give the letter to Felipe, who says he is descending as express-courier. In my letter I tell him not to worry about my hurrying. I [am] also wrote [writing] a letter to the commandant of New Madrid, which I [am] sent [sending]

62. See Cramer, *Navigator,* p. 167.
63. Middle Ecores. See above, p. 186, n. 63.
64. "Reconocer las avenidas de su canal."
65. Probably meaning they did not stop to prepare a meal.
66. Portell. See above, p. 56, n. 65 and p. 178, n. 50.
67. Barnó y Ferrúsola to Gayoso, on *La Flecha,* 2 leagues below Ecores de Perdom [Prud'homme], January 3, 1794, P de C 47.

with a man so that it may animate the people, [saying] that I hope to arrive the tenth of the present month. I have not sent the letter in order not to lose two men who are needed in the pirogue [and] in order to hasten, because if these go I shall probably be a day later in arriving. At eleven-thirty we arrived at Ecores de Perdom [Prud'homme Bluffs]. Light variable south-southeast winds. Today we went to sleep at the lower end of Ecores de la Farina ó últimos [Flour, or Last, Bluffs].[68] We rowed eight leagues, being ninety-four leagues from the principal mouth of the Arkansas River. Night fell, with somewhat cloudy skies. At six o'clock the word was taken, and nothing unusual was reported from the guard.

January 4, 1794. From midnight until five-thirty, when we rowed away, calm, no news. At seven-thirty we began to ascend the Isla de la Harina [Flour Island].[69] When the river is low, the channel has no water. At nine o'clock we were already at the head of it. At twelve o'clock we entered the batura of Pruna Point, and at one we were beyond it. Travelers say that this is the strongest current of the Mississippi, but I have not found it so. Perhaps it is because the river is low. At three o'clock we entered the first of the Acadian Islands.[70] We have passed two. We have rowed eight leagues and we are one hundred and two leagues from the principal mouth of the Arkansas River. Night fell, with cloudy skies. At six o'clock the word was given, and nothing new in the guard.

January 5, 1794. From midnight until five-thirty, when we rowed away, calm, and nothing new. At eight o'clock an opposing rather strong northeast wind began to blow. We have scarcely made any progress. At twelve o'clock we found a beautiful four-oared pirogue upside down on a mud bank. I ordered the water bailed

---

68. See Cramer, *Navigator*, pp. 164–68. Sailing up the Mississippi, at 35°, 15 minutes, is Chickasaw Bluffs (between the Las Casas and Carondelet Rivers); at 35°, 30 minutes, is the third bluff; at 35°, 45 minutes, is the second bluff (where Ft. Prud'homme was); at 36° is the first bluff. The terms Ecores à Margot or Chickasaw Bluffs were usually used interchangeably and often referred to all the bluffs.

69. Farina or Flour Island takes its name from having had flour boats wrecked on it (Cramer, *Navigator*, p. 164).

70. Barnó y Ferrúsola's letter of January 5, 1794, was written from Islas de las Canadianas (P de C 47). Islas de las Canadianas is sometimes also called Islas de las Acadianas.

out and a seam calked. I placed the boat, which is not that good or that fast, on the highest point of an island, well tied and the place marked. I placed a marker at the stern and marked on it the name of the King. At three o'clock we met the patrón, Felipe[71] García, with the sailor Antonio Cotelo, who were coming from New Madrid and were going as mail-express to Natchez. I wrote to that governor[72] [and] to Antonio Soler, remitting to him the knapsack and clothing of the artilleryman Chávez, who died. I also remitted two small chests of my papers, in which there are also all my accounts [kept] when I was storehouse keeper at Nogales, directed to Mr. Duverge, and in his absence to Don Josef Vidal, secretary of that [Natchez] government. This was done in order that we may be freer on board in case of an encounter that I might have with the enemy. At four o'clock the same wind continues, but it is stronger. We camped three leagues below the last of the Acadian Islands. Today, due to the force of the opposing wind, we only traveled two leagues, and we are one hundred and four leagues from the principal mouth of the Arkansas River. Night fell, with stormy horizons. At six o'clock the word was given, and there has been no news from the guard.

January 6, 1794. From midnight until five-thirty o'clock in the morning, when we rowed away, nothing new. Calm. At eight o'clock a rather fresh northeast wind, which is against us. It has continued all day. However, we went to camp opposite the Ribera Bayona [Bayonne River], and we have traveled five leagues. We are one hundred and nine leagues from the principal mouth of the Arkansas River. At six o'clock the word was taken. Night fell, with clear horizons. At seven o'clock, wind to the southeast; at eight o'clock it was to the south, and at twelve o'clock it was to the east, with rain. Nothing new has come from the guard.

January 7, 1794. At seven o'clock in the morning we departed rowing and with sails up. No news. East wind. All last night it rained and it continued to. At eight o'clock it forced me to land. At twelve o'clock the same wind and rain continued. At two o'clock it calmed down a little. We left at three o'clock and saw two barges which, not being able to overcome the current to arrive

---

71. See entry for December 26, 1793, above, p. 212 and n. 54.
72. Barnó y Ferrúsola's letter is dated January 5, 1794, from Islas de las Canadianas (P de C 47).

DIARY

at the principal channel where I was ascending by means of a towline, went on the inside of the island. I was obliged to ascend and then descend in order to examine them, which I did. I found that it was Alexander Harter, American, two passengers, and eight men. Their barges were loaded with salted meat and peltry, with a passport from the commandant of New Madrid destined for New Orleans. After having searched them well and having found nothing, I examined his [Harter's] passport. Because it was so late, I camped on the other side without being able [because it was too late] to leave said island. Today, because of the opposing wind, rain, and the two barges, I have spent the day without traveling more than three leagues. We are one hundred and twelve leagues from the principal mouth of the Arkansas River. Night fell with somewhat squally horizons. At six o'clock the word was given, and nothing unusual occurred in the guard.

January 8, 1794. From midnight until five-thirty, when we rowed away, calm. Nothing new. All day we continued to row, and we went to sleep at the small *praderia* [meadow] of New Madrid. Today we traveled six leagues, and we are one hundred and eighteen leagues from the principal mouth of the Arkansas River. Night fell with clear horizons. At six o'clock the word was taken, and no news has been reported by the guard.

January 9, 1794. From midnight until seven-thirty, when we rowed away, calm, nothing new. We started late today because of the fog, [which was] so thick that nothing could be seen through it, and it lasted until eleven o'clock. All this time I have kept the pirogue following us on the other side of the river in order to examine well the river. At twelve o'clock a south ¼ southwest wind arose and we hoisted the sails, and we came within sight of New Madrid. Today we have made ten leagues, and we are one hundred and twenty-eight leagues from the principal mouth of the Arkansas River. Night fell, with cloudy horizons. The word was taken at six o'clock, and no news has been reported from the guard.

January 10, 1794. From midnight until seven o'clock in the morning, when we rowed away, nothing new. At ten we arrived at the landing place of New Madrid. I gave an official letter to the commandant and *de uno y otro*.[73] I shall send a copy of both of them

---

73. Meaning Barnó y Ferrúsola's letter to Portell and reply of the latter.

to the governor of Natchez.[74] At five o'clock in the afternoon I crossed with the galiot to the other side in order not to be surprised in case of an attack. From Arkansas to this post the people have not prepared meals in order to arrive here sooner, so as to give aid to this post.

The calculation that I have made, according to my estimate, of the distance between the Plaza of Natchez and the post of New Madrid, with distinctions of high and low river, and places most notable for my understanding [sic].[75]

	Leagues High River	Leagues Low River
From Plaza of Natchez to Nogales	35	40
From Nogales to the mouth of the Arkansas	66	120
From the entrance of the Arkansas to the Detachment	5	6
From the Detachment to the St. Francis River	30	45

---

74. Barnó y Ferrúsola to Portell, on *La Flecha,* New Madrid, January 10, 1794, P de C 124; copy in P de C 133. Barnó y Ferrúsola to Gayoso, on *La Flecha,* New Madrid, January 16, 1794, P de C 47. Portell also reported Ferrúsola's arrival in his letter No. 226 to Carondelet, New Madrid, January 18, 1794, P de C 28.

Ferrúsola found New Madrid full of activity, with repairs being made on the fort and the militia sleeping there in order to maintain a constant watch. He informed Portell that he would remain at New Madrid until all rumors of an attack vanished unless orders arrived from Carondelet or Gayoso. He offered 16 men from his crew to aid in the defense preparations during the day, crossing to the opposite bank of the river at night to watch for descending vessels. (Barnó y Ferrúsola to Portell, on *La Flecha,* New Madrid, January 10, 1794, P de C 124; copy in P de C 133; to Gayoso, January 16, 1794, P de C 47; to Gayoso, No. 14, New Madrid, January 16, 1794, P de C 47.)

75. Or "and other places worthwhile mentioning in my account." Original reads: "con distinción del rio alto y bajo y parajes mas remarcables para mi inteligencia."

During January, Ferrúsola was watching the river. He acted as inspector of the defense works going on at New Madrid. A scarcity of able workers delayed the work somewhat, and it was difficult to keep peace between the French and Americans when they worked together, but the presence of *La Flecha* encouraged the men to a more vigorous defense. (See Barnó y Ferrúsola to Gayoso, No. 14, New Madrid, January 16, 1794, P de C 47; same to same, on *La Flecha* before the Fort of New Madrid, January 17, 1794, P de C 47; Portell to Carondelet, No. 226, New Madrid, January 18, 1794, P de C 28; Barnó y Ferrúsola to Gayoso, opposite the Post of New Madrid, January 16, 1794, P de C 47.)

From the St. Francis River to the Batura del Consejo	11	16
From the Batura del Consejo to the Ecores Amargó	10	15
From the Ecores Amargó to those in the middle	5	6
From the Ecores of the middle to those of Perdom [Ecores à Prud'homme] because of the strong current	6	8
From the Ecores of Perdom to those of La Farina, or the last ones	5	6
From the last point of the Ecores of La Farina to the last island of the Acadians	8	10
From the last Acadian Island to the Ribera Bayona	5	8
From the Ribera Bayona to the small meadow of New Madrid	5	7
From the small meadow of New Madrid to the landing place of this post	10	14
	201	301

New Madrid, January 10, 1794

Juan Barnó y Ferrúsola

[rubric]

The diary continues during my stay in New Madrid until my return to the Plaza of Natchez.

January 11, 1794. At eleven o'clock this morning the commandant told me that eight leagues from this place there was a chalán loaded with salted meats which had gone aground within an island, and that he suspected it had not been done on purpose, because the enemy had a storehouse there. I immediately offered to go and inspect it, and he gave me the sublieutenant of the militia force, Don Robert Macay,[76] to direct me to the place. I was entrusted to force it out and bring it to this dock. Today, rowing and with the sails, I made five leagues. At six o'clock the word was given, and nothing happened during the watch.

January 12, 1794. Today at noon we arrived at the place where the chalán was grounded, and after having searched it and not having found anything, I gave orders to the people [on board ship],

76. Probably the most prominent Anglo-American settler at New Madrid during the Spanish regime was Roberto Macay, or McCoy. Spanish records of 1793 list the sublieutenant Macay of the New Madrid militia as a young married man of 29; born a commoner in Montreal, Canada; engaged in the profession of commerce; and possessed of a moderate fortune. In 1786 Macay, then living at Vicennes, descended the Mississippi to New Orleans. On his return in 1787 he found a newly established trading post at l'Anse à la Graisse and decided to settle there. Thus, when Portell formed the first company of militia at New Madrid in 1792, he was commissioned a sublieutenant. During the establishment of Fort San Fernando de las Barrancas in 1795, he was employed to transport supplies from New Madrid to the new post on the royal lanchón *El Príncipe de Asturias*. Gayoso was so impressed with the young man's services that he decided to put him permanently in charge of a small boat, probably *El Príncipe de Asturias*, to perform naval duties on the upper river under Langlois' orders. According to Gayoso's description, Macay was active, intelligent, impartial, and able to speak, in addition to Spanish, the English, French, and Shawnee languages.

In July 1797 Macay was transferred from the rank of lieutenant in the militia's first company of fusileers to a lieutenant in the cavalry company, and a short while later was appointed captain of the second company of militia. So outstanding were his services that, when New Madrid was left without a commandant in June 1799, he was chosen to fill the position until Peyroux's arrival in August. In 1800 Captain Macay was made commandant of a settlement in the Tywappity Bottom, opposite the mouth of the Ohio River. He died in 1840 at the age of 76 and was buried in New Madrid.

(See Portell to Carondelet, No. 119, New Madrid, March 16, 1793, P de C 26; notice signed by Portell, dated in New Madrid, March 16, 1793, P de C 123; Houck, *History of Missouri*, 2, 107, 143; commission of Don Roberto Macay as sublieutenant in the company of militia at New Madrid, signed by Carondelet at New Orleans, December 22, 1792, P de C 2362; in Houck, *Spanish Régime in Missouri*, 2, 33. Copies of commission as lieutenant of cavalry in the militia at New Madrid for Roberto Macay, signed by Carondelet at New Orleans, July 1, 1797, P de C 2363; commission of Macay for captain of the second company of militia at New Madrid, signed by Gayoso de Lemos at New Orleans, December 3, 1797, P de C 2362; both in Houck, *Spanish Régime*, 2, 35 and 39 resp. Gayoso to Carondelet, Barrancas, August 13, 1795, P de C 43; Delassus to Gayoso, New Madrid, June 30, 1799, P de C 2366; in Houck, *Spanish Régime*, 2, 273. See also ibid., 2, 398, n. 3. There is a good deal of correspondence concerning, to, and by Macay in the P de C. And I myself have quite a collection of Macay documentation.)

DIARY 223

and at five-thirty it was already out in the Mississippi and placed alongside the prow of my galiot, since I had discovered that its owner was a hunter of the Bella Ribera [Ohio River] named Prins [Prince], with two enlisted men. All three were Americans, who, because of not knowing the Mississippi, had stopped there. At six o'clock the word was taken, and nothing new has been reported in the guard.

January 13, 1794. This day I arrived at New Madrid with the chalán. At sunset I crossed to the other side to guard well with my galiot, as I am accustomed to.

January 14, 1794. This day there is no news. I continue guarding.

January 15, 1794. The same as the day before.

January 16, 1794. As the day before.

January 17, 1794. Today, after having been searched, the chalán belonging to an inhabitant and hunter of this post, Toni Yust, has arrived. It comes from the Bella Ribera loaded with salted meat. I found no letters or papers.

January 18, 1794. There is nothing new today.

January 19, 1794. As the day before.

January 20, 1794. Today nothing new.

January 21, 1794. Last night Don Enrique Peyroux,[77] with twelve

77. Henri Peyroux de la Coudrenière was born in France and came to Louisiana in 1784 as an interpreter for the Acadians. According to Trudeau, he settled at the old village of Ste. Geneviève, where he built a house and established a salt factory. In April 1787 Miró appointed him commandant of Ste. Geneviève to succeed Francisco de Cartabona. Two years later he was granted 7760 arpents of land near New Bourbon by Lieutenant-Governor Perez. He was a well-educated man, interested in scientific matters, and the author of several publications dealing chiefly with geography. In 1791 he made a visit to Europe via Philadelphia, where he met Thomas Jefferson.

On his return Peyroux found himself the object of Spanish suspicion, and when threats of a French-American attack began to reach Upper Louisiana, Trudeau quietly dispatched him to New Orleans, making François Vallé temporary commandant in his place. Perhaps Trudeau was influenced in his action by certain reports from Vallé, who heartily disliked Peyroux because of an old quarrel with him. According to Peyroux's story, the Vallé family resented some of his land reforms because they made more work for the large landowners, although they were necessary to correct old abuses that were causing quarrels and divisions at the post. The Vallés, seeking the friendship and protection of the Lieutenant Governor, made some coarse remarks about Peyroux's wife and refused to follow his orders. Consequently, he was obliged to arrest François and confine him for 24 hours. For this, the Vallés accused Peyroux of despotism.

volunteers, arrived on a bercha from Sainte Geneviève. Today there has been nothing new.

January 22, 1794. Nothing in particular today.

January 23, 1794. The same as the day before.

January 24, 1794. The same as the day before.

January 25, 1794. This day, after having been searched and nothing found, the chalán loaded with salted meat belonging to Mr. Ricard, with three enlisted men, all Creoles from Illinois, arrived from hunting on the Bella Rivera.

January 26, 1794. An express came today from Cumberland bearing a letter from Colonel Robertson[78] for this commandant. The

---

Whether or not the suspicions against Peyroux were justified, the Vallés, with Trudeau and the parish curé on their side, held the upper hand, and as a result Peyroux was sent to New Orleans. Apparently the evidence was not enough to warrant his immediate removal as commandant of Ste. Geneviève, for in 1795 he was back at the village. Vallé was cautioned to make no show of force against him without positive reason, and continued to act as temporary commandant. In 1796 Vallé became permanent commandant, but Peyroux continued to live at the post. When Lieutenant Colonel Carlos Howard ascended the Mississippi at the end of 1796, Carondelet instructed him to dismiss Peyroux as captain of the regulars if any plausible reason was found. According to Carondelet, Peyroux was "a suspicious, loose tongued fellow." Apparently Spanish suspicions of Peyroux soon disappeared, for in August 1799 he was appointed to succeed Carlos Delassus as commandant of New Madrid. He remained there for almost 4 years, when he resigned, probably as a result of a dispute with Spanish officials over the northern boundary of the New Madrid district. After his resignation he went to France, where he was supposed to have large possessions, and being old and infirm, he never returned. His wife stayed in Louisiana and received all his American properties.

(See Trudeau to Carondelet, No. 154 res., St. Louis, January 15, 1794, P de C 28; Houck, *History of Missouri*, *1*, 347–49; *2*, 137. Peyroux to [Carondelet], Ste. Geneviève, November 14, 1793, P de C 207B; Portell to Gayoso, New Madrid, January 21, 1794, P de C 47; Carondelet to Trudeau, New Orleans, March 3, 1794, P de C 21; draft [Gayoso] to Vallé, on *La Vigilante*, December 10, 1795, P de C 130; Secret Orders to Howard, signed by Carondelet, New Orleans, November 26, 1796, P de C 2364; printed in trans. in MHS *Collections*, *3* (1908), 71–91, and in Houck, *Spanish Régime*, *2*, 123–32; also, excerpts trans. in State Historical Society of Wisconsin *Collections*, *18* (1908), 449–52. Peyroux deserves a biographer. There is a vast amount of correspondence of, by, and concerning Peyroux in the P de C, some copies of which I have in my possession.)

78. Colonel (Brigadier and General) James Robertson, leader of the Cumberland settlement, intrigued with Gardoqui and Miró, covertly communicating with Miró through McGillivray. He became loyal to the United States after the creation of the Southwest Territory in 1790. Head of the Miró district for a while, which he himself aided in naming, Robertson was appointed agent for Chickasaw and advocated settle-

original was sent to the governor with an express of two men that he [Portell] had asked me for from the galiot, whom I gave to him considering that the saving would be for the royal treasury.

January 27, 1794. Nothing new.

January 28, 1794. There is nothing new.

January 29, 1794. Nothing in particular.

January 30, 1794. The same as the day before.

January 31, 1794. The same as the day before.

February 1, 1794. A chalán from Kentucky, after having been searched and nothing having been found, arrived with two families to settle in this post. They are Americans by nationality. Their trade is that of blacksmiths. They bring with them three deserters from the United States, whom the commandant is going to send down the river. The owner of the chalán is named Harant.

February 2, 1794. Nothing new.

February 3, 1794. At ten o'clock in the morning the barge from St. Louis, Illinois, belonging to Mr. Menar, arrived without a load. Mr. Vandenberger [Vanden Bemden][79] is a passenger who has a passport from that commandant. They are to return to that place when they obtain the peltry they say they are owed at this post. I searched both their trunks and bags and found nothing.

February 4, 1794. Nothing new.

February 5, 1794. Two chalanes were sighted at seven o'clock in the morning. As usual I immediately prepared to go to search them and find out who [sic] they were. I came to the first one [man] and found he was an American who was coming from a hunt in Cumberland. The chalán was loaded with salted meat and apples. I searched it, and having seen that he [or it] had nothing, I ordered

---

ment at Chickasaw Bluffs. He warned Portell of filibustering expeditions. There are a vast number of letters from Robertson in the Archives of Spain and a number in the Bancroft Library. (See *Dictionary of American Biography;* Bemis, *Pinckney's Treaty,* pp. 160–63; John P. Brown, *Old Frontiers* [Kingsport, Tenn. 1938], pp. 423–30.)

79. Louis Vanden Bemden, native of Flanders and engineer, settled at Gallipolis. He came to New Madrid in 1794 and was employed to direct rebuilding of fortifications at St. Louis in 1797. (Houck, *History of Missouri,* 2, 155.) Vanden Bemden built the first flour mill in the colony. He died on September 9, 1799. (See Liljegren, "Commission of Don Carlos Howard.")

him to go to the dock and present himself to the commandant. I went in search of the other, and upon passing it [and] examining the people that it had [aboard], according to the instructions that the governor of Natchez gave me,[80] I recognized that among them was Mr. Pisgignoux.[81] Being informed of his forces, I jumped on board with four armed men with [using] much diplomacy, because they had arms in their hands. We greeted each other. Meanwhile I had made a sign to the patrón to have his people ready in case it were necessary, and also the four soldiers who boarded the chalán with me. We conversed, and becoming impatient because I had my men well posted, I ordered him to dress, [and said] that we would go on board my ship in order to arrive at the dock sooner. He did as he was told, and we went aboard. I let him pass ahead, he on the port side and I on the starboard side. He wanted to go up above the cabin and I told him no, please go inside it, because I wanted to give him a cool drink, or at least by my manner I conveyed that idea to him. This was done. I locked him up inside the cabin, putting the key in my pocket. The cabin had been emptied completely. I placed two sentinels to guard him and I went to the commandant to give him the good news. The commandant asked me to please bring him up in order to question him. This I did, with four armed soldiers who went behind me. After having conferred a long time with him, he was accordingly committed to prison, guarded by two sentinels, without any communication whatsoever. This person came from Pittsburg with

80. *Orden del Governador Político y Militar,* Natchez, November 9, 1793, P de C 123; Gayoso to Barnó y Ferrúsola, Natchez, November 7, 1793; copy certified by Vidal, November 10, 1793, P de C 42; draft in P de C 123.

81. Jean Pierre Pisgignoux, "cinq pieds & six pouces de Stature, les Cheveux, & les sourcils chatains, grand nez, bouche ordinaire, & le menton rond" (Orden del Governador Político y Militar, Natchez, November 9, 1793, P de C 123 and other copies). See Nasatir and Liljegren, *LHQ, 21,* 35 ff. See also Liljegren, *LHQ, 22,* 37–38.

Pisgignoux was born in France in 1768. After being taken prisoner by revolutionaries in 1790, he escaped to Santo Domingo and from there came to the United States in 1793. He conversed with French intriguers in the West, especially with Auguste de la Chaise. His testimony was given to Gayoso in Nogales in March 1794 (P de C 152B) and is annexed to Carondelet to Las Casas, No. 106 res., New Orleans, March 20, 1794, and in No. 107 res., dated March 28, 1794, P de C 1447; Carondelet to Alcudia No. 29 res., New Orleans, March 20, 1794, and enclosures. Pisgignoux wrote Jaudenes and Viar, New York, October 1, 1793, encl. in Jaudenes and Viar to Alcudia, No. 198, New York, October 16, 1793, AHN 3895; in *AHAR 1896, 1,* 1002–03; see also pp. 1046–51. See below, p. 227, n. 82.

DIARY   227

Mr. de Luzier's family, and upon entering the Mississippi the family went away to join their father at Ste. Geneviève.

Then [I] passed to the chalán of Mr. Cruzel de San Marcial, [of] French European nationality. He was a doctor of medicine. This man was also in the party and was going to settle in New Orleans. I examined this chalán with the utmost care and found nothing but medicines, books pertaining to his profession, and clothing for his use. Therefore, seeing that he did not know the other man, I said nothing to him. I presented him to the commandant, who said that although he is certain that he has nothing yet, he does not wish to permit him to descend without a previous permit from the Baron. I took all the papers that the enlisted men of the chalán had, and I shall remit them to the governor of Natchez. I shall also send him the arms, books, and clothing of said Pisgignoux, with an inventory. From what I have been able to conceive of this person, he is a very short man, capable of any undertaking, and full of vanity.[82]

82. For this story see above, pp. 82–83. See also Cruzat de St. Martial to Carondelet, New Madrid, February 8, 1794, P de C 210; Delassus [de Luzières] to Carondelet, New Bourbon, March 15, 1794, P de C 210; Ferrúsola to Gayoso, No. 16, Nogales, February 16, 1794, P de C 47; copy certified by Vidal, Natchez, February 20, 1794, P de C 42.

Pisgignoux was descending to New Orleans on the chalán of a French émigré, Dr. Cruzat de St. Martial. Pisgignoux met St. Martial through Mr. Derbigny, son-in-law of Delassus de Luzières of New Bourbon. He traveled with Derbigny from Pittsburgh to Louisville, where they parted, and Pisignoux joined St. Martial, taking with him a letter from Derbigny to Tardiveau stating that Pisgignoux was either a traitor and an imposter or deserved well of the Spanish government.

St. Martial did not completely trust the Frenchman and did not want to take him to New Orleans, but since Derbigny wanted to ascend to the Illinois, there was no other way for him to descend to New Orleans except with the doctor. St. Martial was also detained at New Madrid. Since the delay upset the doctor, who feared that his health would not stand New Madrid's climate, he immediately requested Carondelet for a passport to New Orleans. The Governor General was slow to reply, for when Rousseau and the squadron arrived toward the end of April, St. Martial was still at New Madrid. He tried to load his medicines on the galleys and descend with them, but Rousseau refused to take him. He considered St. Martial an imposter and a braggart, and not much of a surgeon. (St. Martial to Carondelet, New Madrid, February 8, 1794, P de C 210; Rousseau to Carondelet, on *La Venganza*, at Nogales, June 29, 1794, P de C 210.)

No incriminating evidence was found among the confiscated papers of Pisgignoux, but upon questioning, the Frenchman confessed that the projected French expedition was going to occur and that he was to have been a cavalry colonel in it. From his interrogation of Pisgignoux, Portell concluded that, although he was innocent, he was a poorly educated, audacious fanatic, who had expected to be received by the Spaniards

February 6, 1794. Nothing new.

February 7, 1794. The same.

February 8, 1794. Today I left with this commandant—because he officially asked me for them and explained the need he had of them because of the fears I think he has[83]—seven soldiers of the Louisiana regiment [and] the artilleryman Juan Azeytuno, who reinforced and rowed His Majesty's galiot under my command. I also left seventy-eight pounds of gunpowder, one hundred and fifty-four pounds of bullets, and thirteen pounds of fuses [*cuerda-*

---

in triumph. Portell considered him a bad man lacking in understanding, addicted to every vice, and described him a "boceador de café" or a "campanes del públinco." (See Ferrúsola to Gayoso, No. 16, Nogales, February 16, 1794, P de C 47; Portell to Ferrúsola, New Madrid, February 5, 1794; copy attached to copy of Ferrúsola to Portell, New Madrid, January [?] 10, 1794, P de C 133. Portell to Carondelet, No. 236, New Madrid, February 8, 1794, P de C 28; declaration of Pisgignoux, Natchez, March 8, 1794, P de C 152B; Portell to Gayoso, New Madrid, February 10, 1794, P de C 47; Portell to Carondelet, New Madrid, May 2, 1794, P de C 28. For further details see above, pp. 82–83. See also Nasatir and Liljegren, *LHO 21*, reprint pp. 33–36, where several important references are given to sources; Whitaker, *Spanish-American Frontier*; Gayarré, *History of Louisiana*; *AHAR 1896, 1*, 1019–45 passim.)

Ferrúsola and Portell conferred together on the problem of what to do with Pisgignoux and finally decided that Ferrúsola should deliver him, securely bound and handcuffed, to Beauregard at Nogales. They arranged for the galiot to leave at dawn on February 8, carrying in addition to Pisgignoux, two American militiamen convicted of conspiring to desert with some other Americans. However, heavy rains delayed the departure until the afternoon of February 10. (See Portell to Ferrúsola, New Madrid, February 7, 1794; copy attached to copy of Ferrúsola to Portell, on *La Flecha*, at New Madrid, January 10, 1794, P de C 133; copy of reply of Ferrúsola to Portell, on *La Flecha* at New Madrid, February 7, 1794, P de C 124; also a copy attached to Ferrúsola to Portell, January 10, 1794. Portell to Beauregard, New Madrid, February 9, 1794, P de C 47; Portell to Carondelet, No. 236, New Madrid, February 8, 1794, P de C 28; Portell to Gayoso, New Madrid, February 10, 1794, P de C 47; Carondelet to Portell, New Orleans, March 1, 1794, P de C 21; parts in Carondelet to Las Casas, No. 105 res., New Orleans, February 27, 1794, P de C 1447; draft and index in P de C 152B.) Carondelet stated that Pisgignoux should be apprehended and securely bound, then sent to New Orleans together with his papers; also, that there was much suspicious about him, including his part in the Santo Domingo affair (Carondelet to Las Casas, No. 100 res., New Orleans, January 24, 1794, P de C 1447; draft without enclosures in P de C 152B).

83. Ferrúsola exchanged some men with Portell, but Portell's were disinclined to help defend the town. Portell feared that when *La Flecha* left New Madrid the dissatisfied men in the garrison might try to cause trouble. (Portell to Ferrúsola, New Madrid, February 7, 1794, and Ferrúsola to Portell, on *La Flecha*, New Madrid, January [?] 10, 1794, P de C 133; Carondelet to Portell, New Orleans, March 1, 1794, P de C 21; draft also in same legajo. Portell to Gayoso, New Madrid, February 10, 1794, P de C 47.)

DIARY

mecha], having kept a spare top-mast on board in case of urgency.[84] I exchanged the sailor Cristoval de Rojas for Josef María de los Santos, because the former is more useful to him. With the reinforcement of the eight soldiers I have given him, he has forty-eight Spanish soldiers. It rained all day.

February 9, 1794. All day it rained. Nothing new.

February 10, 1794. Today at three-thirty in the afternoon I left New Madrid for Nogales (but the people on board and ashore think that I shall only [not] reach Arkansas, where we have given them to understand the galleys are, and that I shall be back before that [time]), with the important prisoner Pierre Pisgignoux, whom I arrested the fifth of this month[85] on board the chalán belonging to the doctor of medicine Cruzel de San Marcial, and who [Pisgignoux] was fettered and handcuffed, and with two Americans, in order to leave all of them with the commandant of Nogales and at the disposition of the governor of the Plaza of Natchez.

February 11, 1794. Today we awoke thirty leagues from New Madrid, because we drifted during the night as long as there was moonlight. No news and no information of consequence has been extracted from Mr. Pisgignoux.

February 12, 1794. Nothing new. At ten o'clock in the morning, in spite of the rain and the opposing wind, we are [arrived] at Ecores Amargó, and drifting very fast, because we are not able to drift at night owing to the bad weather and our having to pass the Batura del Consejo.

February 13, 1794. Today, at five-thirty in the morning, we left. At one o'clock we were at the St. Francis River. At five o'clock in the afternoon the pirogue of the Indian Chief of the Creek nation, John Hunts, [pulled up alongside and he] came on board. He told me that below the small [river] bank of the Ecores Amargó, he had found, hidden in the ground and covered with sticks, six boxes which contained one hundred and forty guns with bayonets of French make. He said he was descending to give them to the governor of Natchez. He told me that if all the pirogues of his group

---

84. "Habiendome quedado un respeto a bordo por si el caso lo urgía," or "I left a spare top-mast on board in case it was [might be] required."

85. See entry for February 5, above, p. 225, and notes to that entry.

were together, he would give them [the guns] to me, and in order to show me, he gave me one, and it looks like a French gun. I asked him if he had found gunpowder and bullets, and he said he had not. I assume that no attention should be paid to this, because they will keep them for their own use. I have assured him that if he took them all to the governor, he would be well rewarded for them, and that in advance I would write to him. He was very happy and told me to tell him that he would bring absolutely all of them.[86] I gave him a packet of biscuits and he went away very happy. At six o'clock, because of the opposing wind and rain, we were obliged to land.

February 14, 1794. At three o'clock in the morning the rain ceased and a slight wind blew. We left at that time. At ten-thirty in the morning we were twelve leagues above the detachment of Arkansas at the entrance of the White River, where we met the King's pirogue, which is going as an express from the Plaza of Natchez to the post of New Madrid commanded by the sailor Perico el Campechano, with three rowers. [Perico] gave me a letter from the governor of Natchez. I wrote a friendly letter for him to the commandant of New Madrid, telling him that those Indians had found the guns, so that he may be informed. At two o'clock I arrived at the detachment of the White River, and I gave the letter [that] the commandant of New Madrid had given me for the commandant of Arkansas, to the brother-in-law of the commandant, militia officer Mr. Luisman [or Guisman]. At four o'clock we began to drift down the river rapidly.

February 15, 1794. All last night, because the moon was bright and [there was] no wind, we drifted and we awakened below the Seneaux of twelve leagues. Today, at nightfall, I was at the upper head of the Isla Ceré [Cerré Island]. At twelve midnight we were twenty leagues above Nogales. I saw a light ashore and went to investigate. I found militia sergeant Hunau with six militia men of New Madrid who were returning from the Plaza of Natchez to that post with pliegos for the royal service. I received letters through him from the governor and from individuals. We are only seven days away from that plaza. I wrote a friendly letter to the com-

---

86. See also Carondelet to Las Casas, No. 105, res.; Beauregard to Gayoso, No. 408, Nogales, February 16, 1794, P de C 17.

mandant of New Madrid informing him of my pleasant trip thus far and that I would go to Natchez to deliver the prisoners, because I lack five men, and because four of my men had fallen ill since my departure from that post, and that if the governor wished me to make another trip, at least there I would find more men, which I could not do at Nogales.

February 16, 1794. At ten o'clock this morning I arrived at the landing place of the post of Nogales, and delivered to that commandant—and obtained a receipt from him for—the important prisoner, Mr. Pisgignoux, and the two Americans.[87]

On board His Majesty's galiot *La Flecha,* at the landing place of the post of Nogales, February 16, 1794.

Juan Barnó y Ferrúsola

[rubric]

---

87. Ferrúsola delivered his prisoners to Beauregard, who had orders to forward Pisgignoux under heavy guard to New Orleans at the first opportunity. Immediately after his arrival at Nogales, Ferrúsola forwarded the diary of his trip and copies of all his official correspondence with Portell to Gayoso at Natchez. (Ferrúsola to Gayoso, No. 16, Nogales, February 16, 1794, P de C 47; copy certified by Vidal, Natchez, February 20, 1794, P de C 42.)

Ferrúsola expected orders to arrive soon for *La Flecha* to descend to Natchez. The arrangement was satisfactory for him as he needed replacements for his crew, and sailors were hard to find in Nogales. (See entry for February 15, above, p. 230.) When a week passed and no orders came, he wrote Gayoso asking whether he was to remain in Nogales, where Beauregard was using the galiot for his purposes, or to continue his original commission of inspecting vessels that descended the Mississippi. In March the squadron reached Nogales on its way to New Madrid, and Ferrúsola was transferred to the command of *La Castilla,* one of the ascending galleys. (Ferrúsola to Gayoso, *La Flecha* at Nogales, February 24, 1794, P de C 126; Ferrúsola to Gayoso, on *La Castilla* at the military detachment on the White River, March 18, 1794, P de C 47; Ferrúsola to [Gayoso], on *La Castilla* at Batura del Consejo, April 6, 1794, P de C 47. See above, pp 82-84.)

3
Diary of Gayoso de Lemos' Expedition on *La Vigilante*

Introduction[1]

The diary of Gayoso de Lemos' expedition on *La Vigilante* to Barrancas de Margó, given below together with an extension of his trip to the Illinois country, indicates by its style that the writer was from the south of Spain, Andalusia, and perhaps not a very well-educated person. The fact that he uses French words would suggest that the text was not written by Gayoso himself. However, the editor believes that it is a diary of Gayoso's trip, probably written by a secretary.

Written on *La Vigilante*, the diary consists of four parts, all incomplete. Part I, the departure from Natchez, April 16, 1795, covers the period from April 16 through September 7, 1795. It is in P de C 2354. Part II is called "Diary from New Madrid to Illinois [St. Louis]," dated "October [6-27] 1795," and is in P de C 2364. Part III is entitled simply "Diary Written on board *La Vigilante*" and is found in P de C 125. It covers from December 31, 1795, through January 9, 1796, then jumps back to include October 28 through December 8, 1795. Part IV has the same title and is in the same *legajo* as Part III. It covers from December 9 through December 29, 1795. Although the various incomplete parts of the diary are from several different legajos, I have rearranged them so as to form a continuous whole.

Gayoso was on *La Vigilante* throughout his entire trip up the river, a fact that all his letters from April 16, 1795, through the remainder of the year will verify. On May 20 the diary states that *La Vigilante* reached Barrancas. Gayoso, writing on board the galiot, sends that same information to Carondelet in a letter dated Esperanza, May 23, 1795.[2] On August 24 *La Vigilante* reached New Madrid: Diary of Departure, Part I. A letter from Gayoso to

---

1. For background material see above, pp. 104-18. For note on biographical sketch of Gayoso de Lemos see above, p. 11, n. 12.
2. P de C 48.

Carondelet, dated New Madrid, August 25, 1795,[3] states that Gayoso arrived at New Madrid on that day. Part II of the diary, from New Madrid to Illinois, records that on the morning of October 6, 1795, the writer left for Illinois. A letter written by Gayoso to Carondelet, dated New Madrid, October 6, 1795,[4] states that Gayoso was leaving for Illinois on that morning. Early on the morning of November 23 *La Vigilante,* with the writer of the diary, returned to New Madrid: Diary, Part III, written on *La Vigilante,* 1795–96. The same day Gayoso wrote from New Madrid that he had just returned from his trip to the establishments of the Upper Mississippi.[5] He then remained on *La Vigilante* during the entire period that it was on the Upper Mississippi in 1795.

Since Pedro Rousseau was not on *La Vigilante* at this time but on *La Venganza,* and remained at Barrancas when Gayoso ascended to Illinois, he could not be the author of the diary. A letter from Rousseau to Carondelet on *La Venganza,* dated Ecores, April 24, 1795,[6] shows that Rousseau was at Barrancas with *La Venganza* nearly a month before *La Vigilante* arrived there. On October 7, the day after Gayoso left New Madrid for Illinois on *La Vigilante,* Rousseau wrote a letter to him from *La Venganza* at San Fernando de las Barrancas.[7]

Evidence shows that neither Langlois nor Ferrúsola could have written the diary, since both of them were cruising at the mouth of the Ohio when *La Vigilante* left Natchez.[8] Moreover, Langlois wrote a letter to Carondelet dated New Madrid, April 16, 1795,[9] the day *La Vigilante* sailed from Natchez.

Further evidence in the diary itself indicates that Gayoso was responsible for it. All accounts of the events correspond, identically in some cases, to those given by Gayoso in his letters to Carondelet. The description of Gayoso's negotiations with Ugulayacabé and the Chickasaws on May 22 is one example. The details in the entry for May 22, Part I, are given in exactly the same lan-

---

3. P de C 43.
4. P de C 32.
5. Gayoso de Lemos to Carondelet, No. 3, *muy* res., New Madrid, November 23, 1795, P de C 35.
6. P de C 211.
7. P de C 211.
8. Langlois to Carondelet, on *La Flecha,* Ecores, May 15, 1795, P de C 210.
9. P de C 211.

guage, using the personal pronoun "I" in both places, as in the letter from Gayoso to Carondelet, dated Esperanza, May 23, 1795.[10] Furthermore, the writer of the diary speaks of himself as the one who carried out the commission that is known to have been given to Gayoso. In the entry for June 20, Part I, he states that he was the first to sign the treaty with the Chickasaws, signing just to the side of the Royal Seal, and that after him came Beauregard, Rousseau, Bontoux, García, Langlois, Bouligny, Zamora, Fauré, Cruzat, and Perchet. No one but Gayoso, who had been entrusted with the commission of gaining Barrancas from the Chickasaws, would sign first beside the Royal Seal.[11]

Parts of this diary are printed in Spanish in Holmes, *Documentos,* pages 185–249, 289–302. My copy differs slightly from Holmes' printed text, notably because of a sentence missing from the Holmes in each of the following entries in the diary: May 30, June 1, and June 14.

10. No. 6 res., P de C 48.
11. Gayoso to Carondelet, Barrancas, June 18, 1795, P de C 43.

PART I

Diary of Departure for Natchez
on *La Vigilante*

April 16, 1795–[September 7, 1795]

April 16, 1795. On Thursday, the day of departure, at one o'clock in the afternoon, we were accompanied to the *embarcadero* by Lieutenant Colonel Don Carlos de Grand Pré,[1] Captain Don Estevan Minor, Captain Don José Vidal, secretary of the government, Captain Don Gregorio La Rosa, Official Inspector Don Francisco Arroyo, Don Guillermo Vouidan, Don Carlos McKiernnan, Don Guillermo Scot, Don Eduardo McCabe, Don Antonio Gras, Don Manuel Lopez, Don Ezekiel Forman, Father Don Francisco Lennan, Don Juan Girault, Don Antonio Marmillion, Don Francisco Candel, and Don Mauricio Stacpoole.[2] The weather, fair and calm. We made the distance across in front of Natchez—Minor, Vidal, and Arroyo accompanying us with Don Melly Wooly—and we went to eat on the other side of the promontory. The *bercha* of Captain Don Elías Beauregard,[3] rowing with twelve oars, and the *berchita* of Guillermo Betty, rowing with ten, left with us [as a fleet] under the convoy of a ship of war; Beauregard was embarked on his [bercha], and both are to continue their journey.

1. Carlos Luis Boucher de Grand Pré was born in New Orleans probably in 1743. He was appointed a lieutenant of infantry by O'Reilly in 1769, and in 1775 was promoted to captain in the Louisiana regiment. He was in command of Punta Cortada and aided in putting down the rebels in Natchez in 1780. In 1781 he was ad-interim commandant at Natchez. After being at Punta Cortada in 1786, he replaced Bouligny at Natchez in 1786–89 and was appointed by Carondelet as lieutenant governor of Ouachita in 1796, with several posts, including Natchitoches, in his command. Grand Pré died about 1809. While Gayoso ascended the Mississippi River, he was in charge of Natchez.

2. Gayoso was on *La Vigilante* while Beauregard was on his *bercha*, commissioned by Carondelet to take command of the new post of Barrancas. A *berchita* owned by Guillermo Betty who delivered provisions to the Mississippi posts in 1794 and 1795 and to Barrancas, accompanied the expedition (Delinó to Gayoso, No. 67, Nogales, November 16, 1794, P de C 47; Zamoro to Gayoso, San Fernando, December 15, 1795, P de C 48). The berchita *El Mosquito*, conveying lieutenant Perchet, joined Gayoso at Nogales (Carondelet to Gayoso, New Orleans, May 7, 1794, P de C 21; Gayoso to Carondelet, No. 479, Natchez, May 9, 1794, P de C 28; Carondelet to Las Casas, No. 136 [134] res., New Orleans, May 1, 1795, AHN 3899; also in P de C 2354). Most of the men mentioned in the text have been identified in Holmes, *Documentos*, 185–92.

3. For note on Beauregard see above, p. 83, n. 20.

It was observed that the galiot *La Vigilante*[4] was sailing slowly, this being attributed to the poor construction of the oars; the other two vessels sail well, particularly Betty's, which exceeds all of them. After eating, we set sail by rowing, and the bercha of Don Elías Beauregard took my skiff in tow. At nightfall we made for shore to Belt's hacienda, where we encamped, the [two] guests withdrawing in the pirogue of the *galera La Luisiana,* except for Wooly,

---

4. The galiot *La Vigilante* was not a member of the royal squadron, but was used by Colonel Gayoso de Lemos for his official trips on the river. It was made over into a galiot in 1794 from a *lanchón* that the commandant of New Madrid purchased for the royal service from the trader Bartélemi Tardiveau. The new galiot made its first voyage up the river when Gayoso ascended to Barrancas de Margó in the spring of 1795 (trip narrated in this diary). Early in 1796 it returned to Natchez, where it was probably based for the remainder of Gayoso's stay there as governor of that plaza. In September 1797 Gayoso, then governor general of Louisiana, ordered that *La Vigilante* always be kept armed and at his disposition in New Orleans manned by a *patrón,* a *proel,* and 20 rowers who were to serve on the government felucca as well as on *La Vigilante. La Vigilante* was armed with 8 swivel guns and a 6-pound cannon mounted on its prow. In Rousseau's opinion the lanchón that became Gayoso's galiot was better and faster than any boat he had yet seen on the Mississippi, and he wanted to have more small boats like it built for service in the river squadron, for they could go faster than the galleys and regular galiots. (See Rousseau to Gayoso, on *La Venganza,* Nogales, June 29, 1794, P de C 209; Rousseau to Carondelet, on *La Venganza,* Nogales, June 29, 1795, P de C 210; Portell to [Carondelet], New Madrid, July 15, 1794, P de C 29; Carondelet to Rendón, New Orleans, October 16, 1794, P de C 618; certificate of purchase of a lanchón from Bartolomé Tardiveau, signed by Portell, New Madrid, July 22, 1794, enclosed in ibid.; draft [Rendón] to Gayoso, New Orleans, November 20, 1794, P de C 581A; Gayoso to Carondelet, New Orleans, February 6, 1796, P de C 33; Chevalier d'Annemours to le Gouverneur [Gayoso], Fort Miró on the Ouachita, July 27, 1796, P de C 216A; copy certified by Gayoso in P de C 212A. Draft [Carondelet] to Morales, New Orleans, September 2, 1796, P de C 89; Gayoso to Cónde de Santa Clara, No. 94, New Orleans, January 23, 1798, P de C 1501A.)

When *La Vigilante* first appeared as a galiot in 1795 it had 18 oars, but in 1797 Governor Gayoso ordered that 20 rowers be assigned to it, which would indicate that sometime during the intervening period 2 additional oars were added to the vessel. The drawing of the galley that Gayoso used in 1798 shows a boat of 24 oars. However, in a letter to the captain general at Havana, dated January 1798, Gayoso wrote that he was using *La Vigilante* for his trips up and down the river. It would therefore seem that the pictured galley belonging to Gayoso is none other than the former galiot *La Vigilante,* with 4 oars added to it, and perhaps some other changes. This seems even more probable when one examines the drawing and finds that there are seats in the galley for only 20 rowers, indicating that the last 2 seats of oars near the stern of the vessel probably were rather recent additions. (Drawing of Governor Gayoso de Lemos' galley in 1798, in MHS, Voorhees Collection; photostat in my collection; printed in Baldwin, *Keelboat Age,* between pp. 32 and 33.)

DIARY   243

who asked for passage up to Bayú Pierre [Stony Creek].[5] Eighteen oars row the galiot, and it has a complement of two artillerymen.

Friday, April 17, 1795. At dawn I fired a shot as a signal for weighing anchor, and we all left, rowing, with fair weather. We went to eat inside the canal of the Isla de La Pom [Apple Island], where we met a *chalán* loaded with flour and some apples. We purchased a barrel of the latter from it, and I sent another to my house, writing upon this occasion to Vidal. Previous to traversing the distance of the island we noticed a canoe coming toward us, and one [man in the canoe] shouted in order that we might stop; and it was Juan Baptista Trenier,[6] who was bringing letters from Vidal. He was dispatched with an oral word of response. After we finished eating, we continued the journey, and upon leaving the island, we hoisted the sail. I noticed that the galiot was going to the leeward,[7] which made me conjecture that it was badly stowed, but otherwise it acted well. The wind was lessening; nevertheless we continued with the sail until a little below the mouth of Cols [Coles] Creek[8] on the other side, where we encamped. This night I gave orders to Ros that in the morning he embark with Betty and go to the mouth of Cols-Creek in order to receive some provisions that Don Juan Smith should have ready there, and were he not to find them, he should go to the [his] house in order that they might be despatched.

Saturday, April 18, 1795. At daybreak Betty left for Cols-Creek, and [with] *La Vigilante* and the bercha of Beauregard we followed the same coast until we were slightly above [and] opposite said Cols-Creek, where we tied up. Because of the lateness of Betty I realized that they had gone to Smith's house and that the journey of that day was lost, which made me decide to take advantage of it [the delay] by fixing the galiot's stowage.[9] I saw that it [the stowage] was too much to the prow, from which I had some weight re-

---

5. Bayou Pierre, Bayou aux Pierres, or Stony Creek is situated 10 miles below the Big Black River and 60 miles above Natchez. It is a large rivulet. (Collot, *Journey in North America*, 2, 56.) Hutchins says it is 35¾ miles from Natchez (in Imlay, *Topological Description*, pp. 425, 458).
6. Trenier in my copy; possibly it should be Freniere or Freynier.
7. Listing.
8. See above, p. 195, n. 5.
9. I.e. reloading the galiot's cargo.

moved until it [the stowage] remained equal from stern to prow; and since it appeared to me that the defect, which I noticed when we had set out, arose from having it too much to the prow, I determined to place a cover on it, which I did by cutting a stick for the purpose of putting on it [the stick]the larger sail of my pirogue, the *Anguila,* all of which was carried out. Seeing that Betty was late, I sent seventy men[10] in the small boat in order to find out any news there might be, which was done, and the men returned an hour before sunset, bringing with them the provisions; and being doubtful of finding land farther ahead on which to camp, I remained in the same place this night.

Sunday, April 19, 1795. At daybreak we left, passing inside the island, which is farther above Cols-Creek, and upon leaving it, a light wind blew up which did not last very long; we continued rowing and went to camp half a league below the Small Gulf. We met Montimore, and with him I sent my little boat to Vidal.

Monday, April 20, 1795. At daybreak we left, rowing, and we arrived at ten o'clock in the morning at Bayú Pierre, where Mr. Wooly, who sent us four turkeys on board, disembarked. There we found the constable [*alguacil*] Targueson[11] with letters from Vidal. While I answered them, the meal was prepared; and shortly after twelve we departed with signs of a good wind, which turned into rain, inconveniencing us much in the afternoon [and] on account of which we landed; and it having let up a little, we continued as far as a half league below the Gran Golfo, where we encamped, and the covering was placed on the galiot.

Tuesday, April 21, 1795. We left at daybreak. Cloudy weather, which cleared up about ten o'clock in the morning. At noon we landed at the mouth of the islands in order to eat; and with many chalanes passing, Mr. Winters, the principal owner, who assured me that all was tranquil in Kentucky, came on board and gave me a letter from his brother. Many Indian canoes, which were supposed to be those of the Cherokees, were encountered.

After eating, we departed and went to sleep half a league above the Isla Esquermento,[12] on the inner side of which we experienced a strong current.

---

10. "Envié a setenta en el botecillo."
11. Or Fargueson (Ferguson?).
12. Or Esquenmento.

DIARY

Wednesday, April 22, 1795. We left at dawn with fair weather. At eight o'clock in the morning we landed in order to breakfast a little below the three mouths, and upon leaving them we met a canoe with three soldiers whom the Commandant of Nogales had sent to me as reinforcements. We started out again and came to camp at the head of the Island of Nogales.

Thursday, April 23, 1795. We started out at dawn and came to breakfast above Bayú Rapelié. From there we left with the wind at the prow, and a league from the post of Nogales we met a canoe coming from New Madrid which was going to New Orleans, and it delivered to me some letters from various posts. We continued traveling, and at three in the afternoon we tied up at the post of Nogales.[13]

Friday, April 24, 1795. [At Nogales] about nine o'clock at night a strong wind arose, with rain which lasted a very short while.

Saturday, April 25, 1795. We stayed in said post of Nogales, loading provisions, munitions, and other effects.

Sunday, April 26, 1795. We continued loading.

Monday, April 27, 1795. We left the above-mentioned post of Nogales at 2:40 in the afternoon, there having embarked on board the two ships: one sergeant, two corporals, twenty soldiers from the Regiment of Louisiana, and two more artillerymen to garrison them, and ten workmen.[14] There embarked also on the bercha *El Mosquito* the engineer Don Juan María Perchet,[15] who continues traveling with me. And we came to encamp five miles from

---

13. Vicksburg.
14. To garrison the new post at Barrancas de Margó.
15. Juan María Perchet was born in Gerona in 1769, studied and became an engineer, and went to Louisiana in 1794. He made inspections and drew up plans at various posts. After being promoted to captain, he went to Texas in 1802. Perchet was quite argumentative and quarreled with many people while at Barrancas during the expedition and building of Fort San Fernando. He was not very disciplined. (Gayoso to Carondelet, New Madrid, December 3, 1795, P de C 43; Perchet to Carondelet, San Fernando, July 12, August 12, October 9, 1795, P de C 32.) A lieutenant in the Royal Corps of Engineers, Perchet was authorized to use *La Luisiana* for carrying out Carondelet's order to draw up plans of the forts at Nogales, Natchez, Galveston, and Baton Rouge ("Objects to which special attention must be made in the commission placed in the care of the adjutant of the Royal Corps of Engineers Don Juan Perchet," by Carondelet, New Orleans, February 1, 1795, P de C 130). Perchet was also commissioned by Carondelet to draw up plans for the projected fort at Barrancas. (See Carondelet to Las Casas, No. 136 [134] res.)

the fort. Mr. Ree's[16] bercha, which is ascending to the post of Arkansas, left in our company.

Tuesday, April 28, 1795. We left at dawn and breakfasted at the point which is on the other side of La Cup, and from there we left and came to make dinner on the Island of Zasimine or Macocas. We left there, and a short time after our departure we were notified from Beauregard's bercha that its *patrón,* Manuel Diaz, had fallen on a thole and had a rib broken. I sent someone to treat him and to put a bandage on him. This was done, and we continued traveling and stopped to sleep at the Punta e Isla del Cuerno [Horn Point and Island], a distance of about seven leagues from where we had left in the morning. A peso is due the sailors today, since I promised it to them.[17]

Wednesday, April 29, 1795. We left said place at daybreak, and upon leaving the island we met a chalán that was coming from Fort Pitt. We continued our trip and came to breakfast on the lowest point of the three forgotten islands. At this place Mr. Ree took leave of us in order to continue his trip to Arkansas, which he did, and I gave him a letter for the commander of said post. We left after breakfast, and about eleven o'clock in the morning there arose a favorable wind that lasted until two-thirty in the afternoon, at which hour we landed on the Islas las Dos Hermanas [Two Sisters Islands] to eat. And at this time there appeared below said islands a boat with a very heavy loaded pirogue, coming, according to what is presumed, from some upper post of this river. After eating, we calmly pursued our way and came to sleep on the lowest point of the Cuatro Islotes [four small barren islands]. One peso is due the sailors.

Thursday, April 30, 1795. We left at dawn and came to breakfast on the third *islote.* At seven-thirty, on leaving said place, there arose a light favorable wind; it became stronger and lasted until three in the afternoon, when it again calmed down. Upon leaving the Isla la Felipa [Felip Island], we met four chalanes, one of which belonged to Don David Terguison [Ferguson], lieutenant of volunteers of the Plaza of Natchez, and the other to Mr. Winters. The first named delivered various letters to me. Given my need for a pirogue, I bought one from them. We continued jour-

---

16. Holmes say it is Bee; my copy reads Ree.
17. If they made 7 or more leagues per day. See entry for April 30, below, p. 247.

neying, and at the beginning of the long view of the Cabeza del Muerto [Death's Head Point] we met another three chalanes, to which I delivered a letter for José Vidal. We continued our journey and camped opposite the small Isla del Grapen [Island of Grapen], having made six leagues. The sailors did not earn the peso, because the seven leagues that had been agreed to were not made.

Friday, May 1, 1795. We left at daybreak, and about ten o'clock there arose a slightly favorable wind, which lasted until one o'clock, when we reached land to make dinner opposite the Cabeza del Muerto. At this time there appeared a bercha belonging to Felipe Angel, coming from Illinois, who delivered several letters to me, and I gave him others for Don José Vidal. After eating, we continued our trip. We camped about two and a half leagues above the Isla de la Cabeza del Muerto at eight o'clock in the evening, as no land was found until this hour. The sailors [made] one peso.

Saturday, May 2, 1795. We left at daybreak with fair weather. At nine o'clock in the morning there arose a slight wind which lasted until two in the afternoon. On leaving the Isla de Cerré [Cerré Island], we sighted about a league away the bercha of Mr. Ree, who had departed the 29th of April to continue his journey to Arkansas. We continued our trip. At five in the afternoon we camped at an estimated eight leagues from the place we had left in the morning. The sailors earned a peso, since they made more than seven leagues, which had been agreed upon.

Sunday, May 3, 1795. We left at daybreak and breakfasted about two leagues from the place we had slept. There was found Mr. Ree's bonfire, where he had camped the same night. About ten o'clock there arose a light wind, which lasted until twelve. We ate on board in order not to lose time, and we came to sleep more than eight leagues from the place we had camped the night before. The sailors earned one peso.

Monday, May 4, 1795. At daybreak, at the time of leaving, Don Domingo Bontoux[18] arrived in a pirogue equipped with four

---

18. Domingo Bontoux de la Blache was an *émigré* Frenchman and a sergeant major in the French army before the Revolution. Early in 1794 Las Casas sent him from Cuba to New Orleans, with instructions for Carondelet to employ him in the royal service in Louisiana. Carondelet accordingly sent him to New Madrid, where he

oars, which was bringing me sealed envelopes [*pliegos*] from the governor general. I answered the official letters and despatched the pirogue to Nogales.[19] Bontoux continues traveling with us. We left sailing after the day had cleared up well for the ship, since a favorable wind had risen, and about three leagues from where we had started out we caught sight of Mr. Ree's bercha, about a league away, which [torn] is continuing its trip to its destination. At one o'clock the wind ceased, and we continued rowing and came to camp more than nine leagues from where we had left in the morning. About ten o'clock at night some speaking was heard on the river; and having asked who they [sic] were, two chalanes coming from Fort Pitt, loaded with flour, answered. The sailors earned a peso.

Tuesday, May 5, 1795. We left at daybreak with fair weather. At eight o'clock we passed inside the first short cut[20] of the three canals. We breakfasted within, and upon leaving it the sails were hoisted for the crossing, which concluded, they were again lowered. Afterward, at eleven o'clock the sails were hoisted, there having arisen a light favorable wind that lasted us until four in the afternoon; we ate on the way, and afterward we continued rowing

---

was to serve under Portell on the land and under Rousseau on the river. Bontoux ascended to New Madrid at once to carry out his instructions and remained there until October, when he descended to Natchez on the lanchón *La Céréz*. From Natchez he returned to New Orleans, where he stayed until spring 1795. In May, under orders from Carondelet, he joined Gayoso in his expedition to Barrancas de Margó, and remained at Barrancas until late September to assist in the construction of the fort. He then again returned to the capital. In 1797 Bontoux ascended to Natchez and to Illinois and in 1800 was named commandant of the *bombadera Margarita* in the expedition against Bowles. Gayoso considered him an excellent individual, "truly Spanish, active and capable." While at Barrancas he apparently behaved well and displayed activity, zeal, and military knowledge. Portell's report of his conduct at New Madrid however, strikes a different note. He complained that Bontoux acted like a true French flatterer to his face but made all kinds of ridiculous and damaging statements about his command behind his back. (See resumé of orders in 1794, signed by Macay, New Madrid, August 20, 1799, P de C 134B; Carondelet to Portell, New Orleans, May 15, 1794, P de C 21; Carondelet to Gayoso, New Orleans, May 15, 1794, P de C 21; Portell to Gayoso, New Madrid, October 20, 1794, P de C 47; Gayoso to Carondelet, No. 1, on *La Vigilante* at confluence of White and Arkansas Rivers, May 8, 1795, P de C 43; Gayoso to Carondelet, New Madrid, September 27, 1795, P de C 43; Gayoso to Carondelet, San Fernando de las Barrancas, July 18, 1795, P de C 198; Gayoso to Santa Clara, No. 184, New Orleans, July 31, 1798, P de C 1501B, encl. a memorial of Bontoux, July 31, 1798.)

19. See Gayoso to Carondelet, No. 1, on *La Vigilante,* at confluence of Arkansas and White Rivers, May 8, 1795, P de C 43.

20. *Racursi.* There were 3 channels.

and came to camp on the six islotes eight leagues distant from where we had left. The sailors earned one peso.

Wednesday, May 6, 1795. We left at daybreak with the wind at the prow and strong currents, and we came to make dinner two leagues from where we had left in the morning. The slight wind at the prow having calmed down, we then continued our journey; and a league from the Isla del Trigo [Wheat Island] we met a bercha descending from the Arkansas Post enroute to New Orleans. By said bercha the sailor Felipe Drolet was sent to Natchez because he was sick. Shortly afterward we met a chalán coming from Fort Pitt. We continued our trip and came to camp half a league from the small Isla del Trigo, having made four leagues during the entire day. A peso must be deducted from the sailors' wages for not having made the seven leagues agreed upon.

Thursday, May 7, 1795. We left at daybreak with fair weather and came to eat on the isle, which is below the Arkansas River. We continued after having eaten, and at six in the afternoon we entered into the mouth of said river and came to camp a league from its entrance. We made four leagues during the whole day. One peso was deducted from the sailors.

Friday, May 8, 1795. We left at daybreak from said place, with cloudy weather which changed to a storm. About seven-thirty it cleared up and we continued our journey. We came to eat about three leagues from where we had left. We continued and encamped at the second point below the confluence of the White and Arkansas Rivers.

Saturday, May 9, 1795. We left at daybreak, and at six-thirty in the morning we encamped on the point of said confluence, where we remained all day. At the time we landed there appeared a pirogue on the White River which came from the detachment at the mouth of said river and was ascending to Fort Arkansas loaded with flour, in which priogue Blanco and Beltran embarked in order to go to the fort in search of some provisions. About four o'clock there arrived on board *La Vigilante* Captain Don Carlos de Vilemont,[21] commandant of said post. He had come in a pirogue with five men. He slept on board.

---

21. Carlos de Vilemont was the son of an officer in the Spanish colonial service stationed in the province of Louisiana and West Florida. His father died when Carlos was a young boy, and in recognition of his father's services, the King appointed

Sunday, May 10, 1795. We remained in said place. We stowed the ships and gave the crew an opportunity to rest.

Monday, May 11, 1795. At eight-thirty there arrived on board Blanco and Beltran, who had gone to the fort. About eleven-thirty the man named Pedro Pertuy arrived alongside in a pirogue with his woman, whom he was going to marry, and who [Pertuy] asked me to baptize a child of his, aged one month, which I did by giving it the name Manuel. We made something to eat and at twelve o'clock sharp we departed, at which hour Don Carlos de Vilemont, saying he was returning to the fort, bade us farewell. We entered the White River,[22] and at four o'clock in the afternoon we sailed through its mouth into the Mississippi River, and when we were on it [the Mississippi] we found that the wind was favorable. We hoisted the sails and came to camp two and a half leagues from the mouth of said White River.[23] During the night we had a strong wind with rain.

Tuesday, May 12, 1795. We left at daybreak. We ate three leagues from where we left today. We continued voyaging and came to sleep six leagues from where we had left in the morning.

Wednesday, May 13, 1795. We left at daybreak with the wind at the prow, which soon became favorable, but lasted only a short time. We ate about two and a half leagues from where we had left. We continued our voyage and came to sleep seven leagues from

---

Carlos a cadet in the royal army. In 1775 the boy, scarcely 13 years of age, went to Spain to petition for an officer's commission. Two years later he returned to Louisiana, bringing a royal order for a commission as soon as a vacancy should occur. In January 1780 he was listed as a sublieutenant in the Regiment of Louisiana, in 1784 was attached to the new Spanish garrison at Pensacola, and in 1785 was at Natchez. In the spring of 1794 Vilemont was in New Orleans, a captain in the regiment. In May of that year Carondelet ordered him to relieve Delinó of the command of Arkansas Post. Vilemont arrived at Arkansas in July, and Delinó immediately delivered the post to him. He served there until 1797. (See Carondelet to Delinó, New Orleans, May 7, 1794, P de C 21; May 12, 1794, P de C 21; draft in P de C 122B. Delinó to Carondelet, No. 171, Arkansas, June 14, 1794; No. 176, July 13, 1794; both in P de C 29. Census of Arkansas, signed by Vilemont, December 13, 1796, P de C 2364. I have a great deal of Vilemont's correspondence in my collection, obtained from various legajos in the P de C. See also Faye, *LHQ*, 27, 713.)

22. A short distance above the mouth of the Arkansas River, the White River enters the Mississippi, and about 6 leagues inland a navigable channel connected the two rivers with each other (Collot, *Journey in North America*, 2, 25–26).

23. The original reads: "Pusimos la vela y venimos a acampar a dos leguas y media del de esto que se halla a la boca de dicho Rio Blanco."

DIARY 251

where we left in the morning, having passed through a short cut, which saved us three leagues.

Thursday, May 14, 1795. We left in the morning with the wind at the bow. We breakfasted a league and a half from where we left. We continued with the wind contrary. We ate at three leagues from where we left. We continued with the same wind against us and came to sleep at the point above the Ermitage [Hermitage]. We made seven[24] leagues according to our estimation.

Friday, May 15, 1795. We departed at dawn with a light favorable wind, which soon became contrary because the river turned.[25] About two-thirty the light favorable wind returned. We came to camp about six leagues [from where we left] according to our estimation. Ten-thirty at night Glas arrived in a pirogue with six oars and brought me sealed envelopes from the governor general.

Saturday, May 16, 1795. We left very early. I answered the official letters and despatched Glas in the same pirogue for Nogales. During this interval a chalán passed, coming from Fort Pitt. At nine o'clock a light favorable wind arose, which later became stronger. Glas and the six men were furnished with 35 rations and the corresponding *filetes*.[26] We continued our trip with a strong wind, and at three o'clock in the afternoon we passed in front of the St. Francis River, at which time the wind began to calm. We continued rowing and came to camp a league above said river, having experienced a strong current. At three-thirty in the afternoon there appeared a pirogue with three sailors from the squadron, who came down as letter conveyors [and] who delivered to me various letters from the commandant of the galeras,[27] and it [the pirogue] continues with us. We made eight leagues.

Sunday, May 17, 1795. We left very early. About eight o'clock there arose a slight favorable wind which lasted until twelve o'clock, when it calmed down. At eleven o'clock we met three chalanes coming from Ohio. We continued journeying. We made dinner below the Isla Sarpy [Sarpy Island]. We continued afterward and came to sleep at the head of Isla Sarpy, having made seven and a half leagues in all that day.

24. Holmes says "five and one half leagues."
25. Probably going round a bend in the river.
26. A *filete* was a ration of liquor delivered to *engagés* (McDermott, *Glossary of Mississippi Valley French,* p. 76).
27. Pedro Rousseau was commandant of the galeras.

Monday, May 18, 1795. We left at break of day with a slight favorable wind, which about nine o'clock became calm. We continued rowing and came to eat at one-thirty at the extremity of the Batura del Consejo, and seeing then that the ten sailors that Don Pedro Rousseau had sent me as reinforcement were not found there, I had a cannon fired in case they might be within the short cut in front of us, as indeed they were, and half an hour later they arrived aboard. After eating, we continued rowing; we passed within the short cut and came to sleep two leagues from the Batura del Consejo, having made five and a half leagues during the entire day.

Tuesday, May 19, 1795. We left at daybreak. We experienced strong currents this morning. About nine o'clock there arose a slight wind, which lasted until three in the afternoon. We continued rowing, and the galiot and *El Mosquito* came to camp a league from the Isle of Barrancas de Margot, and the bercha *El Tracnar* camped a league further down, since it was not able to pass over the *batura*[28] because it was late. [We made] five leagues.[29]

Wednesday, May 20, 1795. We left early. We hoisted the sails since the wind was favorable and freshening, and we came to land below the Isla del Diamante [Diamond Island], where we made breakfast and awaited the bercha *El Tracnar,* which had been delayed the night before. The said bercha arrived an hour and a half later. During this interval five chalanes from Ohio appeared. Their masters came aboard and they were sent off afterward. I continued sailing at ten o'clock, with the wind still favorable, and when we were entering the isle, a boat appeared, coming from Illinois, loaded with peltry belonging to Carlos Graciot,[30] merchant of

---

28. See above, p. 154, n. 4.

29. "Seguimos al remo y vino [vinieron] la Galeota y el Mosquito [a] acampar a una legua de la Ysla de los [sic] Barrancas de Margot y la Bercha el tracnar a una legua mas abajo por no haver podido rapicar la Batura por ser tarde 5 leguas." This differs slightly from Holmes, *Documentos,* p. 208.

30. Charles Gratiot, 1752–1817, born in Lausanne, Switzerland, in 1752, came to Canada in 1769 and engaged in Indian trade. In 1777 he went to Illinois and lived in that area for a number of years. He knew English and French, and aided George Rogers Clark. In 1781 Gratiot moved to St. Louis and engaged in trade on both sides of the Mississippi. He went to Europe in 1791, having business connections with London and his brothers-in-law, Auguste and Pierre Chouteau. A well-known businessman in St. Louis, he amassed a fortune and served there in public office after 1805. He died in 1817. (No good biography of Gratiot exists, but there is abundant manuscript material about his family. See Houck, *History of Missouri;* J. A. James,

said post, who landed, and I also. At this time a storm began which detained us for about an hour. I dispatched said boat and continued journeying. When we were passing in the middle of the island, we observed that a pirogue was descending from above, which came alongside, and on it came Don Pedro Rousseau and Fauré[31] to meet me. We continued with them, and at four-thirty in the evening we arrived in front of Barrancas de Margot, where the squadron was camped.[32] The latter saluted me and I replied. [We made] three leagues.

Thursday, May 21, 1795. Good and calm weather. I spoke with Ugulayacabé.[33] He breakfasted with me, and about nine o'clock he returned to his camp.[34] The setting up of the tents and the establishing of a camp was started.

Friday, May 22, 1795. Good weather, the wind to the north. At ten o'clock I embarked on the galiot *La Vigilante* with all the officers of the expedition except Manuel García,[35] who remained with the squadron. The galiot crossed over [to] the [Las] Casas River. We disembarked, and from there I went by land with the officers to the place where Ugulayacabé had set up his camp with all his warriors. I began my harangue with said chief by means of the inter-

---

ed., *George Rogers Clark Papers* [Springfield, Ill., 1912–26]; J. T. Scharf, *History of St. Louis* [2 vols., Philadelphia, 1883]. Billon, *Annals of St. Louis.* Many manuscripts relating to the Gratiots are in the MHS. The best printed material on Gratiot himself is contained in J. F. McDermott, ed., *Old Cahokia* [St. Louis, 1949], see esp. chap. 4. See also Nasatir, *Before Lewis and Clark,* and Nasatir and Douglas, *Manuel Lisa.*)

31. Dr. Fauré, the fleet's surgeon. He was at the royal hospital in Natchez beginning in 1785 and served at various posts.

32. *La Vigilante* joined the squadron moored on the west bank of the river at a spot which Gayoso christened Campo de la Esperanza [Hopewell]. See Gayoso to Carondelet, No. 6 res., Esperanza, May 23, 1795, P de C 48, encl. in Carondelet to Las Casas, No. 137 res., New Orleans, June 13, 1795, P de C 2364; in Houck, *Spanish Régime*, 2, 114–18. Rousseau to Carondelet, on *La Venganza* at Esperanza, May 26, 1795, P de C 43; Rousseau to Rendón, on *La Venganza* at Esperanza, May 24, 1795, P de C 602B; Rendón to Gardoqui, No. 60, New Orleans, June 17, 1795, Sto. Dom. 87-1-22 [old numbering]; draft in P de C 638; copy in MHS, Papers from Spain No. 88a.

33. Chief Ugulayacabé, "The Wolf's Friend," was a leader of a faction among the Chickasaw Indians that was opposed to the Americans. He received an annual pension of $500 from Spain. The Americans called him "Ugly Cub."

34. Gayoso summoned Ugulayacabé and the interpreter Benjamin Fooy for a secret preliminary conference. As Ugulayacabé appeared agreeable to the Spanish occupation of Barrancas, there remained to be gained only the formal consent of his warriors. The ceremony was set for 10 A.M. the following day. See above, pp. 112–13 and next day's entry in this diary.

35. On García see above, p. 103, n. 29.

preter Fooy,[36] who accompanied me. I pointed out to him the advantages to his nation that would result from a fort being erected on these Barrancas de Amargot, both for their peace and tranquillity, as well as their having a place to take refuge in case of an unexpected attack. He received me according to the fashion of his nation in the midst of all his people, and, seating ourselves underneath a shade, where said chief was seated, our compliments having been exchanged, I told him that I came to repeat in his own country and before his chiefs and *considerados*[37] what I had privately discussed with him the day before,[38] and right after that I talked in great detail of peace with the Creeks and of the establishment of the projected fort. He answered me, disclosing many difficulties, as is customary among Indian chiefs when they speak before their people. I decided to manifest a decisive resolution,[39] repeating in very few words the two points of my commission. I concluded by telling them that I likewise demanded a clear and definite answer, and in order that he might have an opportunity to deliberate over these points with his considerados, I would withdraw until he should call me, which I did, together with all those who had accompanied me.

After nearly an hour had passed he sent someone to call me, and he told me that since I wished to speak with other chiefs of his nation, it would be necessary to wait for them to come, and upon hearing my resolutions they would resolve on what I proposed.[40] I told him that I was satisfied with his manner of thinking, and

---

36. Benjamin Fooy was born in Holland and lived many years among the Choctaw Indians before moving to Natchez in 1788. He had a land concession in Bayou Pierre, where he raised tobacco, maize, and cattle. He aided the Spaniards in obtaining the cession of Chickasaw Bluffs from the Indians and acted as interpreter. There he had difficulties with García, leading to the latter's arrest. Fooy not only established Hopewell in 1798, but was an experienced Indian trader and operated among the Chickasaw Indians. In 1798 Gayoso authorized him to form a Dutch or German settlement near Campo de la Esperanza, where he lived many years. (Gayoso to Carondelet, Barrancas, July 18, 1795, P de C 198; No. 18 res. New Madrid, September 22, 1795, P de C 32. Fooy to García, Barrancas, November 18, 1796, P de C 203; Gayoso to Fooy, New Orleans, July 18, 1798, August 14, 1798, and March 2, 1799; all in P de C 215B. Houck, *History of Missouri*, 2, 152–53; *Spanish Régime*, 2, 114; Samuel C. Williams, *Beginnings of West Tennessee* [Johnson City, Tenn., 1930], pp. 54–55.)

37. For an explanation of a *considéré*, see above, p. 182, n. 55.
38. See above, p. 253, n. 34.
39. To adopt a resolute and decisive attitude.
40. Line omitted in Holmes.

since he also told me that he did not deviate at all from his word, I gave him my thanks for the concession that he had made to me of the very ground on which we found ourselves. Immediately I asked him to tell me when I could transfer my camp to that side, because my people had nothing to do and I desired to employ them at once in clearing the ground of trees and undergrowth and to begin to construct buildings. He replied that whenever I wished I could go there myself, and he asked me what building it was that I intended to erect. To this I answered that I planned to construct a fort to protect them and to safeguard the lands of my King. This seemed all right to him, and he advised me to make it very strong so that they might not remain embarrassed [defenseless], giving me to understand by this that it should be constructed in such a manner that the Americans could not easily take possession of it; for should they succeed in obtaining it, they would deal severely with those that followed any other faction [*partido*] than that of Payemingo.[41] I assured him that the fort would have sufficient cannons and be constructed in such manner that it would not be easy to capture. This concluded, I took my leave. I proposed to them that they come and dine with me if they wished; Ugulayacabé and nine of his considerados followed me. We all embarked on *La Vigilante* and at three o'clock arrived at Campo de la Esperanza [Hopewell]. After eating, said chief and considerados returned to their camp in the pirogues of the galeras.[42]

Saturday, May 23, 1795. Fair weather. At dawn Captain Don Pedro Rousseau crossed in *La Activa*[43] with fifty sailors, and they made

41. Payemingo was head of the "American" faction of the Chickasaws.

42. The activities of May 21 and 22 are also recounted in Gayoso to Carondelet No. 6 res., Esperanza, May 23, 1795, P de C 48; encl. in Carondelet to Las Casas, No. 137 res., New Orleans, June 13, 1795, P de C 2364; in Houck, *Spanish Régime*, 2, 114–18; also encl. in Carondelet to Alcudia, No. 53 res., New Orleans, June 10, 1795, AHN 3899. See Rousseau to Carondelet on *La Venganza* at Esperanza, May 26, 1795, P de C 43; Gayoso to Carondelet, No. 9 res., San Fernando de las Barrancas, P de C 2364; Rousseau to Rendón, on *La Venganza* at Esperanza, May 24, 1795, P de C 602B; Rendón to Gardoqui, No. 60, New Orleans, June 17, 1795, Sto. Dom. 87-1-22 [old numbering]; draft in P de C 638; copy in MHS, Papers from Spain No. 88a. Gayoso to Carondelet, on *La Vigilante* at Esperanza, May 26, 1796, P de C 31; Gayoso to Alcudia, res., New Madrid, September 5, 1795, AHN 3902; draft in P de C 128. See above, pp. 112–13.

43. *La Activa* was in the same class as *La Flecha*. In the opinion of Colonel Carlos de Grandpré, temporary commandant at Natchez in 1795, *La Activa* was a beautiful ship of very favorable construction for military service on the river (Grandpré to Carondelet, Natchez, February 5, 1795, P de C 212B). *La Activa* and *La Flecha* were

the crossing to the place that I had pointed out to them [as the one] to begin to clear, which they did, without encountering any obstacle. At eleven they withdrew to Campo de la Esperanza. At two o'clock in the afternoon the same number of people with said captain came back to continue the clearing, and they withdrew at nightfall. Ugulayacabé came with other considerados to eat with me, and after finishing, I gave them a small gift and included in it nine small barrels of *aguardiente,* which they transported to their camp.[44]

Sunday, May 24, 1795. Fair weather, the wind from the southeast. The clearing could not be continued on the chosen spot, because the Indians were drunk due to the drink that had been given them the day before, and we wished to avoid the slightest quarrel in the situation in which we found them. About twelve o'clock noon I sent a mail pirogue to the post of New Madrid under the care of the sailor Pedro Servant and two more from the squadron of galeras, with pliegos for the commandant of said post.

Monday, May 25, 1795. After Ugulayacabé and all those who accompanied him had left their camp about eight in the morning, I ordered fifty more men under the care of Don Manuel García, in order that they might continue the clearing.[45] About eight-

---

both active on the Upper Mississippi around Barrancas de Margó, New Madrid, and the Illinois country. *La Activa* ascended with the squadron to New Madrid in 1794. It was not on the Upper Mississippi as constantly as was *La Flecha.*

44. In the presence of all the Indians, Rousseau cut down the first tree. Then the sailors began to work, and by the end of the day they had cleared between 6 and 7 arpents of land. When the Indians saw Rousseau work all day completely unarmed, they asked Ugulayacabé to request Gayoso's permission to name him "Payemingo," meaning fearless. Pleased at this request, Gayoso readily consented, and the name was bestowed with great ceremony, each brave solemnly approaching to shake the captain's hand. (Rousseau to Rendón, on *La Venganza* at Esperanza, May 24, 1795, P de C 602B; Rousseau to Carondelet, on *La Venganza* at Esperanza, May 26, 1795, P de C 43; Gayoso to Carondelet, No. 9 res., P de C 2364; Rendón to Gardoqui, No. 60, draft in P de C 638; Gayoso to Carondelet, No. 6 res., P de C 48.)

45. Both land troops and sailors were willing workers, although not accustomed to much regularity or teamwork. At first each man wanted to be boss and tended to work independently of the others, but Gayoso tried to impress on them the value of regularity and method. At times he became very impatient and declared the men incapable of learning or of the desire to learn. Since they seemed unable to work without specific orders, he had to distribute jobs to them every morning, in addition to his other duties as commander-in-chief of the expedition. (Gayoso to Carondelet, on *La Vigilante* at Esperanza, May 26, 1795, P de C 31; Gayoso to Carondelet, San Fernando de las Barrancas, July 18, 1795, P de C 198; Gayoso to Carondelet, No. 18 res., New Madrid, September 22, 1795, P de C 32.)

DIARY

thirty there appeared a boat coming from St. Louis, Illinois, owned by Mr. Tropé, who, with all his family, his furniture, and effects, continued traveling in order to establish himself in the parish of Mr. Cantrer [Cantrelle]. About four in the afternoon the bercha *El Mosquito,* which had ascended in my company,[46] left from this *apostadero* [landing place] of La Esperanza, loaded with peltry, which he was to leave in Nogales for the account of Ugulayacabé. At nightfall all the laborers retired [returned to camp] without anything unusual having transpired [at the clearing].

Tuesday, May 26, 1795. Fair weather. At dawn Don Domingo Boulini,[47] with fifty men, left for the other side of the river to continue the clearing. At ten o'clock in the morning Mr. Tropé's boat left for its destination, taking pliegos of the royal service for the Baron de Carondelet.

Wednesday, May 27, 1795. Variable weather. The same number of people crossed with Captain Don Pedro Rousseau to continue the clearing. They withdrew at eleven o'clock and [then] returned to the same task.[48] About four o'clock I crossed to the other side

---

46. See entry for April 27, above, p. 245.

47. Sublieutenant Don Domingo Bouligny, born in New Orleans in 1773, first served with the river squadron early in 1794, when he ascended with it to New Madrid as commander of the land troops on the galleys. When *La Flecha* joined the fleet at Nogales, Rousseau put him in temporary command of the galiot to replace Ferrúsola, whom he transferred to *La Castilla.* While at New Madrid, Bouligny acted as second in command of Fort Céleste, taking his orders from Portell. He returned to the lower river with the squadron in June, this time in command of *La Felipa.* At Nogales he left the squadron to continue with his troops to New Orleans, arriving early in July. When Carondelet decided to establish a fort at Barrancas de Margó, Bouligny was again attached to the squadron as commander of the land troops that garrisoned the galleys. At Barrancas he was assigned to the command of *La Felipa* and remained on the galley until the squadron's descent in December 1795, when he was transferred to *La Flecha* for the return trip. In February 1796 Carondelet recommended his promotion from sublieutenant to full lieutenant. In the opinion of Rousseau, Bouligny was a very active and vigilant officer, exacting in duty and always dependable. Gayoso reported that he showed talent and a willingness to serve while at Barrancas but that he had the vivacity of a mouse. (See resumé of orders printed in 1794, signed by Robert Macay, New Madrid, August 20, 1799, P de C 134B; Rousseau to Carondelet, on *La Venganza,* Nogales, June 29, 1794, P de C 210; Bouligny to Carondelet, Barrancas, July 15, 1795; San Fernando, July 28, 1795; both in P de C 32. Gayoso to Carondelet, No. 18 res., New Madrid, September 22, 1795, P de C 32; list of subjects recommended by Carondelet for promotion, enclosed in draft [Carondelet] to Prince of Peace, No. 73 res., New Orleans, February 10, 1796, P de C 178A; original in AHN 3886. Gayoso to Carondelet, San Fernando de las Barrancas, July 18, 1795, P de C 198.)

48. "Volvieron a la misma faena"—i.e. returned to their duty on board ship.

to see in what condition the work was. At four-thirty a chalán appeared, whose owner came in a pirogue to draw up alongside *La Activa,* which was in the Las Casas River. He told me he had sold all his flour to the commandant of the post of New Madrid. I signed his passport and he continued the ship's course to New Orleans. At nightfall the people returned to Campo de la Esperanza, having cleared the growth at the foot of the hill, where I have decided that the construction of the fort [should take place].

Thursday, May 28, 1795. Weather overcast and rain; wind variable. In the morning Don Manuel García left with the above mentioned number of people for the other bank of the river in order to begin the clearing on the bluff, where I have decided to place the fort. This he did, and at eleven o'clock in the morning he returned to Campo de la Esperanza. At two in the afternoon they returned to the same place to continue the same work, and Don Pedro Rousseau, with part of the crew from *La Venganza,* began to make the road from the disembarkation point on the Las Casas River to the site of the fort. All withdrew at nightfall, without anything unusual having taken place.

Friday, May 29, 1795. On this day there arrived a flat boat coming from Fort Pitt loaded with flour and which landed below Campo de la Esperanza. [N.B. This sentence is a postscript found at the end of the entry for May 30 in the original manuscript.]

Don Manuel García left at daybreak with the above-mentioned people to continue the clearing on the site of the fort; Don Pedro Rousseau [left] with his people to continue the road that he had begun; and Don Elías Beauregard [left] with a detachment from *La Luisiana* to fix the road of the bluff in order that the artillery might come [be brought] up.[49] They all withdrew at the accustomed hour. In the afternoon all those mentioned returned except Don Pedro Rousseau, who in the morning had finished the road to the place where the fort is to be built. One tree was left in order that it might serve as a flagpole. The top and leaves that it had were cut off and a topmast was put on it. I gave suitable orders so that on the following day the flag could be hoisted. The people withdrew at nightfall, without anything unusual having transpired.

49. To prepare the road in order to transport artillery to the top of the bluff.

Saturday, May 30, 1795. Good weather—calm. At sunrise the first shot was fired as a signal for weighing the anchor of *La Vigilante*. At seven o'clock the second shot was fired, at which signal all the tents of the troops and sailors that had to march were taken down. Before having breakfast twenty sailors of the squadron made the crossing. At seven-thirty, forty men from the Regiment of Louisiana embarked, distributed among *La Vigilante, La Activa,* and *La Venganza,* and the bercha of Don Elías Beauregard. I immediately embarked, accompanied by all the officers of the squadron and land troops. I had fired the third shot as a signal for weighing the anchor and immediately I began to cross, followed by the boats already mentioned at a distance of fifty *toises*. At eight o'clock in the morning I arrived at the disembarkation point in the Las Casas River. I immediately had disembarked the artillery, which consisted of four 4-caliber cannons in marine gun carriages, and two 2-caliber cannons in land gun carriages, with the corresponding munitions and utensils for trenches and all the troops.

With the crews of the boats that had made this crossing I had the above mentioned artillery taken to the destined place of the fort, escorted by the troop from *La Luisiana*. At that place they were mounted and placed on the esplanade that had been arranged there the day before. All of this was concluded by ten-thirty, at which time I myself climbed with the rest of the troop formed into a column under the command of Don Elías Beauregard, accompanied by the whole body of officers.

The squadron formed in two divisions, one under the orders of Captain Don Pedro Rousseau and the other under the orders of Don Manuel García [and] were placed facing this post, each one on the opposite bank of the Mississippi.

My battery having been set up in front of the flagstaff and above the river, I myself, with all the officers, hoisted the royal flag and saluted it with a cannon shot. As soon as it was seen by the squadron, each vessel saluted it with fifteen cannons, and when that was concluded, the battery of this new post likewise made a royal salute. The squadron then fired a salute and the salvos on land were concluded with three general volleys from the infantry.[50]

---

50. A line in this paragraph is missing in Holmes, *Documentos,* and 2 words are also missing earlier in this day's entry.

This occurrence having taken place on a day so distinguished as the name day of our Most Serene Prince of Asturias, I thought that I should not give it any other name than that of San Fernando de las Barrancas,[51] a circumstance which filled with enthusiasm all the individuals of this expedition, who, with the most expressive demonstrations, manifested their love and loyalty to our August Sovereign. The function all completed, they began to mark out the camp and to set up the tents for the troops.[52] At nightfall His Majesty's galera *La Venganza* withdrew to Campo de la Esperanza with orders to return the following day.

Sunday, May 31, 1795. Appearances of rain. At dawn Don Manuel García crossed to this fort of San Fernando with thirty men and the galera *La Venganza* in order to continue the work, to which an effective beginning was made by an intrenchment of cut-down trees, and the rest of the works were continued as usual. About eight in the morning I was on board the chalán, which was found tied below Campo de la Esperanza, and *La Activa* and the bercha of Don Elías Beauregard went in search of 100 barrels of flour, which I bought from the owner of the chalán for provisions for this post, which boats returned to this disembarkation point with said quantity of flour. The master of the chalán came. I had Captain Don Elías Beauregard, commandant of this fort,[53] give him a certificate that accredited him with being creditor of the amount of the 100 barrels of flour at the prices current in the capital, which he did immediately. I signed his passport and handed him a pli-

51. This name pleased the Indians, who proceeded to show their enthusiasm with expressive demonstrations of their love and loyalty for the Spanish King. (Gayoso to Carondelet, Fort San Fernando, May 31, 1795, P de C 2364; Gayoso to Alcudia, res., New Madrid, September 5, 1795, AHN 3902; draft in P de C 128).

52. In a letter to Alcudia, Gayoso de Lemos gives an account of the cession of Barrancas to Spain and the establishment of Fort San Fernando de las Barrancas at that location. There is enclosed with the letter a certified copy of the treaty with the Chickasaws and a sketch of the grant. (Gayoso to Alcudia, New Madrid, September 5, 1795, AHN 3902; draft without encls. in P de C 128.) I have a colored sketch made from Gayoso's letter. A copy of it is published in Miguel Gómez del Campillo, *Relaciones diplomáticas entre España y los Estados Unidos*, *1* (2 vols. Madrid, 1944), 289, and in other places. The date of the formal taking of possession is also given in draft of [Carondelet] to Rendón, New Orleans, June 15, 1795, P de C 31.

53. Beauregard was appointed commandant of the post officially by Gayoso on May 31, but until San Fernando could be more definitely established, Beauregard was to remain under the orders of Gayoso (Beauregard to Carondelet, No. 1, Barrancas, June 1, 1795, P de C 32.

ego [sealed envelope] for Don José Vidal, in which went another for the Baron de Carondelet, and he went away. The rest of the day passed without anything unusual occurring.

Monday, June 1, 1795. Don Domingo Bouligny crossed from Campo de la Esperanza to this fort at about two-thirty,[54] with thirty men, who, with an equal number from the troops, continue the work. At three o'clock there arrived by land an Indian from the Choctaw nation who, according to what he says, was just promenading, and he told me that from a tributary of the Yazú [Yazoo] River he had heard the cannons that were fired at this fort. The day ended without anything unusual happening.

Tuesday, June 2, 1795. At dawn Don Manuel García, with 30 sailors and an equal number of troops, continued the work. After breakfast I embarked on my galiot with Don Pedro Rousseau [and] with the engineer Don Juan Perchet, Don Domingo Bontu [Bontoux], Don Domingo Bouligny, and Don Antonio Cruzat, and I went reconnoitering these Barrancas de Margó down the river to the Carondelet River. I entered within it [the Carondelet River] and proceeded to a distance of about half a mile. I could not go further, having encountered a mud bank [*embarada*] which impeded me there. I put the vessel to land, and Don Domingo Bouligny, Don Antonio Cruzat, an artilleryman, and the man named Flechar disembarked in order to return by land. I went out into the Mississippi River and continued going up along the edge of the bluffs. At one o'clock I arrived at the disembarkation point of this fort and found Bouligny, Cruzat, and the rest, who had arrived by land. The work was continued as usual, and at nightfall the people withdrew to their places.

Wednesday, June 3, 1795. The work was continued as usual. At one o'clock the King's boat, *El Príncipe de Asturias,* arrived at this fort proceeding from New Madrid under the command of the lieutenant of the militiamen of said post, Don Robert Macay [McCoy]. It came loaded with provisions for the account of the royal treasury, for the use of this post and squadron of galeras. The work continued as usual.

Thursday, June 4, 1795. At dawn an equal number of sailors crossed over to continue the work with the troop. The provisions

---
54. Or they worked until about two-thirty.

began to be unloaded by the troops which the boat *El Príncipe de Asturias* had brought. In the work there was nothing unusual that occurred.

Friday, June 5, 1795. The same number of people were employed on the work. At five o'clock in the afternoon there arrived a chalán proceeding from Kentucky loaded with flour, which is going on to New Orleans. I gave it a letter for Don José Vidal and another for Ygnacio Delinó, and at two o'clock in the morning it [the boat] left. The rest of the day passed without anything unusual occurring.

Saturday, June 6, 1795. At eight o'clock there arrived two chalanes from Fort Pitt, and from that of Don Alexandro Fulton there were purchased fifty barrels of flour for the use of this post at New Orleans prices. The work continues as usual. 3650 [pounds of][55] bacon, which the boat brought, were thrown into the water because it [sic] was found to be spoiled.

Sunday, June 7, 1795. At daybreak *La Felipa* crossed in order to put the flour on it. At ten o'clock in the morning the boat *El Príncipe de Asturias* left for the post of New Madrid, and at ten-thirty the two chalanes from Fort Pitt left for New Orleans, to which were given a pliego [sealed envelope] for the secretary of Natchez.

Monday, June 8, 1795. The work continues, without anything unusual occurring.

Tuesday, June 9, 1795. At eight-thirty there arrived at this post His Majesty's galiot *La Flecha,* under the command of Don Francisco Langlois,[56] which came escorting a chalán from New Madrid that was loaded with oxen for pulling, cattle, and provisions for this post. The work continues as usual. At 12 o'clock there arrived a chalán with flour which is going to New Orleans.

Wednesday, June 10, 1795. A *casa-fuerte* was begun on the side that overlooks the level country. The work continues as usual.

---

55. There is a blank in the original. Gayoso wrote a letter to Carondelet (No. 1, San Fernando de Barrancas, June 12, 1795, P de C 43), in which he told the Governor General that he has asked Portell for provisions, but that the pork there was not of the best quality and caused an epidemic, hence he "dumped it into the river" and purchased goods from a chalán, because they were short and they were expecting visits from the Indians.

56. For Langlois see above, p. 92, n. 12.

Thursday, June 11, 1795. Good weather. The people are at work. At two o'clock there arrived eight chalanes coming from Ohio, at which hour I went out on my galiot to receive them. I later made the crossing to Campo de la Esperanza. I again made the crossing about an hour later, and I continued up the Las Casas River for about a league and returned at nightfall to the disembarkation point.

Friday, June 12, 1795. Fair weather. In view of the scarcity of provisions with which we found ourselves, I ordered that there be taken from the chalanes a consignment of ham and bacon at the price current in Natchez. At nine o'clock five chalanes set out down the river, and at twelve the other three left to continue journeying to the capital. At three o'clock *La Flecha* was unloaded and the maize was taken to the warehouse of the fort. In the afternoon a downpour of rain occurred.

Saturday, June 13, 1795. Good weather. At seven o'clock we began to unload the flour which was on board *La Activa* and the bercha of Beauregard, and immediately it was conveyed to the warehouse of the post. At eleven o'clock the chiefs of the Chickasaw nation, Guillermo Glover and Payehuma and forty Indians of the same nation arrived. The first named chief came with the message from the king of the nation, and the second with that from Ugulayacabé, chief of the same [nation], and they camped near the fort.

I ordered that at nightfall all the boats should cross over to the island, and that at the same time there should come as a reinforcement to the fort forty-two men from the galeras, with an officer from them in order that they might pass the night carrying out the necessary watches, and that at daybreak they should withdraw—all of which was carried out, Don Francisco Langlois coming with said reinforcement. All day and all night passed without anything unusual occurring.

Sunday, June 14, 1795. I summoned all the officers to a congress with the Indians, which I set for 9 o'clock, at which hour the Indians came. I began with the points of my commission, and we continued until one o'clock, when it concluded and a salute of five cannons was made. The same reinforcement people continued with the same officer.[57] The day passed without anything unusual occurring.

---

[57] A line is omitted in this day's entry in Holmes, *Documentos*.

Monday, June 15, 1795. Day broke clear and calm. At six-thirty the galera *La Felipa,* which was on the other side, crossed over here, and as soon as it was tied up fifty barrels of flour were unloaded and were taken to the warehouse.

Seeing the delay of the boat *La Cérés* [*Céréz*],[58] I ordered that a pirogue with nine men go out immediately to see if they could find it [going] as far as the *pequeña pradería* [small meadow], which it did, starting out at nine o'clock.

---

58. After the treaty was signed (see entry for June 20, below, p. 266), Gayoso presented some presents to the Indians. He had been able to bring only a few presents on *La Vigilante* when he ascended the river, and these were distributed to Ugulayacabé and his braves when the Spaniards first began clearing ground for the fort in May. (See entry for May 23, above, pp. 256–57.) The bulk of the presents to be used as payment for Barrancas was supposed to follow him on the lanchón *La Céréz,* together with funds for the expedition and additional provisions and building materials for the fort.

Early in May *La Céréz* left Natchez under orders to proceed at full speed until it met the squadron. The lanchón's patrón knew very little about navigation, however, and as he managed the boat very poorly, its progress was slow. Just 25 leagues above Nogales it sprung a leak and began shipping water so badly that it was necessary to return to Nogales for repairs. As a result of all these delaying factors, the lanchón was unable to reach Barrancas before early July (see entry for July 6, below, p. 270.) Gayoso, who expected *La Céréz* to appear about June 1, was greatly disturbed by its delay. By the 12th his meat supply was down to half a barrel for all the men in both the land and river forces. Luckily, he was able to buy some ham and bacon from passing chalanes, but such meat was very expensive.

As the days passed and the lanchón still failed to arrive, Gayoso sent a searching party in a pirogue down the river to look for it. He feared a serious accident might have occurred, in which case it would be difficult to pacify the Indians and make them believe their gifts were really coming. Having run low on provisions, the search party returned on the 22nd only to report that it saw no sign of the missing lanchón. (See entry for June 22, below, p. 267.)

The restlessness of the Indians increased until finally they announced that they could wait no longer but had to return to their village at once. Gayoso saw that they suspected no lanchón was ever intended to bring them gifts, and he feared the Americans might try to take advantage of the situation. Already a rumor was being circulated that the Spaniards had called the Chickasaws to Barrancas to divide them so that the Creeks could enter their villages without risk. Although the rumor was false, the fact that, while Ugulayacabé was at Barrancas, the Creeks entered Chickasaw country and the villages were saved only by Payemingo's intervention lent plausibility to the story. The Indians were tired of waiting but unwilling to return home empty-handed. Gayoso promised them he would do everything in his power to avoid such a necessity the moment *La Céréz* arrived. This seemed to satisfy them for the time being, for although Glover and a few braves left on June 25, Payehuma and the rest remained to await their gifts. (See entry for June 25, below, p. 268.)

Extremely worried that some accident had befallen the lanchón, Gayoso ordered Manuel Lisa, who was descending to the capital with letters for Carondelet, to search

At four o'clock I went out in my galiot *La Vigilante,* accompanied by the galera *La Venganza,* to test the workings of said galiot. With me went Bontoux, Glover, and Payehuma, and on *La Venganza* went Don Pedro Rousseau, Bouligny, Fauré, and García. We went up to the Carondelet River. I entered it, but after a very short distance I came out again. We started on our return. I arrived at the disembarkation point at eight o'clock and *La Venganza* arrived at nine-thirty. Nothing unusual happened during the day.

Tuesday, June 16, 1795. At daybreak the people went to work. At twelve o'clock there appeared six chalanes which tied up on the

---

carefully for any news or trace of it during his descent. As it was imperative that the gifts *La Céréz* carried be delivered to the Chickasaws, he urged Carondelet to dispatch another vessel with more presents immediately if Lisa reported finding no signs of the lanchón between Barrancas and New Orleans. To speed the progress of the second vessel, he suggested that it might be provided with 2 extra men in addition to its regular crew and, as a precaution against theft, guarded by 8 trusted men from the New Orleans garrison. Gayoso also instructed Commandant de Vilemont at Arkansas to watch closely for news of *La Céréz,* warning him to keep an eye out for its crew in case they had robbed the lanchón and fled with its funds.

The day after Lisa's departure, Gayoso ordered Langlois to take *La Flecha* down the Mississippi as far as the White River to look for the missing boat. The galiot discovered *La Céréz* about 8 leagues above the White River, in a very leaky condition, but with the assistance of Langlois' men, it finally managed to reach Barrancas on July 6. (See entry for that date below, p. 270.)

(Most of the above account has been taken from entries in this diary up to July 6. But see also the following upon which it has been based: Gayoso to Carondelet, No. 6 res., Esperanza, May 23, 1795, P de C 48; encl. in Carondelet to Las Casas, No. 137 res., New Orleans, June 13, 1795, P de C 2364; in Houck, *Spanish Régime,* 2, 114-18. Gayoso to Carondelet, No. 3 res., on *La Vigilante,* 15 leagues from the Arkansas River, May 4, 1795, P de C 31; Grand-Pré to Delinó, Natchez, May 2, 1795, P de C 129; draft in P de C 127. Gayoso to Carondelet, No. 3, Barrancas, July 19, 1795, P de C 43; Gayoso to Carondelet, Barrancas, June 12, 1795, P de C 43; Gayoso to Carondelet, No. 1, San Fernando de Barrancas, June 12, 1795, P de C 43; Gayoso to Carondelet, Barrancas, June 18, 1795, P de C 43; Rousseau to Carondelet, on *La Venganza* in Las Casas River, June 24, 1795, P de C 211; Gayoso to Carondelet, No. 12 res., Barrancas, June 24, 1795, P de C 43; Gayoso to Carondelet, Barrancas, June 24, 1795, P de C 43; Gayoso to Vilemont, Barrancas, June 24, 1795, P de C 48.)

A few days after the arrival of *La Céréz* it was repaired sufficiently to descend to the capital, but it did not leave at once because supplies for its crew and passengers were lacking. By the end of the month it was ready to go, taking with it several men with very bad cases of scurvy. The lack of fresh fruits and vegetables at Barrancas caused a number of scurvy cases to develop in the squadron's crews, and by July one death had already resulted. (See entry for July 11, below, p. 270; Gayoso to Carondelet, No. 3, Barrancas, July 19, 1795, P de C 43; Gayoso to Carondelet, San Fernando de Barrancas, July 29, 1795, P de C 198.)

island on the opposite side of the river. After eating, I went out on my galiot to reconnoiter them; at ——[59] a heavy shower fell. Night fell with overcast skies and drizzling. The squadron crossed over to the other side of the island as I ordered.

Wednesday, June 17, 1795. Day broke clear. The squadron crossed over to the disembarkation place. The same people went to work. At nine the chalanes set out to float down the river. At twelve o'clock there arrived a boat from New Madrid coming from Illinois [and] belonging to Don Juan Bautista Vallé. At five o'clock it began to rain and blow in all directions, and thus it continued until ten o'clock at night. The squadron crossed as ordered.

Thursday, June 18, 1795. Day broke with a strong southeastern cool wind. The squadron remained on the Isla de Fooy. Night fell overcast. At eleven o'clock at night a slight storm came up, and thus it passed, with nothing unusual occurring.

Friday, June 19, 1795. Day dawned overcast and raining. At six o'clock Mr. Vallé's boat put out for New Orleans, to whom [Vallé] I handed some pliegos of the royal service for the Baron. At nine o'clock it stopped raining and the work continued. The rest of the day passed without anything unusual happening.

Saturday, June 20, 1795. Good weather. I gave orders to all the officers so that they might be in [my?] tent at 10 o'clock. Precisely at said hour we all gathered, the chiefs of the Chickasaw nation, Guillermo Glover, and Payehuma having come with the interpreter Don Benjamin Fooy. I took out two maps on which were marked out the confines of this post, demarcated with ——[60] [a gold] colored line, and at the bottom of each was explained in the Castilian language the said boundaries that the Chickasaw nation was granting to us, and underneath [where] the royal seal [was], I signed next to the seal. Afterward I had the following sign: Don Elías Beauregard, Don Pedro Rousseau, Don Domingo Bontoux, Don Manuel García, Don Francisco Langlois, Don Domingo Bouligny, Don José Zamora, Don Luis Fauré, Don Antonio Cruzat, Don Juan Perchet; and afterward the above-mentioned chiefs made their signs, and underneath them Don Benjamin Fooy signed. This ceremony concluded, I lighted my pipe and gave it

---

59. Blank in document.
60. Blank in document. Holmes says "color de oro."

DIARY

to the chiefs to smoke, as is customary among them. After everything was finished, for the sake of a good effect, I had the fort salute them with seven cannons, which concluded, the squadron followed, firing all their artillery.[61]

Since Indians said they had heard a shot like a swivel gun shot below the Isla de Diamante, I ordered a pirogue to go out to see if it was *La Céréz,* and when it returned at nine o'clock, it reported that it had seen nothing. The day passed without anything unusual occurring.

Sunday, June 21, 1795. Good weather. There was no work today, it being a holiday. Nothing unusual has occurred.

Monday, June 22, 1795. Good weather. About ten o'clock there arrived the pirogue that had gone to give aid to *La Céréz,* the one that had descended to the small meadow, and it saw nothing. At seven o'clock they finished, raising the second building [?] of the casa-fuerte.[62] Nothing unusual.

---

61. The limits of the cession as described in the treaty were as follows: the northern boundary ran along Las Casas River, known also as the River of the Two Chickasaws, from the mouth of the Arroyo Gayoso to the Mississippi and including the Island of Fooy; the western boundary extended along the Mississippi from a point about 2 leagues from the mouth of the Las Casas River to the mouth of the Carondelet; the southern boundary ran up the Carondelet River from its mouth to its first branch toward the north; while the eastern boundary followed the Arroyo Gayoso from its mouth in Las Casas River to its source just above the first northern branch of the Carondelet. The intervening space between the sources of the Arroyo Gayoso and Carondelet Rivers was marked by a line connecting the two points at the shortest place. (Gayoso to Carondelet, on *La Vigilante* at Esperanza, May 26, 1795, P de C 31; Gayoso to Carondelet, on *La Vigilante* at Esperanza, June 18, 1795, P de C 43; Gayoso to Alcudia, res., New Madrid, September 5, 1795, AHN 3902; draft in P de C 128.)

Officially the cession included 3,000 arpents of land but Gayoso hoped that the Spaniards might actually control over 10,000 arpents (Gayoso to Carondelet, *La Vigilante* at Esperanza, May 26, 1795, P de C 31). A copy of the treaty is enclosed in Gayoso to Alcudia, res., New Madrid, September 5, 1795, in AHN 3902. Gayoso sent a copy to Carondelet a few days after it was signed. However, the original of the treaty was sent by Gayoso by the hand of Bontoux de la Blache, who descended to the capital late in September. (Gayoso to Carondelet, Barrancas, June 24, 1795, P de C 43; Gayoso to Carondelet, No. 18 res., New Madrid, September 22, 1795, P de C 32.)

62. Or the second story of the casa-fuerte was completed. The original says, "a las 7 se concluyó de levantar al 2° cuerpo de la casa fuerte." Two stronghouses were built and two more were to be built (see Gayoso to Carondelet, San Fernando de las Barrancas, July 18, 1795, P de C 198). Work on the second stronghouse began on July 14 (see entry for that date, below, p. 272). Toward the end of August the third

Tuesday, June 23, 1795. [Today] dawned overcast and cloudy. At seven o'clock there arrived a bercha belonging to Don Manuel de Lisa,[63] which was coming from Port Princet [Vincennes]. Night fell, with rain.

Wednesday, June 24, 1795. Cloudy weather. At three o'clock in the afternoon there arrived three chalanes, two of them belonging to Mr. Shap [Sharp], and the other belonged to the man named Mr. Coy [McCoy?]. I went out in my galiot to receive them. Night fell, with a clear sky and with nothing unusual having occurred.

Thursday, June 25, 1795. Day broke. At six o'clock[64] there arrived a boat and a chalán from New Madrid with provisions for this post. The boat came from Illinois. At nine o'clock Don Manuel Lisa put out in his bercha to descend to the capital with pliegos of the royal service. Immediately, they began to unload the boat from Illinois and the chalán. At eleven-thirty the galiot *La Flecha*, with its commander Don Francisco Langlois and eight men in addition to its crew, left to give reinforcement to *La Céréz*, with orders to go as far as the White River, where the detachment of the Arkansas Post is stationed. At twelve o'clock Guillermo Glover

---

stronghouse was nearly completed, and by the middle of September the fourth and last was almost up (Rousseau to Carondelet, on *La Venganza at Ecores*, August 22, 1795, P de C 211; Gayoso to Carondelet, New Madrid September 12, 1795, P de C 32). In October, Rousseau reported that the fort was completely enclosed except for a fortified curtain in front; a ramp below was begun, and the workmen were already at work on the commandant's house (Rousseau to Gayoso, on *La Venganza* at San Fernando, October 7, 1795, P de C 211; Rousseau to Gayoso, on *La Venganza*, October 12, 1795, P de C 211). By the end of November the entire enclosure was finished, as well as a superb ramp and the commandant's house (Rousseau to Gayoso, on *La Venganza*, at San Fernando, November 25, 1795, P de C 211). Collot describes Fort San Fernando in his *Journey in North America*, 2, chap. 19.

63. When Lisa left he was ordered by Gayoso to be on the lookout for *La Céréz* (see note on *La Céréz* above, p. 264, n. 58; Gayoso to Carondelet, San Fernando, June 24, 1795, P de C 43).

Manuel Lisa's fascinating life has been partially related in both novel and biographical form. A number of Lisa documents are printed in Nasatir, *Before Lewis and Clark*. The best sketch of his life was for many years W. B. Douglas, "Manuel Lisa," in MHS *Collections*, 3, 233–68, 367–406. I have recently expanded those articles into a full biography and written the early life of Lisa, adding much documentary evidence. See Nasatir and Douglas, *Manuel Lisa*. A well written novel of Lisa's life is Shirley Seifert, *Those Who Go against the Current* (New York, 1943). R. E. Oglesby's *Manuel Lisa and the Opening of the Missouri Fur Trade* (Norman, 1963) is a good readable account, but it is not a full biography and has little on Lisa's early life.

64. Gayoso perhaps forgot to mention the weather here as is his usual custom, and he meant to say that at six o'clock the vessel arrived.

left for his nation with a number of people carrying letters for various chiefs of his nation, and Payehuma remained here with the rest of his people. At ——[65] in the afternoon, while the boat was being unloaded, they began to put on board the ship the Indian effects for Illinois. The day passed without anything further unusual happening.

Friday, June 26, 1795. At eight o'clock *La Activa* departed for the *Cipriera* [Cypress Grove] in search of stakes. At ten-thirty the boat left for Illinois, [and] also a canoe with the people that came in the chalán. At six o'clock a pirogue from the squadron was dispatched with pliegos in order to deliver them to said boat. At this time *La Activa* arrived with the stakes. Nothing unusual occurred.

[Saturday] June 27, 1795. It dawned. At five in the afternoon a storm arose which lasted until nine o'clock, when it ceased. During the night some heavy showers fell.

Sunday, June 28, 1795. Day broke clear. The work continues. Nothing unusual.

Monday, June 29, 1795. Good weather. Nothing unusual.

Tuesday, June 30, 1795. As usual.

Wednesday, July 1, 1795. As usual.

Thursday, July 2, 1795. As usual.

Friday, July 3, 1795. As usual.

Saturday, July 4, 1795. As usual.

Sunday, July 5, 1795. Good weather. At one-thirty Don Francisco Langlois with *La Flecha* arrived and on it came the——[66] Second [Sergeant] Baron of Statenfield,[67] and he told us that he had left *La Céréz* below the Isla del Diamante.[68] The work continues as usual.

---

65. No hour is given in the original.
66. Blank in the original document.
67. The Baron de Statenfield was employed as major-domo of the works in the fort at Barrancas at a salary of 6 reales per day. He continued in that position until well into the fall, when a severe illness forced him to descend to the capital for treatment. He left with Perchet in the latter part of October. Gayoso liked the Baron's work, and commented on his punctuality. (Gayoso to Carondelet, No. 3, Barrancas, July 19, 1795, P de C 43; Gayoso to Carondelet, Barrancas, July 18, 1795, P de C 198; Rousseau to Gayoso, on *La Venganza* at Ecores à Margot, October 31, 1795, P de C 211.)
68. See note on *La Céréz*, p. 264, n. 58.

Monday, July 6, 1795. At seven o'clock in the morning the *lanchón La Céréz* arrived, and immediately we began to unload. In inspecting the effects for the Indians,[69] there were found seven damaged and useless dresscoats and some other small trifles. I was informed as to the reason of the delay of said lanchón, and it was because it had to return to Nogales, when it was already 25 leagues from that place, on account of said boat leaking. A chalán arrived with lime for this post.

Tuesday, July 7, 1795. Nothing unusual occurred all day, and the chalán went down the river.

Wednesday, July 8, 1795. I ordered that the present for the Indians be given, which was delivered to them in the afternoon, except for the aguardiente, which I kept from presenting to them until the time of their departure. At three in the afternoon there arrived a pirogue from Nogales with five soldiers, which brought me pliegos from the governor general.

Thursday, July 9, 1795. I had the liquor given to the Indians, since they had told me they were leaving. At four o'clock in the afternoon there arrived seven Chickasaws, who told me that Ugulayacabé should arrive very soon. The day passed with nothing unusual occurring.

Friday, July 10, 1795. Because of the arrival of the Indians the day before, the party that had received their presents delayed [their departure]. At nine o'clock I sent *La Flecha* with Langlois to go and give aid to the boat that was ascending with Don Martin Palao and the transport troop. At six o'clock a pirogue arrived coming from Natchez with three Englishmen[70] who are ascending to New Madrid [and] who delivered a letter to me. Night fell, with nothing unusual occurring.

Saturday, July 11, 1795. At eight the boat *La Céréz* was grounded in order to be examined. At three-thirty Mr. Chouteau's boat, which is ascending to the Illinois, arrived from New Orleans. At four o'clock I dispatched a pirogue to New Madrid with three

---

69. Gayoso ordered the Chickasaw's presents to be unloaded immediately so that Zamora could determine the amount of damage done by the water that was flooding the boat. He found all the garments in the cargo quite ruined and so water-soaked they were falling apart. (See Gayoso to Carondelet, No. 3, Barrancas, July 19, 1795, P de C 43.)

70. See entry for July 12, above, p. 272.

DIARY

sailors, to whom I delivered letters for Don Tomás Portell, asking him for provisions,[71] since we have only enough for nine days. At five o'clock the boat set out again to ascend the river.

71. Located only 44 leagues above Barrancas, New Madrid was the post best suited to serve the new fort as a base of supply and did serve as chief base of supply for Fort San Fernando throughout its brief existence. The Illinois posts also served the new post as a source of supply, especially in the matters of food, while the lead mines near Ste. Geneviève furnished materials for bullets. Sometimes boats from Illinois belonging to private individuals on their way to sell their cargoes in New Orleans took provisions to Barrancas and sold meat and flour. Gayoso ordered such purchases made from Spanish and American boats descending the river. Langlois on *La Flecha*, Macay on the lanchón *El Príncipe de Asturias*, Ferrúsola on the cañonera *El Rayo*, as well as *La Felipa*, smaller chalanes and other boats were used at times to deliver provisions to the new establishment at Barrancas. (See various entries in the diary and the following: Portell to Carondelet, No. 402, New Madrid, May 17, 1795, P de C 33; draft [Carondelet] to Portell, New Orleans, June 1, 1795, P de C 128; draft [Gayoso] to Trudeau, on *La Vigilante* at Esperanza, May 24, 1795, P de C 222B; Portell to Gayoso, No. 2, New Madrid, June 1, 1795, P de C 48; draft [Gayoso] to Portell, Barrancas, June 5, 1795, P de C 222B; Vallé to Portell, Ste. Geneviève, July 9, 1795, P de C 211; Folch to Carondelet, San Fernando, June 7, 1796, P de C 33; Gayoso to Carondelet, No. 1, San Fernando de Barrancas, June 12, 1795, P de C 43; Gayoso to Portell, Barrancas, June 6, 1795, P de C 43; encl. in draft [Portell] to Richardo Waters, New Madrid, June 17, 1795, P de C 43. Gayoso to Portell, on *La Vigilante* at Las Barrancas Blancas, October 8, 1795, P de C 43; Langlois to Carondelet, No. 24, on *La Felipa* at Barrancas, June 28, 1796, P de C 33; Portell to Langlois, New Madrid, February 6, 1796, P de C 48; Portell to Carondelet, No. 433, New Madrid, February 12, 1796, P de C 33; copy in P de C 215A.)

Not all went well with the supplies from New Madrid, especially in the case of meat. Some supplies, unavailable at the upper posts, were obtained from Natchez—as, for example, pitch, tar, tallow, rope, iron, and nails, used for repairing the galleys. In the matter of the supplies trouble broke out with Portell. While both Rousseau and Folch (who replaced Beauregard as commandant at San Fernando in September) lodged numerous complaints against him, Folch's own quarrel with him broke out into an open and regular feud. Although Gayoso, who sided with Portell, tried to smooth matters over between the two commandants, he was not conspicuously successful, for a feeling of mutual animosity existed between Portell and Folch until the latter was transferred from San Fernando in the summer of 1796. (See Gayoso to Carondelet, No. 1, Barrancas, June 12, 1795, P de C 43; certificate of provisions received by Zamora, signed by Rousseau, October 1, 1795; copy certified by Portell, New Madrid, October 19, 1795, P de C 48. Draft [Gayoso] to Carondelet, No. 18, New Madrid, October 5, 1795, P de C 32; Gayoso to Portell, on *La Vigilante*, Ribera Gabury, October 26, 1795, P de C 43; draft [Gayoso] to Grande-Pré, New Madrid, October 5, 1795, P de C 130; Rousseau to Gayoso, on *La Venganza* [at San Fernando], October 12, 1795, P de C 211; Beauregard to Gayoso, No. 19, Barrancas, September 18, 1795, P de C 128; Beauregard to Carondelet, New Orleans, October 19, 1795, P de C 32; 2 letters of Portell to Folch, New Madrid, October 21, 1795, both certified by Gayoso, P de C 43; Folch to Gayoso, San Fernando, October 30, 1795, copy certified by Gayoso, P de C 43; Gayoso to Carondelet, New Madrid, December 3, 1795, P de C 43; Gayoso to Carondelet, New Madrid, December 6, 1795, P de C 43; Gayoso to Carondelet, No. 24,

Note. At dawn Don Pedro Rousseau left to meet Chouteau's boat and at eight he was back with the pliegos. In the morning the Indians left, those who arrived on the ninth remaining.[72]

Sunday, July 12, 1795. Day broke clear. At eight o'clock eight men departed to make bricks. At twelve o'clock a shower fell. This morning I delivered a present to each of the four Indians who had remained here, and they left immediately. At one o'clock there left for New Madrid the canoe of the Englishmen who had arrived on the tenth. At six o'clock in the afternoon a canoe with two men from Arkansas arrived, loaded with peltry and suet. It is ascending to New Madrid. Night fell, clear.

Monday, July 13, 1795. Good weather. The people always at work. This morning a small group of Indians arrived. The rest of the day passed as usual.

Tuesday, July 14, 1795. It dawned clear. At the accustomed time twenty men were sent to continue the clearing on the south side, and the workmen began the second casa-fuerte on the south side. About three o'clock the principal chief of the Chickasaw nation, Ugulayacabé, arrived with his wife and children and a large party of the same nation, who encamped a short distance from the fort.

Wednesday, July 15, 1795. Last night the Indians became inebriated, for which reason Chief Ugulayacabé could not come to see me this day. The work continues as usual.

Thursday, July 16, 1795. I sent all the troops and sailors to —— Fort.[73] About nine-thirty Ugulayacabé came to visit me, with whom I entered into a conference regarding my commission. The chief stated that he was very happy to see the work so advanced. When my conference was over, and to show him that I myself was very happy to see him, I had five cannons fired and the royal flag raised. At ten-thirty a shower of rain fell. The rest of the day as usual.

New Madrid, December 6, 1795, P de C 43; draft in P de C 32. Portell to Carondelet, No. 433, New Madrid, February 12, 1796, P de C 33; Ferrúsola to Vallé, Barrancas, July 7, 1796, MHS, Vallé Collection, No. 6.)

72. From time to time throughout the summer, small bands of Chickasaws continued to visit the Spanish camp and were always given a present before they left.

73. Blank in the original. "To the *casa-fuerte*," says Holmes.

Friday, July 17, 1795. Good weather. The people are at work. At eleven I ordered the present for the Indians brought up to this fort, which was done. At two o'clock the present was taken to the camp of the Indians. Ugulayacabé left [with] Borgan various articles that he could not take with him. In the afternoon, accompanied by Rousseau, I went to see Ugulayacabé, who was distributing the present to his party. All the rest of the day passed without anything unusual occurring.

Saturday, July 18, 1795. This morning all the Indians left for their nation except the chiefs Ugulayacabé and Payehuma, who remained to dine with me. After eating, the two chiefs said goodbye to me and departed. The rest of the day as usual.

Sunday, July 19, 1795. The people are at work, and the day passed without anything unusual happening. It was observed that two laborers were missing from the group.

Monday, July 20, 1795. At eight o'clock Beauregard, Fooy, and Frazer left on horseback in search of the two workmen. At six in the afternoon they returned without having found them. Shortly afterward said individuals presented themselves and were placed in stocks. At nightfall a vessel was sighted coming down the river, and shortly afterward the vessel of the King, *El Príncipe de Asturias,* its commander Don Roberto McCoy, arrived with provisions it was carrying from New Madrid for this post. Nothing more occurred.

Tuesday, July 21, 1795. The boat was unloaded. At the break of day *La Venganza* left to camp on the outer side of the Isla [de] Fooy. Nothing more happened.

Wednesday, July 22, 1795. At daybreak the mail pirogue left for Nogales with sealed envelopes [pliegos] of the royal service for the Baron.[74] The people worked as usual. Nothing unusual occurred.

Thursday, July 23, 1795. The second *cuerpo* [section or story] of the second casa-fuerte having been finished, it was set up, and at twelve it was in place. At four o'clock I went with the officers of the squadron on board my galiot to take a pleasure sail on the Rio

---

74. On July 19, 1795, in his letter No. 2, Gayoso had sent Carondelet the *plan* for the casa-fuerte (P de C 43).

Lobos [Wolf River] for a half league, whence we returned. The day passed without anything unusual occurring.

Friday, July 24, 1795. The works continue as usual. Nothing in particular occurred during the day.

Saturday, July 25, 1795. The work continues as usual.

Sunday, July 26, 1795. There was no work, this being a holiday. The man named Brashears arrived with six of Panton's[75] slaves,

> 75. One of the Spaniards' main talking points for persuading the Chickasaws to permit them to occupy Barrancas was that a Spanish fort there would serve as a protection for the trading post that Juan Turnbull was planning to establish on the bluffs. Turnbull was an Indian trader who dealt mainly with the Chickasaws. He already had some warehouses on the Movila and Yazoo Rivers, and as early as December 1792 Carondelet considered the advantages of allowing him to establish himself on the Margot River as well. By the time the Spaniards finally succeeded in securing the cession of Barrancas, however, Carondelet had forgotten Turnbull. Before the negotiations had even begun, he commissioned the trading house of Panton, Leslie and Co. to establish a warehouse at Barrancas, in order to give Panton, whose company was one of the strongest in North America, an interest in conserving Spain's new post there. Gayoso disapproved of the measure, feeling that Turnbull deserved the trading rights at Barrancas, since he was the choice of the Chickasaws for their purveyor. He could not understand why Panton should think he was entitled to a trading post at Barrancas, since he had never before thought of trading on the Mississippi.
>
> Despite Gayoso's protest, the House of Panton succeeded in establishing itself at Barrancas. Late in July an agent of the company named Brashears arrived from Mobile, with 6 slaves, to begin the warehouse. Gayoso assigned him a position about a mile south of the fort, on the same bluff and possessed of a good landing place. By fall the warehouse was finished and John Forbes, a partner of Panton, arrived with a boatload of goods to stock it.
>
> In August, Gayoso, who still believed that the Chickasaws could be managed best through Turnbull, granted the latter permission to establish another trading post at Barrancas. The House of Panton did not like Turnbull's competition and by various means tried to eliminate it. When Folch became commandant of San Fernando, he sided with Panton, but while Gayoso remained on the upper river, he gave Turnbull his full support. After Gayoso's return to Natchez, Turnbull's influence waned and he was gradually supplanted by Panton.
>
> (See Carondelet to Gayoso, New Orleans, December 18, 1792; copy certified by Carondelet, encl. in Carondelet to Las Casas, No. 61 res., New Orleans, December 21, 1792, P de C 1446. Gayoso to Carondelet, No. 457, Natchez, April 18, 1794, P de C 28; Carondelet to Las Cases, No. 136 [134] res.; Gayoso to Carondelet, San Fernando de las Barrancas, July 18, 1795, P de C 198; Gayoso to Carondelet, San Fernando de las Barrancas, July 29, 1795, P de C 198; Rousseau to Gayoso, on *La Venganza* at San Fernando, October 7, 1795, P de C 211; Gayoso to Carondelet, Barrancas, August 13, 1795, P de C 43; Gayoso to Carondelet, New Madrid, September 12, 1795, P de C 32; Gayoso to Carondelet, New Madrid, December 3 and 6, 1795, both in P de C 43; Folch to Carondelet, San Fernando, June 19, 1795, P de C 33; Whitaker, *Spanish-American Frontier*. For Panton, Leslie and Co. see Whitaker, *Documents Relating to*

who come [came] from Mobile to set up the trading store. At four o'clock in the afternoon a chalán from New Madrid arrived at this post with supplies for the squadron.

Monday, July 27, 1795. The chalán was unloaded. The work continues as usual.

Tuesday, July 28, 1795. Two pirogues departed for New Madrid with the people that came with the chalán. The work continues as usual.

Wednesday, July 29, 1795. Nothing unusual occurred.

Thursday, July 30, 1795. The people at work, and the rest without anything unusual occurring.

Friday, July 31, 1795. The people are at work. Brashears notified that he had heard a cannon shot at daybreak, but to all appearances it was some tree that had fallen, for it turned out to be nothing. At three o'clock in the afternoon two Chickasaws arrived; one was the son of Glover, who delivered to me a letter from his father. The day passed as usual.

Saturday, August 1, 1795. A small present was given the two Indians who arrived yesterday, and they left. The work is continuing as usual.

Sunday, August 2, 1795. In the morning four Indians arrived from Payemingo's faction. About four-thirty a strong wind began to blow, with much rain, which lasted throughout the night. There was no work, this being a holiday.

Monday, August 3, 1795. Good weather. The people are at work. At ten o'clock arrived three Indians and a Chickasaw Indian woman, who encamped on the place designated. The day passed as usual.

Tuesday, August 4, 1795. The people at work. Immediately after the retreat many gun shots on the hillside were heard. I immediately ordered Frazer to go and see what it was. I took all the precautions necessary and [saw to it] that all the people would be on

---

the Commercial Policy of Spain in the Floridas and Louisiana, pp. xxx–xxxix. Documents relating to Panton are printed in Florida Historical Society *Quarterly,* beginning in April 1933 issue. A short biography of Panton is in the *Dictionary of American Biography.* Many Turnbull letters are printed in C. E. Carter, ed., *Territorial Papers of the United States* [24 vols. Washington, D.C., 1934–59], *3.*)

the alert. At the end of an hour Frazer returned and told me that it was the king of the Chickasaw nation who had encamped two miles away from this fort with many of his party [and] who, having heard the drum,[76] believed that the Spaniards were saluting them, and thinking it such, they had answered with gun shots. Nothing of an unusual nature took place during the night. Good watch.

Wednesday, August 5, 1795. At nine-thirty the king arrived at this fort with 166 men, 84 women, and 35 children, who, upon arriving at the fort, shot off their guns. At the time they entered the fort, each of the two casas-fuertes saluted with four swivel gun shots. I received the king in front of my tent underneath a roof shade [*sombrajo*] that I had made for the purpose. When he was already seated, I had a general discharge of the heavy artillery made from the gun ranges [*bateria*] that face the river. We began our discourse, which lasted until two in the afternoon, when we ate with the king and three of his chiefs and considerados. During the night nothing new happened. Good watch.

Thursday, August 6, 1795. I gave a present to the Indians.[77] At six in the afternoon a trader's pirogue arrived from New Madrid. The people are at work. Good watch.

Friday, August 7, 1795. The barrels filled with aguardiente were brought in and were given to the Indians, who later went to their camp. Nothing new occurred.

Saturday, August 8, 1795. The Indians left for their nation. The people are working. At six o'clock there was a lot of wind, but it did not last. Good watch.

Sunday, August 9, 1795. Since today is a holiday, there was no work. A pirogue arrived from New Orleans which delivered to me some sealed envelopes [pliegos] from the governor general. He [the pirogue man] told me that he had left the bercha *El*

---

76. "Haviendo oido la caja."

77. Commenting on the Indian gifts in a letter to Carondelet, Gayoso observed that the Chickasaws generally preferred small gifts of good quality, disliking things of poor quality. They did not like striped or chintz shirts, and they made fun of the whites who gave such shirts as presents. (Gayoso to Carondelet, No. 9, New Madrid, September 23, 1795, P de C 34.)

Socorro, upon which the troop was embarked,[78] at thirteen leagues from here. In the afternoon said pirogue set out for New Madrid.

Monday, August 10, 1795. The people are at work. In the afternoon McCoy left for New Madrid in the boat *El Príncipe de Asturias.* The day passed without anything unusual occurring.

78. Because of the proximity of Barrancas de Margot to the Americans at Fort Massac and Muscle Shoals, Carondelet thought Fort San Fernando should be strongly garrisoned. His first estimate placed 60 men and 8 8-calibre cannon as being strong enough to keep the Americans out, but he later raised the number of troops to 80. When Gayoso ascended to Barrancas in April, he took with him about 30 soldiers, mostly from the Nogales garrison, and Portell was ordered to send the other 30 men from New Madrid together with 4 cannon and munitions. (Carondelet to Las Casas, No. 136 [134] res.; Gayoso to Carondelet, No. 16 res., New Madrid, September 12, 1795, P de C 2354.) Gayoso took 1 sergeant, 2 corporals, and 21 infantry soldiers from Nogales; 2 infantrymen and 2 artillerymen from Natchez (Grand Pré to Carondelet, Natchez, September 2, 1795, P de C 32). In addition, to have a large permanent garrison to protect San Fernando, Carondelet figured that the militias of Arkansas Post and New Madrid could be used as reserves in the event of an American attack. Consequently, he ordered Portell and Vilemont to send as many armed militiamen as they could to Barrancas the moment either of them heard it was being attacked. (Carondelet to Vilemont, New Orleans, June 9, 1795, P de C 22; Carondelet to Portell, New Orleans, June 30, 1795, P de C 22.)

The threat of an attack on Barrancas late in the spring caused Carondelet to order the acting commandant of Natchez, Carlos de Grand Pré, to send 40 troops and 8 8-calibre cannon to reinforce Gayoso's forces. Grand Pré complied in June, dispatching Lieutenant Martin Palao with another lieutenant, 2 corporals, and 37 soldiers on the *bercha El Socorro.* Being heavily loaded, the *bercha* made slow progress. In July, Gayoso sent *La Flecha* down the river to aid its ascent, and on August 11 the 2 vessels finally reached Fort San Fernando. Gayoso names the 32 men on their arrival in his letter to Carondelet, No. 6, San Fernando, August 13, 1795, P de C 43. (See Carondelet to Las Casas, No. 136 [134] res.; Carondelet to Las Casas, No. 137 res., New Orleans, June 13, 1795, P de C 2365; in Houck, *Spanish Régime,* 2, 111-12. Gayoso to Carondelet, No. 2 res., Nogales, April 26, 1795, P de C 43; Grand Pré to Carondelet, Natchez, July 16, 1795, P de C 32; Grand Pré to Carondelet, Natchez, September 2, 1795, P de C 32; entries July 10, above, p. 270, and August 11, below, p. 278 [the diary says Palao arrived with 32 men]; Gayoso to Carondelet, San Fernando de las Barrancas, July 18, 1795, P de C 198; Gayoso to Carondelet, No. 6, San Fernando, August 13, 1795, P de C 43 [the names are given in this letter].)

In addition to Spanish troops, Rousseau suggested that a party of Loup Indians should be kept near the fort to serve as reserves. Gayoso, however, considered such action unnecessary and much too expensive. He thought it sufficient to keep the good will of the surrounding Indians, as was the practice in the other Spanish outposts. (Gayoso to Carondelet, Barrancas, June 18, 1795, and August 13, 1795; both in P de C 43.) The artillery for the fort and galleys, and the proposed artillery on Campo de la Esperanza, etc., to be delivered to Perchet, are discussed in Carondelet to Gayoso, New Orleans, July 2, 1795, P de C 48; and Gayoso to Carondelet, No. 16 res., New Madrid, September 12, 1795, P de C 2354.

Tuesday, August 11, 1795. At ten-thirty in the morning there arrived at this post the bercha *El Socorro* and Lieutenant Don Martin Palao and thirty-two men from the *La Luisiana*,[79] with the galiot *La Flecha,* under the command of Don Francisco Langlois. The troop disembarked, and the day passed without further news.

Wednesday, August 12, 1795. The vessels which arrived the day before were unloaded. The work continues as usual.

Thursday, August 13, 1795. In the morning the first *pieza de leva*[80] was fired as a signal for weighing anchor; the second one was fired at eleven o'clock. At five in the afternoon I left[81] with *La*

---

79. I believe Gayoso means from the Fixed Regiment of Louisiana and not the vessel *La Luisiana.* Gayoso informed Carondelet in his letter No. 6, Barrancas, August 13, 1795 (P de C 43), of the arrival of Martin Palao and 32 troops.

80. A shot fired as a signal for weighing anchor.

81. Informing Carondelet of his departure, Gayoso stated that he would probably return within a month and a half (Gayoso to Carondelet, Barrancas, August 13, 1795, P de C 43). When Carondelet made Gayoso de Lemos commander-in-chief of the expedition to take possession of Barrancas de Margó, he also gave him permission to extend his journey up the Mississippi to include a military reconnaissance of New Madrid and Spain's Illinois posts. The real object in sending Gayoso to Upper Louisiana was not a military tour, although his presence did create a favorable impression of Spain's power and prestige among the inhabitants. His chief purpose was to contact certain American agents from Kentucky and discuss with them the possibility of separating the American West from the United States. (These negotiations—the Wilkinson–Innes intrigues—are discussed above, pp. 119-31. Good accounts of it may be found in Whitaker, *Spanish-American Frontier;* Bemis, *Pinckney's Treaty;* Hay and Werner, *The Admirable Trumpeter,* chap. 6. The documentation on these intrigues in the Spanish archives is immense.)

Gayoso was Carondelet's choice to carry on the intrigue at New Madrid. Carondelet's part in the intrigue and choice of agent was confirmed by Spain. On July 18 he dispatched an order to Gayoso at Barrancas to proceed immediately to New Madrid, entrusting to Manuel Lisa, who was to leave New Orleans in a few days, the enclosed cipher letter with orders to deliver them at once to Wilkinson at Fort Washington. In it is contained the Spanish propositions, and in his letter to Wilkinson dated July 16 (two days before writing the orders to Gayoso) Carondelet stated that he was sending Gayoso to New Madrid to treat secretly with agents from Kentucky concerning the plan of separation. To ensure delivery of the letters, Carondelet also sent a duplicate set by another agent who traveled by sea to New York and from there overland to Cincinnati. (See letter unsigned and unaddressed [Carondelet to Wilkinson], dated at New Orleans, English copy in P de C 2374; draft in Spanish, also unaddressed, in P de C 129; copy [with rubric] enclosed in Carondelet to Gayoso, res., New Orleans, July 18, 1795, P de C 22. The letters to Wilkinson included Carondelet's letter of July 16 and another of July 1. See Carondelet to G. W. [Wilkinson], New Orleans, July 1, 1795; copy encl. in Carondelet to Gayoso, res., New Orleans, July 18, 1795, P de C 22; draft marked muy res. in P de C 48.)

Vigilante and *La Flecha*. On the first named were embarked Cruzat[82] and Mr. Bontoux, and on the second Langlois and Perchet. Upon saying farewell to the fort, it saluted me, and when I left I responded. On passing in front of the squadron it saluted me and I answered. We continued *con buen viaje,* Rousseau, García, and Fauré accompanying us, and we came to camp four [sic] leagues away, on the point of the first Isla de las Desgraciadas [Isle of Misfortune].[83] When we left, *La Flecha* attempted to see if it could pass on the outside of *La Vigilante,* but it did not succeed, since the galiot sails very fast. The latter rows 18 oars and *La Flecha* 16. At seven in the evening those who came to accompany us took leave and returned to the squadron. At that time Beauregard[84] arrived; he came to supper with me, and afterward he went to the fort. Good watch. Nothing unusual.

Friday, August 14, 1795. Day broke, with overcast skies and with the wind to the north. A shot was fired as a signal for weighing anchor. We left at break of day, a fresh wind at the prow. We passed through the principal channel of the Islas Desgraciadas. On passing above the islands we saw in the distance Fort San Fernando. At eight o'clock it began to drizzle, which stopped but from time to time it returned. On the point above the aforementioned isles, we made breakfast and afterward continued, with a strong wind at the prow. We came to make dinner on the batura of the Isla de Vilain [Villein Island]. We continued after eating, with the same

---

82. Sublieutenant Don Antonio Cruzat was a young officer who accompanied Gayoso on his expedition to Upper Louisiana in 1795. He assisted in the construction of Fort San Fernando and was one of the signers of the treaty by which the Chickasaws ceded Barrancas to the Spaniards. When Gayoso ascended to New Madrid, he asked Cruzat, because of his discretion, zeal, and fidelity to Spain, to act as his confidential secretary in matters dealing with the Kentucky intrigue. He seemed to have a great fondness for the young man and regarded him as a son. He described him as docile, well inclined, and having the distinguishing qualities of a useful officer. (Gayoso to Carondelet, San Fernando de las Barrancas, July 18, 1795, P de C 198; Gayoso to Carondelet, No. 18 res., New Madrid, September 22, 1795, P de C 32.)

83. This translation follows my text. Holmes' text reads: "vinimos a acampar a la punta de la primera isla de las desgraciadas a un cuarto de legua."

84. Beauregard remained in charge of Fort San Fernando when Gayoso left to ascend the river. On September 24, 1795, Rousseau wrote to Gayoso de Lemos from Ecores à Margot that the officers were living happily. They were having a better time than when Beauregard was there, the latter having left on September 24. (P de C 211.)

wind, and we came to sleep opposite the head of the Isla de Vilain or del Feo. Threatening weather. We made four leagues.

Saturday, August 15, 1795. We left very early. The weather was cloudy, and wind to the north and at the prow. On the point opposite the batura of the Thousand Islands, we saw the warp of *La Flecha,* which was stopped by the currents, which were very strong [towed] up to the beginning of the batura,[85] where we had breakfast. At eleven o'clock we left with the wind at the prow, although not very strong; we entered on the inside of the Isla de los Chicotes.[86] On it we made dinner. When finished, we left and came to camp above the batura, which is on the other side of the river farther above the Isla de los Chicotes, having made three and a half leagues.

Sunday, August 16, 1795. We left at break of day. About nine o'clock we entered through the Channel of the Devil,[87] where we experienced strong currents. Upon leaving it, we ate dinner on the point of the mainland. A swivel gun was fired in order to call the hunters. We continued; afterward we crossed over the batura that is above the Barrancas de en Medio [Third Chickasaw Bluffs], from where were seen the bluffs. We continued by poling. We entered within the Isla de las Barrancas de Prudon [Prud'homme Bluffs],[88] where we camped, having made ——.[89]

Monday, August 17, 1795. We left at daybreak; cloudy weather.

85. The meaning of this sentence is conjectural, the document being illegible at this point.

86. Collot's map shows most of the points mentioned. Incidentally, there are two different Isles aux Chicots shown on it. See plate 25 in Atlas accompanying Collot, *Journey in North America.* Between the Arkansas and Yazoo Rivers there were two places, Isle à la Tête de Mort and Isles aux Chicots, which are encumbered with driftwood heaped 60 feet high, and where the channel of the river is narrowed. See Collot, 2, 43.

87. "Por el canal del Diablo."

88. On Ecores à Prud'homme. Gayoso gives a long description of this in his letter to Carondelet, No. 17 res., New Madrid, September 16, 1795, P de C 2364; printed in Spanish in Holmes, *Documentos,* pp. 253-59.

The Barrancas de Prud'homme, or Second Chickasaw Bluffs, are 5 leagues further up on the same side of the river, which is narrow at this point (Gayoso to Carondelet, No. 17 res.). The Barrancas de en Medio, or Third Chickasaw Bluffs, are on the same side of the river as Barrancas de Margó, about 10 leagues north. These bluffs appeared to be on the river at two or three places, but they are not long and do not interrupt navigation.

89. Blank in original.

We went outside of the Isla á Prudon [Prud'homme Isle] at seven o'clock, and at seven-thirty we landed at the beginning of the bluffs in order to eat, which done, we left there—remaining on land—Langlois, the engineer, and the Mestizo Luison,[90] in order to reconnoiter above[91] the bluffs. We crossed over the batura on the opposite side, which we followed by poling.[92] The pirogue continued on the side of the bluffs, while we were ascending the batura. I called the pirogue, and Don Domingo Bontoux crossed on it to the shore of the bluffs.[93] Before arriving at the end of said bluffs, Langlois, Perchet, and Mr. Bontoux came aboard, and the second one [Perchet?] informed me that the aforesaid Barrancas de Prudom, whose northern point appears over the river, are very high and constantly appearing over the river a little more than a half league to the south. [The Barrancas] form in their exterior appearance or profile an endless succession of little hills and uneven places, which are perceived within and show more unevenness, forming an infinity of ravines; and rising in some places in the interior of the forest are some heights[94] that dominate considerably even the very ones that appear on the river, causing the

90. Gayoso says a hunter (Gayoso to Carondelet, No. 17 res.).
91. *Por encima*.
92. In his dispatch No. 17 res., dated New Madrid, September 16, 1795, Gayoso summarizes his trip from Barrancas to New Madrid. He said that the Barrancas de Margó were 266 leagues up the river from New Orleans, and the fort was situated at 35° 12 minutes, and 20 seconds. He describes the various bluffs above Memphis, including the Barrancas de Prud'homme. At the latter, on August 17, he had the engineer Perchet, Langlois, and a hunter disembark with instructions to reconnoiter the bluffs. He had Cruzat on *La Vigilante* follow along the opposite bank of the river in order to get full description of the land.

The Barrancas de Prud'homme formed an arc whose *cuerda* was one-half league NNW and SSE. They were 70 to 90 feet in elevation, varying in different places. The judgment of the engineer was opposed to having them as a defense, because vessels could pass, especially in high water at its foot, without fear of being damaged from above. Five leagues further up the river were the Barrancas de Harina, or First Chickasaw Bluffs. Gayoso states that both the Barrancas de Prud'homme and the Barrancas de Harina were of little importance to the Spaniards (P de C 2364; see also Cramer, *Navigator*, pp. 164–65).

93. In his letter cited above, n. 92, Gayoso said that Bontoux followed in a pirogue along the foot of the bluffs, and that Gayoso and Cruzat on *La Vigilante* followed along the river on the opposite side.

From this point in the text to the last paragraph in the diary entry for August 17, the wording is identical to that of Gayoso's letter to Carondelet No. 17 res. (P de C 2364).

94. Or "in the interior of the forest there were some heights."

terrain to be *escabrosa* [craggy]. It is traversed with difficulty, not because the forest is excessively impenetrable, but only because since the land is exceedingly sandy, the waters of the ravines themselves make them almost impassable. The character of these lands is shown more on the exterior of the bluffs, when with great difficulty the engineer [Perchet] himself went down. Since in the place which he did go down and in those places where he had previously attempted to go down—due to the appearance in that place and in those [aforementioned places where he attempted to go down] of some hillocks which sloped down to the edge of the river, he found that these hillocks were caused only by the crumbling of the earth of said bluffs, and were composed only of a very slippery sand of a red color, over which, with much difficulty, one can descend and traverse without sinking in.

The point of view they offer from the river is magnificent, appearing like a perpendicular cliff of rocks of various colors, and the foot of it [seems] as if it were real slate.

Looking upon the hills as an essential point of defense on the river, without counting the obstacles already mentioned, they deserve very little attention, because any ship can pass by the foot, especially in high waters, without fearing grave damage from the ones that may occupy the height.

We continued traveling and came to make dinner on the point of the Isla Otawas [Otawa Island]. After eating, we left by poling. When the sun set, we arrived at the beginning of the Barrancas de Harina [Flour Bluffs], where *La Flecha* was grounded; it had hit against a junk [*chicote*] and sprang a leak, but since there was no question of danger, I continued, and Langlois remained repairing it, which was immediately accomplished and he continued. We came to camp at the end of said Barrancas de Harina, facing the point of the island of that name,[95] having made six leagues.

Tuesday, August 18, 1795. We left very early. We passed through the last passage of Flour Island. Upon leaving it, about six o'clock, we landed on a point of the mainland to breakfast. Afterward we continued. We crossed the batura of the Punta de Ciruelas [Point of Plums]. At its point we put out the line [cordelling], the currents being very strong. On this point there are different *baturas*

95. Barrancas de Harina, or First Chickasaw Bluffs. The island opposite is called Flour Island. See Holmes, *WTHSP, 13,* 38–50; Cramer, *Navigator,* pp. 164–65.

DIARY 283

cortadas. We passed within the first one. Upon leaving it, or upon arriving at the very point of Ciruelas, we were stuck[96] in such a way that we had to throw out part of the ballast into the water in order to lighten the ship. The galiot *La Flecha,* which was on shore, came to give us aid, and upon arriving, it also got stuck, but got out immediately. It cast anchor and its crew came out immediately to help us. We went out the way we had entered, following the passage[97] on the edge of *tierra firme,* we continued rowing and landed on the Punta de Ciruelas itself in order to fix dinner. While we were stuck, a shower fell and a slight wind arose. We left after eating, and at a short distance we put up the sails, as the wind was favorable, but at the end of an hour it turned against us. We continued rowing and poling within the first island of the Canadians, and we came to encamp opposite the head of this one [island] on the mainland. On passing in front of it, a shout was heard on said island. I sent the canoe with Luisin [Luison], and having returned, he told me that it was an Indian with his wife who were coming in their pirogue with bison meat. Indeed, they arrived on board and I bought the meat from them. At nine o'clock there began a strong downpour of rain, with thunder. All night it rained.

Wednesday, August 19, 1795. We left at six-thirty, since the rain had not ceased until that time. On the point which is found between the first two islands of the Canadians we put out the line [*cordela*] because of the excessive current. We continued rowing and poling over the batura, and we came to make dinner above the batura of the fourth island, whence we left sailing, the wind being favorable; and upon arriving on the next to the last island of the Canadians a vessel was sighted, which put to land. The owners came aboard; they were Mr. Dubrar [Du Brean] and the Baron de Bastrop,[98] who were descending with their families to settle

96. Struck bottom or ran aground.
97. The original reads, "salimos por donde haviamos entrado y cojiendo la para [Holmes says, "cogiendo el paso"] a la orilla de la tierra firme seguimos al remo y pusimos en tierra en la misma punta de Ciruelas para hacer de comer."
98. There is a vast amount of manuscript material upon this interesting character and of this projected settlement in Spanish Louisiana. Much is in the Spanish archives. More material is contained in *American State Papers, Public Lands* (1832–61). See M. A. Hatcher, *Opening of Texas to Foreign Settlement 1801–1827* (Austin, 1927); Gayarré, *History of Louisiana, 3,* and esp. *LHQ,* 20 (1937), 289–462.

on the Ouachita. I signed their passports and they departed. We continued sailing and came to camp opposite the last island of the Canadians, the wind having ceased half an hour before the sun set. About nine o'clock a heavy squall [*turbonada*] fell, but it did not last very long. Good watch.

Thursday, August 20, 1795. We left at daybreak, rowing. We had breakfast on the last batura, which has a long view over the [Islas] Canadianas. We continued traveling, and on the batura of the Rivera à Bayon [Bayonne River] there came to the edge of the ship a pirogue which was descending from New Madrid to Barrancas de San Fernando with vegetables and fruit.[99] I bought some and they left. We continued traveling and came to make dinner on the point below the first island of the Río Bayón [Bayonne River]. We continued afterward, and at the head of said island we encountered strong currents, which we passed, rowing, and we came to camp opposite the third Island of Bayón, on a point of the mainland.

Friday, August 21, 1795. The gun was fired as a signal for weighing anchor, and we left at daybreak, the weather being cloudy and drizzling. We had breakfast above the fourth Island of Bayón. We left afterward and since the wind had appeared favorable, we hoisted the sails, but it was in vain, for the slight wind that had begun had calmed down. We came to make dinner on the island of the Small Prairie, whence we departed, with a contrary although not very strong wind, [passing] within said island, we came to sleep on the Small Prairie, with seemingly bad weather, but it dissipated.

Saturday, August 22, 1795. We left an hour before daybreak, with cloudy weather. Upon arriving at the batura, which is above said prairie, a favorable wind arose which lasted us until we reached the end of said batura, where we had breakfast. We later continued rowing. We made the crossing on [to] the first isle, where we encountered a pirogue which was descending with an Indian, women, and three children who were going to hunt. We hoisted the sails, but the wind was so weak that we were obliged to lower the sails. We continued rowing. At ten o'clock a not very strong wind arose, and we continued by sails and oars; we came to make

---

99. See entry for July 11, above, p. 271, n. 71.

DIARY 285

dinner on the point below that of Ansa al Aseite [sic],[1] where we met a man who was descending with his family to Natchez. After eating we set sail and came to sleep on the point below the Falsa Ansa [Cove] of New Madrid.

Sunday, August 23, 1795. At dawn the gun was fired as a signal for weighing anchor, and we left at seven from the camp. At half a league from New Madrid alongside our boat came the gunboat *El Rayo*,[2] with its commandant Don Juan Ferrúsola and Don Tomás Portell, commandant of the post. We continued our voyage, and at nine-thirty the boat docked in front of the fort. I disembarked and met all the officers of the militia, who had come to compliment me. The fort saluted me, and I replied.[3] The day passed without anything unusual occurring.

Monday, August 24, 1795. I was visiting the town and its environs. The day passed without anything unusual happening.

---

1. I.e. Ansa á la grasa or Ainse à la graisse, New Madrid. On the origins of this name see Houck, *History of Missouri*, 2, 105. Described in Collot, *Journey in North America*, 2, 17–19.

2. The lancha cañonera *El Rayo* was a small gunboat ordinarily equipped with 8 oars. It was a member of the river squadron. A full crew for the little lancha consisted of a patrón, a proel, and 8 sailors or oarsmen, and it was armed with a single 12-caliber cannon, probably mounted on the prow. It had no cabin, though it probably had a hold for storing provisions, and it was provided with a mast, sails, rudder, and helm. The chief means of propulsion was by oars and sail. From 1792 until the beginning of 1794 the *El Rayo* was with the squadron on the lower river. Early in 1794 it ascended with the fleet to New Madrid, returning to Natchez in June, where it remained until the following December. Throughout 1795 and 1796 the *El Rayo* was on the Upper Mississippi around New Madrid and Barrancas de Margó, being based at the latter post in 1796. During a large part of 1795 the gunboat was cruising at the mouth of the Ohio. Upon Gayoso's arrival at New Madrid he ordered the *El Rayo* to remain there so that Portell could use it to transport more troops to Barrancas in case the reports of attack increased or were confirmed. (Gayoso to Portell, New Madrid, August 25, 1795, P de C 43; draft in P de C 226A. Gayoso to Carondelet, New Madrid, August 26, 1795, P de C 32.) In the spring of 1797 it ascended to St. Louis with the squadron, returning that summer to the lower river for the first time in fully 2½ years. (The above is based in large part on the numerous letters of Ferrúsola and other Spanish officials found in the P de C. Some material on the *El Rayo* is found in Liljegren, "The Commission of Lieutenant-Colonel Carlos Howard." See also Ferrúsola to Carondelet on *El Rayo*, New Madrid, March 28, 1795, P de C 32; another letter written on the same date in P de C 31; dotation of artillery considered necessary in the plazas and forts of the province [of Louisiana], n.p., n.d., P de C 122A.)

3. See Gayoso to Carondelet, No. 7, New Madrid, August 25, 1795, P de C 43.

Tuesday, August 25, 1795. I gave orders to depart the following day.

Wednesday, August 26, 1795. At four o'clock in the afternoon I left the post of New Madrid for Illinois, and about a half league from New Madrid, where I had landed to make camp, there arrived a mail pirogue from San Fernando with pliegos from the governor general, and these needing immediate answer, I returned to New Madrid to answer them.[4] The rest of the night passed without anything unusual occurring.

An hour before I left, the vessel *El Príncipe de Asturias* left for San Fernando with supplies for that post.

[Thursday] *August 27, 1795.* I remained at said post. Nothing unusual happened.

[Friday] *August 28, 1795.* Nothing unusual.

[Saturday] *August 29, 1795.* Nothing unusual.

[Sunday] *August 30, 1795.* Nothing unusual.

[Monday] *August 31, 1795.* Nothing unusual.

[Tuesday] *September 1, 1795.* Good weather and nothing unusual occurred. A pirogue left for downstream by which I sent a letter to the Baron.

[Wednesday] *September 2, 1795.* Nothing new.

[Thursday] *September 3, 1795.* Nothing new.

[Friday] *September 4, 1795.* No news.

[Saturday] *September 5, 1795.* At eight in the evening Power[5] left in a pirogue for Ohio. No news.

4. The contents of the letters that Gayoso received from Carondelet caused him to change his plans, return to New Madrid, and postpone his trip to the Illinois. Among these letters was Carondelet's of July 18. When he wrote to Carondelet on August 13, he told his superior officer that he expected to be back at Barrancas by October 1. Carondelet's letter of July 18, ordering Gayoso to go to New Madrid (which Gayoso received after he had arrived at New Madrid), told him to remain at New Madrid until November. (Gayoso to Alcudia, res., New Madrid, September 5, 1795, AHN 3902; draft in P de C 128. Gayoso to Carondelet, Barrancas, August 13, 1795, P de C 43; Carondelet to Gayoso, New Orleans, July 18, 1795, P de C 22.)

5. Gayarré describes Thomas Power as a Spanish naturalized Englishman used by Carondelet as an agent in his intrigues with Wilkinson. Power was apparently intelligent, cautious, and had a natural disposition to intrigue. (*History of Louisiana, 3,* 346.) In a letter to Gayoso, Portell said that Power came to Louisiana from the

[Sunday] *September 6, 1795.* At nine *La Flecha* left for Sainte Geneviève in search of maize for San Fernando.[6] Cloudy weather.

[Monday] *September 7, 1795.* Without news.[7]

Canary Islands and that he originated in Ireland (Portell to Gayoso, New Madrid, March 29, 1794, P de C 47). Power had made 2 trips to Kentucky for Portell. Gayoso used him as his messenger to forward the letters to Wilkinson, since Manuel Lisa did not arrive until October.

6. See entry for July 11, above, p. 271, n. 71.
7. This copy of the diary, in P de C 2354, abruptly ends here. It is incomplete.

PARTS II AND III

Galeota La Vigilante. Diary from New Madrid to Illinois,[8] October 6, 1795–December 8, 1795.

Tuesday, October 6, 1795.[9] At nine o'clock in the morning I left the wharf of New Madrid for Illinois,[10] accompanied by the *lancha cañonera El Rayo*, with its commandant Don Juan Barnó y Ferrúsola. About a league from the fort we hoisted the sail, since the wind was southern and favorable at this place; but about a league and a half further we had to lower it, since the wind was against us, caused by the bend where the river turns to the east. At one-fifteen we landed about two leagues from the fort in order to eat. At three-thirty [three-fifteen] we left, with the winds always to the south, which little by little calmed down. At five in the afternoon, at the beginning of the batura of the Isla á Dará, we met a pirogue that was descending from the Illinois loaded with apples. Cruzat went

8. This diary, which may be found in P de C 2364, is incomplete. For the original Spanish see Holmes, *Documentos*, pp. 289–302.

9. While Power had been sent off, certain that he would not return to New Madrid for some time, Gayoso decided to begin his Illinois tour and thus be through with that visit before the agent from Kentucky arrived to parley with him in New Madrid (Gayoso to Carondelet, New Madrid, October 2 and 3, 1795, P de C 211; Gayoso to Carondelet, New Madrid, October 6, 1795, P de C 32; Gayoso to Carondelet, St. Louis, October 30, 1795, P de C 43).

Gayoso de Lemos hoped to accomplish 3 main objectives by his tour of the Illinois country. The first was to impress the inhabitants with Spain's power and prestige. Since the residents of Illinois were predominately French, the district was always a source of anxiety to Spanish officials, who were never quite sure of the complete loyalty of the people. Gayoso's tour, therefore, was partly a good will mission to flatter the inhabitants of the Illinois country and to increase their loyalty to Spain. His second objective was to impress and flatter the Indians in the district in order to attach them more closely to the interests of Spain. The third, of a more military nature than the others, was the inspection of defenses at the Illinois posts.

A fourth purpose, of minor importance, might also be added to the list. In September the commandant of Ste. Geneviève informed Gayoso that the governor of the American Northwest Territory, Arthur St. Clair, was in Kaskaskia to preside over the courts in that district. Gayoso therefore decided to take advantage of the opportunity for a conference with St. Clair in order to sound him out and try to influence him with ideas favorable to Spain. (Vallé to [Gayoso], Ste. Geneviève, September 14, 1795, P de C 211; draft [Gayoso] to Vallé, New Madrid [September], 1795, P de C 130; Gayoso to Carondelet, No. 11, New Madrid, September 25, 1795, P de C 43; draft in P de C 32. Gayoso to Carondelet, New Madrid, October 2 and 3, 1795, P de C 211; Gayoso to Carondelet, New Madrid, October 6, 1795, P de C 32.)

10. Gayoso to Carondelet, No. 23 res., Mina de Fierro, October 9, 1795, P de C 43.

on board, and on his return he handed me two letters. We continued poling the vessel and came to camp a little below the Isla á Dará, on the batura. At nine o'clock at night a pirogue arrived which Don Tomás Portell had dispatched, sending on it Samuel Labery, who had arrived that afternoon from Fort Washington with a pirogue loaded with merchandise. I answered said commandant immediately, [asking him] to permit Labery to continue journeying to Natchez, I myself writing to the Baron[11] and to the intendant about this matter. At ten-thirty that night the pirogue set out for New Madrid. The rest of the night was spent as usual; the river rose one foot. We made two leagues during the day.

Wednesday, October 7, 1795. At daybreak we fired the swivel gun as a signal to weigh anchor, and we left. On the *batura cortada,* which is opposite the Isla á Dará, we put to shore to have breakfast, and as soon as it was done, we left with the wind to the north and at the prow. We made the crossing to the Isla á Favot, where we put to land at eleven in the morning and had dinner, because the wind was very strong at the prow. At one-fifteen we departed with the same wind at the prow, although not so strong, and we came to sleep on the Isla del Lobo [Isle of the Wolf][12] on the outer side. During the night the river rose two and a half feet. We made four leagues during the day.

Thursday, October 8, 1795. We left at daybreak with fair weather, the wind to the north. We had breakfast at the head of the Isla del Lobo, whence we left with an unfavorable wind; and at twelve-thirty [we were] in front of the Bayou Chicacha. On the head of the isle of that name we put to shore in order to eat. When we had finished, we left, and we encamped at nightfall on the point which is above said isle, at the beginning of the Cove. We made three leagues during the day; the river rose one foot during the night.

Friday, October 9, 1795. We departed at daybreak with fair weather and calm. On the Ysla Grande de las Barrancas Blancas [Large Island of the White Bluffs] we put to shore in order to breakfast, at which time a bercha arrived, coming from Ohio with some fifteen Chickasaw Indians, a Negro and a Negress, and two whites. This bercha was carrying gifts to San Fernando for said

---

11. Gayoso to Carondelet, New Madrid, October 6, 1795, P de C 32.
12. See Cramer, *Navigator,* p. 158.

nation.[13] We stopped with them until one o'clock, when we left; and on the same island, opposite the aforesaid bluffs, we fixed dinner at one-thirty, whence we left at three in the afternoon. On the point above the White Bluffs there came alongside a pirogue coming from Ste. Geneviève, and in it was the man named Garno [or Larno], who was bringing letters from the commandant of the post and from various persons; and he told me that on the outside of the island of said bluff, a bercha of Mr. Menard's was descending with pork meat for the king [king's account] at New Madrid. We continued the trip and came to camp near the Mina de Fierro [Iron Mine], having made three and a half leagues the whole day. During the night the river went down one foot.[14]

Saturday, October 10, 1795. We left very early, and we breakfasted at seven-thirty on the second island of the Mina de Fierro, where at eight-thirty the wind arose to the west. We left sailing, and at one-thirty we put to land on the opposite bank of the river, about a quarter of a league below the entrance of the Ohio,[15] where we made dinner; and at three-thirty we left said place, and at a quarter of four we arrived at the cruising station [*apostadero del crucero*][16] opposite the Ohio. At five o'clock that same afternoon

13. Folch reported on this in his letter to Carondelet, No. 7, San Fernando, October 22, 1795, P de C 52.

14. See Gayoso's letter to Carondelet, No. 23 res., written from Mina de Fierro, October 9, 1795, P de C 43.

15. Hutchins, in Imlay, *Topological Description*, pp. 429, 458, says it is 15 miles from Mine au Fer to the Ohio. Collot, in *Journey*, 2, 14, says 18 miles.

16. This was the naval cruising station established by order of the Governor General to watch all vessels descending the Ohio. Langlois in *La Flecha* established the cruising station at the Ohio, operating there in 1794–96. Ferrúsola also cruised there.

Although no permanent settlement ever existed at the mouth of the Ohio during the Spanish period, from the summer of 1794 until the end of 1796 and probably later, a war galiot was assigned to cruise before the Ohio to prevent enemy expeditions against Louisiana from entering the Mississippi by that route. In the fall of 1795 Gayoso visited (see pp. 317–22) the naval station at the Ohio and ordered a small stockade erected on the shore oppposite the mouth of the river to provide shelter for the men from the cruising vessels.

In his military report of 1794 Carondelet suggested that 4 galleys be permanently stationed at New Madrid to guard the passage of the Mississippi River. These could also be used to cruise before the entrance of the Ohio, thus preventing enemy expeditions from entering the Mississippi. In 1796 Carondelet requested Vanden Bemden, a Flemish engineer in New Madrid, to investigate the mouth of the Ohio for a suitable site for a fort and to make an estimate of the price and quantity of men, materials, and time necessary to construct the fort.

there arrived a pirogue belonging to the man named Chatoyé, coming from New Madrid and ascending to Ste. Geneviève. We made five leagues all day. During the night, good watch. The river receded one foot and a half.

Sunday, October 11, 1795. We remained in said cruising station.[17] At eight o'clock Chatoyé left with Garno, I having given him the replies to the letters he brought me. At ten-thirty in the morning I crossed over the batura of the Ohio in *La Vigilante* in order to observe from there and to take measurements [*tomar bases*], which I did, and at one o'clock I had returned to the camp. At four o'clock in the afternoon I returned to the same work in order to confirm the sights I had taken, and at five-thirty I had returned to the camp. During the night nothing unusual occurred. The river receded one foot.

Vanden Bemden complied and sent his report to the Governor General in December 1796. He found that the only place suitable for a fort was opposite the mouth of the Ohio at a spot that dominated the Mississippi above and below. In the river before the spot, and separated from it by a channel 60 fathoms wide, a long sand bar extended into the mouth of the Ohio. On one end of the sand bar a battery could be placed to protect and aid the fort. Vanden Bemden believed that the position was all that could be asked for to completely control the entrance of the Ohio, but the cost of constructing a fort there would be tremendous. The battery on the sand bar would have to be built on piles and raised at least 25 feet to be completely free from the danger of floods. The fort would also have to be raised, and the marshes and flooded lands surrounding it would make land approaches impossible. All the materials for construction, except bricks, would have to be brought from distances varying from 10 to 24 leagues.

When Collot inspected the mouth of the Ohio in 1796, he voiced the opinion that it would be impossible without great labor and immense expense to build any kind of fort or military work near the entrance of the river because of the height of its waters at flood time. Apparently the Spanish government found that the expense of fortifying the mouth of the Ohio outweighed the military importance of the works, for none were ever constructed there by Spain.

See entries in this diary for October 10 and December 14–23; Carondelet's military report, which is Carondelet to Las Casas, New Orleans, November 24, 1794, encl. in Carondelet to Alcudia, No. 48 res., New Orleans, November 24, 1794, P de C 2354; printed in Robertson, *Louisiana under Spain, France and the United States*, 1, 293–345, and in *AHR*, 2, but not as accurately as in Robertson. The same information is found in Carondelet to Aranda, No. 129, New Orleans, November 24, 1794, AHN 3897; also found in British Museum, *Additional Manuscripts*, Vol. 17567, folios 22–63 v.; extracts printed in Houck, *Spanish Régime*, 2, 9–17 (letter to Las Casas); letter from Louis Vanden Bemden, New Madrid, December 21, 1796, P de C [213?]; Collot, *Journey in North America*, 2, chap. 19.

17. Gayoso spent October 11–12 surveying the land around the naval station (*apostadero*) at the mouth of the Ohio.

Monday, October 12, 1795. At ten-thirty [ten-fifteen] in the morning I made the crossing to the aforesaid batura in order to confirm the observation, and at one o'clock I returned to the cruising station, at which time Mr. Lorimier[18] with his two sons, who were coming to see me, arrived in a pirogue. At three in the afternoon I put out in *La Vigilante* up to the point which is below the cruising station in order to confirm from there the sights I had taken from the other side of the river. At five I had returned to the naval station. At five-thirty a pirogue was sighted which was going up on the batura at the entrance of the Ohio. Immediately I dispatched a pirogue with three men in search of it, and at six o'clock they had returned; and it was the man named Ste. Marie, sergeant of the militia of New Madrid, who was ascending to Post Vincennes, [and] to whom I gave a letter for the commandant of Fort Massac and another for Power. At seven-thirty in the evening a fire was observed on the point to the west of the Ohio. Immediately Mr. Lorimier went with four sailors in a pirogue to reconnoiter, and on returning he told me that it was six Englishmen who were going to Ste. Geneviève with a pirogue loaded with whiskey. The night passed without anything unusual occurring.

Tuesday, October 13, 1795. Early in the morning the English crossed to this bank, and asked to continue journeying with me to Ste. Geneviève, which I conceded. At nine-thirty in the morning I left the aforementioned cruising station for St. Louis,[19] leaving in it the lancha cañonera with its Commandant Don Juan Barnó y Ferrúsola, with orders to wait for Power and to ascend with him to find me. We continued our journey along the Ansa, where we encountered strong currents, and we came to eat a little below the entrance of the Isla del Buey. We left after eating and followed the outer side of the island, there being no water within. We had strong currents, which obliged us to encamp at nine-thirty in the evening, not having found a camping place until this hour because of the ruggedness of the bluff, and we slept at the entrance of the Ysla de Sierbo [Buffalo Island], a league and a half away from the entrance of the Ohio.

18. For Lorimier, see above, p. 71, n. 27.
19. From the mouth of the Ohio to the mouth of the Missouri was 230 miles by water and 140 miles by land. See Ashe, *Travels in America,* p. 254. Collot, in *Journey in North America, 1,* 226–27, says 176½; see pp. 211–27 for most of islands mentioned in diary. See also Cramer, *Navigator,* pp. 152–57.

Wednesday, October 14, 1795. We left at seven o'clock in the morning, with threatening weather. We had breakfast at the head of the Isla del Sierbo; we continued afterward with bad weather, drizzling. We entered the channel of the Ysla del Capón, and we came to make dinner at the entrance of said island, on land, whence we left, with rainy weather. We made the crossing over the batura and continued along it by poling, and we came to encamp opposite the Ysla de Gran Detorno. About nine-thirty the wind began to blow hard and it lasted all night. Good watch. [Made] four leagues.

Thursday, October 15, 1795. We could not leave until ten in the morning because of the strong head wind, and having left at that hour by poling the boat, we came to eat at twelve-thirty a quarter of a league from where we had slept. At three we left with the wind still at the prow, and at five, having arrived on the first Ysla de la Curs, we hoisted the sails, because the river runs to the east and the wind was southeast. We came to camp at the point above said island, having made a league and a half. At eleven o'clock it began to rain, and it lasted until the following day.

Friday, October 16, 1795. We left early, with rainy weather and the wind to the north and at the prow. Nevertheless we continued and came to eat on the island below that [island] of the English. We departed with a contrary wind. We met a pirogue with the man named Chodillon and another person, who were descending to New Madrid with pork meat for that post. We continued our voyage and encamped at nightfall on the Ysla del Yngles [Isle of the English],[20] having made two leagues. The river went down a half foot during the night.

Saturday, October 17, 1795. We left very early and came to eat opposite the Tehuapite [Tywappity], where we found the chief of the Loup nation called Cabeza de Cuerbo [Crow's Head], because he always has one around his neck, who was there with five more of his tribe and who had made a shelter and a very large fire in front of it. They made me sit down beneath the shelter, and presuming that the bonfire warmed me too much, they abandoned said shelter in order that I might turn away from the fire. On the

---

20. English Island, called Great Courcy Island by the Canadians, and Taiouwapeti by the Indians. Collot, *Journey, 1,* 214.

bonfire they had a cauldron with meat, which, once they had put it on a wooden dish, they put in front of me so that I might eat with those who were with me, which I did, with Lorimier and Cruzat. Later I had brought them from aboard biscuits and a flask of whiskey, which they received with much pleasure. In the meantime they had carried on board a quantity of fresh meat, which they had hunted expressly for me. We left said place, the Indians following us in their pirogue. The wind strong at the prow. We landed above the chain of rocks in order to eat. During this interval of time the wind again became favorable, [and] we left, sailing. At five o'clock in the afternoon, being at the Cabo de la Cruche [Cape La Cruz], and with the wind calmed down, we threw out the towline [poling, cordelling] and with it we ascended said Cape up to the bayou, which is farther above, where we picked up the oars and came to camp on the Ansa de Cipriera, having made three and a half leagues in all that day. Bolon stayed behind with the Indians in order to hunt. The night passed without anything unusual occurring.[21]

Sunday, October 18, 1795. We left very early. We had breakfast at the Arroyo, which is situated [a little] below Cape Girardeau. Upon leaving there I had a cannon fired. At ten in the morning we arrived at said cape, where I stayed all day.[22] At twelve Bolon arrived and, shortly afterward, the Indians, who at five o'clock in

21. Gayoso had been making very slow progress due to rainy weather and strong opposing winds. (See Collot, *Journey, 1*, 212-14.)

22. On the Spanish side of the Mississippi, about 20 leagues below Ste. Geneviève and some 15 leagues above the mouth of the Ohio, an important trading post known as Cape Girardeau was located. Probably early in 1792 an Indian trader named Louis Lorimier moved to Cape Girardeau from the Ste. Geneviève district, in order to trade with the Indians living between the Missouri and Arkansas Rivers, over whom he enjoyed a great deal of influence and control.

In January 1793 Carondelet recognized the importance of Lorimier's influence over the Indians by granting the trader permission to establish an independent trading post at Cape Girardeau. The grant placed under Lorimier's care all the Indians living west of the Mississippi between the Missouri and Arkansas Rivers, and gave him and the savages the right to hunt and to cultivate all the unoccupied land in that territory. For the first few years after the establishment of Lorimier's post, the only people at Cape Girardeau were Lorimier, his family (his wife was a half-blood Shawnee), and his Indian friends. In 1795 the first white settlers moved to the post from the United States. By 1798 about 30 Anglo-American families had emigrated there, attracted by Spain's free land grants. Except for Lorimier and one or two other Frenchmen, the entire population of Cape Girardeau consisted of Anglo-Americans whose principal occupation was agriculture.

the afternoon came to see me. They shook my hand and showed much joy upon seeing me; I advised them to live in peace and quiet on their lands. I gave them four necklaces of white porcelain in order to make their nation see that I had come to see them on their own territory. I gave them a barrel of whiskey and a few handfuls of tobacco. They took leave of me and left for their cabins. The night passed without anything unusual occurring.[23]

Monday, October 19, 1795. We left at daybreak. At the Ysla de Duverqué we hoisted the sails, because of the wind being southern and favorable at this place. Within said isle we encountered a pirogue that was descending with two hunters to New Madrid. We continued by rowing and by sailing because of the wind being very weak, and we came to sleep in front of the second Ysla del Esquermento, having made ——.[24]

As long as Lorimier served as Spanish commandant of Cape Girardeau, the post had no fort and no regularly laid-out village. While Lorimier had a house for himself, the rest of the inhabitants, as they moved in, settled on farms nearby. The military importance of the post in the defense of Upper Louisiana lay in its use as a listening post for aggressive activities brewing around the Ohio River. Lorimier, who had a perfect understanding of the customs, prejudices, and language of the Indians, and held their unquestioning confidence, was able to give the Spaniards invaluable assistance when the Clark-Genêt expedition threatened the province. Throughout the period of the threatened attack he and his Indians kept watch over all the roads and districts in the vicinity of the Ohio, including the mouth of the river, to prevent a surprise attack. Lorimier also sent his Indians up the Ohio into American territory to spy on the enemy's movements. When the French attempted to draw the Indians away from Spain with bribes and false stories, he successfully combatted their efforts and kept them loyal to the Spaniards. Many times the Spanish government called upon Lorimier and his Shawnee and Loup Indians for help in repelling threatened attacks and to defend the Spanish territories.

See Houck, *History of Missouri*, *1*, 318; *2*, 167, 170–71, 180–82. Trudeau to Gayoso, St. Louis, January 15, 1798, P de C 2365; in Houck, *Spanish Régime*, *2*, 247–58. Nasatir, *Before Lewis and Clark*, *2*, 534–44; Trudeau to Lorimier, August 8, 1792, in Houck, *Spanish Regime*, *2*, 47; Perrin du Lac, *Voyages in the Two Americas*, p. 82; Collot, *Journey*, *1*, 217–22; Stoddard, *Sketches of Louisiana*, p. 214; Memorandum of the Missions of Louis Lorimier, 1787–1796, Cape Girardeau, June 19, 1797, P de C 2365 (see entries for March 18, 1793, and January 1794); Lorimier to Carondelet, Cape Girardeau, September 17, 1793, MS in Bancroft Library; printed in *AHAR 1945, 4,* 204–05.

23. The Indians were greatly pleased with Gayoso's speech, and Lorimier believed that Gayoso's visit produced a very good effect on both whites and Indians in the Cape Girardeau district. Since the other Indian nations in the district had left for their winter hunt, Lorimier said he would repeat the speech to them when they returned, for he thought it would attach them more strongly to Spain's interest. (Lorimier to [Carondelet], Cape Girardeau, December 31, 1795, P de C 211.)

24. Blank in document.

DIARY

Tuesday, October 20, 1795. We left very early. We ate at a quarter of a league below the Torre [Tower], whence we left at three in the afternoon. Upon arriving at the Torre we made the crossing, and on the Cabo de Santa Cruz we again made the crossing to the Cabo San Antonio, on which we encamped at nightfall, having made ——.[25]

Wednesday, October 21, 1795. We left very early. We made breakfast on the Cabo del Ajo, whence we set out and at which time there arose a slightly favorable wind. We hoisted the sails, and with the sails and the oars we continued up to Cabo San Cosme, where we made the crossing in order to make it later over the Cabeza de la Ysla á Ruansa. We did this, and entering through the channel of said island, we ran aground; the anchor was cast, and while we were pulling it by means of the cable, the latter broke. With spars the galiot was set free, and again leaving through where we had entered, we continued following the principal channel. Our pirogue and Bolon's pirogue remained to pick up the anchor, which they succeeded in getting; and we camped outside the Ysla á Ruansa, having made ——.[26]

Thursday, October 22, 1795. The wind being strong and at the prow, we left, cordelling [poling] as far as the outlet of the Ysla á Ruansa, where we had breakfast. We continued rowing and cordelling, and came to make dinner a little below the Ysla á la Percha, whence we left after eating, by cordelling. At this time there arrived on board Mr. Lorimier with his wife and children, who had come in a pirogue and are going to accompany me to Ste. Geneviève. After a second attempt at cordelling [*A la segunda cordela que dimos*], we had to put to shore, the wind being very strong at the prow, which obliged us to camp opposite the entrance of the Ysla á la Percha, at the beginning of the Ansa, having made ——.[27]

Friday, October 23, 1795. We set out early. We crossed over the Ysla á la Percha with a strong wind at the prow, and cold. We made breakfast on the batura of said isle, whence we made the crossing to the Ansa del Monte Brulé, where we sailed by cordelling up to its end, at which place we put to shore at twelve-thirty to eat. We left said place, the wind having calmed down, and we came to sleep

25. Blank in document.
26. Blank in document.
27. Blank in document.

on the Ysla de los Caballos, on the outer side, and Bolon camped within its canal. We made ——.[28] The night passed without anything unusual occurring.

Saturday, October 24, 1795. We departed at daybreak with fair weather; we made the crossing over the mainland. On the batura, farther above, we made breakfast, at which time arrived Bolon, who told me that during the previous night there had been stationed two horsemen, who, immediately upon learning that I was there, left for Ste. Geneviève to give notice. At the time we left, a pirogue was sighted which was descending and which drew up alongside, and it was Mr. Papin[29] coming from Illinois, who was going to Vincent Post [Vincennes] with merchandise. We left with wind at the prow. At twelve o'clock we put to shore at the point located in front of La Salina, where we made dinner, at which time there crossed, starting from La Salina, the man named Sainte Marie, who had just arrived from New Madrid with sealed envelopes [pliegos] from that post and from San Fernando de las Barrancas. After eating, I left, making the crossing on the batura of La Salina, at which time Mr. Jones[30] and Mr. Morison,[31] who also crossed the batura in order to go on to Kaskaskia, came alongside; and after having saluted me, they left for their destination. We continued traveling, putting up the sail, the wind being good even though slight, due to the turn that the river makes to the

28. Blank in document. Many of the names of places mentioned here are in Collot, *Journey, 1,* 222–25.

29. Joseph Marie Papin was born in Montreal on November 6, 1741, and died in September, 1811. (See Houck, *Spanish Régime, 1,* 192; MHS *Collections, 3,* No. 1, pp. 71, 76–77, 88–90.) In 1794 Rousseau charged him with spreading information and counseling the inhabitants against the government (Rousseau to Mon Gouverneur, June 29, 1794, P de C 210). See Liljegren, *LHQ, 22,* 45–50 passim.

30. John Rice Jones was a prominent attorney in Kaskaskia. He was born in Wales, educated at Oxford, and practiced law in London. In 1784 he came to America and settled in Philadelphia. Jones arrived in Kaskaskia in 1789, settled in Vincennes, and dealt extensively in land. In 1801 he became attorney general of the territory. He emigrated to Missouri in 1810 and engaged in mining with Moses Austin at Potosi. He died on February 1, 1824. (See Chicago Historical Society *Collections, 4* [1890], 230–70; Alvord, *Kaskaskia Records;* Carter, *Territorial Papers, 2, 3, 7, 8, 14, 16;* Philbrick, *Laws of Indiana Territory,* pp. ccxxxviii–xlii. For an illustration of one case see Nasatir, *IJHF, 20* (1931), 199 et seq.)

31. William Morrison and his brother, Robert, were prominent men in Kaskaskia both as merchants and in public affairs. (See Philbrick, *Laws of Indiana Territory,* p. cclxvi.)

north, and the wind being from the west. When the galiot appeared above the island, a company of mounted militiamen, who were stationed there in order to receive me, shot off their guns. Immediately I sent Cruzat with the pirogue to tell the commandant that it was impossible to land where he was with his militia because of the strong current that exists at the head of said island, but that I was going to do so at the old post of Ste. Geneviève. At the same time I answered their salute with all my artillery. Cruzat returned on board, and on the same pirogue came Mr. Vallé,[32] commandant of the post, and Father St. Pierre ,who continued traveling with me. The militia went to station itself at the place I was going to disembark, and having made the crossing, I disembarked in tbe old town of Ste. Geneviève,[33] where, mounting on a horse, I directed

32. For François Vallé see above, p. 60, n. 5.

33. Located about 20 leagues below St. Louis and 345 leagues above New Orleans was Ste. Geneviève, the oldest white settlement west of the Mississippi in Upper Louisiana. The country in the district of Ste. Geneviève was rather hilly and uneven, but the river bottom furnished good farming soil, and the land was rich in lead, iron, and salt deposits. Originally the village was located close to the river bank on a flat plain called Big Common Field, but frequent floods finally forced the inhabitants to move to a higher location, and by 1791 the old site was abandoned.

The new village was located about 2 or 3 miles from the river, on the side of a small hill that dominated all the surrounding country. In 1790 it contained 60 houses, and by 1797 the number had risen to 100. Census reports for 1795 placed the population of Ste. Geneviève at 849.

The principal occupation of the inhabitants of Ste. Geneviève was agriculture. Another source of income, and a very profitable one, was found in the lead and salt mines located just a few miles inland from the town. The people also engaged in hunting and the fur trade. The posts of New Madrid, San Fernando de las Barrancas, and St. Louis obtained lead and salt from Ste. Geneviève and also received a large part of their corn and wheat supplies from there.

The civil and military commandant of the village included in his jurisdiction the whole district of Ste. Geneviève. From April 1787 to 1796 Henri Peyroux de la Coudrenière was the commandant, at least in name. Until the end of 1793 he performed the duties of his office, but in January 1794 he was sent to the capital by Trudeau. François Vallé, *fils,* was appointed temporary commandant in Peyroux's place and held the position until his death in 1804, his appointment having been made permanent in 1796.

Most of the inhabitants of Ste. Geneviève were related by blood and hence their society was closely bound together. This fact probably accounts for the custom, not found in other Spanish posts, of the commandant's calling together all the notable residents of the village to discuss and consult with them before making any important decisions. François Vallé was the head of the most numerous and notable families in Ste. Geneviève.

Ste. Geneviève was not a military post like St. Louis and New Madrid. Until the threat of French-American attack in 1793–94, the new village did not even have a

myself to the town a league distant from the bank of the river in this place. The militiamen formed in a column behind me. At eight o'clock in the evening I arrived at the town, and in the street in front of the house of Commandant Don Francisco Vallé there was drawn up in formation the militia on foot, who likewise saluted me with a discharge of musketry. Before arriving at the town the Commandant began to salute me with seven cannon until I had entered his house; then all the inhabitants came and they congratulated me upon my safe arrival; I offered them my services and they withdrew.

---

fort. Its defenses up to that time consisted solely of a company of foot militia under the village commandant. However, when Upper Louisiana was threatened by the Clark-Genêt expedition, the inhabitants of Ste. Geneviève hurriedly constructed a fort to defend their town. They also created a company of mounted militia to aid the foot soldiers, each member furnishing his own horse. The fort was a small, square, stone building situated on the hill above the village. Strategically its position was very poor: it was too far from the river to protect its navigation, and it was dominated on the southeast by the hill upon which it was located.

Carondelet considered Ste. Geneviève as an important point in his plan of defense of Upper Louisiana and thought that a strong detachment of soldiers ought to be stationed there to restrain the Americans in Kaskaskia. In Carondelet's plan Ste. Geneviève formed the center of a line of defense in Upper Louisiana that stretched from St. Louis to New Madrid. Actually the military value of Ste. Geneviève rested upon two points. Her militia could be used to supplement that of St. Louis or New Madrid whenever one of them was threatened with attack, and she was a source of supply for both food and bullets to the other military posts—in particular, to New Madrid.

The district of Ste. Geneviève was bounded on the east by the Mississippi, on the north by the Meramec River, on the south by Cinque Homme or Apple Creek, and stretched westward indefinitely. (See Robertson, *Louisiana under Spain, France and the United States, 1,* 133 [Paul Alliot's Reflections"]; Pittman, *Present State of European Settlements,* pp. 95–96; Stoddard, *Sketches,* pp. 215–17; Perrin du Lac, *Voyages,* p. 44; Collot, *Journey, 1,* 252–56; Trudeau's Report of 1798 in his letter to Gayoso of January 15, 1798, P de C 2365; in Houck, *Spanish Régime, 2,* 247–58. Nasatir, *Before Lewis and Clark, 2,* 534–44; Houck, *History of Missouri,* I, 301, 337–60; *Relación* of the general population of the establishment of Illinois from November 1, 1794, to October 31, 1795, signed by Trudeau, encl. in Trudeau to Carondelet, No. 239, St. Louis, November 28, 1795, P de C 2364; resumé of the general population of western Establishments of Illinois for 1796; in Houck, *Spanish Régime, 2,* 140–43.) The Census of 1796 reported only 773 inhabitants. Probably a number of the residents of Ste. Geneviève moved to New Bourbon, for census reports of the latter post show an increase of 200 in its population in 1796 over that of 1795. In 1796 Ste. Geneviève produced 34,645 minots of corn, 10,185 minots of wheat, and 600 pounds of tobacco. Census reports for the same year showed 1045 head of cattle and 208 horses in the village. In 1796 the mines yielded 800 minots of salt and 165,000 pounds of lead. (See Vallé to Portell, Ste. Geneviève, June 8, 1795, P de C 192; Delassus to Carondelet, No. 38,

DIARY 303

Sunday, October 25, 1795.[34] The galiot ascended to the entrance of Gabury River, one league's distance from where I disembarked, and from said river it is one mile to the town.

Monday, October 26, 1795. I stayed at said post, reconnoitering.

Tuesday, October 27, 1795.[35] I dispatched the mail for New Madrid. At eleven o'clock I left the town of Ste. Geneviève on horseback. I went to where the galiot was. Upon leaving the house of the Commandant [Vallé], he saluted me with seven cannons. The cavalry militiamen were forming behind me, and various officials of it came to accompany me. At eleven-thirty in the morning I arrived at the entrance of the Gabury River, where the galiot was. At the time of embarking, the militia saluted me with discharges of [their] guns. I answered them with all my artillery, and I left said place for Illinois. After having gone about a half league, we put to shore in order to eat, which finished, we left and

---

New Madrid, December 30, 1796, P de C 34; Vallé to Portell, Ste. Geneviève, July 9, 1795. P de C 211; Vallé to Portell, Ste. Geneviève, December 16, 1795, P de C 192. Trudeau to Peyroux, Nos. 1 and 3, St. Louis, January 8, 1794, P de C 207A; Peyroux to [Carondelet], New Orleans, February 26, 1794, P de C 207A; Carondelet to Trudeau, New Orleans, March 3, 1794, P de C 21; Peyroux to [Portell], Ste. Geneviève December 26, 1793, P de C 208A.)

The fort at Ste. Geneviève cost 1442 pesos, 5 *reales*, to build, for which amount commandant Vallé billed the Spanish government. It was surrounded with planks to support the earth and serve as palisades. According to Collot, its artillery consisted of 2 pieces of iron cannon of 2 pounds, although Gayoso, who visited Ste. Geneviève (see diary entries for October 24, 25, 26, and below, pp. 309-11) in the fall of 1795, stated that the village possessed 7 cannon. (See Trudeau to Peyroux, No. 2, St. Louis, January 8, 1794, P de C 207A; expense account of François Vallé, Ste. Geneviève, May 15, 1795, encl. in Carondelet to Rendón, New Orleans, July 7, 1795, P de C 618; Carondelet's Military Report of November 24, 1794; Yealy, *Ste. Geneviève*.)

34. The entry for Sunday, October 25, in Pt. III of the diary, states: "The *galeota* ascended to the Gabury River, where it encamped and I remained at the post." The entry for Monday, October 26, reads: "Without news."

35. Beginning with the entry for October 27, I have taken the text from Pt. III. (The entry for October 27 is a composite from both parts.) Pt. III, which is incomplete, continues until the first sentences of the entry for Wednesday, October 28.

Pt. III of the diary was found in P de C 125, where it is without heading except that its beginning is entitled: "December." It starts with the entry for December 31, 1795, and continues until January 9, 1796, then swings back to Sunday [October] 25 and extends to December 9. Pt. IV, also found in this same *legajo*, is also incomplete and without heading. It begins with the entry for December 9 and goes to December 29. I have rearranged these parts and fitted them into one almost continuous diary. See introductory note to this diary, above, p. 235.

encamped opposite the island of the old Clark Fort, having made ——.³⁶

Wednesday, October 28, 1795. We left very early. At eight o'clock we met a pirogue³⁷ coming from Illinois on which was embarked Madame Vital, with two Negroes. We made breakfast and left. Below the Ansa de Reno we ate; and we left, sailing, even though the wind was weak. At the end of said Ansa the sails were hoisted [and] by means of sailing and cordelling³⁸ [we continued] until we reached the Ysla del Pety Platin [Plattin], where we encamped.

Thursday, October 29, 1795. We left very early. Upon pulling the towline of the pirogue, it broke [*sasobró*], but no misfortune occurred and only a piece of old rope was lost. We started deflecting from our course in order to overtake the pirogue, and we succeeded in this, opposite where we had slept. We continued our journey. After passing the Platin, we put out the line. At said Platin some Indians of the Peoria and Puan tribes were found. At ten o'clock we encountered a pirogue loaded with provisions which was going to New Madrid. We hoisted the sails, with a slight wind, and by sailing and rowing, we continued and came to sleep opposite the Ysla del Cotoñe de Cedro [Island of Cedars].

Friday, October 30, 1795. We left very early. We set out poling and ate breakfast about half a league from Villa de Carondelet,³⁹ whence we left, sailing with a fresh wind, and at eleven-thirty I arrived at St. Louis,⁴⁰ Illinois, at which time I was saluted from the *Fuerte de la Torre* [Fort of the Tower], and I replied.

    36. Blank in document. On "the old Clark Fort" see James, *George Rogers Clark*, e.g. pp. 196–97.

    37. Here ends the diary in Holmes, *Documentos*.

    38. "La vela a los cordeles."

    39. Villa de Carondelet, the village of Carondelet or Videpoche, was located about 5 miles below St. Louis on the west bank of the Mississippi. It was a tiny settlement, pleasantly located but, according to Perrin du Lac, not marked by a display of industry or activity. For a long time its population consisted of about 20 families, mainly French Canadians and Creoles. The principal occupation was agriculture, St. Louis receiving some of its provisions from the village. (Stoddard, *Sketches*, p. 219; Perrin du Lac, *Voyages*, p. 49; Trudeau's Report of 1798, which is Trudeau to Gayoso, St. Louis, January 15, 1795, printed in Nasatir, *Before Lewis and Clark*, 2, 534–44; Houck, *History of Missouri*, 2, 64.)

    40. Gayoso to Carondelet, St. Louis, October 30, 1795, P de C 43. In this letter Gayoso tells of the good effect of his journey to Illinois and the difficulties of navigating the Mississippi in low water.

    There are several histories of St. Louis, viz. by Scharf, Shepard, etc. See J. F.

DIARY 305

Saturday, October 31, 1795. At four-thirty I dispatched the galiot in order that it might go up to San Carlos del Misuri [St. Charles][41] to await me there.

McDermott, ed., *The Early Histories of St. Louis* (St. Louis, 1952). Houck, *History of Missouri*, contains a good account of St. Louis under the Spanish regime. See also Billon, *Annals of St. Louis*. Chouteau's Journal of the founding of St. Louis is printed in MHS *Collection, 3,* 335–66. An account of the founding of St. Louis is found in Nasatir, "Trade and Diplomacy in the Spanish Illinois 1763–1792." The present editor is now engaged on a biography of Chouteau.

St. Louis was founded as a trading post in February 1764 by Pierre Laclède. Situated near the junction of the Missouri and Mississippi Rivers, it was the most important town in Upper Louisiana, the capital of that area, and the only military outpost in the Illinois district. Its advantageous location early made it the trading center of Upper Louisiana and gave the post a position of great strategic importance in the defense of the upper province. (Pittman, *Present State*, p. 94; Stoddard, *Sketches*, p. 218; Perrin du Lac, *Travels*, pp. 47–48; Houck, *History of Missouri, 2,* 7; Robertson, *Louisiana under Spain, 1,* 231, n. 103.)

Most of the inhabitants of St. Louis were French, although in the early 1790s quite a few Americans began to be attracted to the district by Spain's generous system of land grants. In 1791 the total population—including all whites, free and slave mulattoes, and free and slave Negroes—was 1088. (Statistical census and products of St. Louis and its districts, printed in Houck, *Spanish Régime, 2,* 373–78; Houck, *History of Missouri, 2,* 58.) During the next few years the population apparently fell off, for in 1795 the inhabitants numbered only 976. (Lieutenant governor Trudeau reported that the 1795 census showed an increase over the one of the previous year. See Trudeau to Carondelet, No. 239, St. Louis, November 28, 1795, P de C 2364; Relación of the general population of the western establishments of Illinois from November 1, 1794, to October 31, 1795, signed by Trudeau, encl. in Trudeau to Carondelet, No. 239.)

The people lived simply and received little education, the majority being illiterate. There were few farmers, and their methods of cultivation were crude and primitive. The chief occupation was fur trade with the Indians, and it was as a center of trade for the upper province that the post gained its importance. (Perrin du Lac, *Travels*, pp. 47–48; Trudeau's Report of 1798; "Historical and Political Reflections on Louisiana," made by Paul Alliot, trans. and ed. Robertson, in *Louisiana under Spain, 1,* 133–39.)

From 1792 to 1799 Zenon Trudeau served as lieutenant governor at St. Louis. In addition to his regular responsibilities, the proximity of the Americans in Cahokia and Kaskaskia to the settlements in Spanish Illinois added duties of a diplomatic nature to his position. He was on good terms with Governor Arthur St. Clair and tried to maintain harmony in political matters with the judges and magistrates in the American Illinois country. (Trudeau to Gayoso, St. Louis, October 4, 1795, P de C 48; Houck, *History of Missouri, 1,* 318; *2,* 62.)

Always the political capital of Illinois, St. Louis did not become a fortified town until the British-Indian attack upon it in 1780 exposed the necessity for some means of military defense. Early in the spring of 1780, when the first threat of English attack reached St. Louis, the lieutenant governor, Fernando de Leyba, ordered the hasty construction of some fortifications. A round stone tower about 30 feet in diameter and from 30 to 40 feet tall was erected on the crest of a hill behind St.

Sunday, November 1, 1795. Nothing unusual occurred.

Tuesday,[42] *November 3, 1795.* At nine o'clock I left on horseback from St. Louis[43] with Don Zenon Trudeau, Don Agustin Chouteau, Don Benito Vasquez, the priest, [and] Mr. Robison accom-

---

Louis and christened Fort San Carlos. The only other fortifications that time permitted were two intrenchments, one north and the other south of the tower. With these defenses, De Leyba repulsed the British attack, but the need for more adequate fortifications was demonstrated. (Musick, *St. Louis as a Fortified Town*, pp. 28-29; Houck, *History of Missouri, 1*, 306-07; Nasatir, *Journal* of the Illinois State Historical Society, *21*, 291-358; Nasatir, *St. Louis during the British Attack of 1780*, reprinted from *New Spain and the West, 1* (2 vols. Lancaster 1932), 239-61.)

Toward the end of 1780 Francisco Cruzat, who had replaced De Leyba as lieutenant governor, began the work of extending and improving the town's hastily built defenses. He had a wooden stockade about 9 feet high and 6 inches thick erected around the town, and north of the stockade he had a wooden bastion built. The only other item which Cruzat constructed was a semicircular stone building north of the town on the river bank, referred to in Spanish records as "ravelin of the north."

In November 1787, when Manuel Perez became lieutenant governor, he found the fortifications of St. Louis in a sorry state. Cruzat's wooden stockade was completely rotted down, and the town's only defense was the stone tower of Fort San Carlos, the "ravelin of the north," and the rotted north bastion. In accordance with instructions from the Governor General, Perez had the north bastion rebuilt with stone. However, as he provided no banquette or esplanade for it, when Trudeau took office he estimated that it would cost 1,000 pesos to complete the bastion's defense. (Stoddard, *Sketches*, p. 219; Musick, *St. Louis*, pp. 56-60, 68-70, 78; Houck, *History of Missouri, 1*, 309, 312; Trudeau to Carondelet, No. 3, St. Louis, July 25, 1792, P de C 25A. For the administrations of Cruzat and Perez see Nasatir, "Trade and Diplomacy," chap. 4.)

Such was the state of the defenses of St. Louis when Trudeau became lieutenant governor in July 1792. He had scarcely taken the oath of office before instructions arrived for him to begin repairs on the fortifications of the town. Since St. Louis was surrounded by Indian nations and open to the assaults of both the Americans and English, Carondelet felt that the post should be provided with strong military fortifications. Another reason for strong fortifications was the fact that the great distance of the post from the capital made it impossible for reinforcements to arrive in time in case of a sudden attack. Carondelet ordered Trudeau to rebuild Cruzat's stockade if the work could be done for 2,000 pesos. Otherwise, he was to erect a stockade and banquette around the stone tower of Fort San Carlos. The "ravelin of the north" was to be dismantled and abandoned, because the Governor General feared its weak position would make it difficult to defend and susceptible to easy capture.

Trudeau began work on the fortifications of St. Louis in the summer of 1792. He removed the artillery from the "ravelin of the north," but did not destroy the building because he thought it could be used for some other purpose. In the spring of 1793 he completed the work on the fort, at a cost of 3,000 pesos. The structure consisted of a rectangular enclosure of planks of about 192 feet square, with 4 bastions at the corners. Around the outside ran an earthern parapet, forming a sloping esplanade. At the foot of the esplanade a ditch 2 feet deep and 6 feet wide served as a moat. Within the stockade a banquette or bank of earth was constructed around the wall for the defenders of the fort to stand upon in order to see over the parapet.

DIARY 307

panying me. At twelve o'clock we arrived in San Fernando de Florisante,[44] where we ate, and we departed, passing the Marais des Liards, and about five o'clock we arrived at San Carlos del Misuri, where the galiot was, which had arrived there about an hour before. It made the crossing immediately in order to come and look for me. I crossed on it together with all those who [had] accompanied me by land. The militias were there in formation,

---

The dominating feature of the fort was the old stone tower which contained the artillery consisting of 8 cannon. In addition to the tower, the enclosure contained a stone barrack, a kitchen with a prison adjoining, a stone powder magazine, and a well. Although Trudeau thought the fort should be garrisoned by at least 200 soldiers, and Carondelet recommended 4 companies, the regular complement of troops at St. Louis never exceeded 50 men during the Spanish period. (Musick, *St. Louis*, pp. 77–80; Carondelet's Military Report of November 24, 1794; Trudeau's Report of January 15, 1798; Trudeau to Carondelet, No. 3, St. Louis, July 25, 1792, P de C 25A; Carondelet to [unaddressed], New Orleans, April 18, 1793, P de C 2353; copy in P de C 178A.)

In 1796 the French general Victor Collot visited St. Louis and was greatly impressed by the post's advantageous military position. He regarded the town as an essential point in the defense of Louisiana and in the domination of the Upper Mississippi, Illinois, and Missouri Rivers. However, he considered the Spanish fortifications of St. Louis poorly constructed and entirely inadequate for the town's defense. He drew up several plans for the fortifications of St. Louis. (Collot, *Journey in North America*, 2, 249–56.)

The French archives abound with Collot materials. I have collected a very large body of manuscript material relating to Collot and his activities in the Mississippi Valley. Some of this has been used by my former students, such as Lloydine Martin, who wrote her dissertation on Collot; E. R. Liljegren, who wrote on the Commission of Carlos Howard and on Jacobinism in Spanish Louisiana; and L. R. Devlin, who wrote on the Upper Mississippi Frontier. (See Gayoso to Carondelet, Natchez, October 15, 1796, P de C 43; Carondelet to Las Casas, No. 163 res., New Orleans, November 1, 1796, P de C 1447. Several documents are printed in Nasatir, *Before Lewis and Clark*. See also Musick, *St. Louis*.)

The district of St. Louis included all the territory between the Meramec and Missouri Rivers.

41. Located on the bank of the Missouri River about 24 miles above its mouth was the village of San Carlos del Misuri, oldest and most important Spanish settlement north of the Missouri. In 1797 the town boasted about 100 houses and had a population of some 450 persons. In 1795 Don Carlos Tayon was commandant of San Carlos and of the company of militia that defended the town. (Stoddard, *Sketches*, p. 222; Perrin du Lac, *Travels*, p. 48; Houck, *History of Missouri*, 2, 79–86. Many documents mentioning San Carlos are to be found in Nasatir, *Before Lewis and Clark*.)

42. The entry for Monday, November 2, 1795, was either omitted in the original or omitted by my copyist.

43. Gayoso's stay in the St. Louis area and his trip to St. Charles and elsewhere, which he mentions in the following few days' entries, was reported upon at some length by Gayoso in his report to Carondelet, which he wrote immediately upon his return to New Madrid. Gayoso's report is contained in full below, pp. 331–41.

with their Commandant Don Carlos Tayon, who saluted me with discharges from the muskets, and I answered them with all my artillery.

Wednesday, November 4, 1795. At sunrise the galiot was draped with flags, the day being the birthday of Our Catholic Monarch, and we fired three volleys of fifteen shots. After Mass I mounted a horse, and accompanied by various people among those that had come with me and some fifteen militiamen, I went to reconnoiter the lower prairie, where, having arrived, I climbed on the isolated rounded hillock but did not succeed in seeing the prairie in all its expanse because of the smoke that had arisen over the ridge of hills, and through them I returned to San Carlos at one o'clock. At sunset a volley was discharged of 21 cannon shots, and the colors were struck.

Thursday, November 5, 1795. I left said post on *La Vigilante* with Mr. Chouteau and Cruzat. At twelve o'clock I reached the mouth of the Missouri leading into the Mississippi, which I ascended, sailing to the island that is a little above Paysa, where we encamped.

Friday, November 6, 1795. We left early. About eight o'clock we hoisted the sail and at twelve o'clock we arrived at the Illinois River, and, having examined its entrance, we drifted down the river with the wind at the prow and came to sleep at the entrance of the Missouri. About two o'clock in the morning it began to rain.

Saturday, November 7, 1795. We left in the rain. Between seven o'clock and eight o'clock it ceased raining. At eleven-thirty we reached St. Louis, where I disembarked. At twelve-thirty I again embarked with various gentlemen to go and dine at Kaokias [Cahokia]. I made the crossing on *La Vigilante* up to the portage,

---

44. The largest settlement in the district of St. Louis, aside from St. Louis itself, was the village of San Fernando de Florissante. It was situated about 14 miles northwest of St. Louis on a bit of rising ground beside Cold Water Creek. Agriculture was the main occupation, the villagers furnishing grain to St. Louis and New Orleans. When Collot visited the Illinois country in 1796, he noted 30 families in Florissante, many of them Americans and good farmers. During the Spanish period the village supported a company of militia, and François Dunegant served as commandant of the town. (Perrin du Lac, *Travels*, pp. 48–49; Stoddard, *Sketches*, p. 220; Collot, *Journey, 1,* 252; Trudeau's Report of January 15, 1798, to Gayoso; Houck, *History of Missouri, 2,* 66–67; G. J. Garraghan, *St. Ferdinand de Florissante* [Chicago, 1923].)

DIARY   309

where I disembarked and went by land to the town. At this time there arose a strong wind which caused some damage to the *batteau* from St. Louis. While at the table Mr. Cerré arrived from St. Louis, having just arrived from Canada.[45] At nightfall I left Kaokias. I made the crossing on *La Vigilante* to the residence of Mr. Lacroix, whence I departed by land to St. Louis. *La Vigilante* remained at said *Cao* [sic].

Sunday, November 8, 1795. No news.

Monday, November 9, 1795. No news.[46]

Tuesday, November 10, 1795. At ten o'clock I left St. Louis and came to sleep a little below Pety Koiche.

Wednesday, November 11, 1795. We left; clear weather. And after traveling about a quarter of a league, we went aground on a batura [sic], which obliged us to unload all the mats, and seeing that this was not sufficient, I had thrown into the water all the ballast that it had, with which it [the boat] floated immediately. The people had breakfast and we continued traveling. Three leagues above Fort Chartre I met a pirogue that Ferrúsola had dispatched with letters for me,[47] and which continues traveling. At five o'clock in the afternoon I arrived at the Gabury River, whence I went on foot to Ste. Geneviéve.

Thursday, November 12, 1795. The galiot was bedecked with flags, and a salute of 21 cannon shots was made.

At noon and at sunset I had the colors struck, and 21 cannon shots were fired, today being the birthday of our Monarch.

Friday, November 13, 1795. After having breakfast, I mounted a horse, and accompanied by several inhabitants from there [Ste. Geneviève], I went to reconnoiter some surrounding springs and contiguous lands, and by twelve o'clock I had returned.

    45. On Cerré's trip to Canada see Nasatir, *IJHP*, *28*, 337-89; and more fully in Liljegren, "Commission of Don Carlos Howard." For short biographies of some of the more prominent men in St. Louis at about this time see Secret Instructions to Carlos Howard, signed by Carondelet, New Orleans, November 26, 1796, P de C 2364; printed in translation with copious editorial notes in MHS *Collections*, *3* (1908), 71-91.
    46. Gayoso spent the 2 days, November 8-9, in St. Louis, during which time he inspected the military defenses and talked with the townspeople and officials.
    47. Ferrúsola to Gayoso, mouth of the Ohio, November 2, 1795, P de C 212A. This boat also brought a letter from Power to Gayoso.

Saturday, November 14, 1795. After breakfast I went with the same persons to see La Salina at a distance of about a league and a half from Ste. Geneviève, passing via New Bourbon, which I did, and on the road I reconnoitered two springs that existed on this road. By one o'clock I had returned to the house of Mr. [de] Luzières,[48] where I ate, and at nightfall I returned to Ste. Geneviève.[49]

---

48. See short biographical note on Luzières above, p. 179, n. 51. Luzières gives a short sketch of his life in a petition he sent to the governor, dated New Bourbon, September 20, 1797, P de C 214.

49. Luzières to Gayoso, New Bourbon, December 3, 1795, P de C 212A.

New Bourbon was situated 2½ miles from the old village of Ste. Geneviève, on the same hillside as the new town. It was established in 1793 by order of Carondelet as a refuge for French royalist families who had migrated to the American settlement at Gallipolis but were dissatisfied with conditions there. (Trudeau's Report to Gayoso, January 15, 1798; Houck, *History of Missouri*, *1*, 363–67.) By 1795, 183 persons were living in the new village (Relación of the general population of the western establishments of Illinois from November 1, 1794, to October 31, 1795). Census reports for the following year shows the figures to be more than doubled, the population in 1796 being 383, including 109 slaves (resumé of the general population of western establishment of Illinois for 1796; resumé of the general list of the western settlements of Illinois, 1796, in Houck, *Spanish Régime*, *2*, 140–43). In addition to French refugees, a number of Americans settled at New Bourbon, but the Spaniards made sure they were good farmers before accepting them (Portell to Carondelet, New Madrid, March 12, 1795, P de C 31).

The principal occupation of the inhabitants of New Bourbon was agriculture. They cultivated the same "Big Common Field" with their neighbors in Ste. Geneviève and raised the same products. In 1796 New Bourbon produced 11,545 minots of corn and 3400 minots of wheat. The inhabitants possessed 513 head of cattle and 69 horses. (Resumé of the general list of the western settlements of Illinois, 1796; Trudeau's Report to Gayoso, January 15, 1798.)

The first commandant of New Bourbon was Pierre Dehault Delassus de Luzières, one of the French royalists from Gallipolis and a countryman of Carondelet. Luzières held the office throughout the Spanish period in Louisiana. Being in the Illinois country, New Bourbon was under the lieutenant governor at St. Louis, and its position in the Ste. Geneviève district also placed the village under the jurisdiction of the latter commandant.

Shortly after the establishment of New Bourbon, Peyroux suggested that the new settlement be made independent of St. Louis, and its commandant given the same powers that the commandant of St. Louis exercised, including the right to grant lands. Without such independence Peyroux believed New Bourbon would always be full of the intrigues of private interests and mischief-makers. He thought Ste. Geneviève would be much better populated if it had been made independent from St. Louis 20 years before. Peyroux also suggested that the civil acts and publications of New Bourbon be written in French until the Spanish language could be better known. (Peyroux to Votre Seigneurie [Carondelet?], Ste. Geneviève, November 14, 1793, P de C 207B; Trudeau's Report to Gayoso January 15, 1798; Houck, *History of Missouri*, *1*, 363.)

DIARY

Sunday, November 15, 1795. No news.

Monday, November 16, 1975. At nine o'clock I bade farewell to the people of Ste. Geneviève. At nine-thirty I mounted a horse and I rode to the old post of Ste. Geneviève, where the galiot was. I embarked on it with the commandant and various military officers and inhabitants. I made the crossing over to the district of Kaskaskias, where I disembarked. In this place were Mr. Morrison and Mr. Jones. I got on a galera and went to Kaskaskias. Upon our arrival Mr. Edgar,[50] commander of the post, saluted me with five volleys of cannons. We ate there, and at six I returned to the galiot with the same people who had crossed with me, and I made the crossing to the Spanish side, where all who had come disembarked, and I slept on board in order to leave the next day.

Tuesday, November 17, 1795. At six o'clock in the morning Don Francisco Vallé came on board, and once he had bade me farewell, I departed at eight o'clock, drifting down the river. I then answered Mr. Edgar's salute and continued traveling with the wind at the prow. At four-thirty, on passing in front of the Cabo San Cosme, the two sons of Mr. de Luzières came aboard, to whom I gave a few refreshments, and I continued traveling. They saluted me with musket shots and I answered with three swivel gun shots. I came to sleep a little above the Cabo del Ajo.

Wednesday, [November] 18, 1795. I left an hour before daybreak, with the wind at the prow. At two o'clock I arrived at Cape Girardeau, where I stayed until the following day.

[Thursday,[51] November 19] 1795. I left an hour before daybreak, with the weather calm, and at a quarter of two I arrived at the naval station opposite the Ohio, where the gunboat was. There was Don Manuel Lisa with his bercha, and he told me that Don Francisco Vigo,[52] who desired to see me, was at Fort Massac, as did also

50. John Edgar came to Kaskaskia in 1784 and from that time became prominent in all undertakings. (See Illinois Historical Society *Transactions* [1907], pp. 64–73. See also Alvord, *Kaskaskia Records,* and more especially Philbrick, *Laws of Indiana Territory,* pp. cclxiii–cclxiv.)

51. For some reason, in the original beginning here the writer skips a day without meaning to do so. For example it is Wednesday, [November] 18; then Friday 19, Saturday 20, Sunday 21. The diary then drops the name of the days.

52. Vigo informed Gayoso that a former resident of Mobile, who was active in the Clark-Genêt expedition, had arrived at the Falls of the Ohio to promote another expedition under Clark's leadership. Although Gayoso thought that peace between

Commander Gragg [Gregg]. At four-thirty I sent my pirogue to said fort to see if they wished to descend. Without news [as usual].

[Friday, November 20] *1795*. About eight o'clock a chalán was seen descending the Ohio. The gunboat [the cañonera *El Rayo*] went out to reconnoiter all that there was on the Mississippi, and at about this time there came alongside a pirogue and with it Don Francisco Vigo, who remained with me; and the chalán continued to New Madrid, [with everyone] but a French tailor, who remained on board in order to descend with me. The night passed without anything unusual occurring.

[Saturday, November 21] *1795*. At eight o'clock the wind from the west was growing stronger. At twelve o'clock the wind was northwest and very strong; it began to calm down as the sun set.

[Sunday, November 22] *1795*. At eight o'clock the pirogue that I had sent came alongside and immediately another followed, on which was embarked Mr. Wilson, with two soldiers, who gave me a letter from Mr. Gregg, and Wilson told me that Gregg could not come as he had no one to leave in command. He [Wilson] dined with me and left at two o'clock, and I drifted with the gunboat

---

Spain and France would surely destroy the project, he decided to proceed with caution. (See Gayoso to Carondelet, New Madrid, No. 24 res., November 15, 1795; below, pp. 331-41.)

Joseph Maria Vigo, called Francisco Vigo, a merchant of Vincennes and a most fascinating character, was born in Piedmont on December 3, 1747. He joined the Spanish army and was sent with a Spanish regiment to New Orleans. He became interested in fur trade and established his headquarters in 1772 at St. Louis, where he was in secret partnership with De Leyba. Vigo was interested in and aided George Rogers Clark. Twice he went from Kaskaskia to St. Louis to give him assistance. Vigo was imprisoned by the British but later released because he was a Spanish subject. Although he gave freely of his time, influence, and fortune to the American causes, he was never repaid and was thus in want in his old age. Vigo moved from St. Louis to Vincennes before 1783 and became an American citizen. Intermittently associated with the early history of Vincennes and Terre Haute, he was also the executor of De Leyba's will. A year or two after his death on March 22, 1836, the United States Supreme Court ordered Vigo's claims paid, and his heirs received about $50,000. He was a trustee of Vincennes University. (D. Riker, "Francisco Vigo," *Indiana Magazine of History* [March 1930]; Joseph J. Thompson, "Penalties of Patriotism— Francis Vigo, Pierre Gibault, George Rogers Clark and Arthur St. Clair," *Journal of the Illinois State Historical Society*, 9 (1917) 401-49. An enthusiastic biography is Bruno Roselli, *Vigo—A Forgotten Builder of the American Republic* [Boston, 1933]. See Nasatir and Douglas, *Manuel Lisa*.)

and the bercha of Don Manuel Lisa. At seven o'clock in the evening, at the head of the Ysla de Las Barrancas Blancas, we landed and made supper. At eight-thirty we left and drifted downriver all night until two in the morning, when we arrived at New Madrid,[53] the gunboat and my pirogue having remained behind on the Isla á Dará to see if some accident had occurred to the bercha of Don M. Lisa, which had remained behind.

[Monday] *November 23, 1795*. At five o'clock in the morning my pirogue and the gunboat returned, [and the men in them] told me they had not seen the bercha. At nine-thirty said bercha arrived, and Don M. Lisa told me that he had been obliged to land because his bercha had filled up with water, which entered through the first ridges [cracks of the boat].[54] The rest of the day passed as usual.

[Tuesday] *November 24, 1795*. Today forty-two Cherokees arrived at this post, and they encamped here.[55]

[Wednesday] *November 25, 1795*. No news.

53. Gayoso to Carondelet, No. 3 muy res., New Madrid, November 23, 1795, P de C 35.

54. Ibid. On the very day that he arrived in New Madrid, Gayoso prepared a report on the results of his trip to Illinois to send to Carondelet. On the whole he considered the tour a success, even though he was unable to see Governor St. Clair at Kaskaskia, since the Governor had returned to Philadelphia by the time he had arrived. (St. Clair made a tour of inspection of the tribunals and did come to Cahokia and visit Trudeau in St. Louis. Trudeau also visited St. Clair in Cahokia, and St. Clair's visit was a return one. See Trudeau to Carondelet, St. Louis, September 26, 1795, and October 26, 1796.) However, St. Clair wrote a very courteous letter to Gayoso, explaining the cause of his sudden departure and promising to tell the President of Gayoso's good intentions toward the United States.

Colonel Gayoso observed that relations between the Spaniards and their American neighbors on the upper river were good and that St. Clair and Trudeau got along very well. He said that he tried to increase the feeling of good will by gaining the friendship of the residents of Cahokia and Kaskaskia, where he was received with distinction on his visits to both towns. Although he was unable to visit Fort Massac and commandant Gregg found it impossible to meet him at the mouth of the Ohio, the American wrote him a courteous letter. Gayoso believed Gregg would remain on good terms with the Spaniards, because, in addition to a naturally good disposition, he was interested in securing a contract with the royal treasury to furnish supplies to San Fernando de las Barrancas. (Gayoso to Carondelet, No. 24 res., New Madrid, November 24, 1795, P de C 43. See also Gayoso to Carondelet, St. Louis, October 30, 1795, P de C 43.)

55. With his tour of Illinois completed, Gayoso turned his full attention to the main purpose of his trip up the river—namely, the intrigue with Wilkinson, for which story see pp. 129–30, 322–26, and references there cited.

[Thursday] *November 26, 1795.* About eight o'clock . . . a day without news.[56]

[Friday] *November 27, 1795.* No news.

[Saturday] *November 28, 1795.* No news [illegible].

[Sunday] *November 29, 1795.* Mr. Todd[57] left for New Orleans. The rest of the day passed as usual.

[Monday] *November 30, 1795.* Without news.

[Tuesday] *November 31 [sic], 1795.* Manuel Lisa left in a pirogue for Post Vincennes.

[Wednesday] *December 1, 1795.* Don Tomás Power left in a pirogue. He [or it] did not arrive.[58]

[Thursday] *December 2, 1795.* No news.

[Friday] *December 3, 1795.* Without incident.

[Saturday] *December 4, 1795.* No news.

[Sunday] *December 5, 1795.* Without incident.

[Monday] *December 6, 1795.* Don Francisco Vigo went by land to Ste. Geneviève.

[Tuesday] *December 7, 1795.* Without incident.

[Wednesday] *December 8, 1795.* Nothing new.[59]

56. The entry for this day has been faded by water that stained the document, making it impossible to read.

57. This was Andrew Todd, who was descending to New Orleans to ask for privileges of exclusive trade on the Mississippi. (See Nasatir, *IJHP, 29,* 207–32; Nasatir, *Before Lewis and Clark,* 2.)

58. Power, who had been sent on a mission into the United States by Gayoso before the latter had left for Illinois, returned to New Madrid shortly after Gayoso had reached the latter place on his return from his Illinois tour. No sooner had Power arrived than Gayoso ordered him to ascend immediately to Red Banks to bring down the agents who were supposed to treat with Gayoso at New Madrid. Stopping only long enough to load his pirogue with merchandise in order to conceal the real motive for his voyage, Power departed from New Madrid on December 1. (Gayoso to Carondelet, on *La Vigilante,* 6 leagues above New Madrid, December 10, 1795, P de C 43; Power to Portell, New Madrid, June 27, 1796, printed in Clark, *Proofs of the Corruption of James Wilkinson,* pp. 33–35 nn.)

59. Here ends Pt. III, abruptly. It is incomplete.

PART IV

December 9–29, 1795

Thursday, December 9, 1795. At two o'clock in the afternoon we left the post of New Madrid,[60] rowing. We continued by the Cove and came to camp at the entrance of the short cut [*racursi*], a distance of a league and a half from New Madrid. The night passed without anything unusual occurring. A *berchita* of Don Manuel Lisa continues traveling with us under my charge [*por cuenta mía*].

Friday, December 10, 1795. We left early. We hoisted the sail because of the light favorable wind. It became contrary on the bend that the river takes and then it calmed down. At the exit of the short cut we landed in order to have breakfast. At ten o'clock there appeared a chalán. Cruzat embarked on the berchita and went to reconnoiter it, and on his return he told me that there were two Englishmen coming from the Ohio with cattle for New Madrid. On the Ysla á Favot we landed in order to eat, and afterward we left and came to sleep at the entrance of the Ysla del Lobo. Before doing this Father St. Pierre[61] arrived, coming from Ste. Geneviève, [and] descending in the bercha of Doña Verdon, and the latter having been stranded four days ago on the *roche brutale,* he [Father St. Pierre] was obliged to embark on the pirogue in which he was traveling. This Father gave me a letter from Mr. Vallé, commandant of Ste. Geneviève, and another from Mr. de Luzières, in which they gave me news that the man named Micheaux had finally written the latter a letter (of which he inserted a copy for

60. Gayoso left New Madrid for the Ohio naval station to wait for Power and the agents from Kentucky.

61. Father St. Pierre, a barefooted Carmelite and priest of Ste. Geneviève in 1789–95, was ordered by the bishop to descend to New Orleans and not return to Illinois. He was accused of not being a priest, but the evidence was questionable. He left the "service" October 12, 1797, but re-entered as acting priest of Punta Cortada. In Ste. Geneviève, Father St. Pierre had established a school. (Houck, *History of Missouri,* 2, 275; his *asiento* in P de C 538B; Nasatir, *Before Lewis and Clark, 1,* 324, 373; 2, 442. J. Rothensteiner, "Father James Maxwell of Ste. Geneviève," *St. Louis Catholic Historical Review, 4,* [1922], 142–54; Yealey, *Ste. Geneviève;* F. A. Rozier, "Rev. James Maxwell. Missionary at Ste. Geneviève," *United States Catholic Historical Magazine, 1* [1887], 283 ff. on Father Maxwell, who succeeded St. Pierre at Ste. Geneviève.)

me), in which he said that he believed that a second expedition would probably be premeditated against this province by the French rebels—without giving the reasons upon which he based this suspicion.[62]

The night passed without anything unusual having occurred. During the day we made four and a half leagues.

Saturday, December 11, 1795. The wind is at the prow. We left very early from the outlet of the Ysla del Lobo. We had breakfast and then made the crossing over the small islands [sic] of that name, along whose banks we continued. We made dinner at the beginning of the batura below the Island of Chicacha. Then we continued through it by cordelling. We entered by means of the island and continued until eight o'clock at night. Upon leaving the channel, we camped opposite the head of the island [*La cabeza de la ysla*]. During the night the wind blew hard. Good watch. The river receded a half-foot. We made in the whole day today two and a half leagues.

Sunday, December 12, 1795. We left very early, at which time was sighted the bercha of Dama Verdon. I immediately dispatched Cruzat in the berchita to reconnoiter and to deliver to said Verdon

---

62. Rumors of a projected American attack on Barrancas de Margó were rife at this time, although Gayoso somewhat discounted several of them. But when he received the news from the commandants of Ste. Geneviève and New Bourbon of a projected French attack, he became a bit perturbed. Gayoso was not too upset, however, since the recent armistice between France and Spain made a French attack on Louisiana rather unlikely. Micheaux, being connected with the project or the news concerning it, gave Gayoso some serious worry, but that too was dispelled a few days later when he had an unexpected opportunity for meeting with Micheaux and talking over matters in person. As a result of his conversation with Micheaux, Gayoso countermanded his orders to the commandants of Ste. Geneviève and Cape Girardeau to arrest Micheaux. (See Dehault de Lassus [de Luzières] to Carondelet, New Bourbon, December 3, 1795, P de C 211; Delassus [de Luzières] to Carondelet, Ste. Geneviève, December 5, 1795, P de C 211; Micheaux to Lusieres de la Suze [Delassus de Luzières], Kaskaskias, December 2, 1795, encl. in Delassus [de Luzières] to Carondelet, Ste. Geneviève, December 5, 1795; Lorimier to Monsieur, Cape Girardeau, December 11, 1795, P de C 208A; Gayoso to Carondelet, on *La Vigilante,* 6 leagues above New Madrid, December 10, 1795, P de C 43; Gayoso to Carondelet, No. 27 res., on *La Vigilante,* 6 leagues above New Madrid, December 10, 1795, P de C 43; draft [Gayoso] to Folch, on *La Vigilante,* 7 leagues above New Madrid, December 11, 1795, P de C 127; Gayoso to Carondelet, No. 28 res., on *La Vigilante,* opposite the entrance of the Ohio, December 17, 1795, P de C 43; draft in P de C 128. Draft [Gayoso] to Vallé and Lorimier, *très. res.,* on *La Vigilante,* December 17, 1795, P de C 130.)

a letter for the governor general. During this interval a favorable wind arose from the south. The sails were hoisted but then taken down in order to wait for the berchita as soon as I saw that it had out-distanced the ones of the galiot, and we followed with a fresh wind up to the point which is opposite the Mina de Fierro, where I landed at eleven o'clock in order to await the bercha and the pirogue. The first one arrived at twelve and the second at one-thirty. As soon as we had eaten, we left rowing, with a not very favorable wind, and we came to camp on the second island of the Mina de Fierro, having made four leagues and a half in all that day. The river receded one foot.

Monday, December 13, 1795. We left early with a north wind at the prow. We had breakfast on the last island of the Mina and then continued along the Ansa, and in the middle of the latter we landed in order to eat. We then continued and came to sleep at the head of Clark Island, on the mainland.

Tuesday, December 14, 1795. We left early. We made the crossing and came to have breakfast on the Point of Spain, one mile away from opposite the entrance of the Ohio. At nine o'clock in the morning we arrived at the naval station, where I had my tent set up, and I commenced to make an enclosure in the manner of a redoubt in this form △, in order to put the people under shelter.[63]

Wednesday, December 15, 1795. At four o'clock in the afternoon there appeared a chalán on the Ohio. As soon as it was on the Mississippi, I went to reconnoiter it in the berchita, and in the chalán was a family from Fort Massac that was descending to New Madrid to establish itself there. The day and night passed without anything unusual occurring. Good watch. The river rose a half foot.

Thursday, December 16, 1795. At four o'clock in the afternoon a bercha was sighted which was descending the Mississippi, following close around the point of the Ohio. I dispatched Cruzat in the

---

63. This was done to use as an excuse for his remaining there until Power would arrive. But despite Gayoso's careful attempts to keep the negotiations with the Kentucky agents secret, he was unable to prevent a certain amount of talk and speculation among the sailors as to the real reason for his long delay on the upper river. (Gayoso to Carondelet, on *La Vigilante,* 6 leagues above New Madrid, December 10, 1795, P de C 43; declaration of Power, sworn to before Fitch, New Orleans, March 14, 1809, printed in Clark, *Proofs,* pp. 67–71 nn.)

bercha to see who it was, and in spite of the attempts that he made, he could not reach it before it entered the Ohio; but having landed in the American district, Cruzat went on board with the purpose of seeing the new state of things that might have occurred. At six he returned to the naval station and with him Mr. Richard, owner of the bercha that was going to Cumberland, who told me he had on board the man named Micheaux. Immediately I embarked in order to go and see him to investigate, if I could, on what he based the notice he had given to Mr. [de] Luzière. I arrived at the place they were encamped, and Mr. Micheaux received me with many signs of friendship. He did not take long to enter into a political conversation. As soon as we were through, I took leave of him and left for the naval station.[64] The night passed without anything unusual occurring. The river rose four inches.

Friday, December 17, 1795. The [building] of the redoubt of stakes is continuing. The day passed without anything unusual occurring. The river rose six inches.

Saturday, December 18, 1795. At eight o'clock the man name Lachanse arrived, coming from New Madrid. He is ascending to Ste. Geneviève in a pirogue. At the same time there arrived with him a little pirogue with two Americans who are continuing within the Ohio. I gave to Lachanse various letters for Ste. Geneviève and St. Louis, and then he left.

At five o'clock in the afternoon a chalán was seen within the Ohio. I embarked on the galiot and went to tie up on the batura in front of the entrance in order to wait for it to go out into the Mississippi, and it having done so, I went on board to reconnoiter it, and it was Owert [Owens?] of Natchez, who was descending with a load of apples and whiskey for that plaza. The night passed without anything unusual occurring. The river remains the same, without rising or receding.

Sunday, December 19, 1795. At noon I dispatched Chodillon to Cape Girardeau in search of shoes and some vegetables for me. The day passed without anything unusual occurring. The river is still in the same state.

---

64. See note to entry for December 10, 1795, above, p. 318, n. 62. On Micheaux see James, *George Rogers Clark*. For material on Micheaux's earlier intrigue see Whitaker, *Spanish-American Frontier*; some documents in *AHAR 1896, 1*, and *1903, 2*; Micheaux's narrative reprinted in Thwaites, *Early Western Travels, 3*; and many other references. See also Nasatir, *Before Lewis and Clark, 1*, 164–66.

Monday, December 20, 1795. Nothing new has occured; the river went down four inches.

Tuesday, December 21, 1795. At [?] in the morning I crossed on *La Vigilante* over the batura of the Ohio to take some measurements [*para tomar bases*] on the Point of Spain in order to measure or to take the width of the river at that place. I left orders with the sentry of the camp that as soon as he saw a boat on the Ohio, he should fire a swivel gun shot. In fact, at twelve-thirty we heard a swivel gun shot, and shortly afterward we saw crossing to the naval station a pirogue that emerged from the Ohio, and I recognized it to be the one belonging to Power. I immediately embarked and directed myself to the naval station, where I found Power.[65]

At five o'clock in the afternoon a chalán was seen descending the Ohio. I immediately embarked on the galiot and went to wait at the batura, which is in the middle of the Mississippi River, and as soon as it entered said Mississippi, I recognized it to be the [vessel of the] man named Ste. Marie, a sergeant of the militia of New Madrid, which was going [to New Madrid] loaded with pork meat.

During the night the river receded eight inches.

Wednesday, December 22, 1795. The weather is cloudy and it rained nearly the entire day. During the night the wind changed to the north and the weather cleared up slightly. The river receded six inches.

Thursday, December 23, 1795. Drizzling all day. At eleven-thirty Chodillon arrived from Cape Girardeau. During the night the wind changed to the north and it blew harder. Don Tomás Power was obliged to unload his pirogue, because it had filled up with water. About eight o'clock in the morning Mr. Podras and Bernody arrived in a chalán, and they continued on to New Orleans. The river receded about two inches.

Friday, December 24, 1795. Wind to the north, and it was cloudy. At nine-thirty we started to drift toward New Madrid. We hoisted

---

65. Power arrived at the mouth of the Ohio, where Gayoso was waiting for him. He was accompanied by a flatboat bearing Benjamin Sebastian, the agent chosen to represent the Kentuckians. As stated in the next entries in the diary, while the trio were prevented from descending to New Madrid on account of a snowstorm, they departed on December 24 and arrived the next day at noon at New Madrid. (See Gayoso to Portell, on *La Vigilante,* opposite the mouth of the Ohio, December 19, 1795, P de C 43; declaration of Power, sworn to before Fitch, New Orleans, March 18, 1809.)

the sail. It then began to snow and it also hailed. We continued nevertheless. At three o'clock in the afternoon, at the entrance of Bayou Chicacha, we met Mr. Podras, who was being detained because of the bad weather. The bercha went to reconnoiter a pirogue which was above the Pequeña Ysla del Lobo [Little Isle of the Wolf]. It was carefully observed that there was a bonfire on land, but presuming that it was [made by] Indians, we continued up to the second Pequeña Ysla del Lobo, where we put to land because of the weather being bad. Then it was perceived that the gunboat was descending and was tied up behind the galiot, whose lancha went to bring me the provisions for which I asked.

Saturday, December 25, 1795. We departed early, with snow and hail falling. At twelve o'clock we arrived at the post of New Madrid.[66] Nothing unusual occurred. The river rose about four feet. Still snowing.

Sunday, December 27, 1795. Mr. Podras arrived in his chalán. The river rose about six feet from where it had been, and during the night it began to wash away the banks. The lanchón *El Príncipe de Asturias* broke its moorings and went on drifting down, since the land where it was moored had also given way, which obliged me to order that the galiot, as well as the lancha cañonera, should go to take shelter in the Bayou San Juan.

[Monday] *December 28, 1795.* Mr. Podras left on the 27th. I dispatched a *correo* [express] to the squadron to descend. The river rose about eight feet. The weather was good. Nothing unusual occurred.

[Tuesday] *December 29, 1795.* I gave my orders to march the following day. The river rose about four feet. The weather was good, and without anything unusual occurring.[67]

---

66. As soon as they arrived at New Madrid, Gayoso and Sebastian retired to the house that Gayoso had rented, to begin discussions on a commercial agreement concerning the navigation of the Mississippi. Since they soon discovered that their powers were too limited to permit them to reach an agreement, Gayoso suggested that they descend to the capital to continue the discussions with Carondelet. Sebastian agreed, and on the afternoon of December 30 they embarked on *La Vigilante* for New Orleans, accompanied by Power in a berchita.

67. With Pt. IV, the diary ends abruptly here. Beginning with December 31 we revert to the beginning of Pt. III. See Introduction to Diary 3 p. 235.

[Thursday] *December 31* [30], *1795*. At four o'clock in the afternoon I embarked[68] on *La Vigilante* and drifted down the river. At five o'clock the berchita did the same, and on it embarked Don Tomás Power and Mr. Vaden. We put to shore at nightfall on the point below New Madrid——[torn] the side of this, at which time I had a swivel gun fired so that the bercha might know we were there. About half an hour later the people on the bercha were heard talking, and I had a second swivel gun fired, to which the bercha replied with a fusillade to make known that they were—— [illegible] on the shore and a short while later——[illegible] we

68. Gayoso's trip to the upper river caused considerable expense. He complained that they overcharged him for work on the house he had apparently purchased and had had repaired in New Madrid. But since Gayoso's trip was secret, especially the nature of it, even Gayoso told Carondelet that his expense accounts should not be made public. He claimed that they charged more than double the value of the house he had had in New Madrid. (I do not have the complete documentation, but I do have a great many accounts of the costs and expenditures made by Gayoso on this voyage, chiefly for expenses at New Madrid and for his return trip. Among them the following are indicative: Gayoso to Carondelet, res., New Orleans, March 16, 1796, P de C 89, with Rendón to Carondelet, New Orleans, March 8, 1796, in same legajo; itemized expense account, encl. No. 1, in Gayoso to Carondelet, New Orleans, March 16, 1796, encl. with Rendón to Carondelet, New Orleans, March 8, 1796, P de C 89; Carondelet to Rendón, New Orleans, March 21, 1796, P de C 600 [Rendón's letter of March 8 was also sent on same date to Gayoso, P de C 89]; statement of account of Portell for Gayoso, New Madrid, December 9, 1795, P de C 600; account of receipts and expenses formed by Portell of moneys he received and distributed by order of Gayoso, New Madrid, December 9, 1795, attached to letter of Rendón to Carondelet, New Orleans, March 9, 1796, P de C 89; accounts presented by Jacob Mayers and John Rein for carpentry work on house and kitchen repaired for Gayoso, signed by Portell, New Madrid, December 28, 1795, P de C 600; another account of same, same date, attached to Rendón to Carondelet, New Orleans, March 9, 1795; Carondelet to Rendón, muy res., New Orleans, December 29, 1795; copy sent to Ministry in No. 13 res. [marginal note], P de C 600. Langlois to Gayoso, New Madrid, August 28, 1795, P de C 48; Zamora to Gayoso, San Fernando, September 8, 1795, P de C 48; draft [Carondelet] to Rendón, New Orleans, December 29, 1795, P de C 211.)

The King approved the expedition of Gayoso and Rousseau to Barrancas. (See Rendón to Gayoso, New Orleans, February 27, 1796, P de C 34, in which he transcribes the royal order of approval of Gardoqui, dated November 18, 1795.) Moreover, Gayoso requested money for his intrigues and negotiations with Wilkinson (e.g. see Gayoso to Carondelet, New Madrid, December 3, 1795, P de C 43; draft [Carondelet] to Alcudia, No. 61 res., New Orleans, October 4, 1795, P de C 178A; draft [Gayoso] to Zamora, New Madrid, November 24, 1795, P de C 130; Zamora to Gayoso, San Fernando, September 17, 1795, P de C 48.

saw their fire. All night passed without anything unusual occurring. The river rose a foot.

[Friday] *December 31, 1795.* We left before the break of day, having fired a swivel gun. About a quarter of a league [away] we joined the bercha and we proceeded together. The wind was strong and at the prow. At the beginning of the Ansa de la Pequeña Pradería [Cove of the Small Meadow] we landed and made breakfast. We left with calm weather and came to camp a little above the first island of the Canadians. The river rose half a foot.

[Saturday] *January 1, 1796.* At four o'clock in the morning we left with a strong wind to the prow. The weather being clear, we ate on board. At ten o'clock the wind had calmed down somewhat. At nightfall, below the Ysla de los Chicotes, we met a pirogue which Don Francisco Langlois had dispatched with a letter from Don Vicente Folch[69] for me. The latter continued with us. At six o'clock at night we put to land on the Thousand Islands, where we slept. The river rose one foot.

[Sunday] *January 2,* [1796]. We left early. Before arriving at the Yslas Desgraciadas, we landed——[illegible], having sighted a boat whose master, when it had arrived, came to me and said that it belonged to Mr. Longine and that it was ascending to St. Louis and that he had left two pliegos which he had for me with the commandant of San Fernando, believing me to be traveling. We had breakfast. Afterward we left with a strong wind to the prow. At ten o'clock in the morning we sighted Fort San Fernando, and at eleven-thirty we arrived there, putting to land on Gayoso Creek since there was no land [place] in the landing stations. As soon as I was on land an orderly from the fort arrived, who delivered to me the above-mentioned pliegos from the commandant. I ate on board and then disembarked and went to the fort. During the night the river rose four inches. At eight o'clock the wind rose from the south, and about nine-thirty it began to rain, and it stopped at break of day.

[Monday] *January 3,* [1796]. The weather being good and clear, I climbed to the fort at eight o'clock and gave the necessary orders pertaining to the post at——[torn] Ugulayacabé——[torn] came to

---

69. For Vicente Folch see above, p. 116, n. 59.

DIARY

see me. The rest of the day passed without anything unusual occurring. The river rose eight inches.

[Tuesday] *January 4, 1796*.[70] The weather is clear. At two o'clock in the afternoon I left the Post of San Fernando. Opposite the fort I continued rowing [*me mantuve sobre los remos*], because Don Vicente Folch, Don Francisco Langlois, and Folch [sic] were eating with me, and as soon as these people went ashore by means of the pirogue, I allowed myself to drift a league below the Ysla del Diamante. Night overtook us. We drifted all that night, putting six men on guard until twelve o'clock, and six more until the following [morning].

To talk [Spoke] to Turnbull about the Negroes for Ugulayacabé. Brashears; settlement of accounts with Beauregard.[71]

[Wednesday] *January 5, 1796*. ——[illegible] opposite the San Francisco River, twenty leagues distant from San Fernando, we continued with the wind to the prow without stopping to land. We landed at nightfall twelve leagues above the White River because of the weather being bad, with snow and hail falling, and we remained there all night.

[Thursday] *January 6,* [*1796*]. We left early, with the wind to the prow. At one o'clock we arrived at the detachment of the entrance ——[torn] of the White River. I gave a letter to the corporal of that detachment for the commandant of Arkansas, and then we left, sailing with a favorable wind, which later calmed down. On the small Ysla del Trigo night overtook us. We continued——[illegible]——[blindly?] all this [night].

[Friday] *January 7, 1796*. Daybreak found us on the Ysla del Chicote. We continued drifting without landing at the Cabeza del Muerto. At twenty-five leagues above Nogales night overtook us. We drifted all night without landing.

[Saturday] *January 8, 1796*. Daybreak found us slightly above the ——[torn] of Zasivine, five leagues away from Nogales. A little below the Yazoo we put to shore in order to eat breakfast, and at nine-thirty we left. At eleven o'clock we arrived at the post of Nogales. The fort saluted me and I answered it, and I remained there

---

70. During his two-day stop at Barrancas de Margó, Gayoso inspected the fort and prepared some instructions for the commandant of the post.

71. These may be merely notes to remind the writer about such items.

all day visiting the fortifications. At ten o'clock at night I started drifting down the river.

[Sunday] *January 9, 1796.* Day broke when we were seven leagues above Bayou Pierre. We continued without stopping up to said Bayou, where I landed[72] and remained about half an hour and then left.

72. The diary stops abruptly, actually with the entry of January 8. The entry for January 9 is somewhat mixed up in my copy. On January 9 Gayoso was at Bayou Pierre, located about 60 miles above Natchez. Arriving at Natchez, Gayoso invited his companions to his home, where he entertained them royally. Power stayed only a short time, then continued his descent to the capital, arriving toward the end of January. A few days later *La Vigilante* reached the capital with Gayoso and Sebastian on board. Discussions with the Kentuckians were begun at once, but while the negotiations were in process, Carondelet received the news and order of October 28 informing him of the signing of the Treaty of San Lorenzo el Real. Toward the end of February additional orders from Madrid arrived for Carondelet, ordering him to close the negotiations with the Kentuckians, since navigation of the Mississippi River was conceded to them in the treaty. (See declaration of Power, sworn to before Fitch, New Orleans, March 18, 1809; Gayoso to Prince of Peace, No. 4 res., New Orleans, February 4, 1796, AHN 3902; Acts of Council of State for May 27, 1796, printed in Nasatir and Liljegren, *LHQ, 21,* reprint pp. 61–72; draft of reply [Alcudia] to Carondelet, San Lorenzo, November 25, 1795, attached to Carondelet to Alcudia, No. 54 res., New Orleans, July 1, 1795, AHN 3899. See also accounts in Whitaker, *Spanish-American Frontier,* p. 213; Hay and Werner, *Admirable Trumpeter,* p. 149; Bemis, *Pinckney's Treaty,* pp. 348–49; Gayarré, *History of Louisiana, 3,* 359.)

4
Gayoso de Lemos' Trip to Illinois: A Report
1795

Introduction[1]

Here we have a translation of Gayoso's full report on his tour of the Illinois posts, the original of which is found in P de C 2364. Further information on the places mentioned is contained in the notes to Gayoso's diary, above, pages 291–313. This document is printed in Spanish in Holmes, *Documentos,* pages 263–85. Holmes earlier printed it in English translation in the *MHR,* 55 (1960), 5–17, with at least one paragraph omitted. My translation differs somewhat from his.[2]

1. For background material see above, pp. 126–28.
2. See the description of Trudeau in his long letter addressed to Gayoso de Lemos, St. Louis, January 15, 1798, P de C 2365, in Nasatir, *Before Lewis and Clark,* 2, 534–44, and in Houck, *Spanish Régime,* 2, 247–58. Houck, in *History of Missouri,* gives the early history of the various towns and villages in the state.

Report

New Madrid, 24 November 1795

My esteemed Governor and friend: Yesterday I arrived from my voyage,[1] and although the journey is [was] painful, I would not have wished to miss knowing those countries, even had it been more arduous [for me]. I have been as far as the Illinois River itself, after having visited all the establishments we have, except Fort Carondelet,[2] for the season did not permit it. I shall take the time necessary to inform Your Excellency officially, since I have much to tell; nevertheless, I do not wish to delay assuring Your Excellency of the good disposition and loyalty of all the inhabitants of these most remote establishments.[3] I will tell about each post or

---

1. Gayoso's diary of his voyage to the Illinois country and return to New Madrid is given in full above, pp. 291–313. For notes on many of the men and places mentioned in this document see notes to Diary 3, above, pp. 291–313.

2. Fort Carondelet of the Osages was built by the Chouteaus under a six-year exclusive monopoly of the Osages' trade, granted by Carondelet to Auguste Chouteau in 1794 and confirmed by the Spanish Court. A complete documentary history of that fort and of the relations of the Spaniards with the Osages during the Spanish regime is contained in my as yet unpublished "Imperial Osage." Many documents relating to Fort Carondelet are published in my *Before Lewis and Clark*.

3. In his letter of December 16 Carondelet states: "I have seen with the greatest satisfaction the relación of the trip you made to the Illinois. What you as well as Don Zenon Trudeau said about the affection of those inhabitants for the Spanish government has especially given me the greatest satisfaction. It is clear that freedom of trade will make all the settlements of the Upper Mississippi prosper in a few years, and by means of the subjection of the Osages, agriculture will be established; the exploitation of the lead, coal, salt mines, etc., which the fear of those same savages had caused to be abandoned, will be advanced. I am thinking of means to engage the Court to support and foster the efforts of our Company of Discoverers, and if I remain in the province—that is, in the captaincy-general, as the rank of field marshall to which [Las] Casas tells me I have been promoted seems to indicate—I have no doubt that we shall succeed in driving the English from the Missouri. While I was engaged in thinking about this important object, I received the letter of recommendation that you gave to Don Andrés Todd, whose arrival gave me the greatest pleasure, since if we can persuade him to establish a branch of his firm here, it is evident that we shall drive out the trade of Michilimackinac. I entertained him well and I

inhabited place, although it may not be more than two words. Cape Gerardo [Girardeau] is an excellent location; the land is very good and well covered with trees: Don Luis Lorimier lives here, and it is beginning [to be] a considerable establishment. This subject has very particular merit and influence among the Indians; he is of good character, determined and active and, above all, very loyal.

Ste. Geneviève has a considerable population, and it is admirable how well developed the town is, considering how recently it has been transferred there from its original location. Its inhabitants are very united, of good disposition, and blindly ready for whatever is ordered them by the royal service or with respect to the economy of the town. Captain Don Francisco Vallé is a subject of very appreciable qualities, a lover of peace and of good order; all his actions are so many more testimonies and proofs of the fervor with which he loves the King; he has the confidence of the people, who, guided by him, will make the greatest sacrifices. Father San Pedro [St. Pierre], priest of the post, is worthily esteemed by all [and] is very charitable and attentive to his ministry; the attendance at the church and the frequency with which the inhabitants observe the sacraments is [are] the greatest proof of his merit.

At the old site of the town of Ste. Geneviève there exist only the houses of Mr. Peyroux and Mr. Du Bardó [Hubardeau?]. The former's being there is not strange, because he must change his residence, but the latter's is [strange] because of one of those preoccupations for which there is no excuse.[4]

---

will support his petition to the Court to return to him the value of the merchandise that was confiscated from him two years ago, directing him to the Ministry of State, who sees things in a larger way and with more understanding. Within a week he will leave for Canada." (Carondelet to Gayoso, New Orleans, December 16, 1795, original in Bancroft Library.)

On November 14, 1795, Trudeau wrote to Carondelet: "Monsieur de Gayoso has at last, as I desired, made his trip to St. Louis, where he spent eleven days, during which time he glanced over our establishments and the country of which I hope he will give you favorable information, which will only increase the projects that you have long formed for their prosperity." (P de C 211; in Nasatir, *Before Lewis and Clark, I,* 369.)

4. Or "the former [Peyroux] is not disloyal due to the fact that he probably will change his ways; but the latter is [disloyal] due to one of those preoccupations which have no pardon." The original reads: "En el antiguo sitio del Pueblo de Santa Genoveva solo existen las casas de Mr. Peyroux y de Mr. Du Bardó; el primero no

The town [*población*] of New Bourbon is already considerable, and it will not be long in becoming united with Ste. Geneviève. In[5] this town resides Mr. de Luzières, a subject quite respectable in his behavior [and] without note, except for the interest he takes in the prosperity of the country in general, with which he is occupied, really adapting himself to the situation and the nature of its inhabitants in an admirable manner.

On La Salina there is a small town [*población*] composed of the people who work in the manufacture of salt, which could be greatly increased, since there is no more than one pit, which produces barely fifteen *minotes* of salt a day. It would be best to promote this branch of industry because of its being a prime necessity; half of those who work [in it] are Anglo-Americans.

The lead mines are twenty leagues from Ste. Geneviève, but there are other mines that are not being worked. There is also a great amount of mineral wealth in good iron and coal.

At ten leagues from Ste. Geneviève one begins to see the ruins of the establishments that the Indians destroyed, which, had they remained, would extend to St. Louis in the same way as they do in the immediate vicinity of your capital. At a short distance from St. Louis is the town of Carondelet, which is beginning to develop; it is made up of agricultural inhabitants, but [they are] not very wealthy.

St. Louis presents a beautiful aspect from afar due to its advantageous position. The town is made up of quite large and attractive houses; it is of a fair size, and its inhabitants [are] dedicated to agriculture and commerce; but the latter occupation is more prevalent. From all the information I had received, I myself believed that

---

es estraño por que deve mudar de destino, pero el segundo es por una de aquellas preocupaciones que no tienen disculpa."

Peyroux had trouble with Vallé. He was suspected and out of office for a while. During Peyroux's absence from office, Vallé acted as commandant, and in 1796 Carondelet appointed Vallé as commandant of Ste. Geneviève, and Peyroux continued to live at the post. Trudeau said that Peyroux had settled at the old village of Ste. Geneviève, where he built a house and established a salt factory. In 1796 Carondelet instructed Carlos Howard to dismiss Peyroux as a captain if any plausible reason occurred. Carondelet said that Peyroux was "a suspicious, loose-tongued fellow," who nearly 2 years before had promised to give up his post but never did so. (Carondelet to Howard, New Orleans, November 26, 1796, P de C 2364; in Houck, *Spanish Régime*, 2, 130. See biographical note on Peyroux above, p. 223, n. 77.)

5. This sentence in my copy differs from that printed in Holmes, *Documentos*.

most of the inhabitants of St. Louis were dissatisfied with our government. Now that I have carefully tried to investigate their views, I cannot help but claim the contrary. There is no individual with whom I have not spoken on the subject. I have been in their homes and at their gatherings, and I have not recognized a thing, even remotely, that might be reprehensible; on the contrary, all show the greatest affection for the King. I observed the dress of the women at a very magnificent assembly I attended in the house of Mr. Chouteau, and I saw neither a tricolored ribbon nor an adornment that could arouse suspicion as to the manner of thinking of the families; only the wife of Mr. Robidou had a dress of three colors, but I attribute it to the lady's bad taste; besides, it was older than the French Revolution, and her husband and she herself are persons of good character. In addition to what I was able to judge myself, I have learned through Don Zenon Trudeau that my point of view was right. In this town there is only one ungovernable person, and he is Mr. Papin, but his relatives and a large family restrain him, and he alone is not able to arouse suspicion.[6] Likewise, I find it impossible to forget the well-known enthusiasm of Mr. Chouteau, [as well as] his enterprising and ready character regarding whatever interests the royal service.

I have admired the mercantile ambition of all the businessmen, which is likewise extended to promoting the cultivation of the land, desiring an increase in population in order to make it [the land] more valuable. Nor can I omit mentioning the name of Mr. Cerré, about whom there was some groundless suspicion, but surely that was due to misinformation, since he is a peaceful inhabitant who concerns himself with nothing but his trade and his work, and, on the contrary, he ought to be considered a useful and trustful vassal.

The directors of the Company of New Discoveries are prompted by the most laudable ambition and are worthy of the government's favor.[7] Monsieur Soulard has justified the first good opin-

---

6. See, in connection with Papin, the story of his "New Year's" revelry which alarmed Carondelet so much and on account of which in part Carlos Howard was sent to take care of sedition in St. Louis in 1796. This story is related by Liljegren in his "Commission of Don Carlos Howard," and in shorter form in his "Jacobinism in Spanish Louisiana," *LHQ*, 22, 45–50.

7. The history of the Company of Discoverers of the Upper Missouri (the Missouri Company) is given in full and with documents in Nasatir, *Before Lewis*

ion I formed of him, and his behavior has removed the doubt in which the note found on Mr. Bonnevie [had] placed him, since he informed me voluntarily about the correspondence that he carries on with Pentro [Pentreaux], [the motive for] which is merely to acquire news that he communicates to Don Zenon Trudeau. This is true.[8] Given this supposition, [and] relying on a trustworthy subject such as Soulard has turned out to be, the connection is useful rather than harmful.

Lieutenant-Governor Don Zenon Trudeau has the affection of all the inhabitants, and all have assured me that their happiness consists in the permanence of this chief, whose character, being so

---

and Clark. A good summary of the work of the company may be found in Nasatir, *MVHR, 16*, 359–82, 507–30; Nasatir, *Missouri Historical Review, 25*, 219–39, 432–60, 585–608; Nasatir, "Formation of the Missouri Company," ibid., *25* (1930), 3–15; and Nasatir, "Jacques Clamorgan," *New Mexico Historical Review, 17* (1942), 101–12.

8. In his letter No. 19 res., written from New Madrid on September 26 (P de C 2364; draft in P de C 226A), Gayoso informed Carondelet about the rumors he had heard about the French incommoding the province—rumors he did not believe or take too seriously. But he searched the trunk of Bonnevie, who had just arrived from the Ohio and who was waiting for permission from Delassus to go to New Orleans. Bonnevie, a former naval lieutenant of France and a resident at New Madrid, had taken an oath of allegiance to Spain. Since Gayoso found a mémoire, he took Bonnevie prisoner. He found out that he was aided by other men in the Illinois and that he had got some information from Pentreaux, who had changed his name to Lucas and had received information from the correspondence of Soulard's father in France to his son in Illinois. Gayoso suspected the men, as well as St. Vrain, who had had conferences with Bonnevie and Pentreaux in Kaskaskia, and also either Vanden Bemden or Derbigny. Bonnevie was sent to New Orleans, where he had a trial and was cleared. Due to peace having been made between Spain and France, Carondelet freed him and sent him to Havana, whence he intended to go to Santo Domingo. (Carondelet to Gayoso, New Orleans, December 16, 1795, Bancroft Library. See Liljegren, *LHQ, 22,* 46.)

For documentary evidence in the case of Bonnevie see Deluzières to Gayoso, New Bourbon, October 2, 1795, P de C 212A; Bonnevie to Deluzières, Fort Massac, August 27, 1795, P de C 211; certified copy encl. in Deluzières to Gayoso, New Bourbon, October 2, 1795. Gayoso to Carondelet, New Madrid, October 2 and 3, 1795, P de C 211; Deluzières to Carondelet, New Bourbon, December 3, 1795, P de C 211; Gayoso to Carondelet, No. 19 res., New Madrid, September 26; instructions to Bontoux, New Madrid, September 23, 1795, P de C 226A (Bontoux took Bonnevie to New Orleans as a prisoner on orders and instructions of Gayoso); Gayoso to Grand-Pré, New Madrid, September 26, 1795, P de C 32; draft in P de C 130. Gayoso to Carondelet No. 12, New Madrid, September 27, 1795, P de C 43; draft in P de C 32. Certificate issued by Carondelet (freeing Bonnevie), New Orleans, November 20, 1795, P de C 119; Rousseau to Gayoso, on *La Venganza*, San Fernando, October 7, 1795, P de C 211; Carondelet to Rendón, New Orleans, November 27, 1795, P de C 32.

well known, needs no praise. The priest Father Don Didier is also respected by all [and] is highly attentive to his ministry, which may clearly be recognized in the devotion of the people who go to church. It would be unfair to forget the only Spanish Officer who resides in these countries, Don Benito Bazquez [Vasquez,] a subject generally esteemed and pitied because of his small fortune; he has acquired distinguished merit ever since he came to this province in the time of Señor Ulloa.

San Fernando [Florissante], at five leagues from St. Louis, is exactly like a hamlet of Spain; it is a small town, but its inhabitants are favorably inclined and good farmers.

The little town [*pueblo corto*] called Marais des Liards is two leagues from San Fernando; it consists of some seven Anglo-American families and a portion of the Araonanes Indians, who live as whites, and all are very peaceful and industrious.

San Carlos de Misuri [St. Charles][9] is three leagues from this last town, but by a direct road it is only eight leagues from St. Louis. One may cross the Missouri in a passenger boat [*barca de pasage*] to go to the town, which is fairly large. It consists of two streets, many ordinary houses, and various factories that are working, which denotes that the town is prospering. All are farmers and very peaceful and industrious. Likewise, they all wish that somehow an increase of their population might be promoted. A great number of the inhabitants make trips to the upper part of the Missouri. Hearing the name of the King gives these people pleasure; they pronounce it with veneration and they live in the hope that with his protection they will be the happiest people in the world. I found myself in this town on the day of San Carlos, which was celebrated with the greatest joy, the priest of St. Louis having come for the church ceremonies (having been replaced in St. Louis by

9. When, with Gayoso, Trudeau was visiting St. Charles on November 4, 1795, celebrating the King's holiday and the day of the patron saint of St. Charles and of its commandant, one of the inhabitants had his two wrists fractured. Trudeau had him carried to St. Louis to the only physician in the area, Dr. Reynal. Since the injured man was a poor person, Trudeau said he would pay. However, Dr. Reynal's bill, which Trudeau thought would amount to between 50 and 60 livres, amounted to 1385. Trudeau said the amount charged was exorbitant. The injured man was still with Trudeau, who asked Carondelet for a place for him in the charitable hospital in New Orleans. He was an old man, whose tongue was paralyzed. Montegut at New Orleans estimated the bill should have amounted to 151½ piasters. (Trudeau to Carondelet, St. Louis, August 4, 1796, P de C 212A.)

the one from Cahokia). Since my galiot arrived as prearranged at St. Charles, I ordered that the colors be hoisted and a salute be given, which greatly pleased the inhabitants. Don Carlos Taillon [Tayon], captain of the militia and commandant of this establishment, is a subject of great merit and very suitable for that position, since in addition to diligently performing his duties, he is valiant and determined, which makes him be respected by the Indians. This town is already too large to be without a permanent priest. The people are naturally devout and it pains them to see themselves deprived of spiritual aid. In Cahokia there is a French priest, Father Janin, a commendable subject, who would like this position.

Farther below San Carlos, on the bank of the river, there is a promontory called the Mina de Carbon [Coal Mine]; it is literally formed of a great mass of coal covered by a layer of earth. Iron is found in the same district, as is true for different places in the whole vicinity of Illinois. I have neglected to speak about the land, having delayed making mention of it [until arriving at this place] at this time. The whole Illinois country is delightful, good terrain, well forested, with frequent springs, which will be increased as the country is opened up. From Cape Girardeau up to San Carlos of Missouri, the land is high in general, with some unevenness, and in all this expanse is found lead, iron, and coal. At the back of San Carlos begin immense plains that reach up to where the hunters have advanced in all directions, skirting the heights of which I have spoken, from Cape Girardeau to San Carlos. The climate is very mild, favoring the production of all kinds of European fruits except oranges and lemons; it is good for the production of wheat, corn, all seeds known in Europe, and cotton and hemp; all cattle would prosper if the population were larger in order that the thefts the Indians are accustomed to make would be impeded, although recently in this district they have not been so frequent.

It would be of the greatest importance to increase the emigration of good quality people to Illinois, since I consider it the most direct passageway to the Kingdom of Mexico, and if this exceedingly important matter is not attended to, it will not be many years before English traders are introduced there, and they will be followed by [armed] forces. It would be best to form a cordon of small posts from the Missouri, beginning from San Carlos [and]

Carondelet, and continuing until we are united with those of the *Provincias Internas*. In this way we would command greater respect from the Indians, we would keep their trade, and we would effectively protect the Kingdom of Mexico. In my official report I shall develop my remarks on all these important matters.[10]

It is with the greatest pleasure [?] that I assure Your Excellency of the good disposition of our people of Illinois. Some subject [of Your Excellency] who has not observed well has degraded their character, but it [all that] is unfounded. Your Excellency is not aware of the jealousy that always exists among the merchants and [of the fact] that they necessarily have connections in [with] foreign countries. Hence they have taken the opportunity to promote suspicious ideas against those [people] of St. Louis, but I flatter myself that I know the men of St. Louis and I affirm that those of Illinois are good vassals. Vigo has intimately known Peyroux in Philadelphia, and knows all his activities at the time he was commissioned by Your Excellency, and he assures me that he is a royalist and that he has not been in communication with the revolutionists, even indirectly.[11]

I forgot to tell you that in the whole country of Illinois 1500 armed men of good quality can be assembled.[12]

Your Excellency will think it strange that I have said nothing about New Madrid.[13] I am keeping this for another occasion, and for the present may I say only that it is a very young [*tierno*]

10. I have dealt in summary fashion with these matters in my "Shifting Borderlands," *Pacific Historical Review*, *34*, 1–20. They are dealt with at some length in the volume entitled "Pedro Vial and the Roads to Santa Fé," which Noel Loomis and I have prepared and which is now published. Much documentation on this subject is contained in my *Before Lewis and Clark* and in other of my publications.

11. See in this connection Nasatir and Douglas, *Manuel Lisa*, pp. 11–13, 34–35. See also Diary 3, entries for November 19 and 20, 1795, above, pp. 311–12; Liljegren, *LHQ*, 22, 41–42.

12. On November 30, 1795, Trudeau wrote to Carondelet about the construction of barracks in the fort at that place. He says: "I enclose for Your Excellency the *estado* [account] of the expenditures of said barracks, which Señor Governor Don Manuel Gayoso has seen and which he found beautiful and well constructed, thus giving me hope for the new approval of Your Excellency, which I solicit—that is, that the certificates I have issued [will] be paid" (Trudeau to Carondelet, No. 242, P de C 32).

13. Another sidelight on Gayoso's stay in New Madrid is reflected in Carondelet's letter to Gayoso of December 16, 1795 (Bancroft Library), in which he tells him: "I have now to speak to you about a matter which I loathe so much that I do not imagine it to be possible. Know, then, that there is a very valid rumor here that you are taking a wife in New Madrid, notwithstanding that it is believed you are

country, and that most of the inhabitants work by impulse rather than by inclination, particularly those who have come from the United States, except for Waters [Dr. Richard Jones Waters], who is a subject of principles and whom one is able to trust. I assure Your Excellency that I consider Portell to have infinite merit due to his way of handling them as he does; nevertheless I am convinced that some well-to-do families from Monongahela probably will come here now, and when there is a foundation of sound inhabitants, it will be an important post because of its nearness to the Ohio, and for this reason it is best to promote it. When I send Your Excellency the map of the confluence of the Ohio and the Mississippi, I shall tell you what I think of that location.[14] As a safe estimate, this river is more than 600 fathoms wide and cannot be less because of repeated operations[15] that I made on a base of 700 fathoms carefully measured on the bank opposite our landing place [naval station].

I still have not seen the site of the mill since I came, but I assume that it is finished. I don't know where the wheat will come to them from, except the United States.[16] Chouteau has a mill in St. Louis that grinds all the flour of that district and of San Carlos and much

---

pledged to the daughter of Wats and have even lived with her under the promise of marriage, your having been formerly married to her sister, now deceased. Reflect on what you are doing if you are having any affair of this kind there, because our bishop takes such matters very seriously and would certainly make you regret it if, after having solicited a license to marry Wats' daughter, with whom it is sure that you have lived publicly in Natchez, you were intimate with another in the same manner. The Intendant has been told that the house you have had built [had the misfortune of having had built, for you] in New Madrid is destined to lodge your paramour, but I believe, and so I told you, that since it is indispensable to conceal the true motive of your delay [staying longer] in that post, you could only feign in public some apparent motive such as plans for settling down there. Whatever the case may be, I believed it my duty to warn you as a friend."

14. "As for New Madrid it would be my opinion to leave it in the class of a civil establishment, transferring the fort farther up and as near as possible to the mouth of the Ohio" (Carondelet to Gayoso, New Orleans, December 16, 1795, Bancroft Library). This letter is in reply to Gayoso's letters of September 27, October 30, and November 23, and is not in direct reply to Gayoso's report. The first two of the letters mentioned are in P de C 43, and the third is in P de C 129. There is also another letter of Gayoso to Carondelet, dated November 23, in P de C 23.

15. See Diary 3, entries for October 11–12 and December 21, above, pp. 293–94; 321. Gayoso had a stockade built there.

16. Carondelet said there would be plenty of wheat that could be raised in the Spanish possessions in addition to that obtained from the Americans (Carondelet to Gayoso, New Orleans, December 16, 1795, Bancroft Library).

wheat that comes from Ste. Geneviève; in spite of this it is stopped half the time. In Ste. Geneviève, Vallé's mill is going to be rebuilt, [and] with that [mill] not one grain will remain unground in that district; besides, there is Mr. Doge's [Dodge's?] mill in New Bourbon, which will also provide a large supply. I would say that when there is one more mill in New Madrid the laborers will apply themselves more to their work and will have larger harvests; the same will be necessary to make the mills of St. Louis, Ste. Geneviève, and New Bourbon work, without considering that it is very probable that one may be established in San Carlos on account of its being a country which already produces as much wheat as St. Louis. Where, then, will the wheat for New Madrid come from? It is not cultivated here yet, and even if all the inhabitants dedicated themselves to it, they would not be able to keep the mill in operation for one month in the year. These reflections are accurate. It is true that much wheat could be obtained from Kaskaskia, for they have told me there that as soon as the above-mentioned mill is finished, and if they are paid regularly for their wheat, they will dedicate themselves to cultivating it. But on the other hand, in the same town another mill is going to be established, and because they are not making it as perfectly as they plan to make this one, the former will be finished first. My opinion is that it has been a poorly conceived speculation by Don Pedro Tardiveau, welcomed with discreet enthusiasm by the Chevalier de Luzières and the other associates, and facilitated by the extraordinary ability of Mr. Vanden [Bemden], without considering where the wheat was to come from.[17] Vanden [Bemden] is a diamond in the rough, harsh in his behavior, rude and inconsiderate at first sight, but knowing his character, he does not have a bad heart, and even letting him follow his nature, which he cannot refrain from doing, he can be very useful; moreover, he is accommodating. Derbini [Pedro Derbigny] is docile and young and looks after Vanden [Bemden] because of the interests of his [Derbigny's] father-in-law, but he [Derbigny] is a poor young man without malice.

It is impossible that there be wickedness in the heart of Mr. de Luzières, but because of his goodness he can be deceived; he assured me that he will never again give any more recommenda-

17. Gayoso wrote Carondelet from New Madrid on September 27, 1795, about the mill being erected by Vanden Bemden.

tions to anyone. Madame de Luzières has not that good character; she would be happy in a city, but she cannot conform to the social behavior of working people; thus she remains alone. The sons are good boys, but not having been subjected to a hard life, they do not find any resources within themselves that might help their parents, notwithstanding that the poor fellows do what they can.

Now, at four o'clock in the afternoon of the 25th, Power has just arrived, but as I am unable to decipher his letter to send it to you on this occasion, I will send it by special express. However, you will know what he says by his letter, which I am remitting to you, along with another for Gilberto [Leonard].

Power assures me that Sebastian and another man not yet decided upon will come to negotiate between roughly the 10th to the 20th of December.[18] I do not have time to speak of Perchet or whom *se le parezca* [he resembles].[19]

Receive, Sir, the cordial affection of your most devoted and faithful servant, who kisses Your Excellency's hand.

Manuel Gayoso de Lemos

[rubric]

[To]

Baron de Carondelet

---

18. See above, p. 314, n. 58; 321, n. 65. Sebastian arrived with Power at the mouth of the Ohio on December 21, and together they went to New Madrid, where Sebastian and Gayoso held conferences. Sebastian agreed to go to New Orleans to confer with Carondelet and left New Madrid with Gayoso on December 31, arriving in New Orleans at the end of January. (See Diary 3, entries between December 21 and 31, 1795, above, pp. 321, 324; Carondelet to Prince of Peace, No. 69 res., New Orleans, January 30, 1796, AHN 3886; copy in P de C 2374. Gayoso to Prince of Peace, No. 4 res., New Orleans, February 4, 1796, AHN 3902; Nasatir and Liljegren, *LHQ, 21,* 64. See also E. Warren, "Benjamin Sebastian and the Spanish Conspiracy in Kentucky," in *Filson Club Historical Quarterly, 20* [1946], 107–33; Whitaker, *Spanish-American Frontier;* Bemis, *Pinckney's Treaty.*)

19. Perchet was the engineer at Barrancas de Margó, and some differences arose between Gayoso and him concerning the plans and construction of Fort San Fernando there. There is a great deal of documentary evidence concerning Perchet in the P de C.

Index

Abenaquis (Indians), 127
Acadian Islands, 217, 218
Activa, La (galiot), 39, 40, 84, 95, 96, 99, 108, 114, 126, 128, 129, 130, 133, 137, 138, 145, 212 n., 255, 258, 259, 260, 263, 269; with Howard expedition to St. Louis, 138; described, 154 n., 255–56 n.
Agulera, Josef, 198
Alcudia, Duque de la. *See* Las Casas, Luis de, Duque de la Alcudia
Alexandre Island, 209
American Northwest Territory, 291
Amistad, La (flatboat), 158 n.
Angel, Felipe, 247
Anglo-Spanish alliance (*1793–95*), 4
Anguila (pirogue), 244
Ansa de Cipriera, 297
Ansa á la grasa (or Ainse à la graisse), 285 n.
Ansa del Monte Brulé, 299
Ansa de Reno, 304
Appalachian Mountains, 3
Apple Creek, 302 n.
Apple Island (Isla de La Pom), 243
Aranda, Conde de, 17
Araonanes Indians, 336
Arkansas Indians, 65, 108, 133, 162, 167, 170
Arkansas Post, 22, 25, 28, 35 n., 63, 81, 116, 268, 277 n., 325; commander warned of French invasion, 77; location, history, 164–65 n.; Rousseau stops for repairs at, 164–66; described, 165–66
Arkansas River, 35 n., 63, 67, 81, 90, 113, 163, 187, 205
Arroyo, Francisco, 166, 241
Arroyo Gayoso, 267 n.
Atakapas Indians, 65
Audrain, Pierre, 41, 179
Austin, Moses, 300 n.

Azabal, Juan, 198
Azeytuno, Juan, 213, 214, 228

Balize, 20, 37, 68, 153 n.; hurricane strikes, 98 n.
Barges (lanchones), described, 50. See also *Príncipe de Asturias, El*
Barja, La (paquebot), 67
Barnó Ferrúsola, Juan Francisco José, 92 n., 93 n., 118, 123, 154 n., 236, 285, 291, 295, 309; commands cruise to upper province, 76–77, 81–83, 191–92, his account of cruise, 193–231; hastens to fortify New Madrid, 82, 192–220; captures Pisgignoux, 82–83, 192; success of expedition, 83; patrols New Madrid area, 94; and humiliating *El Rayo* voyage, 99–100; arrives at New Madrid (*Feb. 12, 1794*), 101, 102; textual style, 192; transferred to *La Castilla*, 257 n.; delivers provisions, 271 n.
Barrancas de Harina (Ecores à Farina; First Chickasaw Bluffs; Flour Bluffs), 107, 185, 186 n., 217, 282; location, 281 n.
Barrancas de Margó (Ecores à Margot), 22, 35 n., 54, 62, 63, 64, 65, 72, 76 n., 85, 90, 93, 98, 101, 133, 152, 172, 173, 177 n., 180, 186 n., 229, 253, 279 n.; distance from New Orleans, 36; strategic position, 65–66, 105–07; reasons for fort at, 105 n.; Spanish Fort established at, 105–18 (*see also* Fort San Fernando de las Barrancas); American interest in, 106, 107–08; surrounding country described, 107; projected U.S attack on, rumored, 318 n.
Barrancas del Medio (Middle Bluffs; Third Chickasaw Bluffs), 107, 116,

Barrancas del Medio (*cont.*)
  186 n.; location, 280 n.
Barrancas de Prud'homme (Ecores de Perdom; Second Chickasaw Bluffs), 106, 107, 152 n., 174, 185, 186 n., 217; location, 280 n.; described, 281–82
Basel, Treaty of, 4, 5, 7
Bastrop, Baron de. *See* Neri, Felipe Enrique, Baron de Bastrop
Baton Rouge, 22, 34, 105
Batura del Consejo, 229, 252
Bayonne Islands, 284
Bayonne River, 218, 284
Bayou Chicacha, 292, 322
Bayou Mardigras, 75
Bayou Pierre. *See* Stony Creek
Bayou San Juan, 322
Bayú Rapelié, 245
Beauregard, Elías, 29 n., 113, 114, 116, 157 n., 158 n., 161–62 n., 228 n., 231 n., 237, 241, 242, 243, 271 n., 273, 279, 325; biographical note, 83 n.; prisoners delivered to, 83; Rousseau meets, 156; loyalty questioned, 156 n.; signs treaty for Barrancas land, 266; engaged in fort-building, 258, 259; appointed San Fernando commandant, 260 n., 279 n.
Belle Rivière. *See* Ohio River
Beltran (Mr.), 249, 250
Berchas, 50; described, 50 n. See also *Mosquito, El; Socorro, El; Tracnar, El*
Berchita, 50 n. See also *Betty*
Bernody, Mr., 321
Betty (*berchita*), 113
Betty, Guillermo, 241, 242, 243, 244
Big Black River, 156 n.
Billy (Englishman), 196
Blancó, José, 213, 249, 250
Blount, William, 129, 130, 136
Bolon (Mr.), 297, 299, 300
Bonnevie, Mr., 335; biographical note, 335 n.; captured, sent to New Orleans, 124 n.
Bontoux de la Blache, Domingo, 237, 247–48, 265; biographical note, 247–48 n.; engaged in fort-building, 261; signs treaty for Barrancas land, 266; carries treaty south, 267 n.; on upper-river cruise, 279, 281
Borgan (Mr.), 273

Bougigne (Mr.), 161
Bouligny, Domingo, 95 n., 129, 237; biographical note, 257 n.; commands troops on upper-river defense, 85; engaged in fort-building, 257, 261, 265; among land-treaty signers, 266
Boulliers, Alexandro de, 30; given fleet command, 26–27
Bourbon Family Compact, 4
Bowles (Mr.), 248
Bowles, Augustus, 56 n.
Bowles, William, 32 n., 33 n.
Bradbury, John, 53 n.
Brashears (Panton trader), 274, 275, 325
Brouyain (Mr.), 171
Brown, E. M., 152
Bruin, Peter Bryan, 196; biographical note, 196 n.
Bryan, Guy, 179; biographical note, 179 n.
Buffalo Island (Ysla de Sierbo), 295, 296
Bullboats, described, 49

Cabeza de la Ysla á Ruansa, 299
Cabeza del Muerto. *See* Death's Head Point
Cabo del Ajo, 299, 311
Cabo San Cosme, 299, 311
Cabo de Santa Cruz, 299
Cahokia, 55, 126 n., 127 n., 305 n., 308, 337
Campo de la Esperanza, El (Hopewell), 113, 116, 135, 137, 253 n., 255, 256, 257, 258, 259, 263; ships headquartered at, 134
Canada, 4, 74, 79, 139, 142, 309; impending British attack from, rumored (*1796*), 136–37; Spanish spies sent to, 139; fears Spanish attack (*1800*), 141
Canadian Islands, 175, 176, 185, 283, 284, 324
Candel, Francisco, 241
Cantrer (Cantrelle), Mr., 257
Cape Girardeau, 34, 35 n., 71, 127, 297, 311, 318 n., 320; trading post, history of, 297–98 n.; Gayoso describes, 332
Cape La Cruz (Cabo de la Cruche), 297
Carondelet (town), 333
Carondelet, Baron de. *See* Hector, François Luis, Baron de Carondelet
Carondelet River, 107

INDEX

Cartabona, Francisco de, 223 n.
Casa Calvo, Marquis de, 71 n., 142 n.
Castilla, La (galley), 69, 72, 76 n., 83, 84, 89, 95, 100, 104 n., 108, 126, 128, 129, 130, 231 n.
Cat Island, 210
Catholics. *See* Roman Catholics
Cayenne Island, 209
Céréz, La (lanchón), 50 n., 94, 98, 115, 116, 248 n., 264; ill-fated Indian-gift voyage, 264–65, 267; sought by Lisa and *La Flecha*, 268; found by Langlois, 269; arrives at Barrancas, 270
Cerré, Jean Gabriel, 155, 309; biographical note, 155 n.; Gayoso reports on, 334
Cerré Island, 230, 247
Chalanes. *See* Flatboats
Channel of the Devil, 280
Chafale (Choctaw chief), 199
Charpentier, Louise, 60–62 n.
Chatahoochee River, 6
Chatogé, 294
Chausson, Pierre, 167
Chávez, Joseph, 211, 212, 213, 214
Cherokees (Indians), 181, 244, 313; alliance with Spanish, 11, 12; rumored threat to Cumberland, 60, 161; vs. Creeks, 102
Chicacha. *See* Bayou of Chicacha; Island of Chicacha
Chickasaw Bluffs, 35, 36, 112, 125, 225 n.; First, 281 n. (*see also* Barrancas de Harina); Second, 280 (*see also* Barrancas de Prud'homme); Third, 280 (*see also* Barrancas de en Medio); American settlement threats to, 24–25 n.; Spanish plan for trading post, fort on, 66; Spanish establish fort at, 105–18 (*see also* Barrancas de Margó; Fort San Fernando de las Barrancas); described, 106–07
Chickasaws (Indians), 65, 68, 70, 90, 95, 101, 105 n., 112, 133, 160, 167, 276, 292; alliance with Spanish 10, 11, 12; gifts to, 55, 272 n., 273, their preference in, 276 n.; wheat for, 65; Spanish plan for trading post and fort among, 66; divided allegiance, 67; in league with British, 106; warned of U.S. plans, 107–08; vs. Creeks, 108, 115, 264 n.;

Chickasaws (*cont.*)
drunk, 110, 272; yield Nogales lands, 158 n.; speech by tribesman, 167–70; hostile, 205 n.; Spanish negotiate with, for fort site, 253–55; and Barrancas fort-building, 263; occasional visitors to Barrancas, 272 n.; and Barrancas trading posts, 274 n.; visit Gayoso, 275
Chicago, Spanish spies sent to, 139
Chicó Island (Gran Isla Chicó), 203, 216
Choctaws (Indians), 105 n., 160, 199, 200, 254 n.; alliance with Spanish, 10, 11, 12; yield Nogales lands, 158 n.
Chodillon (pirogue passenger), 296, 320, 321
Chouteau, Auguste, 127 n., 133 n., 168, 252 n., 270, 272, 306, 308, 331 n., 334
Chouteau, Pierre, 252 n.
Clark, George Rogers, 17 n., 20, 24, 25, 27, 71 n., 155 n., 252 n., 312 n.; role in Clark-Genêt expedition, 78
Clark, William, 124; flatboat expedition, 69–70
Clark Fort, 304
Clark Island, 319
Clark-Genêt expedition, 32 n., 73, 107, 119, 143–44, 298 n., 302 n., 311 n.; Genêt's role, 74; reported planning attack on New Orleans, 74–76, 80; and upriver defenses, 76–77, 81–83; Clark's role, 78; Mitchell reports on, 78; problem of multiple defenses against, 78–80; reported boat-building for, 80; reported failure of, 90–91; threatens Natchez, 153 n.
Coal Mine (Mina de Carbon), 337
Cold Water Creek, 308 n.
Coles Creek, 27, 195, 243, 244; location, 195 n.
Collot, Victor, 134, 136, 139, 303, 308 n.; opinion on Ohio fort site, 294 n.; impression of St. Louis, 307 n.
Company of Discoverers of the Upper Missouri (Missouri Company), 331 n., 334, 334–35 n.
Concorn Island, 209
Confederación, Spanish fort at, 125 n.
Congress, U.S., 19; refuses statehood for Kentucky, 16; and Clark-Genêt expedition, 78
Connolly, John, 28 n.

Cotelo, Antonio, 218
Council Island, 171
Council Shoals (Bature du Conseil), 186, 213
Cove of the Small Meadow (Ansa de la Pequeña Pradería), 324
Coy (McCoy?), Mr., 268
Creeks (Indians), 68, 111, 229–30, 254; alliance with Spanish, 10, 11, 12; reported attack on Cumberland, 161; vs. Cherokees, 102; vs. Chickasaws, 108, 115, 264 n.
Creoles, 199, 304 n.
Crevecoeur, Mr., 40
Crow's Head (Loup chief), 296
Cruzat, Antonio, 40 n., 237, 291; biographical note, 279 n.; fort-building duties, 261; among land-treaty signers, 266; on upper-river cruise with Gayoso, 297, 301, 308, 317, 318, 319, 320; improves St. Louis defenses, 306 n.
Cuatro Islotes, 246
Cumberland, 76, 102, 111, 173, 224 n., 225, 320; feared U.S. attack on, 59–60; reported Indian attack on, 161
Cup, La (island), 246
Cypress Grove (*Cipriera*), 269

D'Argès, Pierre Wouves, 17, 40 n.
De Leyba, Fernando, 305 n., 306 n., 312 n.
De Pauw, Charles: biographical note, 75 n.; sought for arrest, 77, 191
Death's Head Point (Cabeza del Muerto; Isle à la Tête de Mort), 159, 187, 201, 247, 325
Degoutin, José Deville, 117 n.; given San Fernando command, 134
Delassise, Eulalie, 59 n.
Delassus de Luzières, Carlos Dehault, 56 n., 59 n., 71 n., 88 n., 135, 141 n., 142 n., 177 n., 179 n., 224 n., 335; biographical note, 135 n.; makes retreat plans, 140–41
Delassus de Luzières, Pierre Charles Dehault. *See* Luizières, Pierre Charles Dehault Delassus de
Delaware Indians, 71 n.
Delaware River, 30 n.
Delinó, Ignacio, 28, 67, 81, 83 n., 90, 96, 161, 250, 262; commands Nogales,

Delinó, Ignacio (*cont.*)
157 n., and Arkansas Post, 161–62 n.; develops Arkansas Post 164–65 n.
DePauw University, 75 n.
Derbigny, Pedro, 227 n., 335; Gayoso describes, 340
Des Moines River, 141 n.
Détour des Anglais, 69
Devil's Island, 173, 216; described, 174 n.
Diamond Island (Isla del Diamante), 252, 267, 269, 325
Diaz, Manuel, 246
Didlier, Father, 336
Doge (Dodge?), Mr., 340
Drolet, Felipe, 249
Du Bardó (Hubardeau?), Mr., 332
Du Brean, Mr., 283
Du Paw, Mr. (Charles De Pauw?), 175
Dubois, Toussaint, 156 n.
Dunegant, François, 308
Duparc, Guillermo, 34 n., 93 n.
Duverge, Mr. 218
Dwet, Ezekiel, reports French boat-building, blockading, 80–81

East Florida, 1, 2, 6, 10
Ecores. . . . *See* Barrancas . . .
Edgar, John, 311
El Campechano, Perico, 230
England, English, 16, 22, 33 n., 106, 180, 272, 305; and borderlands conflicts, 1; fights for Northwest and Upper Mississippi Valley, 2; encroaches into Spanish Louisiana, 3; traders, 3, 10, 11, 142, 337; as threat to Louisiana, 3–4, 7, 8; grants navigation rights to U.S., 6; at war with Spain, 131; and U.S., rumored to declare war on Spain (*1796*), 134; suspected designs on Upper Louisiana, 136; impending attack from Canada rumored, 136–37; fur trappers in Spanish territory, 137; reported inciting Indians, 140, 141; policy of maintaining pressure, 141; on Missouri, 331
English Island (Ysla del Yngles), 296
Esperanza, La (ship), 135 n.

Fauchet, Jean Antoine Joseph, 5, 91
Fauré, Dr. Luis, 42, 237, 253, 265, 279;

INDEX

Fauré, Dr. Luis (*cont.*)
 biographical notes, 42–43 n., 253 n.;
 among land-treaty signers, 266
Favorita (goleta), 104 n.
Felip Island, 210, 246
Felipa, La (galley), 72, 76 n., 84, 89, 93 n., 95, 108, 118, 128, 130 n., 137, 193 n., 257, 262, 264, 271 n.; sent to New Orleans for repairs, 134; with Howard expedition to St. Louis, 138
Feluccas, described, 50 n.
Ferguson, David, 246
Ferrer, Joseph, 198
Ferreyra (Terreyna), Manuel, 195
Ferrúsola. *See* Barnó y Ferrúsola, Juan Francisco José
Fina, La (galiot), 38 n., 44, 99, 104 n.
Flatboats (chalanes): maneuverability, 36–37; described, 49; types, 51–52. See also *Amistad, La*
Flecha, La (galiot), 30 n., 40, 45, 72, 84, 89, 90, 92, 93 n., 98, 99, 102, 103, 111, 115, 118, 123, 128, 129, 130, 133, 135, 138, 141, 142 n., 143, 145, 256 n., 257 n., 262, 263, 265 n., 271 n., 277, 278, 279, 280, 282, 283, 287; carries reinforcements to New Madrid, 63–64; cruise to defend upper province, 76–77, 81–83, 191–92, diary account, 193–231; repaired, renovated, 134; account of New Madrid trip (*1793*), 151–88; description, uses of, 154 n.; in search for *La Céréz*, 268, 269; races *La Vigilante*, 279
Flechar (Mr.), 261
Fleet, Spanish fresh-water (His Catholic Majesty's Light Squadron of Galleys): Carondelet requests, 22; Miró first to suggest, 24–25; vessels on guard at Arkansas Post and Natchez, 25–27; Gayoso's plan for, 30–31; Carondelet forms squadron of galleys, 31–32; and special problems of the Mississippi River, 33–36 (*see also* Mississippi River); military purposes, 36–37; domestic uses, 37–38; types of vessels, 38–42, galleys, 38–39, galiots, 39–40, 41, *lancha cañonera*, 41; means of propulsion, 41–42; surgeon, 42; close supervision of Carondelet, 42, 43; *contador*, 43; number of men in, 43–

Fleet, Spanish (*cont.*)
 44; sailors' pay, rations, 44; discipline, 44–45; first ascends Mississippi, 45–46; struggles with Mississippi current, 46–47; and obtacles in river, 47–48; daily schedule, 48; policing duty on river, 48–55; treatment of Americans, 55–56; formalities, searching procedures, 56–57; and friendly Indians, 57–58; dispatched downriver to counter French, 68–69; plans to remobilize for Ecores expedition, 70–73; hurricane damages, 72; squadron ordered to New Madrid, 84, 85–86; urgency of need for squadron, 87–89; arrival in New Madrid, 91–92; squadron remarkable for speed, distance covered, 91–92; squadron descends to Nogales, 92–94, to Natchez, 95–96; squadron reordered to New Madrid (*August 1794*), 96–97; Rousseau ordered to wait in Nogales, 100–01; role in establishing Fort San Fernando, 105–18; squadron begins reascent to New Madrid (*February 1795*), 108; rerouted to Barrancas by Gayoso, 108–09; Rousseau stresses need for repairs to, 125–27; prepared for battle at the bluffs, 128–29; ships descend for repairs, 129–30; based at San Fernando (*1796–97*), 132, 133–34; to St. Louis, 137–38; activities, *1797–1802*, 141–42 n.; history of, summarized, 143–55; success in fulfilling purpose, 143
Flemish, as settlers, 15
Floridas, the, 4, 6. See also East Florida; West Florida
Flour Island, 282
Floch y Juan, Vincente, 83 n., 271 n., 274 n., 324, 325; biographical note, 116–17 n.; replaces Beauregard, 116, 117 n.; deals with U.S. ultimatum, 129; replaced at San Fernando, 134
Fooy (island). *See* Island of Fooy
Fooy, Benjamin, 104 n., 117 n., 135, 253 n., 266, 273; biographical note, 254 n.; quarrel with García, 126 n., 254 n.; role in Chickasaw fort negotiation, 253–54
Forman, Ezekiel, 241
Fort Arkansas, 249

Fort Carondelet, 331; historical note, 331 n.
Fort Céleste, 80, 123, 177–78 n., 257 n.; Rousseau describes, 183–84
Fort Charles III of the Arkansas, 164 n.
Fort Massac, 94, 111, 116, 277 n., 311, 319; seen as looming threat, 98
Fort Nogales (Walnut Hills), 22, 23, 28, 35, 52, 56, 57, 62, 63, 66, 72, 83, 85, 87, 105, 125 n., 156, 157, 158, 188, 191, 192, 197, 198, 228 n., 245, 246, 325; location, history, 157–58 n.; American settlement threats to, 24–25 n.; established, 29 n.; commander warned of French invasion, 77; relinquished to U.S., 139–40
Fort Pitt, 59, 63, 101, 158, 262; boat-building at, 80, 111; vessels from, 246, 248, 249, 251, 258
Fort Placaminas (Plaquemine), 22, 23, 32, 37, 69, 75, 139, 143; location, 69 n.; hurricane strikes, 98 n.
Fort San Estevan of the Arkansas, 164 n.;
Fort San Fernando de las Barrancas, 11 n., 32 n., 33 n., 65, 76 n., 83 n., 93, 126, 144, 152 n., 222, 279, 292, 300, 324, 325; first rumors of its planning, 102–03; established, 105–18; strategic location, 105–06, 118, 267 n. (*see also* Barrancas de Margó); site described, 106–07; Spanish acquire site, 109–13; formal possession ceremonies, 113–14; named, 114, 260; treaty signed for site, 114, 266–67, limits of cession in, 267 n.; Carondelet's plans for, 116–17; U.S. acquires, 118; U.S. formal inquiry on, 124–25; rumored impending U.S. attack on, 128–29; river squadron based at (*1796–97*), 132; men, munitions to be transferred to St. Louis, 136; demolition, evacuation, 137; sources of supplies for, 271–72 n.; garrisoning of, 277 n.; trade with Ste Geneviève, 301 n.
"Fort Santa Margarita" (nonexistent), reported French designs on, 74, 75
Fort of the Tower, 304
Fort Washington, 161, 278 n.
Foucher, Pedro, 56 n., 177 n.
France, French, 16, 24, 94, 124 n., 179,

France, French (*cont.*) 180; holdings in North America, 1, 2–3; retrocession of Louisiana, 2, 5; traders, 3; Revolution, 3, 4; National Assembly, 4; Louisiana inhabitants petition for reannexation, 4; as threat to Spanish Louisiana, 4–5, 7, 8; treatment by Spanish naval officers, 57; threat of war with, 67–68; war breaks out with, 68; invasion of Louisiana feared (with U.S.), 74–75 (*see also* Clark-Genêt expedition); settlers, 92; victories in Spain, 101; influence in illinois, 291; armistice with Spain, 318 n.
Frazer (Mr.), 273, 275, 276
French Canadians, 304 n.
Fulton, Alexandro, 262

Gabury River, 127 n., 303, 309
Galiots, in Mississippi fleet, 38, 39–40. See also *Activa, La; Fina, La; Flecha, La; Vigilante, La*
Galleys: suitability for Mississippi, 30 n.; military maneuverability, 36–37; domestic uses, 37–38; in Mississippi fleet, 38–39; means of propulsion, 41–42. See also *Castilla, La; Felipa, La; Leal, La; Luisiana, La; Venganza, La; Victoria, La*
Gallipolis, 175, 310 n.
Gálvez, Bernardo de, 4, 7, 9 n., 32 n., 106
Gálveztown, 22
Galveztown (brigantine), 32 n.
Gannón (sailor), 195, 211
García, Felipe, 212 n., 216, 218
García y Muniz, Manuel, 135, 237, 253, 256, 279; biographical note, 103–04 n.; quoted, 38 n.; commands *La Luisiana*, 103–04; quarrel with Fooy, 126 n., 254 n.; given river-fleet command, 133; headquarters at Island of Fooy, 133–34; instructs Collot in navigation, 134; to New Orleans with Howard, 138; arrested, 254 n.; engaged in fort-building, 258, 259, 260, 261, 265; signs treaty for Barrancas land, 266
Gardoqui, Diego de, 28 n., 224 n.; role in Kentucky intrigue, 17
Garno (Mr.), 293, 294

INDEX

Gayoso Creek, 324
Gayoso de Lemos, Manuel, 12, 29 n., 40, 45, 54, 64, 76 n., 82, 88 n., 93 n., 96, 97, 99, 100, 137, 144, 151, 152, 168 n., 178 n., 193, 271 n.; biographical note, 11–12 n.; signs Nogales treaty, 11; naval flotilla plans, 26 n.; presents plan for defense of Natchez, 30–31; naval and post commander, 48; on mail service, 58 n.; sends galley to New Madrid, 63; warns forts of French invasion, 77; concurs on holding Nogales, 80; disagreements with Carondelet, 86, 95; with Rousseau on upriver trip, 89, 90; opinion of García, 104 n.; orders occupation of Barrancas, 108; instructions for occupying Barrancas, 108–10; orders squadron to Barrancas, 108–09; appointed commander of Barrancas occupation, 112; arrives at Barrancas, 112–13; negotiates for fort site, 112–13; diary account 253–55; role in formal possession of fort, 113–14; anguished by delay of Indian-gift boat, 115–16, 264, 264–65 n. (see also *Céréz, La*); assigns vessels to Barrancas defense, 118; reply to Innes on secession-support offer, 121; *Report* to Cardonelet on Illinois visit (*1795*), 127–28 n., 128, 313 n., Introduction, 330, text, 331–41; health, 133; orders Rousseau on New Madrid trip, 153; effectiveness as governor, 153 n., 154 n.; takes Rousseau's command, 154–55; role in establishing Fort Nogales, 157–58 n.; evidence of his authorship of diary, 235–37; opinion of Bontoux, 248 n.; supervises fort-building, 256–78; report on Bouligny, 257 n.; describes ceremony for formal possession of fort, 266–67; view on trading post for Barrancas, 274 n.; entertains Chickasaw "king" and party, 276; role in Kentucky intrigue, 278 n.; regard for Cruzat, 279 n.; three objectives of his Illinois tour, 291 n.; visit to Illinois (*Diary*, parts II, III), 291–314; dines with Loups, 296–97; visits Ste. Geneviève, 301–03; visits St. Louis, 304–09; meets with Micheaux, 318 n., 320; meets with

Gayoso de Lemos, Manuel (*cont.*)
Power, 321–23, 326 n.; expense of his trip to upper river, 323 n.; rumored "taking a wife" in New Madrid, 338–39 n.; differences with Perchet, 341 n.

DOCUMENTS

Diary: Introduction, 235–37; Part I, *Apr. 16–Sept. 7, 1795* (departure from Natchez), 241–87; Parts II and III, *Oct. 6–Dec. 8, 1765* (New Madrid to Illinois), 291–314; Part IV, *Dec. 9–29, 1795* (on board *La Vigilante*), 317–26

Report (*Nov. 24, 1795*) on tour of Illinois posts: Introduction, 330; text, 331–41

Genêt, Edmond Charles, 5, 88 n., 91; role in Clark-Genêt expedition, 74
Georgia, 107
German Coast, 105
Germans, 180; as settlers, 15
Gingenbre (Genjambre), Mr., 197
Girault, Juan, 241
Girondin government, 5
Glas (Mr.), 251
Glover, Guillermo (Chickasaw chief), 263, 265; at formal land-granting ceremony, 266; leaves Barrancas, 268–69; son of, 274
Godoy, Manuel de, 7; urged to promote Kentucky secession, 121; authorizes Kentucky negotiations, 122
González, Luís, 213
Gouble Island, 202
Grand Gulf, 156, 188, 197, 244; location, 156 n., 197 n.
Grand Prairie, 180
Grand Pré, Carlos de, 255 n., 277 n.
Grand Pré, Luis Boucher, 241; biographical note, 241 n.
Grapen (island). *See* Island of Grapen
Gras, Antonio, 241
Gratiot, Charles (Carlos Craciot), 252; biographical note, 252–53 n.
Great Bluffs Island (Isla aux Ecors), 216
Greenville, 101
Gregg, Commander, 312, 313 n.
Guiana, 2 n.

Guijon, Amalt (Amable Guion), 212
Gunboats. See *Lanchas cañoneras*

Harbey, Mr. 215
Harrison, William Henry, 156 n.
Harter, Alexander, 219
Havana, Cuba, 25, 38
Hector, François Luis, Baron de Carondelet, 5, 8, 20, 27, 93 n., 134, 151, 177 n., 180, 261, 273 n., 286 n., 336 n.; policy with Indian nations, 9–12; quoted, 13, 67, 98 n.; opposes counter-colonization, 15; free-trade views, 15–16; 4-battalion defense plan, 22; pleads for more troops, 22–23, 24; rule described, 29; succeeds Miró, 29; forms river squadron, 31–32, 36; understanding of the Mississippi, 33–34, 35; close naval command of, 43, 44; orders gentle behavior toward Americans, 55–56; hears reports of American threats (*1792*), 59–60, 65, 67–68, 69–70; dispatches reinforcements to New Madrid, 62–65; actions to secure Ecores, 65–67; postpones Ecores expedition, 67, 74; pleads for fair play from U.S., 68; shifts forces downriver to counter French, 68–69; remobilizes to establish Ecores position, 70–73; secret orders for Ecores expedition, 72–73; prepares for Clark-Genêt attack on New Orleans, 74–76, 80; dispatches *La Flecha* upriver to patrol, 76–77, 81–83; fears Clark-Genêt attacks at multiple points, 78–79; and problem of defending Nogales, 80; hears report of French boat-building, blockading, 80–81; orders squadron to New Madrid (*January 1794*), 84, 85–86; strategy favored by circumstances, 86–87; ordered to seek Chickasaw aid, 95; approves Rousseau's descent to Nogales, 94; reorders squadron to Madrid (*August 1794*), 96–97; alarmed by U.S. threat on Ohio, 98–99; orders squadron holdover in Nogales, 100–01; orders reascent to New Madrid (*February 1795*), 108; appoints Beauregard for Barrancas post, 113; strategic plans for Fort San Fernando, 116–17; sends Gayoso to further

Hector, François Luis (*cont.*)
Kentucky intrigue, 119, 123; corresponds with Godoy on secession prospects, 120–21, 122; belief in an independent West, 121; shrugs off U.S. San Fernando inquiry, 125; Gayoso's *Report* to, on Illinois visit (*1795*), 127–28 n., 128, 313 n., Introduction, 330, text, 331–41; implored to authorize fleet repairs, 128; approves downriver fleet return, 129; rebuffed by Wilkinson on intrigue (*1797*), 131; exempts Rousseau from duty, 133; plans San Fernando evacuation, 136; appoints Howard for anti-British mission, 137; recommendations for Natchez, 153–54 n.; view of Nogales, 158; opinion of Delinó, 161 n.; opinion of Peyroux, 224 n., 333 n.; commissions Perchet, 245 n.; orders to Bontoux, 247 n., 248 n.; sends Vilemont to Arkansas Post, 250; decisions on San Fernando traders, 274–75 n.; strong garrisoning of Fort San Fernando, 277 n.; involves Gayoso in Kentucky intrigue, 278 n.; military interest in mouth of Ohio, 293, 293–94 n.; plan for Ste. Geneviève, 302, and St. Louis defenses, 307 n.; ordered to close Kentucky negotiations, 326 n.; establishes New Bourbon, 310 n.; praises Gayoso for Illinois trip, 331–32 n.; instructions regarding Peyroux, 333 n.; admonishes Gayoso on love-life, 338–39 n.; on wheat-supply problem, 339 n.
Henry, Andrew, 156 n.
Hermitage (island). See Island of the Hermitage
Hero (brigantine), 104 n.
Hollanders, as settlers, 15
Hopewell. See Campo de la Esperanza
Horn Island, 246
Horn Point, 246
Howard, Carlos, 88 n., 144, 224 n.; given Upper Louisiana command, 136; to lead expedition to the Illinois, 137; evacuates San Fernando, 137–38; fortifies St. Louis, 138, 139; returns to New Orleans, 138, 140; other assignments against British, 139–40; instructed in regard to Peyroux, 333 n.

INDEX

Hubardeau, Mr., 332
Hunau (militia sergeant), 230
Hunts, John (Creek chief), 229–30

Ile aux Chicots. *See* Stump Island
Illinois, Spanish, 71 n., 119, 144, 168, 169; Gayoso's visit to, 291–314; crops, natural resources, 337; wheat-supply problem, 339–40
Illinois Indians, 108
Illinois River, 127 n., 128, 139, 144, 291–92, 307 n., 308, 331
Ilvain, Hugh, quoted, 54
Indians, 3, 45, 244, 283, 284, 291 n., 332, 337; encouraged against U.S., 9–12; alliance with Spanish, effect of, 12; and Treaty of San Lorenzo el Real, 13; treatment by Spanish navy, 57–59; Spanish fear U.S. trade with, 65; Carondelet's military plans for, 79–80; Spanish seek aid from, in upper-river defense, 85, 95; gifts to, 90, 103–04, 108, 109, 127, 133, 270, 272 n., 275, 297–98; English reported inciting, 140, 141; in Illinois, Spanish overtures to, 291 n. *See also* Abenaquis; Araonanes Indians; Arkansas Indians; Atakapas; Cherokees; Chickasaws; Choctaws; Creeks; Delaware Indians; Illinois Indians; Kickapoos; Loups; Mascoutins; Natchitoches; Opelousas; Osage Indians; Ottawas; Peorias; Puans; Sacs; Shawnees; Sioux Indians; Talapuche Indians; Texas Indians
Innes, Harry, offers Kentucky-secession support, 120–21
Iowa, 141
Irish, 137, 180
Iron Mine (Mina de Fierro) (cliff), 35, 293, 319
Isla... *See also* Ysla...
Isla au Bled. *See* Wheat Island
Isla del Buey, 295
Isla á Dará, 291, 292, 313
Isla de Diamante. *See* Diamond Island
Isla Esquermento, 244, 298
Isla á Favot, 292, 317
Isla del Feo. *See* Villein Island
Isla del Trigo. *See* Wheat Island
Isla de Vilain. *See* Villein Island
Island of Cedars (Ysla del Cotoñe de Cedro), 304
Island of Cedars (*cont.*)
Island of Chicacha, 318
Island of Fooy, 104 n., 266, 267, 273; becomes fleet headquarters, 133–34
Island of Grapen, 201, 247
Island of the Hermitage, 170, 186, 251
Isle of La Coupée, 160, 202
Isle of Misfortune (Islas Desgraciadas), 279, 324
Isle à la Tête de Mort. *See* Death's Head Point

Jacobins, 4, 86, 101, 108, 137
Jamaica, 2 n.
Janin, Father, 337
Jaudenes y Nebot, José, 64 n., 74, 208 n.; reports Clark-Genêt plans, 74; works as informant, 77–78
Jay, 17 n.
Jay-Gardoqui treaty, proposed, 16
Jefferson, Thomas: quoted, 13; reassures Spanish agents on U.S. aims, 73
Jones, John Rice, 300, 311; biographical note, 300 n.
Josepha, Don, Marquis de Maison Rouge, 15
Junta de Estado, 19

Kaskaskia, 55, 127 n., 178, 291 n., 300, 302, 305 n., 311; on Clark-Genêt route, 78; as wheat source, 340
Keelboats, described, 49–50
Kentucky, 76, 90, 96, 171, 173, 278 n.; tobacco from, 9 n., 54; Spanish scheme for, 16–20 (*see also* Kentucky intrigue); population, 27; and Clark-Genêt expedition, 76, 78; Mississippi navigation conceded to, 326 n.
Kentucky intrigue (Spanish support of secession), 16–20, 27, 28, 30, 54, 64 n., 105 n., *119–31*, 278 n., 279 n., 313 n.; Gayoso sent to further, 119, 122–24, 126 n., 127–28; to capitalize on Westerners' dissatisfaction, 119–20; and offers for support from secession-minded, 120–21; Spanish Council of State position on, 121–22, 131; and U.S. ultimata on San Fernando, 124–25, 129, 130; Madrid orders close of, 326 n.

Kickapoos (Indians), 87
King, Spanish, 323 n., 336
Kinnaird, L., "Spain in the Mississippi Valley," 152

La Coupée (island). *See* Isle of La Coupée
La Chaise, Auguste de, 226 n.; biographical note, 74–75 n.; sought for arrest, 77, 135, 191; rumored return of, 136
La Chappelle, Antonio, 214
La Rosa, Gregorio, 241
Labady, M., 168
Labery, Tomás, 292
Lacassagne, Michel, 121
Lachanse (Mr.), 320
Laclède, Pierre, 305
Lacroix, Mr., 309
Lafayette, 75 n.
Lake Pontchartrain, 32 n.
Lake Ste. Marie, 181
Lanchas, described, 50
Lanchas cañoneras, described, 31 n. See also *Rayo, El*
Lanchones. *See* Barges
Langlois, Francisco, 76 n., 92, 94, 102, 103, 111, 115, 118, 236, 237, 262, 263, 278; biographical note, 92–93 n.; to defend Ecores, 101; among land-treaty signers, 266; sent to seek *La Céréz*, 268; finds *La Céréz*, 269; delivers provisions, 271 n.; on upper-river cruise, 279, 281, 282, 324, 325
"Laramie's Station," 71 n.
Large Island of the White Bluffs, 292
Largeau, L., 71 n.
Las Casas, Luis de, Duque de la Alcudia, 29, 68–69, 71 n., 86, 95, 247 n., 260 n., 331 n.; orders seeking Chickasaws' help against U.S., 95
Las Casas River (River of the Two Chickasaws), 107, 110, 113, 253, 258, 259, 267 n., 363
Le Sieur brothers, 177
Leal, La (galley), 33 n., 38, 44 n., 99, 104 n.
Lean Bear (L'Ours Maigre) (Cherokee chief), 181
Lemos. *See* Gayoso de Lemos, Manuel

Lennan, Francisco, 241
Leonard (Gilberto), 341
Limestone, boat-building at, 80
Lisa, Manuel, 115, 124, 264–65 n., 268, 278, 287 n., 311 n., 313, 314, 317; bibliographical note, 268 n.; conveys intrigue letter, 123
Little Isle of the Wolf (Pequena Ysla del Lobo), 322
Little Prairie, 185, 186
Longine, Mr., 324
Lopez, Manuel, 241
López y Angulo, Intendant, 142 n.
Loomis, Noel, 79 n.
Lorimier, Louis, 60, 87, 94, 98, 127, 295, 297, 299, 332; biographical notes, 71–72 n., 297–98 n.; to support Portell, 71
Los Adaes, 3
Los Santos, Josef María, 229
Louisiana: retrocession by France, 2–3, 5; English threat to, 3–4; problem of Spanish rule over French inhabitants, 4; French threat to, 4–5; French petition for reannexation, 4–5; and aggression by Americans of western U.S., 5–8; state of defenses, 8, 20–21, 29–30; Carondelet's defense policy, 9–12, 22; conflicting objectives of Spanish policy, 12–13; and counter-colonization, 13–15, 20; fresh-water fleet, 22–58 (*see also* Fleet, Spanish fresh-water); population, 27; mail service, 58 n.; lull in threat from North (*1794*), 94–95; insurrection fears aroused by French victories in Spain, 101; threatened by reported U.S. troop buildup, 101–02; Montgomery death eases Cumberland threat, 102; San Fernando established, 105–18 (*see also* Fort San Fernando de las Barrancas); and reported U.S. expedition to Barrancas, 111–12; Upper, envisaged as independent state, 136; fur trade imperiled, 136, 137; transfer to U.S., 145; problem of wheat supply, 339–40. *See also* Regiment of Louisiana
Loups (Indians), 71 n., 72 n., 181, 298 n.; called to account for destroying barge, 180; entertain Gayoso party, 296–97
Lucas, Mr., 335 n.

INDEX

Luisiana, La (galley), 38, 39, 69, 87, 94, 95, 97, 98 n., 103, 104, 105, 108, 126, 132, 133, 138, 242, 245 n., 258, 259, 278; sent to be disarmed, 134; with Howard expedition to St. Louis, 138
Luisman (Guisman), Mr., 230
Luison (hunter), 281, 283
Luzières, Carlos Dehault Delassus de. *See* Delassus de Luzières, Carlos Dehault
Luzières, Madame, 341
Luzières, Pierre Charles Dehault Delassus de, 135 n., 179, 227, 310, 317, 320, 340; biographical note, 179 n.; commands New Bourbon, 310 n.; Gayoso describes, 333; and family, Gayoso's opinion of, 340–41

McCabe, Eduardo, 241
Macarty (Macarthy), Agustín: biographical note, 194 n.; eludes boat chase, 194
Macay (McCoy), Roberto, 40, 118, 222, 261, 268, 273, 277; biographical note, 222 n.; delivers provisions, 271 n.
McGillivray, Alexander, 9 n., 10
McKee, John, 129, 130
McKiernnan, Carlos, 241
Mackinack. *See* Michilimackinac
Macocas (or Zasimine) Island, 246
Manchac, 105
Mandans, 137, 139
Marais des Liards, 127 n., 307; Gayoso describes, 336
Margarita (bombadera), 248 n.
Margot River, 59, 274 n.
Marmillion, Antonio, 241
"Marseillaise," the, 4
Marshall, Humphrey, 17 n.
Martin, Mr., 195
Mas, Miguel, 200, 201
Mascoutins (Indians), 87
Mathurin, 75 n.
Memphis, Tenn., 34, 65
Menar (hunter), 210
Menar, Madame, 206
Menard, Pierre, 71 n., 156, 293; biographical note, 156 n.
Meramec River, 302, 307 n.
Metzinger, Juan Baptista, 94, 134; ordered to Natchez, 87; takes *La*

Metzinger, Juan Baptista (*cont.*)
Luisiana upriver, 132; on inspection duty, 135
Mexico, 24, 72 n., 337, 338; Regiment of, 23; Clark-Genêt attack feared on, 79
Miami River, 71 n.
Micheaux, André, 88 n., 130 n., 317–18; ordered aarrested, 124 n.; meets with Gayoso, 318 n., 320
Michilimackinac, 142 n., 331 n.
Minnesota River, 142
Minor, Estevan, 241
Miró, Esteban, 12, 116 n., 157 n., 177 n., 223 n., 224 n.; biographical note, 9 n.; 4-point defense plan, 9–10; and Indian alliances, 10; countercolonization policy, 13–15, 20; and Kentucky secession scheme, 16–20; recommends fresh-water navy, 20–21; first suggests armed vessels, 24–25; instructions to Boulliers, 26–27; cites four military threats, 24–28 n.; Carondelet succeeds, 29
Misfortune (island). *See* Isle of Misfortune
Mississippi River: free navigation of, as political issue, 6, 12, 16, 17, 19; Junta prescribes duty for navigation, 19–20; course of, 34–35; and logistical problems, 35–36; and Ohio, strategic advantages of, 36; types of vessels on, 38–42 (military), 48–52 (nonmilitary); problems of navigating, 46–48; night floating in floods, 52–53; shallow season, 97; maps of, 151–52, 185, 188 n., 339; navigation conceded to Kentuckians, 326 n.; width at confluence of Ohio, 339
Mississippi Valley, 5, 6; colonial conflict over, 1–2; Upper, 2, 3, 137; economic, political control negotiated, 7
Missouri Fur Co., 156 n.
Missouri River, 15, 127, 307 n.; 331 n., 336; Upper, 137
Missouri Valley, 140
Mitchell (Michel), Medad (Medard, Thomas), 64, 65, 151, 152, 185, 188 n., 208; biographical note, 64 n.; brings news of Clark-Genêt expedition, 78, 82, 206–07, 209

Mobile. *See* Movila
Molina, Antonio, 193
Molina, Bernardo, 135; takes *La Victoria* upriver, 132; patrols Iowa country, 141
Monongahela, 339
Monte de Vigia, 157 n.
Montegut (Mr.), 336
Montgomery, John, 71 n., 99; role in Clark-Genêt expedition, 81; assassinated, 102
Montimore (Mr.), 244
Moore, Guillaume, 158
Morgan, George, 177 n.
Morrison, Mr., 300, 311
Morrison, Robert, 300 n.
Morrison, William, 179 n., 300 n.
Mosquito (bercha), 113, 245, 252, 257
Moustier, Eléonore François-Elie, 2 n.
Movila (Mobile), 22, 32 n.
Movila River, 274
Muhlberger, Capt., 5
Murray, William, 121
Muscle Shoals, 59, 116, 277 n.

Napoleon, 2
Natchez, 6, 7, 11 n., 21, 22, 34, 35 n., 36, 52, 62, 64, 105, 137, 143, 144, 153, 326 n., 339 n.; district, 14; defenses, 24, 25, 26, 27; naval facilities, 48; prepared for Clark-Genêt attack, 80; relinquished to U.S., 139; history, description, 153–54 n.
Natchitoches (Indians), 65
Natchitoches, military post at, 22, 32 n.
Nava, Victorio de, 116 n.
Navarro, Martín, 13; biographical note, 9–10 n.; free-trade recommendations, 14, 15; and Kentucky intrigue, 18, 19
Negroes, 292, 304, 305 n., 325; danger of revolt among, 79; suggested as oarsmen, 99; uprising in Louisiana, 135. *See also* Slaves
Neri, Felipe Enrique, Baron de Bastrop, 15, 283
New Bourbon, 127 n., 179 n., 310, 318; historical note, 310 n.; Gayoso describes, 333; wheat mill in, 340
New Madrid, 14, 22, 23, 32 n., 33 n., 56, 85, 96, 97, 98, 108, 134, 285, 286, 293,

New Madrid (*cont.*)
298, 300, 303, 312, 313, 322, 323 n., 338; description, history, 177–78 n.; distance from New Orleans, 35–36; American threat seen to, 59, 60; reinforced against Americans, 62–65; to supply Ecores fort, 68; commander warned of French invasion, 77; Clark-Genêt attack feared, 78, 80; steeled for Clark-Genêt forces, 80; Ferrusola's role in fortifying, 82–83, 101, 102, 192; squadron ordered to (*January 1794*), 85–86; urgency of need for reinforcement, 87–89; greets squadron, 91–92; fleet departs from, 92; squadron again ordered to (*August 1794*), 96–97; Rousseau describes stay at, 177–85; distance from Natchez, 220–21; supplies Fort San Fernando, 271 n.; trade with Ste. Geneviève, 301 n., 302 n.; wheat-supply problem, 340. *See also* Fort Céleste
New Mexico, 16
New Orleans, 7, 13, 15, 17, 65, 72, 83, 88 n., 139; revolutionary demonstrations in, 4; fire (*1788*), 9 n.; defense of, 23; Clark-Genêt attack feared on, 74–76, 80; hurricane strikes, 98 n.; Republican revolt feared, 104; envisioned as free port, 121
New Spain, 1, 4. *See also* Floridas; Illinois, Spanish; Louisiana
Nicholas, George, 121
Nogales (fort). *See* Fort Nogales
Nogales, Treaty of, 11–12
Nootka Sound, 7
Northwest, the, 2

O'Fallon, Dr. James, 28, 157 n.; quarrel with Clark, 78
Ohio, 251
Ohio River (Belle Rivière), 3, 20, 22, 27, 36, 37, 64, 85, 86, 93 n., 96, 99, 103, 134, 135, 160, 171, 178, 223, 293, 319, 320; Falls, 36, 37, 80, 311 n.; —Mississippi, strategic advantages, 36; U.S. fort established near mouth, 94–95 (*see also* Fort Massac); Spanish cruising station at mouth, 293, 293–94 n.; width at confluence of Mississippi, 339

INDEX

Ohio Valley, 5, 6
Old Northwest, 7
Old Southwest, 5
Opelousas (Indians), 65
O'Reilly, 241 n.
Oro, Antonio de, 88 n.
Osage Indians, 87, 168, 169, 331 n.; Spanish troubles with, 170 n.
O'Sullivan, John, 28 n.
Ottawa Indians, 181
Otawa Island (Isla Otawas), 282
Ouachita, 22, 284
Owert (Owens?) (Mr.), 320

Pacific Coast, English power on, 140
Palao, Martin, 270, 277 n., 278
Panton, Leslie and Co., 9 n., 13, 117; establish trading post at Barrancas, 274
Panton, William, 10, 13
Papin, Joseph Marie, 300, 334; biographical note, 300 n.
Paris, Treaty of (1763), 1, 2; effect on France, 3
Payehuma (Chickasaw chief), 263, 264 n., 265, 269; at formal land-granting ceremony, 266; dines witht Gayoso, 273
Payemingo (Chickasaw chief), 69, 70, 109, 113, 255, 264, n., 275
Paysa, 308
Pensacola, 22; troop strength, 23
Pentreaux, 335; ordered arrested, 124 n.
Peorias (Indians), 304
Perchet, Juan María, 113, 116, 237, 245, 341; biographical note, 245 n.; fort-building duties, 261; among land-treaty signers, 266; on upper-river cruise, 279, 281, 282, 309; differences with Gayoso, 341 n.
Perez, Manuel, 223 n.; improves St. Louis defenses, 306 n.
Perrin du Lac, 164 n., 304 n.
Pertuy, Manuel, 250
Pertuy, Pedro, 250
Peyroux de la Coudrenière, Henri, 40 n., 62 n., 71 n., 222 n., 223, 310 n.; biographical notes, 88 n., 223–24 n.; resigned to defeat, 87; commands Ste. Geneviève, 301 n.; house of, 332, 333 n.; trouble with Vallé, 333 n.; loyalty upheld, 338

Peyroux de la Coudrenière, Madame, 203
Philadelphia, Pa., 120, 125, 338; Spanish *chargés* in, 68, 74, 77–78, 208 n.; Spanish spies sent to, 139
Pike, Zebulon Montgomery, 142–43
Pinckney's Treaty, 137 n.
Pirogues, described, 49
Pisgignoux, Jean Pierre: biographical notes, 226 n., 227–28 n.; reports impending French attacks, 74–75; believed to be French agent, 75; sought for arrest, 77, 191; capture of, 82–83, 192, dairy account, 226–27, 229, 231
Placaminas (fort). See Fort Placaminas
Placaminas Turn, 69
Podras, Mr. 321, 322
Point of Plums (Punta de Ciruelas), 123, 282, 283
Point of Spain, 319, 321
Pontenson, Juan, 205
Pope, John, 54
Portell, Madame, 216
Portell, Thomas, 33 n., 56, 82, 83, 88, 90, 93 n., 98, 102, 116, 123, 125, 151, 177 n., 178, 181, 184, 187, 188, 225, 227, 228 n., 257, 271, 277 n., 285, 286 n., 292; biographical note, 56 n.; fears American attack, 59; Ecores rations order to, 67; reports U.S. flatboat expedition, 69–70; to inspect U.S. boats, 70, 72; pessimistic on New Madrid defenses, 87; checks out war rumors, 102; issues war warnings, 111–12; effectiveness as New Madrid commander, 178 n.; report on Bontoux, 248
Potosi, 300 n.
Power, Thomas, 102, 123 n., 124, 127 n., 130, 286, 291 n., 295, 314, 317 n., 319 n., 341; biographical note, 286–87 n.; meets with Gayoso, 321–23, 326 n.
Prairie du Chien, 37, 40; Spanish spies sent to, 139
Price, Arce, 205
Prince (Prins) (hunter), 223
Príncipe de Asturias, El (lanchón), 50 n., 118, 222 n., 271 n., 273, 277, 286, 322; at Barrancas, 261, 262
Protestants, encouraged as settlers, 14
Providence, R.I., 74

Prud'homme Bluffs. *See* Barrancas de Prud'homme
Prud'homme Isle (Isla á Prudon), 281
Pruna Point, 217
Puans (Indians), 304
Puglio, James, *El Desengaño del hombre,* 57 n.
Punta Cortada (Pointe Coupée), 105, 212; insurrection feared at, 104

Rascins (Prascins) Island, 202
Rayo, El (lancha cañonera), 41, 45, 72, 76 n., 84, 95, 100, 102, 118, 123, 128, 130 n., 133, 135, 271 n., 285, 291, 312; history, description, 285 n.; with Howard expedition to St. Louis, 138
Red River, 3
Ree, Mr., 246, 247
Regiment of Louisiana, 22–23, 24, 33 n., 38, 83, 114, 154, 245, 250, 259, 278; troop strength in *1790s,* 22–23
Regiment of Mexico, 23
Republican clubs, in Louisiana, 4
Reynal, Dr., 336 n.
Richard, Mr. 320
Richars, Me. (Mme?), 196
River of the Two Chickasaws. *See* Las Casas River
Robertson, James, 68, 69 n., 106, 112, 224; biographical note, 224–25 n.; reported plans for bluffs, 65
Robidou, Mrs., 334
Robison, Mr., 306
Rojas, Cristoval de, 199, 200, 201 n., 205, 229
Roman Catholics, 14, 15, 137, 317 n.
Rousseau, Pedro Andrés, 26 n., 33 n., 38, 116, 129, 227 n., 236, 237, 243, 248 n., 251 n., 252, 253, 271 n., 272, 273, 277 n., 279; biographical note, 32–34 n.; appointed to river-fleet command, 32; under strict command, 42; ordered to Natchez, 45; makes daily squadron account, 48; commands supply trip to New Madrid, 62–65, diary account, 153–88; instructions against Americans, 66; ordered to establish Ecores fort, 67–68; instructed to seize U.S. boats, 70; secret instructions for Ecores expedition, 72–73; ordered to take fleet upriver, 84; given command of

Rousseau, Pedro Andrés (*cont.*) squadron to New Madrid (*January 1794*), 85–86; squadron departs, 89–90; delayed at Barrancas, 90–91; arrives at New Madrid, 91; takes squadron to Nogales, 92–94; opinion of Langlois, 93 n.; takes repaired vessels to Natchez, 95–96; reordered to New Madrid (*August 1794*), 96–97; delayed by illness, 97–98; suggests colored oarsmen, 99; improvises defense with galiots, 99–100; ordered to wait at Nogales, 100, 101; begins reascent to New Madrid (*February 1795*), 108; ordered to Barrancas by Gayoso, 108–09; prepared for fight at Barrancas, 109–10; negotiates with Chickasaws for fort site, 110–11; reports on war vessels, 125–27; seeks authorization for galley repair, 128; prepares squadron for battle, 128–29; on limitations of grandes galeras, 132; ill health forces from duty, 133; writing style, 152; use of patrones, 163 n,; maps by, 188 n.; engaged in fort-building, 255–56, 257, 258, 261, 265; given new name by Indians, 256 n.; opinion of Bouligny, 257; signs treaty for Barrancas land, 266

Sacs (Indians), 87
St. Charles (San Carlos del Misuri), 127, 128, 305, 306 n.; historical note, 307 n.; Gayoso describes, 336–37
St. Charles' Day, 127 n., 336
St. Clair, Arthur, 126 n., 156 n., 291 n., 305 n., 313 n.
St. Francis River, 35, 171, 185, 186, 210, 211, 229, 251
St. Louis, 22, 35, 60, 62, 71, 96, 112, 126, 127, 128; historical note, 304–07 n.; capture feared, 78; mobilized against Clark-Genêt attack, 79–80; militia, 87, 89, dismissed, 94; Trudeau fortifies, 87–88; San Fernando men, munitions transferred to, 136, 137; Howard expedition arrives at, 138; fortified against British threat, 138, 139; limitations on fortifying, 139; planned retreat from, 141; trade with Ste. Geneviève, 301 n., 302 n.; trade with

INDEX

St. Louis (*cont.*)
  Villa de Carondelet, 304 n.; Gayoso visits, 304–09; Gayoso describes 333–36; wheat milling in, 339, 340
St. Martial, Cruzat de, 82, 227, 229
St. Peters (Minnesota) River, 124
St. Pierre, Father, 301, 317, 332; biographical note, 317 n.; Gayoso praises, 332
St. Vrain de Lassus, Santiago, 142 n., 143, 179; n.; patrols Mississippi, 141; Gayoso's suspicions of, 335 n.
Ste. Geneviève, 22, 35 n., 62, 88 n., 102, 112, 127, 134, 223 n., 224 n., 293, 295, 299, 300, 309, 310, 311, 317, 318 n., 320, 332; history, 301–03 n.; defenses built for, 87; Gayoso describes, 332; wheat milling in, 340
Ste. Marie, Sergeant, 295, 300, 321
Salcedo, Governor General, 33 n.
Salina, La, 300, 310, 333
San Carlos del Misuri. *See* St. Charles
San Fernando (fort). *See* Fort San Fernando de las Barrancas
San Fernando de Florissante, 127 n., 307; historical note, 308 n.; Gayoso describes, 336
San Francisco River, 325
San Ildefonso, treaty of, 5
San Juan del Bayú, 22
San Lorenzo el Real, Treaty of, 6, 7, 118, 130, 131, 139, 140, 143, 326 n.; effect of, 13, 20
San Marcos de Apalache, 22, 33 n.
Santa Fé, 4; Clark-Genêt attack feared on, 79
Sarpy Island, 212, 251
Scot, Guillermo, 241
Scott, Robert, 158 n.
Sebastian, Benjamin, 130, 321 n., 322 n., 326 n., 341; secessionist sentiments, 121
Sebilla, Tiburcio, 198
Secret Committee of Correspondence of the West, 64 n.
Semit (or Somit) (Mr.), 166
Servant, Pedro, 256
Shawnees (Indians), 71 n., 72 n., 87, 181, 268, 297 n., 298 n.; request Spanish-language instruction for tribesman, 182–83
Simcoe, John Graves, 79
Sioux Indians, 142

Slaves, 274; insurrection threatened at Punta Cortada, 104. *See also* Negroes
Small Chicó Isle (Yslot Chicó), 202
Small Gulf (Pequeño Golfo), 195; location, 195 n.
Small Prairie, 284
Smith, Juan, 243
Smuggling, 55
Socorro, El (bercha), 277, 278
Soler, Antonio, 218
Soler, Cayetano, 142 n.
Soulard, Monsieur, Gayoso reports on, 334–35
South Carolina Yazoo Co., 28, 157 n.
Spain, Spanish: holdings in North America, 1–2; Court, 3, 8, 17, 19, 21, 23; and threat of British invasion from Canada, 4; strained relations with U.S. over Louisiana, 6–8; conflicting objectives in Louisiana, 12–13; fresh-water fleet, 22–58 (*see also* Fleet, Spanish fresh-water), loath to grant military subsidies, 23–24; French victories in, 101; encourages Kentucky secession movement, 119–31 (*see also* Kentucky intrigue); Council of State decision on Kentucky issue, 122, reasons for, 131; at war with England, 131; rumored Anglo-American plans to declare war on (*1796*), 134; armistice with France, 318 n.
Stacpoole, Mauricio, 241
Statenfield, Baron of, 269
Stoddard (Mr.), 135 n.
Stony Creek (Bayou Pierre), 155, 196, 243, 244, 254 n., 326; location, 155 n., 196 n., 243 n.
Stony Creek Islands (Islas du Bayou de Pierre), 196 n.
Stump Island (Ile aux Chicots), 161, 280, 325

Talapuche Indians, 60
Talleyrand, 5
Tardiveau, Bartélemi, 40, 96, 179 n., 242 n.; biographical note, 40–41 n.
Tardiveau, Pedro, 340
Targueson (constable), 244
Tartell, Antonio, 199
Tayon, Carlos, 307 n., 308 n.; Gayoso reports on, 337

Tennessee River, 25
Terre Haute, 312 n.
Texas, 16
Texas Indians, 65
Thomas (Chickasaw Indian), 168 n.; speech quoted by Rousseau, 167–70
Thousand Islands, 173, 215, 280, 324
Todd, Andrew (Andrés), 314, 331 n.
Todd, John, 155 n.
Tombigbee, 22
Tombigbee River, 125 n.
Tower, the (Mississippi landmark), 299
Tracnar, El (bercha), 252
Treaties. *See under headings* Basel; Nogales; Paris; Pinckney's; San Ildefonso; San Lorenzo el Real
Trenier, Juan Baptista, 243
Tropé, Mr., 203, 204, 257
Trudeau, Zenon, 88 n., 98, 127 n., 135, 223 n., 224 n., 301 n., 305, 306, 313 n., 331 n., 334, 336 n.; biographical note, 59–60 n.; sees impending Cumberland attack, 59–60; ordered to aid Portell, 60–62; ordered to support New Madrid, 70–71; ordered to mobilize St. Louis, 78–79; rallies defenses, fortifies St. Louis, 87–88; hosts Gayoso, 128; improves St. Louis defenses, 306–07 n.; quoted, 332 n.; Gayoso reports on, 335–36; asks payment for construction, 338 n.
Turnbull, John (Juan), 66, 109, 110, 117, 325; trading experiences at Barrancas, 274 n.
Two Sisters Islands (Islas las Dos Hermanas), 246
Tywappity Bottom, 222
Tywappity River, 296

Ugulayacabé (Wolf's Friend; Ugly Cub) (Chickasaw chief), 69, 70, 90, 109, 256, 257, 263, 270, 324; biographical note, 253 n.; diplomatic exchange with Rousseau on fort-building, 110–11; negotiates with Gayoso, 113, diary account, 253–55; receives gifts, 264 n., 273; visits Gayoso, 272; Negroes for, 325
Ulloa Señor, 4, 336
United States of America, 22, 24, 45, 116, 145, 302, 333; Revolutionary War, 2, 3, 5, 6, 24; and borderlands conflicts, 1,

United States of America (*cont.*)
3; as Spanish enemy, 3; strained relations with Spain over Louisiana, 6–8; Indians encouraged against, 9–12; threats to Louisiana reported, 59–60, 65, 67–68, 69–70; and Clark-Genêt expedition, 75, 77, 78, 79 (*see also* Clark-Genêt expedition); restrains hostile Westerners, Frenchmen, 94–95; fort near Ohio mouth, Spanish fear, 98 (*see also* Fort Massac); rumors of troop buildup, 101–02; and Barrancas de Margó, 106, 107–08; building boats at Fort Pitt, 111; acquires Barrancas de Margó, 118; formal inquiry on Fort San Fernando, 124–25; rumored planning attack on San Fernando, 128–29; delivers ultimatum on San Fernando, 129; and England, rumored to declare war on Spain (*1796*), 134; suspected designs on Upper Louisiana, 136; acquires Natches, Nogales, 138, 139; anti-British posts seen as threat to Spanish (*1799*), 140; cannot rid Mississippi Valley of English (*1805*), 142–43; forces, proximity to Fort San Fernando, 277 n.; attack on Barrancas rumored, 218 n.; wheat from, 339
Unzaga, Luis de, 4

Vachard, Pedro, 212
Vaden, Mr., 323
Vallé, François, 60 n.
Vallé, François, *fils*, 60, 223 n., 224 n., 301, 302, 303, 317; biographical note, 60–61 n.; replaces Peyroux, 87, 88 n.; Gayoso lauds, 332
Vallé, Juan Bautista, 266
Vallière, Josef, 25
Van Dieman's Land, 88 n.
Vanden Bemden, Louis (Luis), 96, 225, 335; biographical note, 225 n.; investigates mouth of Ohio for fort site, 293–94 n.; Gayoso describes, 340
Vasquez, Benito, 127 n., 306, 336
Vaugine, Mr., 161
Venganza, La (galley), 39, 69, 72, 84, 89, 95 n., 104, 108, 110, 111, 114, 126, 128, 129, 130, 133, 144, 259, 260, 273; with Howard expedition to St. Louis, 138
Verdom (or Verdon), Mr., 203

INDEX

Verdon, Doña (Dama), 317, 318
Viar, José Ignacio de (Josef de), 64, 208 n.; reports Clark-Genêt plans, 74; works as informant, 77–78
Vicksburg, 34
Victoria, La (galley), 38, 39, 69, 76 n., 87, 94, 95, 97, 98 n., 103, 105, 126, 132, 133, 138
Vidal, José (Josef), 218, 241, 242, 243, 247, 261, 262
Vigilante, La (galiot), 38, 40, 44, 47, 113, 114, 123, 127, 128, 279, 294, 295, 308, 321, 323, 326 n.; history, description, 242 n.; acquired, 96; Gayoso account of expedition on, 235–37, 241–326; races *La Flecha*, 279
Vigo, Francisco (Joseph Maria), 311, 312, 314; biographical note, 312 n.; vouches for Peyroux, 338
Vilemont, Carlos de, 109, 115, 162 n., 249, 265 n., 277 n.; biographical note, 249–50 n.
Vilemont, Luis de, 102 n.
Villa de Carondelet, 304
Villebeuvre, Juan de la, 160
Villein Island (Isla de Vilain; Isla del Feo), 215, 279
Vincennes, 87, 134, 184, 268, 295, 300, 312 n.
Vincennes University, 312 n.
Vital, Madame, 304
Vouidan, Guillermo, 241

Wabash River, 184
Walnut Hills. *See* Fort Nogales
War of *1812*, 143
Waters, Dr. Richard Jones, 178, 339
Wats (Miss), 339 n.
Watts, Margarita ("Peggy"), 11 n.
Wayne, General, 59, 101; inquiry about Fort San Fernando, 125
West Florida, 1, 2, 15; U.S.–Spanish Boundary dispute over, 6–7; and countercolonization, 14; expense of

West Florida (*cont.*)
forts, 23
West Florida (English sloop), 32 n.
Wheat Island (Isla au Bled; Isla del Trigo), 162, 205, 249, 325
White, James, 17
White Bluffs, 293
White River, 47 n., 113, 115, 163, 249; military detachment, 28, 81, 164–65 n., 166, 167, 187, 206, 207, 208, 230, 268, 325; location, 250 n.
Wilkinson, James, 25, 27, 28 n., 54, 76, 96, 278 n., 286 n.; biographical note, 17–18 n.; promotes Kentucky intrigue, 17–20; opinion on galleys, 30 n.; asserts time ripe for intrigue (*1794*), 119–20; informed of Gayoso trip, 123; letters to New Madrid, 128; dismisses Cardonelet plan (*1797*), 131
Winters, Mr., 244, 246, 312
Wolf River (Rio Lobos), 274
Wooly, Melly, 241, 242, 244

Yazoo River, 6, 35, 125 n., 151, 157 n., 188, 261, 274, 325; defenses on, 28–29 (*see also* Fort Nogales)
Ysla de las Barrancas Blancas, 313
Ysla de los Caballos, 300
Ysla del Capón, 296
Ysla de la Curs, 296
Ysla de Duverqué, 298
Ysla de Gran Detorno, 296
Ysla del Lobo, 317, 318
Ysla á la Percha, 299
Ysla del Pety Plattin, 304
Ysla del Sierbo. *See* Buffalo Island
Ytelagana (Itelaghana) (Choctaw chief), 200–01
Yust, Toni, 223

Zamora, José, 43, 237; among land-treaty signers, 266
Zasimine (or Macocas) Island, 246
Zasivine, 325